Design–Type Research in Information Systems:

Findings and Practices

Rustam Vahidov
Concordia University, Canada

Managing Director:	Lindsay Johnston
Senior Editorial Director:	Heather Probst
Book Production Manager:	Sean Woznicki
Development Manager:	Joel Gamon
Development Editor:	Michael Killian
Acquisitions Editor:	Erika Gallagher
Typesetter:	Adrienne Freeland
Cover Design:	Nick Newcomer, Lisandro Gonzalez

Published in the United States of America by
Information Science Reference (an imprint of IGI Global)
701 E. Chocolate Avenue
Hershey PA 17033
Tel: 717-533-8845
Fax: 717-533-8661
E-mail: cust@igi-global.com
Web site: http://www.igi-global.com

Library of Congress Cataloging-in-Publication Data

Vahidov, Rustam, 1969- Design-type research in information systems : findings and practices / by Rustam Vahidov.
    p. cm.
  Includes bibliographical references and index.
  Summary: "This book demonstrates that Design-Type Research is a legitimate scientific activity, particularly in the context of the field of Information Systems"--Provided by publisher.
  ISBN 978-1-4666-0131-4 (hbk.) -- ISBN 978-1-4666-0132-1 (ebook) -- ISBN 978- 1-4666-0133-8 (print & perpetual access) 1. Management information systems-- Design and construction. 2. Information technology--Research. I. Title.
  T58.6.V33 2012
  658.4'038011--dc23
                              2011040623

British Cataloguing in Publication Data
A Cataloguing in Publication record for this book is available from the British Library.

To Natalia

Table of Contents

Chapter 12
Some Example Meta-Artifacts Inspired by Science and Nature 243

Detailed Table of Contents

The purpose of this chapter is to explain the meaning of such important concepts as artifact, design, and design-related research. Traditionally, the term "design research" refers to a field of study that aims at providing insights into designing. This chapter presents a general notion of design. It briefly presents the history of studies of design. The term "design" has a number of definitions, some of which are covered in the chapter. It also considers design as viewed from the perspective of problem solving. The notion of an artifact in relation to its environment and internal organization is described. General methodology of design in terms of key stages is briefly discussed. The role of representation in design is emphasized.

The purpose of this chapter is to provide insights into the nature of scientific research with the emphasis on the design perspective. Early science had started out of the practical needs of human cultures. From the modern perspective the artifactual nature of early scientific constructs is particularly manifest. The design viewpoint can be applied to the major classes of sciences both in form of reverse and forward engineering. Scientific method has been crafted by the philosophers of science throughout the millennia. There are analogies between the major aspects of the scientific method and artifact design process. Inventiveness and creativity play an essential role in the development of human knowledge. Some major scientific breakthroughs have been made thanks to the invention of thought experiments. Some philosophers of science view theories as tools—the artifacts that do not necessarily relate to real entities. Critical treatment of competing theories supports this view.

Information Systems (IS) are complex artifacts which could be viewed as playing the role of an interface between the organizational structure and processes and the technological capabilities. IS design is influenced by—and has an influence on—its outer environment: organizational context. Much of past research in IS is of explanatory nature and has largely focused on the processes and functions of outer environment, including organizations and individuals. There is not sufficient theoretical elaboration on the organizational and technological connections of the IS artifacts. Some of the most prominent theoretical models of IS do not incorporate the very nature of information systems to a substantial extent. The information content of these models is also questionable. IS research has been criticized by some members of the research community for lack of identity and lack of relevance.

Chapter 4

Is science fundamentally different from the design of novel artifact concepts? This chapter aims to examine if there are essential differences between traditional science and design-type research. Human capacities allow us to perceive and understand the world as well as act on it to make changes in a purposeful fashion. As the subjects of knowledge and creation grow increasingly abstract, the differences between creating and understanding tend to fade away. While science studies natural phenomena, the focus of design is on artifacts. Could this be the definitive dividing line between design and science? Regarding the ontological status of the artifacts the opinions are split, some suggesting that they are distinct from natural objects, while others seeing continuity, the position which is defended in this chapter. Other possible differentiation criteria (e.g. design is application of science) are also discussed and it is argued that none of these makes design essentially distinct from science.

Chapter 5

Information systems are socio-technical artifacts whose design should fit to serve the needs of organizations as well as the individuals who employ them. The central purpose of this chapter is to argue that design of new IS concepts can be regarded as a scientific research activity. To this end, several important questions need to be tackled, including the following ones: What is the meaning of observation in design-type research? Is there a notion of a theory in design-type research that corresponds to that in traditional science? If so, what are its building blocks? How does design-type research relate to the issues of truth and discovery? This chapter makes an attempt to provide the answers to these and other related questions.

Chapter 6

The concept of a design theory includes, among others, the components of meta-requirements and meta-systems. As an artifact, according to Simon, it is characterized in terms of its outer and inner environments, and the interface, design-type research projects may focus on one or another aspects of meta-artifacts. The purpose of this chapter is to describe a representational framework incorporating different views of meta-artifacts. The chapter introduces such a framework based on Zachman's model for information architecture. The two dimensional model includes perspectives and categories dimensions. The former is defined in terms of four layers, including analytical, synthetic, technological, and implementation layers. The latter includes the categories of motivation, structure, behavior, and instantiation. At each layer alternative meta-artifact conceptualizations may be proposed by different researchers, implying a third dimension in the framework. A complete design research work on any given layer would correspond to a research project. A work targeting the entire matrix would constitute a design-type research program. Efforts by different design researchers on alternative conceptualizations could be regarded as research stream.

The representational framework introduced in the previous chapter could help design researchers organize their work by choosing to focus on analytical, synthetic, or technological kinds of projects. This chapter presents the case of electronic negotiation systems as an example of the application of the framework. Theoretical background of negotiations allows deriving the analytical picture of systems designed to support them. The chapter discusses two system concepts: one providing an example of a synthetic meta-artifact for conducting electronic negotiations; and the other one representing the case of design-type research with the emphasis on obtaining a sound technical meta-system. Alternative meta-requirement or meta-system concepts could be devised at each layer of the framework.

If design-type research shares deep roots with the traditional scientific research, then the principles advanced by the philosophers of science should be applicable to it as well. The purpose of this chapter is to show how these principles could be interpreted through the lens of design-type research. Induction in DTR implies extracting features of the implemented particular solutions with subsequent generalization. Deduction means inferring meta-requirements and, subsequently, features of meta-systems based on kernel theories. Ockham's razor as a criterion favors simpler designs. Popper's falsifiability criterion means that design of meta-artifacts should be informative. Lacatos's protective belt translates into separating the immutable core of a design theory from the part that is potentially modifiable. Kuhn's paradigms in design establish a given core design statement for a particular kind of meta-artifact, which drives focused research in that area. Feyerabend's anarchy encourages alternative design visions. The aesthetics criterion plays an important part in recognizing forms in meta-artifacts.

This chapter aims at illustrating the application of important scientific principles using a sample design-type research project, which featured the development of a method for online shopping support. Existing schools of thought are described as potentially competing paradigms. A deductive approach is utilized to derive the required features of the artifact based on kernel theories. Falsifiability criterion is met by the development of the concrete form (in terms of structure and behavior) and the proposal of specific testable hypotheses. An example of auxiliary protective hypothesis is given. Ockham's razor is used in order to refute a more complex version of the method.

Development of the informative classification scheme for information system artifacts would be highly useful for design researchers in focusing and organizing their research projects and identifying gaps. There have been few dated attempts at IS classification mostly focusing on intra-organizational systems. This chapter stresses the need for newer frameworks, which would accommodate for recent developments in IS from the design-type research perspective. The chapter outlines one possible approach, which incorporates individuals, groups, organizations and markets as possible components. Classification could span through the layers of the representational framework presented earlier to produce the families of meta-requirements and synthetic and technological meta-systems. Design research frontier helps in identifying possible developments from the existing meta-systems towards true future system forms. Along this path design researchers are expected to encounter phantom forms.

Chapter 11

The purpose of this chapter is to demonstrate that traditional science is a kind of design. Scientific research can be viewed as a type of reverse engineering. Alternatively, one could entertain a highly hypothetical thought about how an engineer would have designed the world as we experience it. The artifact nature of scientific knowledge can be seen in different sciences through examples. Mathematics is the domain of the purely abstract, where the difference between the invented and discovered disappears. History of Astronomy provides examples of how the sense of beauty led the scientists to invent early models involving celestial bodies. Creativity and inventiveness are often needed in Physics to construct artifacts involving the unobservable. Purpose and corresponding design distinguishes Biology, which focuses on living forms displaying high levels of sophistication in their organization.

Chapter 12

Science reveals the workings of the mechanisms behind the natural phenomena. If one can entertain an idea of nature exhibiting definite features of design, then, perhaps human designers could learn from it some of its structures and methods to solve problems faced by human designers. Imitating the natural may be beneficial to tackle tough problems. The chapter provides few such examples. In the first case, the workings of the nervous system, including the brain as revealed by the science have been forward engineered by researchers in artificial neural networks. In the second case, the most versatile designer, i.e. the evolutionary process, has been employed to design solutions for problems in various areas of human activity. In the third case, the "non-scientific" vagueness inherent in human judgment has been harnessed in a fascinating way to provide useful solutions.

Preface

What is the purpose of this book? Perhaps the best way to convey its very essence is through a hypothetical dialogue between two researchers in the area of Information Systems. The two colleagues come from different research perspectives. Let's call one of them T-Researcher, and the other one D-Researcher. They have both recently joined the same department in a North-American university. They decided to have a lunch together and talk about their research interests and discuss the possibilities of future collaboration.

T-Researcher (TR): I've heard your paper has been recently accepted in journal X. That's great news! Congratulations!

D-Researcher (DR): Thank you, yes it always gives one a sense of accomplishment. By the way, I also saw your paper in the latest issue of journal Y. Congratulations to you!

TR: Thanks, it took a while to get it out. So what is your paper about?

DR: I proposed a method for supporting shopping process for online buyers.

TR: You mean you have compared different existing methods, perhaps in experimental settings and found that one of them is superior to others?

DR: No, I have actually *invented* this new method. I also described the structure for a system that could incorporate it.

TR: You mean, you have built a website that incorporates some features and functions which the existing sites lack? Is this what your paper is about?

DR: It's not exactly true. The website itself was not my objective, but it helps objectifying the more abstract concept.

TR: OK, if I understand correctly you came up with the new method, which is an artifact, to test your theoretical model in order to advance knowledge?

DR: In a way, yes. But that's not the major point. The artifact *is* the knowledge.

TR: I know that science uses artifacts of all kinds as *instruments* to advance scientific knowledge. For example, telescopes help astronomers to study vast outer spaces. But a telescope is just a tool. It is not knowledge.

DR: A concrete given embodied telescope is just an artefact, but what about the concept itself in abstract form. May it not be regarded as knowledge?

TR: Artifacts are invented or designed. And isn't design in general just an application of science? Science discovers laws and advances theories, which are then used by practitioners to build useful objects, i.e. the artifacts.

DR: The wheel had been invented long before science existed.

TR: Yet, it is somewhat unusual to regard these objects as knowledge. Perhaps study of the methods used to produce them to some extent could be called research. I don't want to appear rude, but I am just trying to understand. In regards to our field, you are saying that anyone who writes a piece of software (an artifact), which is "novel" in some respect is a scientist? Programming then is the act of scientific research? The software itself is knowledge?

DR: No the software is not knowledge in itself. In fact it is of *secondary* importance.

TR: Now I am really confused. You are saying that designing artifacts is a kind of science. Science aims at producing knowledge. An artifact, according to you is a kind of knowledge. Therefore, the kind of scientific work you do should aim at producing artifacts. But then you are saying that the artefact itself is of secondary importance?

DR: Yes, but there is no contradiction here. I just need to clarify a bit what is meant by the artefact. Knowledge has to be general in some sense. Any given concrete artifact by itself can rarely be general. It could be built in one way or the other, while exhibiting the essential form within it. In the design of concrete artifacts many design decisions could be made to fit it to a specific context of operation. The prototype website that I used in my experiments could be designed and built differently, but yet it had to implement the concept. Therefore, in this designing-sort of research the primary outcome is an abstract artifact, or a type of artifacts. These cannot be built in their pure form. Prototypes are used mostly for demonstration and evaluation purposes.

TR: But still, science is all about discovering things. You are talking about inventions. Science studies the natural, while design is about artificial.

DR: Some artifact forms can be regarded as discoveries. Think about it. Suppose a designer-scientist invents a given artifact form, and provides its description in general abstract fashion. If some years later this abstract artifact "exists" in form of multiple concrete artifacts, then may it not be regarded as a discovery? I would say that a wheel form was truly a discovery, as it is so pervasive nowadays. We can argue about design vs. science forever. Tell me what your paper is about.

TR: Well, I had investigated the effects of culture on the adoption of technology. My model actually worked out beautifully: nice pattern of factor loadings, very good support of hypotheses...

DR: Adoption of what kind of technology?

TR: Information technology, of course.

DR: And how did you represent or incorporate this technology in your model?

TR: Well, it's not explicitly in there. It is one of the external variables.

DR: How can it be an external variable if the theory sounds technology-centric? Indeed, how come Information Systems are often black boxed or omitted completely from theories in the very *discipline* of Information Systems?

TR: Well, this is the way most behavioral studies work in IS. This isn't Computer Science after all... And yet, I cannot understand how inventing could be at par with rigorous scientific research.

After the lunch, somewhat upset D-researcher went to his office to start writing this book.

DISCOVERING THE NON-EXISTENT

In the simulated dialogue the T-Researcher comes from the traditional, i.e. descriptive and explanatory type of science. The D-Researcher is a design-oriented scientist. The dialogue is really hypothetical, and somewhat polarized in terms of the opposing views. Yet design-oriented researchers in Information Systems would probably recognize some of its elements. Those coming through the schooling in traditional understanding in science, in particular, social disciplines often have difficulties accepting design as a legitimate type of science. Not all design is science of course. But a class of design projects, the author believes, are akin to scientific research.

This book is about design-type research, mostly focusing on the area of Information Systems (IS). What is meant by design-type research? In fact, different versions of the term have been used in the recent past, including: design research; design science; design science research; and design-oriented research. The term "design research" actually has been around for over four decades (Cross, 2007). It refers to the study of design in general, in other words it is an interdisciplinary (or, rather meta-disciplinary) field, which deals with the issues of methodology of design, design principles and guidelines, philosophy of design, and the like. It looks to produce knowledge for helping partitioning designers to be effective and efficient in their projects. The outcome of such projects, i.e. design (as a noun) of specific artifacts is not the primary focus. This book is not about design research in this sense.

Design as research, on the other hand looks to produce artifacts, which could be regarded as knowledge. For example, a researcher in operations management area could develop a new method for job scheduling. A computer scientist (in Artificial Intelligence subfield) may develop a novel type of neural networks. Likewise, someone in the IS field may propose a new system concept for business intelligence applications. All of the above activities develop innovative solutions. The artifact is the major outcome of their research. This is constructive type of research. The artifact is knowledge. As knowledge, it must display some level of generality. Thus, the artifacts produced by design-type research are actually classes or types of artifacts, i.e. meta-artifacts. The use of the term "design research" to refer to this type of work would be confusing. Lately, the term "design science research" appears to be used more frequently. In this book the term "design-type research" is primarily adopted as, in the author's opinion, it better reflects the essence of such science, although alternative versions are also used, in particular when citing other researchers' work.

In like-minded homogeneous scientific communities the question of legitimacy of the mode of conducting research is rarely raised. In computer science, let's say, all of the research work is about developing (designing) solutions, i.e. artifacts. In IS area, however, there is a mix of people targeting the human/social side, and thus conducting descriptive and explanatory studies, vs. those occupied with generating innovative solution concepts. The former community has been predominant in the area (especially in North America) within the past few decades. However, design-type research have been rapidly gaining strong popularity lately, especially due to a number of influential publications which raised the awareness and outlined some guidelines and principles of this mode of science (Hevner, March, Park, & Ram, 2004; March & Smith, 1995; Walls, Widmeyer, & El Sawy, 1992).

Journals regarded as the "top" outlets in the field make significantly more emphasis on behavioural studies than on design-type ones. This situation naturally favours the behaviourist perspective on information systems research and hinders the developments on the design side. In this respect, the Editor of the *ACM Transactions on MIS* raises a question as per why some quality design-oriented outlets do not get the adequate level of recognition. As an example, he notes that predominantly design-oriented journal of *Decision Support System* is not in the top "basket", while its ISI Impact Factor (IF) in 2009 has only been second to *MIS Quarterly* (Chen, 2011)? He writes in this respect: "The significant rise in IF may be partly due to the high-quality design-oriented research that DSS has favored, encouraged, and published over the past few years.

In a recent "Memorandum on design-oriented information systems research", a number of leading European (predominantly German) researchers have strongly voiced their concerns regarding the resistance of the internationally renowned journals in the information systems area towards accepting design-oriented research work (Österle, et al., 2011). While acknowledging the value of behaviourist approach, they nevertheless note that: "...leading exponents of the discipline have complained for years that research in the field has lacked relevance for the practitioners' community, which could be surmised from the fact that very few Ph.D.s from the IS discipline have ended up working in business." And further: In the effort to have their work published in these journals, researchers, and young researchers in particular, have no other choice but to comply with the journals' evaluation criteria for paper submissions. Basically, these criteria say that publications providing statistical evidence of empirically identified characteristics of *existing IS* are favored over publications presenting innovative solutions that are considered highly beneficial for business" (italics added).

However, the questions posed by the representatives of the traditional (explanation-focused) school of science are legitimate. If science is about describing and explaining, i.e. understanding and knowledge, how can design fit within its framework? Science is about discovering, design is about inventing. How could an invention be regarded as a discovery? If some type of design could be considered a science, then how could scientific method and principles applied to it? There is a need for establishing legitimacy of design-type science.

This book sets out to address the above issues. In particular, invention is viewed as search for the world-forms that do not yet exist. Design-type research is about discovering the non-existent. Alternatively, some researchers propose that science itself is a type of design (Glanville, 1999). Scientific theories may as well be regarded as inventions, or artifacts, certainly in light of teachings of some of the philosophers of science (Feyerabend, 1975; Popper, 1969). So is science a kind of design, or design a kind of science? It does not really matter. The position of the book is that design of meta-artifacts is *equivalent* to scientific research. Moreover, the philosophy, methodology and principles of traditional science can be applied to design-type of science as well.

ORGANIZATION OF THE BOOK

The book primarily targets design-oriented research in the context of Information Systems. The discussions in various chapters do occasionally deviate from the field of IS to the related design-oriented disciplines, such as Computer Science, Software Engineering and Artificial Intelligence as these latter often serve as the source of knowledge in the design of information systems. Also, some chapters venture into the issues related to design of artifacts in general, in order to reveal meta-design principles, methods, and practices.

Chapter 1 discusses the notion of design in general. It mostly relies on the findings of "design research" as study of designing. It briefly outlines the history of design and provides a number of definitions of the term. Artifact as the key product of design is also described in relation to its environment. General methodology of design is briefly presented in form of a multi-stage process. The role of representation in design is emphasized.

Chapter 2 discusses the nature of the traditional science. It points that early science had started out of the practical needs of human cultures. It further argues that design viewpoint can be applied to the major classes of sciences in form of reverse engineering. Scientific method has been crafted by the philosophers of science throughout millennia. The chapter discusses the analogies between the major aspects of the scientific method and design processes.

Chapter 3 presents the developments in IS research. Much of past and current research in IS has been of explanatory nature and has largely focused on the processes and functions of outer environment, including organizations and individuals. There is not sufficient theoretical elaboration on the organizational and technological aspects of the IS.

Chapter 4 sets out to explore the differences between traditional science and design-type research. While science studies natural phenomena, the focus of design is on artifacts. Could this be the definitive dividing line between design and science? Regarding the ontological status of the artifacts the opinions are split, some suggesting that they are distinct from natural objects, while others seeing continuity. Other possible differentiation criteria are also discussed and it is argued that none of these makes design essentially distinct from science.

Chapter 5 aims at advancing arguments in support of scientific nature of design-type research and clarifying the meaning of important scientific terminology in this respect. In particular, the term observation in design refers to an implemented system instantiated within given organizational context. Reflecting on the notion of truth the chapter shows that design projects could be viewed as attempts to uncover the true forms, just like traditional scientific research may be regarded from the utility point of view.

Chapter 6 introduces a framework for representing IS meta-artifacts based on Zachman's model for information architecture. The two-dimensional model includes perspectives and categories dimensions. The former is defined in terms of four layers, including analytical, synthetic, technological, and implementation layers. The latter includes the categories of motivation, structure, behavior, and instantiation.

Chapter 7 illustrates the framework using the example of electronic negotiation systems.

Chapter 8 proposes how scientific terminology and principles could be applied to design-type research. In particular, it discusses deduction and induction, Ockham's razor, Popper's falsifiability, Lacatos's protective belt, Kuhn's paradigms and Feyerabend's anarchy.

Chapter 9 illustrates application of these principles using an example design project for supporting online shopping.

Chapter 10 stresses the need for IS classification frameworks, which would accommodate for recent developments in IS from the design-type research perspective. The chapter outlines one possible approach. Classification could span through the layers of the representational framework presented in earlier chapters to produce the families of meta-requirements and synthetic and technological meta-systems. The notion of design research frontier that helps identifying possible developments from the existing meta-systems towards true future system forms is presented.

Chapter 11 shows how important developments in different traditional sciences could be viewed as design problems.

Finally, Chapter 12 shows example meta-artifacts which have been inspired by nature and science.

REFERENCES

Chen, H. (2011). Editorial: Design science, grand challenges, and societal impacts. *ACM Transactions on Management Information Systems, 2*(1), 1–10. doi:10.1145/2037661.2037663

Cross, N. (2007). Forty years of design research. *Design Studies, 28*, 1–4. doi:10.1016/j.destud.2006.11.004

Feyerabend, P. K. (1975). *Against method: Outline of an anarchistic theory of knowledge*. London, UK: NLB.

Glanville, R. (1999). Researching design and designing research. *Design Issues, 15*(2), 80–91. doi:10.2307/1511844

Hevner, A. R., March, S. T., Park, J., & Ram, S. (2004). Design science in information systems research. *Management Information Systems Quarterly, 28*(1), 75–105.

March, S. T., & Smith, G. F. (1995). Design and natural science research on information technology. *Decision Support Systems, 15*, 251–266. doi:10.1016/0167-9236(94)00041-2

Österle, H., Becker, J., Frank, U., Hess, T., Karagiannis, D., & Krcmar, H. (2011). Memorandum on design-oriented information systems research. *European Journal of Information Systems, 20*, 7–10. doi:10.1057/ejis.2010.55

Popper, K. R. (1969). *Conjectures and refutations: The growth of scientific knowledge*. London: Routledge & K. Paul.

Walls, J. G., Widmeyer, G. R., & El Sawy, O. A. (1992). Building an information system design theory for vigilant EIS. *Information Systems Research, 3*(1), 36–59. doi:10.1287/isre.3.1.36

Acknowledgment

I would like to thank Dr. Vijay Vaishnavi of Georgia State University (GSU, Atlanta, GA) for introducing me to the subject of this book over a decade ago in his Ph.D. seminar at GSU. I would further like to extend my gratitude to Dr. Gregory Kersten, the director of the Interneg Research Center at Concordia University (Montreal, Canada) for his insights, in particular for his advice and help in preparation of the chapter on electronic negotiation systems. I am also greatly indebted to Dr. Bijan Fazlollahi of GSU for helping me become a researcher. Lastly, I would like to thank Ms. Gulnara Kurmangaliyeva for convincing me to write this book.

Rustam Vahidov
Concordia University, Canada

Chapter 1
Design

ABSTRACT

The purpose of this chapter is to explain the meaning of such important concepts as artifact, design, and design-related research. Traditionally, the term "design research", refers to a field of study that aims at providing insights into designing. This chapter presents a general notion of design. It briefly presents the history of studies of design. The term "design" has a number of definitions, some of which are covered in the chapter. It also considers design as viewed from the perspective of problem solving. The notion of an artifact in relation to its environment and internal organization is described. General methodology of design in terms of key stages is briefly discussed. The role of representation in design is emphasized.

DESIGN: WHAT IS IT?

Herbert Simon, in his seminal book the *Sciences of the Artificial* points that we live in a predominantly human-made world (Simon, 1996). Human activity has dramatically changed the world from the way it used to be in pre-historical time. We have the ability to change the nature and produce artifacts that make our lives more comfortable, safe, and pleasant. Artifacts and their effects can be found everywhere we look: our cities and towns, domesticated plants and animals, our cultures and governments, our knowledge, and even our bodies.

Artifacts are the end products of design activity. In a book called *Knowledge as Design* the author invites us to entertain a possibility of suddenly doing away with all human-made artifacts (Perkins, 1986): "Suppose that … someone wishes that there is no such thing as design… Let us … follow rigorously the consequences of this wish. The clothes vanish from our bodies, never having been invented. The floors and pavements on which we walk slip away into nothingness. We find no books, no artificial lighting, not even a primitive hearth. And perhaps, if language itself can be

DOI: 10.4018/978-1-4666-0131-4.ch001

considered a design, we do not even understand what the mouthings mean."

Design has been recognized as the first tradition among the many traditions of humankind, including arts, religion, science, and technology (Nelson & Stolterman, 2003). Different design thinkers mention four possible origins of design, including creation of universe (Religion, and so-called "Intelligent Design"); prehistoric objects (early human artifacts); industrial revolution; and early twentieth century (scientific approaches to design).

Design as a human-directed activity had originated with the development of early humans. The humanoid species Australopithecus and later Homo Habilis used to make primitive tools now referred to as "Oldowan industry." The name derives from the Olduvai Gorge in Tanzania where the characteristic stone tools were discovered. The tools included simple "choppers" obtained by the means of chopping off "flakes" from a stone core. The early humans had recognized the multiple uses of such rather rough instruments for multiple purposes, ranging from working with the wood to cracking nuts from about 2.5 million years ago.

Further elaboration of the primitive tool-making process had subsequently led to improved, more effective and efficient set of tools, collectively referred to as Acheulean Industry. These tools dating from about 1.65 million years ago were shaped to provide sharper edges to form such instruments as hand-axes. Thus, the birth of design pretty much parallels the development of early humans. Ever since then design has been one of the defining characteristics of humankind. The evolution of technological development abounds with wonderful inventions that shaped our world throughout the human history (see, e.g. McNeil, 1990). Design has been the driving force behind what we recognize as technological progress.

The Merriam-Webster dictionary provides the following meanings of the word "design" as a noun:

- A particular purpose held in view by an individual or group
- A mental project or scheme in which means to an end are laid down
- A deliberate undercover project or scheme
- Aggressive or evil intent—used with *on* or *against*
- A preliminary sketch or outline showing the main features of something to be executed
- An underlying scheme that governs functioning, developing, or unfolding
- A plan or protocol for carrying out or accomplishing something (as a scientific experiment)
- The arrangement of elements or details in a product or work of art
- A decorative pattern
- The creative art of executing aesthetic or functional designs

Thus, (brushing aside the somewhat negative connotations) the word means either a proposed or adopted purpose, a plan to achieve some purpose, or some sort of arrangement of parts that result in specific properties, or functions of the new whole. The scholars of design have also tried to define the word to capture its very essence. Here are just a few examples of attempts to define design either as an outcome, activity, or ability:

- "…the process of inventing physical things which display new physical order, organization, form, in response to function" (Alexander, 1964)
- "…a structure adapted to a purpose" (Perkins, 1986)
- "…transformation of information from the needs, demands, requirements and constraints … into the description of a structure which is capable of fulfilling these demands." (Hubka & Eder, 1996)

Figure 1. Design process

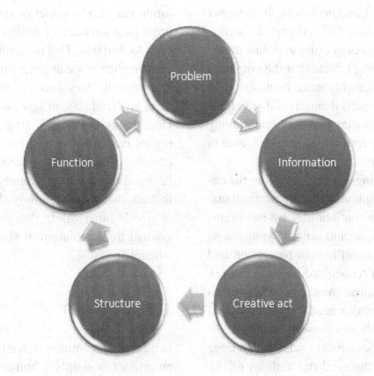

- "…purposeful activity directed towards the goal of fulfilling human needs, particularly those which can be met by the technology factors of our culture." (Asimow, 1962)
- "…the ability to imagine that-which does-not-yet-exist." (Nelson & Stolterman, 2003)

In all these meanings, there is a sense of creation by the designer(s). In other words, there is an act of building something new, something that does not yet exist, be it a process or an entity. Design is a purposeful activity that seeks to endow the entity being created by a sought function (or a set of functions). The function of an artifact is achieved by defining the appropriate structure by arranging the basic elements, or building blocks in such a fashion that would fulfill the function in the best fashion. Design activity is that of transformation of information from requirements to specifications for producing a technical solu-

tion. The actual construction of the artifact relates to the implementation process, which results in a "newly-born" object which fulfills a function which addresses the problem at hand. Often, the problem may not be covered fully, or its structure changes as a result of applying a new solution, which may lead to a new perceived need, and the whole cycle repeats. Figure 1 summarizes the essence of the above definitions in a schematic fashion.

A newly designed artifact could be uniquely applicable to a given concrete problem situation. However, some artifacts could also be adapted to broader classes of design situations. This could be the case when these situations are sharing certain essential similarities. Often, generic designs could be adapted to local situations, whereby a designer would combine general design knowledge, obtained, for example through years of schooling with experience and intuition to better fit particular requirements.

Design, above all is concerned with the synthesis (Simon, 1996). In other words, the designer has to be able to combine different parts, elements, concepts and processes in order to define a new whole (Asimow, 1962). Note that the emphasis here is on finding the right arrangement, the good fitting of parts. The parts themselves do not have to be designed, they may pre-exist, embodying generic design concepts, which are applicable in a variety of contexts.

Thus, synthesizing is a key capability the designer should be employing. In fact, the synthetic capacity is utilized continuously by our brains in everyday perception and action. Synthesis, as the key characteristic of human perception and cognition has been recognized by Kant (1999). He believed that human mind can be viewed as a set of functions, which need to be synthesized appropriately with the raw sensory data for facilitating cognitive tasks. Modern science to a large extent appreciates the synthetic abilities of our brains. For instance, the images constituting our visual perception are built by our minds that utilize a toolbox of models to present information in a meaningful way to us from raw signals received by the photo-sensitive cells of retina. We utilize built-in design powers to perceive. There is no perception without synthesis.

Yet in a deliberate design effort, one is primarily concerned with how designers consciously go about synthesizing good answers to the problems of reality. The designing process has been described as: applied creativity; problem solving; learning; evolution (of problem solutions and problems); social process; and even as a game (in a sense, that design is a challenge) (Dorst, 2006). It is generally believed that creativity is a source of good ideas. From the creativity point of view designers are often encouraged to approach the problem in unusual ways, to go through divergent ideation, and to think outside the box (Ackoff, 1978). Good approach to design, it has been argued, should move gradually from the general to concrete (Dorst, 2006). A quick leap from a problem definition to a detailed solution may lead to inferior outcomes, as not all promising avenues of design possibilities have been looked into. This is essentially a "premature convergence" issue in general problem solving. As Dorst puts it: "Designers spend part of their times in an artificial state of ignorance" (Dorst, 2006). Uncertainty in the early stages of design in this regard is something positive, as it appears. The concrete designed and constructed artifact should be freed of all the uncertainty. The message is, though, that the uncertainty should be removed *slowly*. In other words, design is considered as a gradual transformation of abstract artifacts into concrete ones.

THE ARTIFACT

In the regular common understanding of the term, an artifact is simply a human-made object. An artificial entity. The term itself derives from the Latin roots "ars" (art) and "factum" (something made). The Merriam-Webster dictionary provides the following meanings of the term:

- Something created by humans usually for a practical purpose; *especially*: an object remaining from a particular period;
- Something characteristic of or resulting from a particular human institution, period, trend, or individual
- A product of artificial character (as in a scientific test) due usually to extraneous (as human) agency

Note the historical connotation of the word as it was conventionally used to signify the appearance of early human—produced tools and works of primitive art with the development of archaic human societies. Conceiving artifacts is a job of designers. We, the humans have the ability to recognize that the world can be modified by means of making, arranging and re-arranging the elements provided to us by nature in order to improve the quality of our living. As noted in Nelson & Stolterman (2003) we get involved with the design activities, because we somehow perceive a *lack of wholeness*, in a sense that the world is not in some sort of "desired" state. From this viewpoint we are, as it were, continuously engaged in a process of constantly making artifacts, which we "plug" here and there in the "gaps" we find in our environment to bring the latter into a more attractive state. It is curious to ask whether we will ever be able to achieve the feeling of "wholeness" in perceiving the world? The two notable conceptualizations of the artifact have been proposed by Alexander and Simon, and we shall take a more detailed look into their meanings below.

Artifact as a Form

The artifact is thus a concrete object constructed in accordance with the designer's understanding of the problem and the corresponding synthetic solution with the purpose of making the world a better place to live (in some sense). Christofer Alexander had called the very structural essence of the designed artifacts "the form" (Alexander, 1964). Thus, he regards the form as the ultimate object of design. The designer can then be referred to as a "form-maker." There is a need for form-making, because the world is *irregular*. The world, so to speak, tries to "compensate" for its irregularities by "fitting itself to them." As a result of such fitting the form emerges.

Thus, according to Alexander, forms arise as the results of the irregularities. One interesting consequence of such interpretation of the form is that not all forms have to be designed by humans. Let us take a simple and somewhat "down-to-earth" example. Irregularities in the Earth's internal high-temperature processes lead to global geophysical processes, called "plate tectonics." These processes lead, in particular to clashes between the continents and appearance

of seas and mountain ranges. For instance, as the chunk of earth, which is much of the present-day India (and Afghanistan and Tibet) split off from Gondwana and moved northwards at a rapid speed of 16 cm per year to join Asia, it raised the Himalayas. (in fact, it is still moving northwards even nowadays). Mountains and mountain-ranges are naturally-produced forms.

On a larger scale, the uneven distribution of matter in the Universe leads to large matter chunks formed by the gravitational force. These are the star forms. These heavy objects attract other not-so-heavy objects and participate in a sort of "cosmic" dance with the latter to compensate for the irregularities caused by the concentration centers of gravity in relatively small areas of space. This interplay of forces and irregularities leads to the "planetary systems" form. At even a larger scale stars form galaxies, often in a spiral-like shape. Now, interestingly, it is not known exactly what kind of irregularity causes these patterns (although some partial explanations have been provided, e.g. so called "density waves"). Perhaps, astrophysicists need to engage in more "reverse engineering" kind of inquiry to reconstruct the forces and the mechanism behind the form.

Perhaps the most vivid example of the nature's own production of forms is in the biosphere. Living organisms display a very high order of organization shaped by the Darwinian natural evolution process. Various adaptations and co-adaptations of the organisms have been shaping them into a plethora of different forms by means of complex interactions among the individuals, species, sexes, and the environment.

Yet, when we speak of humans producing forms, there is a difference in the fact that the latter have been conceived in a thinking mind of a conscious designer. The human-engineered forms are not simply the outcomes of superposition of sets of natural forces; they owe their appearance to long successions of mutations coupled with the selective pressures that characterizes evolution. It is a brainchild of human synthetic ability that helps us both model the environment, and put together solutions to the problems posed by it. The difference between human-made forms and those produced by the inanimate nature is that the latter are produced automatically in response to the forces of nature and the processes induced by them. The inanimate forms represent, in Dennet's terms the "forced moves" (Dennett, 1995), meaning that in a given set of natural circumstances the form had no other choice, but to spring into existence. The word "form" here relates to that which is common in a set of similar objects. For example, while every mountain is unique, there is something "mountainly" in each mountain. Human form-makers, in contrast, typically face a design situation, where they have to use their analytical, problem-solving, creative, and technical skills to generate the form from a (often huge) set of possible alternatives. Thus in form-making human designers have freedom compared to an inanimate nature. This freedom, in a sense, *is* a problem.

Darwinian evolution process has been responsible for the production of all kinds of forms among the living beings. The three major (shall we call them) meta-forms correspond to the three kingdoms of plants, animals, and fungi. The multitude of species representing a hierarchy of forms has evolved throughout the history of life on earth in a constant battle for survival. The tree of life is rather bushy, and it does not per se lead to a progress of some sort, however the latter is understood, but simply contains the forms that are best fit for the current state of environment (Gould, 1996). The living beings, along with their interaction with the environment and among themselves represent a complex eco-system, where, one could imagine, small changes or random events could lead to a completely different set of forms. Due to a stochastic nature of mutations and recombinations—the workhorses of the evolution—the forms appearing are not so much deterministic in nature. Sudden environmental events could also lead to a completely new shape of the biosphere with the changed set of actors. It is not easy to imagine what the life might have been like if it were not for a cosmic event that led to the extinction of the dinosaur form.

Darwinian process is a prolific designer capable of producing artifacts of stunning complexity. However, it suffers from two basic deficiencies. First, in order for the evolution to produce a design, the latter should be accessible from the existing forms in a set of simple steps, each of which proves to be advantageous. The second issue with the evolutionary way of form-making is that it is tremendously wasteful, random, and requires long periods of time. The first living forms on Earth – the prokaryotes had appeared about 3.5 billion years ago, it is believed. These were simple bacteria without nuclei. The eukaryotes, the cells with the nucleus holding DNA (which make up our own organisms) have appeared approximately about two billion years ago. It took about 1.5 million years for the nature to figure out how to make a eukaryotic cell from two prokaryotic ones. A human designer would have probably taken much less time before he or she would have suggested in a flash of creativity to put a smaller no-nucleus sell into a larger one, so that the former becomes the nucleus. Furthermore, multi-cellular organisms had appeared "only" about 700 million years ago. Now, it is hard to imagine that a human would take over a billion years before he or she would figure out the way of sticking the single cells together somewhat in a Lego-like fashion. Of course, these analogies are far-fetched and not literally applicable, yet the message is that human form makers are much faster and much less wasteful than the nature itself.

Interestingly, an analogy had been suggested in the past between something like the blind Darwinian evolution, and the human designer. Dennett provides an example of Hume's writings, where the latter speculates via one of the characters, whether a not-so-intelligent designer could have been responsible for the high level of organization the world manifests (Dennett, 1995). This "dumb" designer would simply try out randomly different arrangements to see if they lead to a "better" world. Then, given enough time, isn't there a possibility that he or she would eventually end up with the well-organized world? (Actually, there is a rather inelegant method of design based on a random search: it's called "the trial-and-error" method. Most of the time, however, the designers have some understanding of the nature of problem to be able to search for solutions in a much more efficient fashion.)

Thus, forms can spring into existence as the result of human activity, or natural processes. The distinctive characteristic of human form-making include: freedom of choice, efficient search, and ability to make large changes (meaning that human designers can introduce several vital changes in a single step, e.g. in an XOR fashion). The understanding of the *existing* naturally-produced forms is a matter of traditional scientific research. The generation of *new* forms has been conventionally called "design." Human-generated forms exhibit more of purposefulness in their organization and function. Forms of the inanimate nature do not. Biological forms are closer to human-made artifacts on the purposefulness scale. And yet, however diverse these different categories are, they are all forms. At some level of abstraction, it is probably possible to ignore the issue of where the form came from and study its structure and behavior. At that level the difference between the natural and artificial would vanish, but let us postpone this discussion until later.

Forms are fitted to contexts, i.e. functional requirements (Alexander, 1964). Alexander posits that if one knows the context fully, one knows the form. In other words complete and precise description of the problem *yields* the solution, almost in an automatic fashion. Rather metaphorically, this could be represented as in Figure 2. Imagine the two profiles are the context, and then vase is the resulting form, although in this particular case the form and its context could be exchanged. But there is a deeper meaning in the figure from the design perspective: it implies that both context and form

have to be "designed" in some way. The definition of the context itself, sort of results in an artifact, in a kind of context-form. The Dutch graphic artist Maurits Cornelis Escher has produced many works of art of such nature, where the form can serve as a context, and context as a form.

A good design is produced when a form fits its context. The problem is, however that contexts are not easy to define in a comprehensive fashion. Thus, Alexander suggests, instead of fits to focus on misfits of form-context, as the latter are easier to spot. Moreover, the boundaries between form and context may not be fixed, but flexible, and an adaptation in co-fitting the solution and the problem is often necessary. It has been suggested that in the design process a co-evolution of a problem-solution pair takes place (Maher, Poon, & Boulanger, 1996). In a recent empirical study involving professional designers who were presented with the problem of designing a litter system on the trains, a protocol analysis has revealed that the participants indeed had gone through solution generation—problem modification—solution revision processes (Dorst, 2001). Thus, this confirms the view that form and context boundaries often go through sort of oscillations before settling down in some stable state.

The parallels with the misfit and co-adaptation of forms and contexts could be also found in the Information Systems practice. Innovative IT solutions were not always welcome among the business user groups. If an IT artifact required re-orientation of some sort in performing daily activities by the workers, they perceived it as a lack of fit between what technology had to offer and how the task should be performed. One of the most famous examples includes the implementation and adoption of Enterprise Resource Planning (ERP) systems.

Automation of record-keeping to support various business processes has been a huge improvement in early years of computing. However, the creation of different systems for different functional areas of the business also meant that

Figure 2. The context and the form

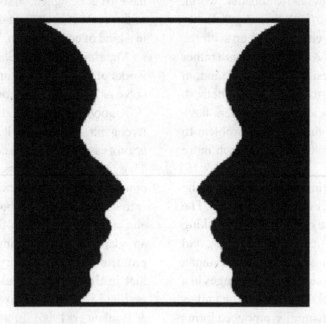

there were barriers in communicating information across those areas. This is a well-known "islands of automation" phenomenon. This rather attractive and "teasing" gap (irregularity) being present, it was only a matter of time that a corresponding form would pop up at some point. The philosophy behind ERP systems focused on delivering the holistic product that would do away with barriers and provide a consistent informational infrastructure to smoothly support all the essential functions across the enterprise (e.g. Sales, Finance, Manufacturing, Inventories, etc.). Although typically it meant installing a formidable software artifact, a properly managed implementation process could lead to the appreciable benefits for an organization (Markus & Tanis, 2000).

However, initially many companies that were eager to embrace ERP solutions had to swallow a bitter pill. Aside from the technical problems, they found out that the software imposed its own logic on the structure of the organization and its business processes (Davenport, 1998). ERP builders adopted the "best practice" approaches in constructing their software, which was not

necessarily what particular businesses demanded. Instead of simply providing smoothly operating infrastructure for the organizational structure, the ERP systems essentially demanded a new structure. To adopt ERP meant changing business practices, which could not have been painless for all. The form demanded the adaptation of the context.

Figure 3 represents schematically the idea of forms and the context. In many cases, if there is a problem (context) there is an old form, a design that was used to fill the gap. However, the misfits in the form-context pairing prompt the further design processes (note that the shape of the context is most frequently unknown to the designer). The new form is thus proposed that promises a much better fit with the context. The new form may be constructed via the assembly of already existing, more basic forms.

Alexander has further defined the design pattern language to systematize and the design process, and make it more effective and efficient (Alexander, Ishikawa, & Silverstein, 1977). Design patterns represent a set of typical successful

Figure 3. Old and new forms

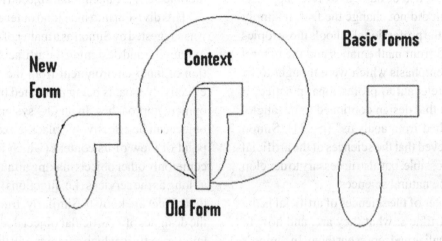

(architectural) design solutions that could be employed in new projects according to rules that trigger under certain conditions. While every design project could be unique in some sense, the larger the proportion of already known design elements in the new solution, the less effort is required on the designer's side, and the higher are chances of successful end product.

In Software Engineering the Object-Oriented (OO) approach to system development has been strongly advocated, in part because it promotes the use of already known working components. This is called "reuse," and objects allow for painless and a less risky way of promoting it. The metric known as "reuse leverage" is expressed as the ratio of the portion of software that has been reused in a given project to the total software. In an ideal (though hardly real) situation, all of the software would have a 100% leverage, meaning that the new software form has been assembled from the old known forms. Software Engineering has also adopted the idea of patterns from Alexander, by which it refers to the common problem situations, and the typical arrangement of software objects to address those situations.

Artifact as an Interface

Nelson and Stolterman point that the objective of design is to produce the "ultimate concrete" (Nelson & Stolterman, 2003). They have pictured the two-dimensional layout with abstraction on one axis and the complexity on the other. Moving from the higher abstraction and lower complexity levels to their opposites parallels the transitions from the universal to general, particular, full particular, and, finally, the ultimate particular. Thus, the designer's work is viewed as building the ultimate particular that would address the concrete design problem situation in full detail. In this relation, it is interesting to consider alternative conceptualizations of the designer's artifact, in particular that proposed by Simon.

Herbert Simon, among other major achievements, has been credited for introducing the very notion of the "Sciences of the Artificial" (Simon, 1996). In this work he had voiced his concern about the lack of design teachings in academic institutions, and their overly reliance on natural sciences: "In view of the key role of design in professional activity, it is ironic that in this century the natural sciences almost drove the sciences of the artificial from professional school curricula…The use of adjectives like "applied" concealed, but did not change the fact. It simply meant that in the professional schools those topics were selected from mathematics and the natural sciences for emphasis which were thought to be most nearly relevant to professional practice. It did not mean that design continued to be taught, as distinguished from analysis" (p. 111). Simon strongly believed that the sciences of the artificial not only are possible, but also necessary to develop at par with the natural sciences.

At the center of the sciences of artificial is the question of artifacts: what they are, and how to best conceptualize and represent them. In Simon's view, when speaking about an artifact one could approach them from two perspectives, or "environments." The "outer" environment represents the required functions of an artifact and the conditions in which artifact is supposed to function. This is similar to the context of the form in Alexander's terms. The "inner" environment is the internal organization of an artifact, the way its components are arranged and the patterns of their interaction.

This dualistic view, Simon argued, has significant advantages. From the "outer" vantage point, one can view the designed object as a "black box," ignoring its internal details, while still being able to make predictions about its behavior in different contexts, knowing what functions it is supposed to perform. For example, most of the theoretical investigations of so-called "intelligent agents" actually focus on their externally exhibited properties and behaviors, while ignoring their internal mechanics. Similarly, from the inner point of view, the artifact designer may abstract away from all the details of the outer environment and focus only on those that are relevant to the function of the artifact. Thus, the environment, in a sense is being black-boxed. The artifact itself is characterized as the "interface" between its outer and inner environments. Somewhat similar to Simon, Kroes recently described artifacts as having a dual

nature: on one hand they are physical entities, on the other they are intentional objects (Kroes, 2002).

This division into inner and outer environment was suggested by Simon as a matter of convenience in studying and designing the artifacts. The insulation of inner environment from the outer one is, effectively what is being promoted by OO development approaches. In an OO system, any given object can be effectively "black-boxed" from the point of view of its context (which implies most commonly other objects making up an application) as long as the services (i.e. functions) provided by that object are known. Similarly, from the inside, the designer of a particular object does not need to know exactly in which contexts will this particular object function. Thus, the rest of the application is being "black-boxed." This proves to be, indeed, quite a convenient isolation, as the application itself may change in the future and still be able to use the services of a given object without having to modify the latter. In other words, the inner environment only "knows" whatever is necessary and sufficient for it in order to produce necessary services in a changing outer environment.

The idea of an artifact as an interface deserves a deeper insight here. Simon notes, that ideally "we might hope to be able to characterize the main properties of the system without elaborating the detail of *either* the outer or inner environments. We might look toward a science of the artificial that would depend on the relative simplicity of the interface as its primary source of *abstraction and generality*" (p.9, italics added). To explain his point he quotes an example of a patent on a motor controller. Motor itself could be used in a variety of contexts, thus it is not tied to any particular context. But what's more interesting, the description of the mechanism itself does not mention any concrete elements, but necessary functions, in a rather abstract way. The function-oriented terms, like "reversing means" are used to describe the inner environment. In essence, the artifact from the outside is described as a function, and in the inside its organization is also given in terms of abstractly defined functions in their interrelationships. The object is described in vague terms from the inside and the outside. This is, effectively an *abstract* artifact. According to Simon, the ideal description of a design is in form of an abstract artifact.

The idea of an abstract artifact is presented schematically in Figure 4. The inner workings of an artifact could be realized by several candidate implementations. These would leave the required functions unaffected. These functions may then be needed to address a subset of requirements in different contexts. Again, it's hard not to make a parallel with OO terminology. A given function may be performed by different objects differently. These are thus defined as abstract functions to achieve polymorphism – a mechanism that significantly improves the flexibility of treating different objects in the same fashion. In fact, the term "interface" is used to refer to a collection of abstract behaviors that could be invoked by different client objects, and implemented by provider objects. Since OO design and implementation has been widely embraced by the professionals,

and the OO philosophy shares many similarities with the Simon's idea of artifacts, this adds a tremendous real-world support for the usefulness of the concept of artifact as an interface, and the related notion of an abstract artifact.

Now, going back to the "ultimate concrete" view of the artifact, there seems to be a contradiction with the Simon's "interface," or the abstract artifact conceptualization. In a concrete design situation the designer, no doubt should be working out the artifact solution which is specified to the minute details, to leave little space for the vagueness of interpretation by the builders. For example, in system and software development the user requirements and the design specifications ideally need to be as detailed as possible to limit the freedom of interpretation on the builders' side. Ensuring the conformity of the system to these specifications is the job of the quality assurance function. The dual perspectives on an artifact do not suggest per se that the artifact is abstract. It's when *both* the inner and outer environments are abstracted the notion of the abstract artifact rises. It is probably not coincidental that Simon brings

Figure 4. Artifact as interface

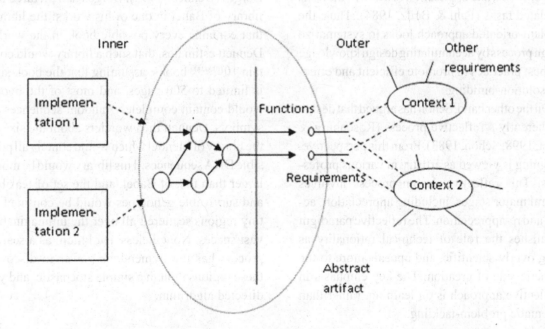

an example of a patent, rather than a concretely designed object in connection with the abstract view of the interface. Patents relate to *inventions*, rather than particular designed objects. Thus, although a designed artifact in a given particular context must be specified rather precisely, inventions can and must entertain some vagueness to be applicable to a wider class of problems in different internal realizations. The abstract artifacts are the key focus of this book.

DESIGN PROBLEM SOLVING

When considering the activity of designing two types of views have emerged: those of systematic problem-solving and reflective practice. Design is required when addressing some sort of a need, or, in other words, solving some problem (e.g. planning a series of actions to achieve a given set of objectives, such as saving for retirement). Pahl & Beitz, for example, emphasize that design method should encourage a problem-directed approach which must be applicable to every type of design activity. Furthermore, it should foster innovativeness and understanding, search for optimal solutions, and application of known solutions to related tasks (Pahl & Beitz, 1984). Thus, the problem-oriented approach looks to systematize design process by accumulating design knowledge and best practices to promote efficient and effective solution-building.

On the other hand, Schön has argued that design is inherently a reflective process (Rosenburg & Dorst, 1998; Schön, 1983). From this perspective, designing is viewed as artistry in various professions. This reflective design process involves several major stages, including appreciation, action, and re-appreciation. The reflective paradigm diminishes the role of technical rationality as being overly scientific, and appeals more to the aesthetic side of creation. The key emphasis in a reflective approach is on learning, rather than systematic problem-tackling.

Both problem-directed and reflective views on designing are valuable for fostering improved design processes. The former emphasizes systematicity and reuse, thus being somewhat analogous to deduction. The latter places a great deal of importance on learning, which is in many respects similar to induction. The deductive and inductive processes have long been recognized as valuable vehicles of inquiry in scientific research.

In human behavior the individuals have to handle problem situations all the time. A problem is often defined as a gap between the initial and desired states of affairs (MacCrimmon & Taylor, 1976). From the design perspective the gaps can be viewed as misfits between the form and the context in Alexander's terms. Solving the problem involves finding a set of transformations that would lead from the initial situation to the desired one. Thus, problem solving in general, and artifact design in particular, can be viewed as a search process.

Adoption of the search perspective can be useful in understanding the characteristics of the design situations and the magnitude of the design space. In regard to search spaces, Daniel Dennett uses a metaphor borrowed from poet Jorge Luis Borges (Dennett, 1995). Borges had pictured the library of Babel in one of his works: the library that contains every possible book in the world. Dennett estimates, that such a library would contain $10^{1,000,000}$ books, assuming that the book size is limited to 500 pages, and most of the books would contain completely random sequences of symbols. Dennett then wonders about the size of the library of Mendel which would contain all possible DNA sequences. This library would be much larger than that of Babel, and the set of feasible and survivable genotypes would be confined in tiny regions scattered all over the unimaginably vast spaces. Nonetheless, evolution, as a search process has the tremendous power to discover these regions though a simple stochastic, and yet directed algorithm.

In regard with design problems one could use an imagination to encode the key design decision variables and as the symbols in the "design book." Then the size of the design space could be estimated quite easily (assuming absence of the constraints). Unlike natural selection, which produces multiple fit solutions, design problems typically involve search for one "best" artifact. Thus, there is a single point (or "book") in a typically considerable design space (library) that needs to be found.

Search problems are one of the major topics in Artificial Intelligence. Suppose we start out with the original design (either an existing solution, or a preliminary new one) as an initial node in the space. We could go about searching by exploring the neighboring nodes in a systematic fashion, e.g. breadth-first or depth-first. For example, in a breadth-first search we would make small modifications to all of the design variables one by one producing a new set of "child" designs. As we produce these new candidates, we could test them for the "eureka" signal, that is to see if we have achieved the desired state. If not we would move on to the children of children of the initial point, and so on until we hit the jackpot. If we could get some sort of workable heuristic that would tell us how far off we are from the target, we could even employ something like a "greedy" search, by exploring the most promising nodes first. This systematic procedure could hypothetically be applied to a rather wide class of design situations. However, there is a catch.

In order to employ such algorithmic processes the procedure at least has to be able to recognize the desired node. The set of the design variables with particular choices of their values represents a "genotype" of the artifact. This genotype should be related somehow to a corresponding "phenotype," i.e. how the artifact's features come into interplay with the design context (problem) to produce measurable effects on problem criteria. This would imply that every candidate artifact must be built and thoroughly tested to assign it a "goodness" value. This is hardly doable due to the enormous cost and time requirements. Moreover, the problem criteria are most often in conflict with each other: improving on one of them would result in an adverse effect on others. Often human designer's judgment is required in making trade-offs. Furthermore, moving in the right direction following some heuristic may not be a straightforward process, as the relationship of genotype to phenotype may be complex, and the sequential search methods may not be able to reach the ideal configurations. So, to summarize, in design search spaces it is unclear what constitutes the desired state, and also what is the best set of search steps to getting to a desired state even if it could be recognized when reached. Problems, where initial or desired state or the set of transformations leading from one to the other are uncertain are known as ill-structured (MacCrimmon & Taylor, 1976). Ill-structured problems cannot be "programmed" or "algorithmized" effectively, although they could be partially structured, meaning that even though the entire solution process cannot be performed algorithmically, there could be certain guidelines, past similar cases, heuristics, and other hints.

There is also a common opinion that modern designers often have to deal with the "wicked" problems (e.g. Nelson & Stolterman, 2003). Wicked problems (Rittel & Webber, 1973), have some "ugly" characteristics, including the following:

- There is no definitive formulation of a wicked problem.
- Wicked problems have no stopping rule.
- Solutions to wicked problems are not true-or-false, but better or worse.
- There is no immediate and no ultimate test of a solution to a wicked problem.
- Every solution to a wicked problem is a "one-shot operation"; because there is no opportunity to learn by trial-and-error, every attempt counts significantly.
- Wicked problems do not have an enumerable (or an exhaustively describable) set

of potential solutions, nor is there a well-described set of permissible operations that may be incorporated into the plan.

- Every wicked problem is essentially unique.
- Every wicked problem can be considered to be a symptom of another problem.
- The existence of a discrepancy representing a wicked problem can be explained in numerous ways. The choice of explanation determines the nature of the problem's resolution.
- The planner has no right to be wrong (planners are liable for the consequences of the actions they generate).

Thus, design problems truly need human insight, creativity, and judgment. In the oft-cited Simon's problem solving model there are phases described as intelligence, design, choice, and implementation and monitoring (Simon, 1977). In the intelligence phase problem is identified and clarified. The design phase deals with generating and consideration of potential solutions, with the subsequent final choice and implementation of the action plan. Well structured problems have all of their phases outlined algorithmically. In ill-structured (including wicked) situations, at least one phase lacks a clear procedural approach.

Pahl & Beitz view design work as a process of information conversion (Pahl & Beitz, 1984). They proposed the "General Problem Solving" method for design tasks in industrial engineering based on the analysis-synthesis pattern. The method is described as a sequence of steps including: task, confrontation, information, definition, creation, evaluation, decision, and solution. Needless to say each of these steps typically requires a considerable cognitive effort on part of the designer. Hubka & Eder described the design process as being creative, in other words, intuitive, iterative, recursive, opportunistic, innovative, ingenious, unpredictable, searching for elegance and beauty and so on (Hubka & Eder, 1996).

Creative approach to problem solving is thus an essential skill needed to become a good designer. While much has been written on creativity, it is difficult to provide precise guidelines for achieving it. Well known creativity-enhancing techniques include such recommendations as "thinking outside the box" (Ackoff, 1978), and stressing divergent processes in the initial stages of problem solving, and the convergent ones towards the end of solution formulation (Basadur, 1994). To stimulate creative approach to design problem solving Ackoff et al. suggest an "idealized design method" (Ackoff, Magidson, & Addison, 2006). The key is to imagine what the ideal solution would be like, relaxing constraints and ignoring technical obstacles, and then work backwards towards the present state. Thus, in this method the authors suggest fixing the desired state and subsequently finding a feasible solution closest to that state (while realizing that the ideal state is most often not achievable realistically). They describe the following stages of their method: formulating the mess, ends planning, means planning, resource planning, design of implementation, and design of control. Ackoff gives an example of his experience with producing "idealized design" in terms of proposing the desired properties for a new type of telephone – the problem that he had encountered in the Fifties. The telephone "wishlist" at the time included features like touch-tone dialing, mobility, and others, most of which are commonplace nowadays.

The idea of starting with the desired outcome, rather than working from the initial state forward is natural in the context of design. Hubka & Eder note (Hubka & Eder, 1996): "In designing, we frequently look for *candidate causes* that are likely to be able to achieve the *desired effects*. The causal chain (from cause to effect) familiar from analysis and science need to be reversed" (p. 9). This "backward chaining" process seems to be applicable equally well to forward, as well as reverse engineering. Dorst notes, that functional thinking of design has parallels in the natural world and can provide insights into the structure of organisms based on the knowledge of their habitat (Dorst, 2006).

Along similar lines, Rosen advised an anticipatory approach to design (Rosen, 1985). According to Rosen, in design the significance of the lost Aristotelian fourth cause (the "final" cause) regains its importance. This teleological stance, however, may be a difficult idea to grasp, because philosophically it implies a causality problem, namely that future states somehow affect the present actions (Zamenopoulos & Alexiou, 2007). Nonetheless, having a desired, albeit "idealized" picture of the artifact seems to be beneficial as it encourages a creative stretch and facilitates generation of "good" ideas.

Identifying the characteristics of "good" creative ideas that could lead to successful designs is not a straightforward process; though there has been some work done in the past in this direction. Goldschmidt & Tatsa have applied linkographic analysis in an empirical study to tackle the question (Gabriela, Goldschmidt, & Tatsa, 2005). Linkography is an analysis method that focuses on links among design idea, decisions and moves (Goldschmidt, 1990). Their findings suggest that good ideas are those, which are extensively interlinked with other ideas. This is analogous to what the web search engines consider to be "good" websites, i.e. those that have many links with other sites.

DESIGN PROCESS

Pahl & Beitz distinguish the original design, i.e. specification of new type of a product or solution from adaptive design, i.e. changes to an existing design due to the modification of requirements (Pahl & Beitz, 1984). For the original design a new type of problem requirements are considered and a novel design solution sought, which would constitute a significant deviation from the solutions used to address the old "version" of the problem,

or similar problems. For adaptive design, there is an original solution which needs to be changed to minimize "misfits" with the newly evolved problem context. Thus, adaptive designs are more structured than the original ones, and hence require less effort on the designer's part. In information systems development both of these design modes are incorporated within the system development lifecycle.

There are many descriptions of the design process all sharing basic similarities. In the context of engineering design Asimow identifies the following phases prompted by what he refers to as "primitive need" (Asimow, 1962):

- Primary design process:
- Feasibility study;
- Preliminary design;
- Detailed design;
- Phases related to production-consumption cycle:
- Planning for production;
- Planning for distribution;
- Planning for consumption;
- Planning for retirement.

We will briefly describe here the primary design phases. The objective of the feasibility study is, in a nutshell, to build the case for design. As Dorst notes: "design is perceived as a necessary evil by companies" (Dorst, 2006). It often implies making changes to the marketing, production, distribution, and other vital processes within an organization, not to mention the risks of failure. The first important step in feasibility study is to answer the question: does the need exist indeed? For product design problems this would probably imply conducting consumer surveys, forming focus groups, and employing other marketing research techniques. Once the need has been identified, the problem is further investigated and clarified, and the design project is assessed in terms of technical and financial feasibility.

In preliminary design alternative solution candidates are considered and assessed with respect to the design criteria. As it has already been noted earlier, it is important not to jump ahead to detailed design, before full consideration is given to all the promising candidates. This ensures that the "due process" of design is maintained. It is also in line with the stress on divergent processes at the early phases of the process emanating from the general problem solving principles.

The detailed design refines the selected solution to incorporate the technical detail and prepare specifications necessary for building an artifact. The whole design process has a high degree of correspondence with the phases of human problem solving/decision making.

Hubka & Eder outline the following stages (Hubka & Eder, 1996):

- Clarifying the task
  Results in problem specifications for the design;
- Conceptualizing
  Use of abstract models to generate framework, outline, and functionality;
- Embodying
  Deciding on materials and components; and
- Detailing
  Complete manufacturing information.

Earlier the problem solving approach to design including confrontation, information, etc. proposed in (Pahl & Beitz, 1984) has been mentioned. In their complete design process description, the problem solving stages should be utilized iteratively for each of the design phases, which include clarification of the task; conceptual design; embodiment design; and detail design. This is similar to some of the modern system development processes based on a "spiral" model.

In systems development context, the phases typically include analysis, overall and detailed design, construction, testing, and maintenance. The identification and proper management of these cases led in the past to what is referred to the structured approach as opposed to "no approach." When the phases are carried out in a sequence, we arrive at a waterfall model. Later more agile methods have appeared, which allowed for a more iterative processes that could deliver some version of a product at an earlier stage. In any case the design process can be described as the process of analysis, synthesis, implementation, and maintenance.

The maintenance phase deserves a special attention. According to Hubka & Eder, designing a novel system or process accounts for 0.1 to 10% of all design projects. In systems development most of resources are also being spent on maintaining old systems, rather than developing new ones. The maintenance phase could actually be treated as a repeated sequence of earlier three phases. It thus translates into some sort of cyclicality in the model. Maintenance involves modifications to existing products, such as software in order to correct defects, provide new functionality, or make modifications according to change in requirements.

Design does not have to be a reactive and irregular activity. Ideally, it could be turned into a strategic tool. In this respect Kotler & Rath define design as "the process of seeking to optimize consumer satisfaction and company profitability through the creative use of major design elements (performance, quality, durability, appearance and cost) in connection with products, environments, information, and corporate identity" (Kotler & Rath, 1984). A systematic assessment of the existing design solutions and investigation of the new possibilities for development in alignment with company's business strategy is referred to as design management. A proactive approach towards design management by a company would involve defining and implementing the "design agenda" (Cooper & Press, 1995).

Comparing engineering and information systems design processes, one can easily see the similarities at some level of abstraction. Essentially, both of them undergo analysis-synthesis cycle. Later in the book we will also try to show, yet at a higher level of abstraction the similarities between designing in general and conducting scientific research. Note, that all of the phases can also be described in terms of synthesis. The analysis phase involves investigating the problem, and yet it results in a synthesis of problem representation. Then follow the conceptual and detail syntheses, followed by technological synthesis. Strictly speaking, all phases of design involve some sort of design. Thus, we see the scope of design in a broad perspective, in particular, we see analysis also as a kind of design activity.

DESIGN REPRESENTATIONS

In design one of the key issues to tackle is the choice of representational means to communicate the designer's vision of the artifact. Goldschmidt claims that in design "the ultimate goal is to arrive at a satisfying representation of the designed entity…We may argue that *to design is to represent*, and in no case is there design without representation" (Goldschmidt, 2004) (italics added). Since the representational means depend heavily on the concrete area of design, here we will limit our focus on some examples from systems design.

Software Engineering and Systems Development use an arsenal of tools to represent and evaluate various design solutions and solution elements at different levels of refinement. Representations are used to clarify, understand, improve, communicate, test, and document various aspects of artifacts. Flowcharts, hierarchy charts, Petri nets, entity-relationship diagrams, z-specifications, data flow diagrams are just a few of the variety of representational tools for describing the structure of an artifact and its processes. Some of the above tools are more formal (e.g. Z-specifications), and some are less (semi-) formal (e.g. data flow diagrams). Formal representations allow for rigorous validation of an artifact and they originate largely

from Computer Science and Software Engineering. However, for complex and open systems developing and using formal models tends to be inadequate considering the effort required (not to mention the training needed for the system stakeholders). That is why substantial testing of constructed systems is a necessity.

In traditional structured approach that largely assumes a "waterfall" model different phases of development are relatively independent. Systems for business tend to be data—centric as large volumes of data are needed to properly track records of transaction information for operational and reporting purposes. Thus, business processes are viewed from an angle of data flows and storages. For decomposing and analyzing the processing of data and tracking the routes of information passage the representational modeling tool known as data flow diagram has been developed. These diagrams would later be considered in designing and implementing a software system. Good design of software had to follow system principles. Modularity, cohesion, and loose coupling were considered to be among the prime principles in guiding the design process. The software itself used to be organized in a sort of hierarchical fashion with division into modules and submodules, with the breakdown continuing until a single module would perform a single function (functional modularity). In a pre-plus-plus version of C language there were no modules, other than those organized as functions.

In other words, the analysis would result in a representation more fitted to business processes, while the design of a system would be more oriented towards IT representation. There is a sense of mismatch between these two types of representation. Examining a DFD diagram one would hardly be able to see immediately the architecture of the system supporting the required data flows and processes. This mismatch made it difficult to adopt iterative approaches to development, whereby one could relatively painlessly move forth and back between analysis, design, and implementation of software-based systems. When planning out a new house (to adopt an example from Zachman), the initial tentative sketches, and the complete technical plans and specifications relate to the same artifact, which takes more and more detailed shape through the refinement process. There is continuity here, a sense that different representations employed in the process relate to the same artifact being designed. In (by now traditional) structured approach the different representations did not seem to be referring to the same artifact.

Object-oriented development has gained its momentum as a means of coping with the complexity and manageability of substantial software projects. Object-oriented languages like SmallTalk and C++ have centered around the notion of an object as an independent interacting entity and a building unit for software-based systems. The beauty of object-oriented analysis, design, and implementation, supplemented by the complex of representational tools called the Unified Modeling Language (UML) is in the continuity of different levels of representation supported by the very notion of the object. Here, the organization of the artifact, its functioning, its shape becomes apparent in the analysis phase, and is further refined through the subsequent phases. There is a sense of continuity, and with it comes the possibility of moving with a relative ease between different stages of development. There is no significant mismatch between the analysts,' designer's, and builder's perspectives.

Choice of representational tools plays a key role in improving the quality and maintainability of the artifacts. The idea of objects basically echoes that of Plato's forms. Incidentally, Alexander also chose to use the term "form" as a key structure of architectural artifacts. In fact, the idea of Patterns was borrowed from Alexander and advocated for OO development. Patterns in OO could be viewed as a toolbox of generic solutions involving objects to commonly encountered development problems. Some of the notions associated with OO approach, most notably the idea of abstract classes, their functions and attributes, as well as the hierarchy of abstract and concrete classes have interesting implications for design research, especially in light of the view adopted in this work that stresses abstract artifacts as a proper focus for design researchers.

DESIGN STUDIES AND PHILOSOPHY OF DESIGN

Much of the insights into the nature of artifacts and design processes have originated in the field discipline called "design research." The design research tradition has had over forty years of history during which it had its own ups and down (Cross, 2007). Nigel Cross argued that design is the third way of knowing the world, in addition to the other two: the Science and the Humanities (Cross, 2006). Designing is a process, and understanding the nature, conditions, and the consequences of successful design is referred to as "designerly ways of knowing." Design itself has been characterized as an agent for promoting knowledge flow at the intra- and inter- organizational levels (Bertola & Teixeira, 2003).

Galle defines design research as "not just how to design, how designers work, what design is, but all of this, and more, scholarly knowledge and understanding of whatever is called design" (Galle, 2008). From the point of view of instructional design, Richey and Kleing define design research as "the systematic study of design, development and evaluation processes with the aim of establishing an empirical basis for the creation of instructional and non-instructional products and tools and new or enhanced models that govern their development" (Richey & Klein, 2007). Hubka & Eder write: "The term *Design Science* is to be understood as a system of logically related knowledge, which should contain and organize the complete knowledge about and for designing" (p.73). According to them, Design Science must explain the causal connections and laws of the area. The objectives of design science include:

- Direct improvement of situation in practice;
- Scholarly contributions to the design knowledge through research projects and dissertations; and
- Improvement of design education at schools.

They further note that design science should incorporate common scientific tools and techniques, such as conjectures, hypotheses, observations, data analysis, generalization, and others. In order to substantiate the scientific approach to the study of design, they put forward a thesis, claiming that

- Designing is a rational activity that could be decomposed into smaller steps;
- Design process can be studied and presented in a general form; and
- Design can be teachable.

Cross has identified three forms of design research: research into design, through descriptive studies and observation; research for design, involving development of tools and methods to facilitate design; and research through design, which implies learning from design experiences, abstracting and generalizing (Cross, 1995). Two classes of systems are used in Design Science: process systems and technical systems (Hubka & Weber, 1998).

Dorst notes that developing the scientific side to the design profession is a logical step in the area of design (Dorst, 2006). However, he warns against being "overly" academic, as design is inherently creative process. He notes that while abstracting away from the peculiarities of design contexts may result in true valid models and concepts, the very fact of ignoring details makes it difficult to apply those tools to practical design problems.

Regarding the comparison between design and science, Buchannan opposes to the science view

of design. He points that while in the traditional sciences the subject matter of the field is given, in design it is created by the designers (Buchanan, 1995). He further posits that there is a difference between discovery and invention. For discovery, there has to be something out there waiting to be discovered. In invention that something does not exist until it is conceived and brought into existence by the designer.

Asimow notes on the distinction between research and design (Asimow, 1962): "In research the outcome of synthesis is one or more alternative hypotheses, in design it is one or more alternative design concepts. It is true, that both outcomes are concepts, but the hypothesis of research is a generalization, while the concept in design is a specialization. *Research is directed toward obtaining a class of answers; design, toward a specific answer*. The end product of research is a finding which will be true in many situations; of design, a piece of hardware. Research proceeds from abstract to the general; design from the abstract to the concrete. Research provides new technical ideas for design ... which are not limited to a particular design." (p. 47).

Hubka and Eder propose that there is a hierarchy of design knowledge, including general and specialized Design Sciences (Hubka & Eder, 1996). They define the constituent areas of Design Science:

- Theory of technical systems;
- Theory of design processes;
- Branch knowledge (knowledge about concrete technical systems); and
- Design process knowledge.

In relation to information systems design, one could also identify the general knowledge that is applicable to all systems, as well as "branch" knowledge, which relates to particular classes of systems. For example, system principles, including such guidelines as modularity and loose coupling could be regarded as part of the theory of technical systems. The systems development methodology constitutes the design processes part. The principles of organization and development of, say decision support systems relate to the "branch" knowledge of this particular subfield.

One emergent topic related to the studies of design is the philosophy of design (Galle, 2002). Although there is hardly a thorough and precise definition of what constitutes such a philosophy, perhaps the best way to understand it is to think of it as meta-design science. As such it should focus on the questions of the nature, objectives, methods of design research, and other similar issues. Love notes: "*Philosophy of Design* is different from *design philosophy*. It is the disciplinary equivalent of Philosophy of Science, or Philosophy of Technology—whereas design philosophy is associated more with the philosophical study of design method" (Love, 2000). Example questions in Philosophy of Design according to Love include: What is design? What is design theory? How can theories be tested? Dorst critically examines the past work in design studies from the point of view of a descriptive framework (Dorst, 2008). The framework includes object (design problem and solution), actor (designer), context of activity, and the process. He notes that past work has mostly focused on the last component of the framework and points at the necessity to direct research efforts into other three areas identified by the framework. Philosophy of design is still in its infancy, and its boundaries and problems are yet to be defined. Nonetheless, this is an admirable effort, and there is a hope that it will grow in the future to establish its own tradition, principles and guidelines similar to the philosophy of science.

"Design research" is a somewhat confusing term. Perhaps, the name of the leading journal in the area "Design Studies" is much better suited to describing what kind of research takes place in the field. Simply put the objective of the design studies in the improvement of design process. This is not what this book is about. "Design Science Research" in the IS field refers to kind of projects that aim at introducing new system concepts. In other words, producing a novel solution to a class of business problems is a type of "design research." It seems that a term like "Design-type Research" better fits the description, and it will be predominantly used throughout the remainder of the book.

DESIGN FUTURE

Let us revisit the idea of "lack of wholeness" in the world that drives design activities. Will we, as humans ever be able to see the world complete to our satisfaction, and thus not requiring any new artifacts? The Great Russian poet Alexander Pushkin wrote a fairy tale titled "The tale of the fisherman and the fish." As the tale goes, there was an elderly couple living in poverty, until one day the old man caught a golden fish. The fish spoke in human language and promised to fulfill any wish if the fisherman let her go. Initially, the old man released the fish back to the sea, but later his wife would send him back repeatedly to ask the fish for more and more wealth, until the fish made her "tsarina." The old lady wouldn't stop, though until she angrily sent her husband to ask the fish to make her the ruler of the sea. At this point, apparently the fish had had enough as she simply swam away from the fisherman. When he returned home he discovered that all of their riches were gone and they are back to where they started with their old hut back in place.

To ask for more is part of the human nature. It's as if the Schopenhauerian "will" leads us from setting one objective to erecting another one, when the previous one has been achieved. Thus, it is doubtful that the world will ever be "complete" (assuming the abundance of resources). The development of human artifact-making was slow in the beginning, taking a million years or so to move from simple choppers to a sharper set of tools, but would pick up steadily eventually leading to industrial revolution of the seventeenth century, and the computer revolution of the present. Ray Kurzweil in the "Age of Intelligent Machines" observes that the development of human technology has been exponentially growing, with a relatively slow and steady growth in the past, and a dramatic explosion in recent times (Kurzweil, 1990).

Alexander makes a distinction between what he calls the "unselfconscious process" of design and the "self conscious" process (Alexander, 1964). The former applied to the times when ground-breaking innovations were rare, and the human technology remained relatively unchanged from generation to generation. Self conscious processes characterize the fast-paced progress of present-day technology. The unselfconscious process, he claimed, produces good forms, since the "misfits" to a relatively stable context (problem environment) are apparent. Self-conscious processes are not so easy to judge, because the context changes as well, and there is little time to spot the misfits. Thus, in the modern world there is a much heavier burden on the designers' shoulders. Design of the multitude of artifacts—good and bad affects the environment that poses the design problems, this environment itself being to a large extent of the artificial nature.

Figure 5. Interplay of technology and context

Figure 5 shows schematically the interplay between new forms of artifacts (in particular, technological artifacts) and their problem contexts. It is based on the analogy with the mutual induction of electric and magnetic fields in electromagnetic waves. Technological change brings a change in the context, which produces the new sort of requirements, which results in a new form, which again changes the context, and so on. At every step the old form and context are somewhat negated in a fashion similar to the "law of negation of negation" of Hegel and Marx. Often the newly born tools and other artifacts have a very short lifespan.

"Everything that can be invented has been" is a statement attributed to Charles H. Duell, the Commissioner of the U.S. Patent and Trademark Office in 1899. This had proved to be a tremendously false illusion. No matter how confident we are in our present-day technology, we shouldn't think that much of the progress is already behind. There is more design work to come, and hence an increased importance of the research into design, and design-type research.

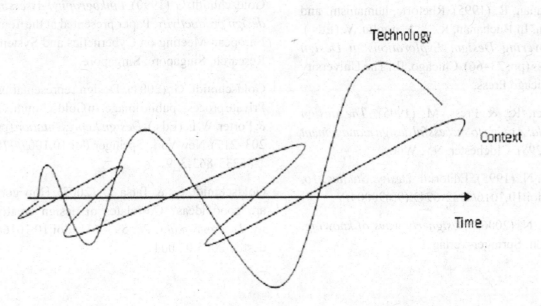

REFERENCES

Ackoff, R. L. (1978). *The art of problem solving: Accompanied by Ackoff's fables*. New York: John Wiley and Sons.

Ackoff, R. L., Magidson, J., & Addison, H. J. (2006). *Idealized design: Creating an organization's future*. Upper Saddle River: Wharton School Publishing.

Alexander, C. (1964). *Notes on the synthesis of form*. Cambridge, MA: Harvard University Press.

Alexander, C., Ishikawa, S., & Silverstein, M. (1977). *A pattern language: Towns, buildings, construction*. Oxford: Oxford University Press.

Asimow, M. (1962). *Introduction to design*. Englewoods Cliffs, NJ: Prentice-Hall.

Basadur, M. (1994). Managing the creative process in organizations. In Runco, M. A., & Chand, I. (Eds.), *Problem Finding, Problem Solving, and Creativity* (pp. 237–268). Norwood, NJ: Ablex.

Bertola, P., & Teixeira, J. C. (2003). Design as a knowledge agent: How design as a knowledge process is embedded into organizations to foster innovation. *Design Studies*, *24*, 181–194. doi:10.1016/S0142-694X(02)00036-4

Buchanan, R. (1995). Rhetoric, humanism, and design. In Buchanan, R., & Margolin, V. (Eds.), *Discovering Design: Explorations in Design Studies* (pp. 23–66). Chicago, IL: The University of Chicago Press.

Cooper, R., & Press, M. (1995). *The design agenda: A guide to successful design management* (*Vol. 298*). Chichester, NY: Wiley.

Cross, N. (1995). Editorial. *Design Studies*, *16*, 2–3. doi:10.1016/0142-694X(95)90004-Y

Cross, N. (2006). *Designerly ways of knowing*. London: Springer-Verlag.

Cross, N. (2007). Forty years of design research. *Design Studies*, *28*, 1–4. doi:10.1016/j.destud.2006.11.004

Davenport, T. H. (1998). Putting the enterprise into the enterprise system. *Harvard Business Review*, (July-August), 121-131.

Dennett, D. C. (1995). *Darwin's dangerous idea: Evolution and the meanings of life*. New York, NY: Simon & Schuster.

Dorst, K. (2001). Creativity in the design process: Co-evolution of problem-solution. *Design Studies*, *22*, 425–437. doi:10.1016/S0142-694X(01)00009-6

Dorst, K. (2006). *Understanding design: 175 reflections on being a designer*. Amsterdam, The Netherlands: BIS Publishers.

Dorst, K. (2008). Design research: A revolution-waiting-to-happen. *Design Studies*, *29*, 4–11.

Galle, P. (2002). Philosophy of design: An editorial introduction. *Design Studies*, *23*, 211–218. doi:10.1016/S0142-694X(01)00034-5

Galle, P. (2008). Candidate worldviews for design theory. *Design Studies*, *29*, 267–303. doi:10.1016/j.destud.2008.02.001

Goldschmidt, G. (1990). *Linkography: Assessing design productivity*. Paper presented at the Tenth European Meeting on Cybernetics and Systems Research. Singapore, Singapore.

Goldschmidt, G. (2004). Design representation: Private process, public image. In Goldschmidt, G., & Porter, W. L. (Eds.), *Design Representation* (pp. 203–217). New York: Springer. doi:10.1007/978-1-85233-863-3_9

Goldschmidt, G., & Tatsa, D. (2005). How good are good ideas? Correlates of design creativity. *Design Studies*, *26*, 593–611. doi:10.1016/j.destud.2005.02.004

Gould, S. J. (1996). *Full house: The spread of excellence from Plato to Darwin*. New York, NY: Harmony Books.

Hubka, V., & Eder, W. E. (1996). *Design science*. London, UK: Springer-Verlag. doi:10.1007/978-1-4471-3091-8

Hubka, V., & Weber, W. E. (1998). Theoretical approach in design methodology. In Frankenberger, E., Birkhofer, H., & Badke-Schaub, P. (Eds.), *Designers: The Key to Successful Product Development* (pp. 12–28). London, UK: Springer-Verlag.

Kant, I. (1999). *Critique of pure reason*. Cambridge, UK: Cambridge University Press.

Kotler, P., & Rath, G. A. (1984). Design: A powerful but neglected strategic tool. *The Journal of Business Strategy*, *5*(2), 16–21. doi:10.1108/eb039054

Kroes, P. (2002). Design methodology and the nature of technical artefacts. *Design Studies*, *23*, 287–302. doi:10.1016/S0142-694X(01)00039-4

Kurzweil, R. (1990). *The age of intelligent machines*. Cambridge, MA: MIT Press.

Love, T. (2000). Philosophy of design: A metatheoretical structure for design theory. *Design Studies*, *21*, 293–313. doi:10.1016/S0142-694X(99)00012-5

MacCrimmon, K. R., & Taylor, R. N. (1976). Decision making and problem solving. In Dunnette, M. D. (Ed.), *Handbook of Individual and Organizational Psychology* (pp. 1397–1453). Chicago, IL: Rand-McNally.

Maher, M. L., Poon, J., & Boulanger, S. (1996). Formalizing design exploration as co-evolution: A combined gene approach. In Gero, J. S., & Sudweeks, F. (Eds.), *Advances in Formal Design Methods for CAD*. London, UK: Chapman and Hall.

Markus, M. L., & Tanis, C. (2000). The enterprise system experience: From adoption to success. In Zmud, R. W. (Ed.), *Framing the Domains of IT Management: Projecting Future...through the Past* (pp. 173–207). Cincinnati, OH: Pinaflex Educational Reseources.

McNeil, I. (Ed.). (1990). *An encyclopaedia of the history of technology*. London: Routledge. doi:10.4324/9780203192115

Nelson, H. G., & Stolterman, E. (2003). *The design way: Intentional change in an unpredictable world: foundations and fundamentals of design competence*. Englewood Cliffs, NJ: Educational Technology Publications.

Pahl, G., & Beitz, W. (1984). *Engineering design*. London, UK: Pitman Press.

Perkins, D. N. (1986). *Knowledge as design*. Hillsdale, NJ: Lawrence Erlbaum Associates.

Richey, R. C., & Klein, J. D. (2007). *Design and development research*. Mahwah, NJ: Lawrence Erlbaum Associates.

Rittel, H., & Webber, M. (1973). Dilemmas in a general theory of planning. *Policy Sciences*, *4*, 155–169. doi:10.1007/BF01405730

Rosen, R. (1985). *Anticipatory systems: Philosophical, mathematical and methodological foundations*. Oxford, UK: Pergamon Press.

Rosenburg, N. F. M., & Dorst, K. (1998). Describing design as a reflective practice: Observations on Schön's theory of practice. In Frankenberger, E., Birkhofer, H., & Badke-Schaub, P. (Eds.), *Designers: The Key to Successful Product Development* (pp. 29–41). London, UK: Springer-Verlag.

Schön, D. A. (1983). *The reflective practitioner: How professionals think in action*. New York, NY: Basic Books.

Simon, H. A. (1977). *The new science of management decision*. Englewood Cliffs, NJ: Prentice-Hall.

Simon, H. A. (1996). *The sciences of the artificial* (3rd ed.). Cambridge, MA: MIT Press.

Zamenopoulos, T., & Alexiou, K. (2007). Towards an anticipatory view of design. *Design Studies*, *28*, 411–436. doi:10.1016/j.destud.2007.04.001

Chapter 2
Science

ABSTRACT

The purpose of this chapter is to provide insights into the nature of scientific research with the emphasis on the design perspective. Early science had started out of the practical needs of human cultures. From the modern perspective the artifactual nature of early scientific constructs is particularly manifest. The design viewpoint can be applied to the major classes of sciences both in form of reverse and forward engineering. Scientific method has been crafted by the philosophers of science throughout the millennia. There are analogies between the major aspects of the scientific method and artifact design process. Inventiveness and creativity play an essential role in the development of human knowledge. Some major scientific breakthroughs have been made thanks to the invention of thought experiments. Some philosophers of science view theories as tools—the artifacts that do not necessarily relate to real entities. Critical treatment of competing theories supports this view.

SCIENTIFIC PREDISPOSITION

"All men by nature desire to know"—this quote by Aristotle aptly underlines humans' natural predisposition towards finding out the workings of the world around them. The curiosity towards understanding the hidden mechanisms of nature might have been a powerful trait that helped the individuals endowed with such capacities

to better survive in a hostile environment. This quality, some believe, has been favored by natural selection and humans utilized it to build internal representation of their environments and conduct thought experiments (Roger, 2007).

In *Darwin's Dangerous Idea* Daniel Dennet introduces the "Tower of Generate-and-Test," where he places different types of living organisms on different levels with respect to their perceive-and-act cycles (Dennett, 1995). The Darwinian creatures are those with pre-wired

DOI: 10.4018/978-1-4666-0131-4.ch002

stimuli-response pairs who have no capacity for changing their behaviors flexibly. The Skinnerian creatures can learn from the action choices their made in a reinforcement fashion. They obtain feedback from the environment and in the future rely on actions that led to pleasurable experiences in the past. The Popperian creatures have a capability to model relevant aspects of reality with the purpose of making their choices before committing to an action.

Humans are Popperian creatures. We have the capacity to perceive the environment, and also, as a result of such perception to build knowledge about its workings. Immanuel Kant proposed that in order for any meaningful perception to appear, certain structures must exist a priori in human mind (Kant, 1999). These "pure" categories, he suggested, are necessary for humans to perceive objects in the world and promote cognition. He listed twelve categories along four major topics: quantity, quality, relation, and modality. Examples of categories include unity, causality, necessity, possibility, reality, and others. Thus, according to Kant human beings have a set of pre-given mental qualities by means of which they can perceive objects and phenomena and make connections between them. In other words, these categories enable human knowledge. Many of these notions (most notably, causality) are also often described as the attributes of Science.

Human cognition is enabled by the psychological apparatus at our disposal. Our brains are capable of performing a variety of precious tasks, such as perception, action, memory, learning, concept formation, and others (Coren, Ward, & Enns, 1999). Concept learning, for example, enables humans to form concepts that relate to classes of objects sharing certain similarities (Bruner, Goodnow, & Austin, 1967). Using concepts humans can classify a variety of objects and events into a set of formed categories and respond to them adequately.

Thus, apparently there are philosophical, psychological, and genetic roots for the general human predisposition towards knowledge: the object of science. Perhaps, the so-called Personal Construct Theory (PCT) proposed by Kelly most strongly underlies the claim that humans are, in a certain aspect, naturally-born scientists (Kelly, 1955). Kelly saw humans as personal scientists who form their own "constructs" in order to model the aspects of the world around them. This quality is utilized by humans so that they could anticipate events. In other words, according to Kelly, people build their own internal private theories, form private hypotheses and make observations that either fit or don't fit their "theoretical" models.

Kelly had formulated his theory in terms of postulates and corollaries. The Fundamental Postulate states: a person's processes are psychologically channelized by the ways in which he or she anticipates events. Some example corollaries include:

- A person anticipates events by construing their replications.
- Persons differ from each other in their constructions of events.
- Each person characteristically evolves for his convenience in anticipating events, a construction system embracing ordinal relationships between constructs.
- A construct is convenient for the anticipation of a finite range of events only.
- A person's construction system varies and he successively construes the replications of events.

According to PCT, human beings are involved in building up their construct-artifacts around what is called the "core" constructs. The latter incorporate the most essential deeply held values and principles relating to the very notion of "self." Humans can and do make modifications to their constructs as they gather more data on an ongoing basis. Thus, we adapt our private theoretical models in response to "reality checks" so that they enjoy a higher validity level. However, the core constructs are relatively immune to such changes. This suggestion has intriguing connections with Lakatos' "protective belt" that will be discussed later in the chapter.

Understanding the person's core constructs is important for the purposes of providing appropriate counseling services when needed. However, there is another interesting application based on PCT. Suppose, there is an area of expertise for which knowledge is not formalized or well-structured. An expert human who's had extensive experience in the area must have developed his or her own private theory about objects, events, and the causal links in the domain. Thus, the task of extracting such personal constructs would be quite valuable in explicating this tacit knowledge. Repertory grid technique has been developed on the basis of PCT with the purpose of extracting personal constructs, in particular for knowledge acquisition purposes (Boose & Bradshaw, 1987; Gaines & Shaw, 1993).

BIRTH OF SCIENCE

Since humans have natural predisposition towards knowledge, the birth of science in human societies was a matter of time. Before the method of scientific inquiry came into the focus of philosophers, early proto-sciences have evolved largely to solve practical problems. Perhaps the first field to appear was mathematics, although arguably it is not a typical kind of a Science, in that it studies purely abstract objects.

The first evidence of counting dates back to about 35,000 years ago (Mankiewicz, 2000). The archeological excavations in Africa have revealed a bone with notches that was probably used as a primitive calendar. Another similar bone was produced about 20,000 years ago with the special markings, which possibly related to the phases of the moon. The first notable development of Mathematics took place in Mesopotamia. The Sumerians that lived in the area have developed their way of recording quantities by about 3000 BC (Nissen, Damerow, & Englund, 1993). The need for record-keeping, and thus for appropriate means to represent quantities grew out of the practical requirements. Now, assume we knew nothing about our modern numerical systems, then how would we go about recording quantity of, say jars of oil, or bags of grain? A straightforward way would be to use a symbol for a given type of object and draw it as many times on a clay tablet as there are units to record. This proving to be somewhat cumbersome, later someone had a brilliant idea to represent a number and an object separately, the number describing the quantity of objects in question. Still later on, the sexagecimal system of numbers was introduced that we still use nowadays for counting seconds in a minute and minutes in an hour.

The hexagesimal system was also in use in Babylonian times with numbers written in cuneiform script. The Babylonians have composed multiplication tables and produced problem texts that described concrete practical problems to be solved by mathematical means (Aaboe, 1964). They also had tabulated the squares and cubes of numbers, developed algebraic methods for solving problems, and made use of the Pythagoras' theorem, although not in abstract formulation.

Pythagoras, though not only made a grand contribution to mathematics, but also to pseudomathematics, for he is commonly regarded as the father of numerology (Dudley, 1997). As the humans realized that numbers could be applied to any objects and quantities in the world, it probably didn't take too long before they started ascribing special meanings to numbers. The study of the properties of integer numbers is the subject of the reputable subfield of mathematics, known as the number theory. It focuses on such topics as the properties of primes and Fermats' last theorem. However, divination of numbers is an unsubstantiated practice which could be traced back to ancient Indian and Chinese cultures, and the Judaist mystical tradition of Kabballah. Pythagoras, who is often regarded as the father of numerology, is credited with the invention of Tetraktys – ten dots arranged in a triangle that was considered to be sacred by his followers. Different cultures have traditionally viewed some numbers as "special," e.g. 1, 2, 3, 7, 9 and 23. And of course, the number 13, commonly associated with bad luck, the fear of which even has its own name: Triskaidekaphobia. Numerology survives today as many people tend to find attractive the mystical side of pure numbers. There are numerology books and websites; for example one could navigate to certain websites (e.g. http://www.paulsadowski.com/Numbers. asp[1]), type some information about oneself, and learn his or her number, along with the description of personality (the author's number, for instance, turned out to be 11).

Ancient Mathematics was often linked with astronomical measures, e.g. for composing calendars. Astronomy is the oldest science about the real world around us. Ancient societies took deep interest in the celestial affairs for religious and practical purposes (Berry, 1961; Cambridge, 1997). In Babylon the detailed observations of motions of the moon and sun were recorded in order to keep an accurate calendar. In Egypt Astronomy was used to predict floods of the Nile River and position the pyramids. In China a complex Lunisolar calendar was used to help timing the agricultural activities.

The humans' natural synthetic abilities often lead them to seek out patterns even if they are not present. The arrangement of stars in the skies is rather random, and yet the ancients, who were used to the idea of animating natural objects, linked them to invent non-existent images. The exact origins of constellations are not known as they go back to pre-historic times. The Babylonians had introduced some constellations in addition to the older known ones. The Babylonians had also pioneered the idea of ecliptic—a path along which the sun and the planets traveled, now familiar to us as Zodiac. In Egypt only five constellations were known. The Chinese had devised twenty-eight constellations, and the Greeks had forty-eight, which are still in use today.

It was also common to populate the skies with gods, spirits, and animals. The Sumerians associated Earth, Air, and Heaven with gods Ki, Enlil, and An respectively. The Egyptians believed that the sky was a body of the goddess Nut, the Earth related to god Qeb, with the god of Air Shu placed in between. The Chinese invented a nine-fold model of heavens, each level guarded by a particular animal, with the Emperor of Heaven occupying the highest level. Thus, it is not surprising that creative minds of the early proto-scientists went further to synthesize their mathematical knowledge, and that of the positions and motions of celestial bodies with the animistic view of the nature to ascribe extra-meaning to the configurations of astronomical objects. If skies can produce meaningful patterns for human affairs, then taking the reasoning one step further, would it be too illogical to assume that the moment when an individual is born one could study the state of the heaven to try to read that person's destiny? Well, to a modern scientist this would seem to be a rather bold suggestion. However, the undisciplined proto-science of the ancients did not lack creativity, and had no critical scholarly reviewing bodies. The pseudo-science was part of the science, as there was no demarcation principle to distinguish one from the other. Astrology had appeared in several cultures, including China, India, and Chaldea. In Chaldea, for example, horoscopes were composed by 410 BC (Ronan, 1982). Later this astrological tradition spread to Egypt and then to Greece, where Ptolemy had systematized it in his Tetrabiblos. Despite the opposition from Christian Church the horoscopes were in use throughout the ages, and are much in favor among many nowadays. Thus, although it is a form of pseudo-science, nevertheless astrological systems represent a tremendously successful artifact.

The origins of physical science (including what we would call today Physics and Chemistry, which were not viewed separately in ancient times) perhaps could be most reliably traced back to the thinkers of ancient Greece. Thales of Miletus (who is often regarded as the first "Western" philosopher) was looking for the essential substance that could be regarded as the basis of all material things. He noticed the essential role of water as it was abundant in the seas and all life depended crucially on its availability. Thus, in Thales' view water was the fundamental material of which all things were made. The same role of the "mother of all substances" was ascribed to air by Anaximenes, and to Fire by Heraclitus of Ephesus. Empedocles had considered the four elements, including earth, air, fire, and water to be the basic building blocks of all substances. The idea of reducing the substances to constituent elements is consistent with the modern Chemistry, which originated sometime in the 17th – 18th centuries. Leucippus and Democritus introduced the atomistic view of the material objects, which pre-dated Einstein's demonstration of the existence of atoms by over 2000 years.

As the ancient world had developed the occult traditions the magical practice was commonplace in different cultures. Some of its practices included attempts of transformation of the substances to one another that are referred to as Alchemy (Battistini, 2007). Alchemist traditions were developed in China, India, Mesopotamia, Persia, Egypt, and later in the Arabic world. Most common purposes of alchemists were to derive philosopher's stone, gold, and elixir of life.

Regarding the development of early (proto-) sciences several observations relevant to the central topic of the book can be made. First, the earliest sciences, including Mathematics and Astronomy were developed largely in response to practical needs (Nagel, 1961). Thus, knowledge was sought in response to solving classes of important problems relevant to supporting activities of daily lives. This problem-solving view of the origins of science shares the similar motivation with the design tradition.

Second, the synthetic abilities of human minds were responsible for designing knowledge artifacts that were used to describe and understand phenomena and operate with quantities. The linking of lunar and solar motions to the agricultural and religious practices, the emergence of constellations, the consideration of matter in terms of basic constituents were all enabled by remarkable synthetic abilities of human minds. Creativity—the key desired trait of a designer—played essential role in the development of ancient proto-knowledge. From the perspective of our current scientific knowledge, the artifactual status of early sciences is especially conspicuous. One is tempted to say that becoming a designer was a pre-requisite for developing into a scientist.

Third, the inventive capacities of early human scientists often led them too far off the boundaries of the scientific into the areas of occult, mystical, pseudoscientific. We saw that each of the aforementioned areas had an irrational counterpart: mathematics – numerology; astronomy – astrology; physical science – alchemy (also noted in Sagan, 1996). This "over-inventiveness" mostly came about as an influence of magic views and practices dominant in the early civilizations. These magical practices themselves were spectacular artifacts arising from the animistic view of the nature. In order to promote discipline and criticality in conducting scientific enquiries, the process needed to be managed by a set of principles, guidelines, and models. The scientific method artifact was about to start taking shape and would be further developed through the millennia yet to come.

MODERN SCIENCE

The business of science is to promote human knowledge. Some essential definitions of knowledge in Merriam-Webster dictionary include (http://www.merriam-webster.com/):

- The fact or condition of knowing something with familiarity gained through experience or association;
- Acquaintance with or understanding of a science, art, or technique;
- The sum of what is known: the body of truth, information, and principles acquired by humankind.

These definitions of knowledge do not preclude the subject of pseudo-sciences, such as astrology and numerology also count as knowledge. The pseudosciences have developed their own techniques and principles, and one could become aware of them through practice and experience. A French writer of the 17th -18th centuries Alain-René Lesage in his novel titled *The History and Adventures of Gil Blas of Santillane* describes in a comic fashion the practice of one physician who treated his patients exclusively with water (Le Sage, 1972). Many patients died of such treatment, but the Physician wouldn't let go of his cherished method. This method would also constitute knowledge of some sort, although of a doubtful nature.

Plato has distinguished knowledge from belief in that the former demands justification, which led to the view of knowledge as "justified true belief" (Plato, 1973). It is not clear-cut, though what constitutes a thorough justification. Would a claim that water is the basic component of all life suffice to justify the true belief in its panaceic powers by Lesage's physician? Wouldn't the universal applicability of numbers account for a sufficient justification for the practice of Numerology?

Thus, although knowledge seems to be referring to all kinds of human ideas about the real and the abstract, not all of it could be reliably trusted. When referring to knowledge Bunge considers its various types as a set of cognitive fields (Bunge, 1984). These may contain genuine or fake knowledge, and all the examples of sciences and pseudosciences given above would be considered as such fields. Revisiting Plato's

view of knowledge, one could easily see that the pseudoscience fields largely rest on the adoption of belief (however poorly). The core belief systems of pseudosciences hardly, if ever, change: the fact which lowers them to the status of dogmas. So what then distinguishes the more "scientific" types of fields?

The development of knowledge systems has interesting analogies with information systems development. In the latter the key activity to ensure their quality (conformance to user requirements and design specifications) testing is required. In the past the idea behind such testing was to ensure that the systems functioned properly. However, this philosophy has changed with the maturity of the field towards adopting a more critical approach. Modern testing practices have adopted the destructive attitude, in other words, the purpose of testing is to demonstrate that the system being developed is *not* functioning correctly. This constructively destructive position guides the quality assurance professionals to design test cases which are most likely to uncover the hidden defects.

Science, likewise, is characterized by its critical approach, as opposed to the dogmatic approach of pseudoscience. Einstein has critically re-considered Newtonian mechanics to advance the special theory of relativity. Problems identified with the critical examination of classical thermodynamics when applied to an idealized object called the black body eventually led to the development of Quantum Physics. Carl Sagan writes in this respect: "…the reason science works so well is partly that error-correcting machinery. There are no forbidden questions in science, no matters too sensitive or delicate to be probed, no sacred truths. That openness to new ideas, combined with the most rigorous, skeptical scrutiny of all ideas, sifts the wheat from the chaff. It makes no difference how smart, august, or beloved you are. You must prove your case in the face of determined, expert criticism. Diversity and debate are valued" (Sagan, 1996, p. 31).

Thus, instead of the weaker term "justification" the stronger "critical approach" would better characterize scientific practices. As opposed to belief fields, sciences are described as research fields, which foster criticality and observation, and, as a result constant change as their modus operandi. Knowledge, just like other human-made artifacts (such as information systems) must be well-designed. The only way to promote valid knowledge designs is to subject them to thorough testing. The testing does not end with a single experiment or an observation. Human- designed systems and other products are being tested constantly by their users. If a defect or malfunction is detected, the artifact may need a fix (such as a software patch), or it could be recalled altogether, scrapped and re-designed. Scientific theories in face of contradicting evidence are also susceptible to "patch"-like corrections or complete refutations to yield the way for better models.

TYPES OF SCIENCE AND THE "S-APPLY CHAIN"

Sciences can be classified into broad categories depending on their methods and type of subject matter. First, there is a distinction between formal sciences and empirical ones (Strahler, 1992). This distinction is based upon the primary method that a given discipline employs to test its claims. In formal sciences the method of logical proof is used to ascertain the conformance of claims with the set of basic assumptions (or axioms) and rules of inference. Mathematics is the primary representative of this category. Empirical sciences study the phenomena of the different aspects of reality, and as such they employ the observation-based methods of testing. These are further commonly divided into pure and applied sciences. Pure sciences focus on advancing understanding of the workings of nature per se. Applied sciences focus on applying the findings of pure sciences to solve practical problems. Applied sciences are said to produce prescriptive, rather than descriptive knowledge. The examples of the applied sciences include Engineering and Medicine. Pure sciences divide further into natural and social types. Natural sciences divide into physical and biological categories. Figure 1 shows the partial classification of sciences in a hierarchical format.

The distinction between pure and applied disciplines is not as clear-cut in all cases as it would seem. In case of, say mechanical engineering, the applied nature is evident, as the notions of forces, momentums, velocities, resistances, frictions, and the like are directly borrowed from physics to engineer practical mechanical artifacts. Consider, however the case of an area such as organizational behavior. Is it a pure science, or applied one? The area is concerned with the behavior and nature of people in organizations, and behavior and nature of organizations in relation to their environments (Miner, 2006, p. 3). It is an applied discipline that is based on other fields, most notably sociology and psychology. Yet, it has been noted that there is a significant gap between the theoretical developments in the field and its target practice domain (Miner, 2006, p. 8). Theories here include those relating to human decision making, motivation, team building, leadership, and the like. Many of these theories have a descriptive and explanatory nature, which is characteristic of pure sciences.

The term "applied" in a general sense could be used in the context of two related disciplines, whereby one of them borrows and uses the concepts and principles of the other to advance its own knowledge and practice. An analogy with supply chains here may provide some critical insights. In a supply chain the raw materials enter at one of the chain end and go through a series of transformations by the participants of the chain until a final product is delivered to a customer. In the context of sciences, the more general knowledge at the root of the knowledge tree becomes gradually more specialized as we move towards the leafs. All objects and phenomena in

Figure 1. Types of sciences

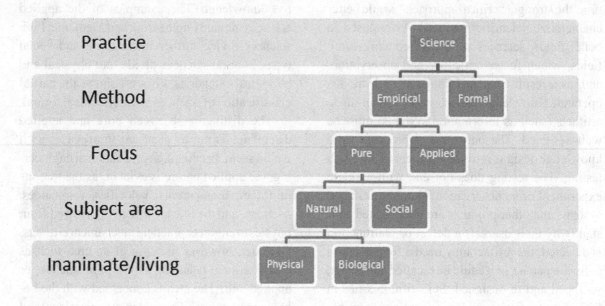

the world obey the physical laws, but it would be rather cumbersome to follow a reductionist view and study, say the biology of animals in terms of fields and molecules composing their physical bodies. Physics, in a sense could be "applied" to feed other disciplines emanating from it. The view of transformation and refinement of general knowledge towards more specific disciplines is sort of a supply chain, that we will call here the Scientific "apply chain" (S-apply chain).

Note that the hierarchy of sciences provided above shows different disciplines in an organized format for convenience purposes. It does not show the patterns of influences of different sciences on each other. For example, physical sciences have impact on the development of knowledge in biological sciences. Mathematics and Computer Science have impact on some of the social sciences, such as Economics. Disciplines often have multiple parents.

In object-oriented systems development, when it comes to sub- to super-class (more specific to more general) relationships the more specific one inherits some properties from a more general, or abstract one. For example, the class "Faculty" may be inheriting some properties and behaviors from a class "Instructor." However, it also inherits some of the features of a "Researcher" class. Thus, in reality, if one wants to show all possible inheritance patterns among classes, one would end up with a network, rather than a hierarchy. However, such "multiple inheritance" practices are commonly discouraged as they lead to complexity, and thus difficulties associated with the development, testing and maintenance of software-based systems. Instead, a hierarchical organization is preferred and multiple inheritance is forbidden in later OO languages, such as Java and C# as compared to some earlier ones, e.g. C++. The designer must work around this intentionally introduced constructive limitation to implement multiple inheritance in different ways.

So, the tree of sciences does not show the patterns of influences among them, but if it did, one could track different paths including various S-apply chains. At the end of any S-apply chain there are terminal disciplines, which must ideally be feeding the practice. These terminal disciplines are the ones that are generally referred to as "applied sciences." Figure 2 shows a somewhat simplified example of an S-apply chain. The end product of the chain is application of genetic engineering to practical problems of agriculture, such as raising better crops or healthier farm animals. Mathematics, as the pure study of the abstract feeds physics with the necessary toolkit (Physics serves as sort of a "model" for mathematics). Part of physics informs the chemical science, and so on until the terminal field is reached.

Any given discipline should participate in some s-apply chain to be of any use at all. Any knowledge must be sought to serve a purpose of some sort, be it a practical purpose, or just satisfaction of human curiosity. If the terminal discipline has no target human curiosity to satisfy, and is not useful for human practice, the discipline's very *Raison d'être* is questionable, to say the least. In some applied disciplines the link with the target audience is weak, and there is an appreciable gap between the terminal node of the S-apply chain and the target customer. This is the case, as it was stressed for example in a citation presented earlier, with organizational behavior.

The gap between theory and target audience may exist for two reasons, depending on the potential value of the theoretical content to the related area of practice. If the former does have a value, but it is not appreciated by the professionals, it's most likely because of communication problems. Perhaps, the researchers are using an overly academic communication style and language, or there is a lack of motivation to open up more outlets

focusing on channeling scientific findings out to the target professional audience. It is a common practice, especially in business schools to base promotion decisions primarily on the "scholarly output" criterion. The "scholarly output" is hardly palatable to the professionals, though. To eliminate such anomalies, perhaps the motivational system for the scholars needs to be re-assessed.

Yet, the gap of this nature would still be considered the "good news" that could be reduced by employing proper communication vehicles. On the other hand, if the discipline does not link with the target audience because of its theoretical content having no value to the latter, that discipline is in real trouble. If scientifically derived knowledge does not (or does only marginally) help us cope with practical situations, and does not satisfy our curiosity (is not what we desire to know), then its right for existence is highly doubtful.

TYPES OF SCIENCE: THE "ABCDE" VIEW

Classification of sciences into formal, natural, and social as presented above is a conventional way of categorizing areas of human knowledge. Other types of classification schemes can also be thought of. Since the current book focuses on the nature of relationship between traditional and design-centric sciences, I will offer a view on classes of science that would better fit the purposes of bridging the gap between the two: the ABCDE view.

Figure 2. Example of s-apply chain

Note that the conventional classification does not adequately incorporate the design – oriented sciences. These are simply relegated to the "applied" category. But being applied, as it has been argued above, simply means being at the end of the S-apply chain. Applied disciplines are not necessarily producing designs to be used by the practitioners. Neither they are always concerned with design principles and guidelines. On the other hand, a field like Computer Science is artifact centric, and yet arguably pure (or at least has a pure part to it). Software Engineering, as well has a pure twist to it, here the focus being on well-designed software structures per se, without reference to any particular application domain.

The ABCDE view divides the sciences into two broad categories: one including the disciplines that look to describe and explain various phenomena (natural or social), while the others offering a design view into classes of natural and artificial objects and processes. The proposed organization of the sciences is shown on Figure 3. While it is admittedly a much simplified perspective and a rather rough approach to categorizing the sciences, the point here is to gain insight into the different types of nature of scientific investigations through adopting a "bird's eye" view on the subject matter of the individual disciplines.

The 'A' category includes sciences that put primary emphasis on the form, rather than any material content. These are the sciences of the purely abstract, mathematics being the ultimate representative. Various subjects of mathematics (e.g. Algebra, Geometry, Set Theory, Number theory, Differential Calculus, etc.) represent a set of abstract concepts and tools potentially applicable to any other sciences. Using math one could specify an artifact, or explain a phenomenon. The difference between the designed and the existing disappears here. The 'B' and 'C' categories refer to disciplines where the adoption of design or function perspective is convenient. The 'D' and 'E' categories include the traditional sciences to which the application of the term "empirical" is most adequate.

While normally, a science such as Biology would be considered empirical as well, it is placed in the design view category, for organization of the animal bodies and behaviors, as well as the structures of the plants can be conveniently described from the teleological perspective. Kant, to some extent had revived the Aristotelian fourth

Figure 3. "ABCDE" classification of sciences

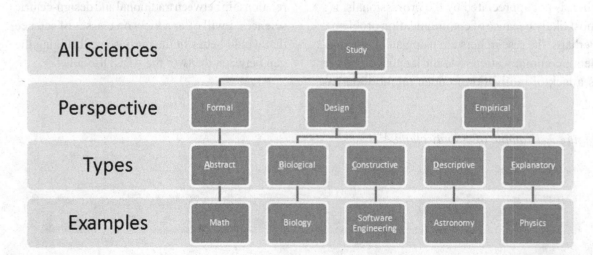

cause by introducing the principle of purposiveness of nature (Kant, 1987). He claimed that humans should approach the nature "as if" it was organized with the purpose. Kant listed several propositions emanating from the principle, stating, for example, that nature takes the shortest path, and there is subordination in nature of species and genera. The teleological position could help us proceed from knowing the ends to understanding the means, according to Kant.

Such thinking, probably applies best to sciences studying complex objects like plants and animals. "Biology is Engineering" is the title of one of the chapters in Dennett's book (Dennett, 1995). This categorization based on the convenience of adopting a given perspective is largely similar to Dennett's other idea: that of assuming one of the three stances for describing phenomena of different complexity levels (Dennett, 1987). He proposed that in order to describe the mechanisms behind a given process or a behavior one could accept either physical, design, or intentional stance for the convenience of description and prediction.

The 'E' category refers to sciences that take explanation as their major objective. Physics is an obvious candidate. Newton's law of gravity, for example, "explains" how any two bodies influence each other in terms of their masses. Other examples from human sciences include psychology and economics.

The "D" category includes kinds of sciences whose primary occupation is to describe and classify. This is not to say that the "E" sciences do not use classifications, but in "D" sciences the descriptive aspects come to occupy the major place. For example, astronomy is concerned with the description of the celestial bodies, including distances to them, their positions in the sky, their chemical composition, size, temperature, motion, and the like. These objects are also placed into the accepted astronomical classification scheme. Thus, an object could be an asteroid, a comet, a planet, a satellite, a star, a nebula, a galaxy, a pulsar, a quasar, or a black hole. These classes

could subdivided further, e.g. a star could be a white dwarf, a red giant, etc. some of the classes have somewhat fuzzy boundaries separating them, e.g. between planets and asteroids. Botany and zoology are the branches of biology whose primary purpose is to describe and classify various plant and animal forms. The hierarchy of major biological classes proceeds from Kingdom to Phyla, to Class, to Order, to Family, to Genus, and to Species.

In Physical Geography the Earthly objects are described in detail and classified as Oceans, Seas, Lakes, Rivers, Continents, Islands, Peninsulas, Mountain ranges, etc. In chemistry much of the effort is devoted to the composition and properties of various substances. The two major types of substances include organic and non-organic ones. The examples of the latter include acids and salts. Organic compounds include the element carbon as a key binding element that could form long molecules. Examples include alcohols and carbohydrates.

Regarding social sciences, in human history, for example, the significant historical events are described in temporal and political contexts. The examples of significant forms here include (having much in common with political sciences) upheavals, revolutions, conquests, monarchies, power regimes, empires, democracies, etc.

TYPES OF SCIENCE: THE DESIGN VIEW

What if we tried to adopt a designer's (engineer's) view on the sciences and treat their content as artifacts? After all, scientific knowledge is not given to us by the superior deities, but developed in a laborious fashion through theorizing, observations and experiments. From the ABCDE perspective, the design-stance sciences are closest to the engineer's perspective. Constructive disciplines aim at building innovative artifacts, methods and tools. Example disciplines include software engineering and artificial intelligence. Thus, constructive sciences are essentially concerned with engineering innovative solutions.

What about biological sciences? While the design perspective may be justified in examining the living forms, is it the same kind of engineering as in constructive sciences? In investigating the organization and behavior of living animals and plants one might as well keep in mind that the purpose of any living being is to survive and reproduce. Then, given the environment in which that plant or animal must survive, one could infer its characteristics. Dorst (2006) cites an example of Paul Colinvaux, who wondered how plants in an ocean would have to be structured in order to survive. Plants need nutrients to work on and Sun's energy to move on their work. The problem is, the nutrients in the Oceans are not at the surface, but deep below. Now, this is a creativity challenge. Two alternatives answers are possible. First, there could be small plants circulating between the deep (get the nutrients) and the shallow (get the sunlight) waters, and these are the algae. Or, alternatively, there could be plants with large leaves on the surface, and deep roots down below the waters. Such plants were found in Sargasso Sea.

In (Dawkins (1976) the author invites the reader ponders upon why trees in a forest are tall. Maintaining a large tree structure is costly for evolution. He asks the reader to consider two points, first, trees need to get sunlight to facilitate photosynthesis, and second all genes (and trees as gene complexes) behave selfishly. If the trees grow densely, they face a prisoner's dilemma-kind of a game. In this game, in a nutshell, if the players co-operate they get a light punishment. If one of them co-operates and the other is selfish, the later one gets rewarded rather handsomely, while the latter one is punished severely. If both of them behave selfishly, both get punished moderately. Since the trees are composed of selfish genetic complexes, they behave selfishly, try to get more sunlight, grow further, and end up being tall while incurring the related costs. If

they could somehow "cooperate," they wouldn't have to raise costly structures. The question is answered. The motivation and the process have been reverse engineered. A variety of other "why" questions can be answered in a similar fashion, and Dawkins does answer them brilliantly in his books, where he provides excellent examples of reverse engineering.

The "why" question is common for all sciences requiring explanation. How does a researcher answer the "why" question? Suppose he or she is studying a particular set of phenomena and is wondering why specific observations take place? Why iron bar extends once it's heated? Why light forms strips on the screen when passing through two narrow slits? Why planets move around the sun? The scientist does not see the mechanisms of nature open wide. He or she views such mechanisms as kind of a black box. And it's his or her job to turn it into a white box. And how this can be done? Through the reverse engineering way. Why there is a Brownian motion phenomenon? Design a model of matter consisting of small particles jiggling the paint spots here and there in a haphazard fashion. And with the higher temperature the jiggling becomes more energetic. Re-invent the atoms of Leucippus and Democritus. Physics is reverse engineering.

What about the "D" sciences? How can design relate to, say Chemistry? The mechanisms of molecular bindings are explained by Physics. The elements could bind together through co-valent bonds, whereby the atoms of different elements could share their electrons, like in water. Or one element could "steal" the electron of the other, and thus the two, being oppositely charged would become attracted to each other, like in Sodium Chloride (NaCl). While Chemistry is concerned with elements, substances and their properties, assuming that atom is indivisible, Physics has a deeper view into the structures of atomic nuclei and the players involved. It is through the physical knowledge that elements like Lawrencium (Lr), Rutherfordium (Rf), Dubnium (Db), Seaborgium

(Sg), Bohrium (Bh), Hassium (Hs), Meitnerium (Mt), Neptunium (Np), Plutonium – (Pu), Americium (Am), Curium (Cm), Berkelium (Bk), Californium (Cf), Einsteinium (Es), Fermium (Fm), Mendelevium (Md), and Nobelium (No) have been derived. Thus, Physics provides the basic mechanism for engineering new types of objects for a descriptive part of chemical science. Astrophysics, based on the current understanding of nature and the composition of the universe predicts such objects as neutron stars and black holes, which have become the standard notions of the modern astronomy. Thus, as far as the D-sciences are concerned, the engineering perspective is that of forward engineering. Figure 4 illustrates how the ABCDE sciences are viewed from the design perspective.

SCIENTIFIC METHOD

The development of early sciences demanded a design of a method necessary for conducting rigorous scientific inquiries. The scientific method refers to the body of knowledge including the principles, processes and guidelines advanced by various scientists and philosophers of science for guiding research activities with the purpose of obtaining reliable knowledge. In Losee (1972) an excellent brief overview of the development of the scientific method is presented and the present section largely draws on this source.

In mathematical studies, Euclid had noted that mathematical (geometrical, to be precise) statements (theorems) could be proved to be true by a logical process if a set of known true propositions exists. This set would include the statements that would not require a proof. Thus, these statements must be in some way self-evident so that they could be taken at a face value. The non-provable adopted conjectures are known as axioms, and the claims which are proved with their help are theorems. The axiomatic method is also utilized in other disciplines that have formal aspects to them, e.g. computer science and artificial engineering. Early attempts in artificial intelligence were directed towards automatic theorem proving. The Artificial Intelligence language Prolog allows the user to enter a set of "axioms" and then can answer the questions about the truth or falsehood of other related claims through the built-in inferencing capability. One of the common methods of proving the validity of statements is known as reduction ad absurdum. In this approach a statement is first assumed to be false, and then the inferencing proceeds to discover a contradiction (such as A and not-A).

With regards to the empirical sciences, Aristotle is commonly regarded as the first philosopher of science. Aristotle has recognized both the value of induction and deduction in developing knowledge about the phenomena of the physical world. As Plato, he rejected the idea of sense-perception being the source of knowledge. Instead, he posited that the sciences should be directed towards un-

Figure 4. Design view on sciences

Orientation	Reverse Engineering	Forward Engineering
Empirical view	Explanatory	Descriptive
Design view	Biological	Constructive

derstanding the deeper essential workings behind observable phenomena. Aristotle had advanced the four-causes framework to explain the structure and behavior of the objects and processes. The formal cause relates to the structure of the thing. The efficient cause explains what initiates the change in the object. For example, a person throwing a stone would be considered an efficient cause in relation to the change in the position of a stone. The final cause describes the ultimate "natural" place or state of an object, towards which it has an inner tendency to move. The material cause is that which makes a thing unique (particular).

One of Aristotle's major preoccupations was with getting at the essence of a thing by inferring its formal structure through observation of particular instances. In this inductive progression from the particular observations to the general picture he outlined two primary methods. The first one is enumeration-based as it proceeds by listing the characteristics of the observed particular instances of a given type of an object to find out the ones that are common to the type. For example, consider the "chicken" class in terms of the presence or absence of the following characteristics: <feathers, beak, two-legs, color: white, color: black, color: red>. Suppose now that somebody observes two black, one white and one red-with-black chickens. This could be represented as:

$$<T\ T\ T\ T\ F\ F>$$
$$<T\ T\ T\ F\ T\ F>$$
$$<T\ T\ T\ T\ F\ F>$$
$$<T\ T\ T\ T\ F\ T>$$

Applying the logical "AND" operation one could then arrive at the description of the characterization of a chicken class as having the properties of being two-legged, beaked animals. With such type instances of the birds one could further derive the properties of the general bird class.

The enumeration-based induction is simple and straightforward, provided all essential object properties are listed. One could imagine a computer program going through a database of object instance records and deriving the hierarchy of types. In doing so the software could use statistical techniques like cluster and discriminant analyses and knowledge discovery methods, such as inductive trees. The instances could be collected by observers, which, to stretch the imagination, could also be robots equipped with cameras and image-recognition software. Thus, the observer robots could be scattered throughout the regions of interest to study, let's say plants, and send them to the database for the analyst software to add new knowledge. These artificial "scientists" could even "publish" new findings in a special outlet.

The point of this rather frivolous scenario is to stress that the enumeration-based induction is largely a well-structured programmable process that requires little creativity. It cannot provide much insight into the nature of the phenomena, and Aristotle was well aware of its limitation. In the second type of induction, a scientist does need to use creativity to make a qualitative leap from observations to explanation. For example, to understand the workings of a lunar or solar eclipse, one has to re-construct the mechanics of the process resulting in a phenomenon. No enumeration can provide such an explanation.

The method of enumeration seems to be more appropriate for the description-oriented sciences as it really deals with discovery of classes. In medieval times, the Aristotelian method was expanded with the aim to discover the cause-effect kind of relationships between phenomena (Losee, 1972). Duns Scotus had proposed the method of agreement, which is similar to the enumeration method of Aristotle. It works as follows: if in all cases of a given event happening some circumstance is invariably present, then that circumstance could be the cause. Ockham had advanced the method of difference, which approaches pointing at causality in a slightly different fashion. It states that if in all instances in which effect is present a given circumstance is present, and when the effect is absent, the circumstance is absent as well, then the circumstance is hypothesized to be the cause of the effect. In essence the methods of agreement and difference are looking for perfect correlation between events to establish the causality.

In addition to induction Aristotle has also recognized the value of deductive reasoning to infer new knowledge from the statements known to be true. He introduced the idea of syllogisms – logical structures that describe how to derive valid conclusions from given premises. For example, knowing that all birds have wings, and ostrich is a bird, one could conclude that the ostrich has wings. One problem with the syllogisms related to the possibility of drawing correct conclusions from false statements. Grosseteste proposed a falsification method based on the rule of logic "modus tollens" to eliminate false premises (Losee, 1972). The rule says that if a hypothesis implies a consequence, and if the latter can be shown to be false, then the hypotheses must be false as well.

The deductive reasoning process was cherished by Descartes as the only reliable source of knowledge. Descartes was unimpressed by the knowledge that the science of his time had generated. He had discovered to himself that much of this knowledge rested on a shaky ground (Descartes, 1996). He noted that sense-perception was susceptible to errors and embraced disciplined thinking as a way of obtaining solid knowledge. Since strict thinking relies on the rules of logic, which requires some sort of axioms, he had to find such a starting point, the validity of which was immediately apparent, and did not require a proof. He proceeded to critically examine different claims that were taken for granted. Destroying the system of these claims he finally arrived at the idea that his own existence could not be questioned (the famous "Cogito ergo sum"). He then proceeded to infer further knowledge by applying rules of inference and accepting further axioms that seemed to be valid to him at the face value. Thus, he inferred the existence of god and that of the world, and even physical laws, such

as conservation of motion, for example. Thus his method of science relied much more heavily on thinking, rather than observation. Spinoza, who was influenced by Descartes' philosophy used a purely deductive approach to "prove" the existence of god and the related attributes in form of theorems. Little did the rationalists know that logic has its own limitations. As Kurt Gödel's famous incompleteness theorem showed that there are some true facts in mathematics that could not be proved, unless new axioms are adopted. The addition of the new axioms, though would lead to the new true unreachable statements.

Perhaps because Aristotle valued form much higher than sense-perceptory data he did not extend his method to empirical testing of the derived knowledge. One of the first advocates of experimental approach to test the conclusions derived by induction and deduction was Roger Bacon (Grant, 2007). He had argued that without experimental procedures humans would never be able to understand the phenomena fully. He had himself performed experimental studies examining the properties of light and its spectrum. Francis Bacon, whose major views have appeared in his *Novum Organon* (Bacon, 2000) has further stressed the importance of experimental studies for establishing a solid ground for knowledge development. "By far the best proof is experience" proclaimed he in defense of employing empirical methods in science. Bacon advised that the practice of generalizing from a limited set of observations to general knowledge should be approached very carefully. He distinguished between the true and accidental correlations in establishing causality and proposed the use of tables of presence, absence, and degrees to spot the latter. He had also pointed at the importance of practical applications of scientific knowledge and the significance of deduction in this respect.

William Whewhell's work is frequently mentioned in connection with what is now referred to as hypothetico-deductive method. He held that scientists should proceed inductively from observations to formulating hypotheses which could be testable by means of further observations (Whewell, 1967). If the newly collected data contradict the claim, the latter is falsified. Otherwise, the hypothesis is confirmed. Karl Popper had severely criticized use of induction as a method of obtaining knowledge. He also maintained that research should proceed with advancing hypotheses deducible from the theories (Popper, 1968). Popper had argued that even if the hypothesis is not falsified by the observation, it does not mean that the theory is valid, only "corroborated."

DEVELOPMENT OF KNOWLEDGE AND ARTIFACTS

The descriptive and prescriptive views on the method of scientific research have interesting parallels with the process of artifact design and implementation. Both of these processes have a problem solving flavor, whereby insight and creativity is required from the scientist or a designer. Normally, in artifact design the analysis and synthesis phases are the primary major activities required to adequately address the design situation. Similarly, Newton has referred to stages of scientific research as analysis and synthesis (Losee, 1972).

To see the deeper connections between science and design, let us revisit Alexander's form view of an artifact. To design a form, the designer must perceive some sort of irregularity that could be viewed as arising from the influence of "fields" or "forces" in the problem environment. Let's think of a designer as a researcher studying the nature of the irregularity to propose an adequate "theory" that would do the job of better fitting the irregularity than the current "theory." The irregularity itself is not defined completely, but through a finite set of observations. In critically viewing the current "theory" the designer-researcher may spot the anomalies: cases in which the accepted theoretical model does not agree with the observations.

These are the misfits. Based on the observational evidence, a new theory would thus be proposed, that presumably better fits the set of the available observations. The designer-resercher then will generate hypotheses in accordance with the theoretical core and put them to test to uncover the potential misfits. If the new observations result in misfits, a new theory must be generated; otherwise the theory being tested is corroborated.

Now, let's view this process in light of system development. If we call the original observations "requirements," the old theory "design of legacy system," the new theory "overall design of new system," and the hypotheses "detailed design," we would pretty much arrive at the model of system development. Figure 5 compares the research and system design processes side by side in a flowchart-like fashion. Gathering observations in systems development is analogous to gathering of requirements. The methods of requirements collection could be through interviews, questionnaires or direct observations of system users. The requirements could be represented in different formats, such as textual or using representational modeling elements, e.g. data flow diagrams. The development of theories in research means coming up with the core set of constructs expressing key theoretical propositions (e.g. "speed of light remains constant independent of the observer"). This is in many aspects similar to developing a system concept and proposing the overall architectural and behavioral principles. Theories are then used to deduce hypotheses that are testable in practice. Thus, the hypotheses involve observable variables and in a sense represent refinements of the theory to relate its conceptual content to the empirical content of the field under study.

The detailed design in systems development also serves the purpose of refinement of a more abstract overall design. In testing theories, the researcher has to decide how the observations will be collected. In an experimental test, he or she must design the experiment, prepare the measurement instruments, experimental tasks,

Figure 5. Comparison of research and design processes

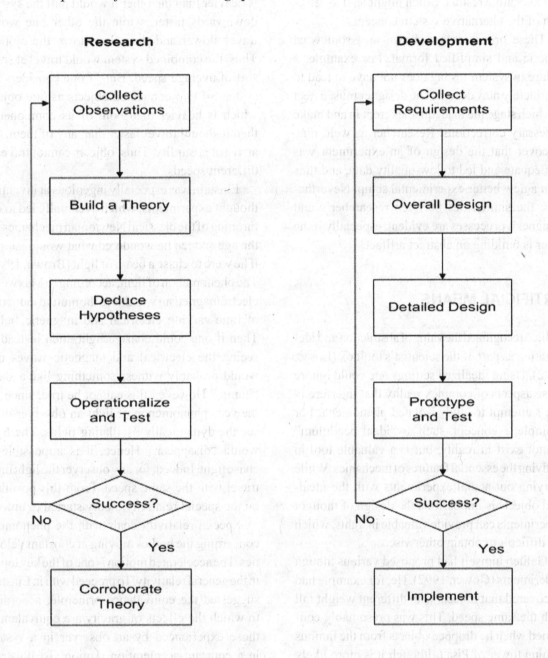

treatments, and take into account other important considerations. Proper experimental design is of critical importance, since the inadequate operationalization decisions could lead to incorrect conclusions. In systems development the system prototype is developed and put to test. Likewise, the inappropriate construction decisions could

lead to wrong conclusions concerning the design concept. Hypotheses testing in research could lead to their rejection, in which case the researcher should learn from the new observations, which could help him or her to consider alternative theoretical models. System testing, likewise, could yield negative results, which might lead to selection of the alternative system concept.

These processes are shown in a somewhat generic and simplified format. For example, a failure in system testing does not have to lead to completely new design. The designer must detect at which stage the inadequacies crept in and make necessary corrections. Researcher as well, may discover that the design of an experiment was inadequate and led to low-quality data, and thus plan a new better experimental setup. Nevertheless, the similarities between researcher's and designer's processes are evident, especially if the latter is building an abstract artifact.

ARTIFICIAL MEANS

Galileo recognized the value of abstraction and idealization as part of the scientist's toolbox (Losee, 1972). Using idealized settings one could ignore those aspects of complex reality that interfere in one's attempt to study isolated phenomena. For example, a concept, such as "ideal pendulum" cannot exist in reality, but is a valuable tool in studying the essential features of mechanics. While carrying out actual experiments with the idealized objects is impossible, the design of thought experiments can provide valuable insights, which are difficult to obtain otherwise.

Galileo himself had proposed various though experiments (Gower, 1997). He, for example had discovered that objects with different weight fall with the same speed. This was presumably confirmed when he dropped objects from the famous leaning tower of Pisa (although it is more likely that he actually rolled round objects on a tilted board). But this was testing of the idea. He had originally invented a mental experiment to get at it. He used the "reductio ad absurdum" method, whereby he first assumed that objects of different masses travel at different speeds in free fall. He then imagined two objects tied with the rope falling together as a system. Since one of them

is heavier than the other it would pull the system downwards faster, while the other one would travel slower and thus slow down the motion. Thus, the combined system would travel at some sort of average speed. But, if one considers the system of two connected objects as one object, which is heavier than both of its components, then it should travel faster than any of them. We arrive at absurdity. Thus, objects cannot travel at different speeds.

Einstein was especially ingenious at inventing thought experiments, which eventually led to dethroning of the classical Newtonian mechanics. At the age sixteen he wondered what would happen if he were to chase a beam of light (Brown, 1993). The phenomenon of light, according to Maxwell's electromagnetism was due to the mutual induction of time-varying electrical and magnetic fields. Then if one could chase a light, then instead of seeing the electrical and magnetic waves one would probably witness something like a static "hump." However, this cannot be true, since for the very phenomenon of light an observer must see the dynamically oscillating fields. The light would "disappear." Hence, it is impossible to chase light. Indeed, for any observer the light must travel with the same speed. From this postulate on the special relativity theory started to unfold.

Special relativity deals with the phenomena concerning the bodies moving at constant velocities. The accelerated motion is one of the key topics in the general relativity. To proceed with it, Einstein suggested the equivalence principle, according to which the effects of gravity are equivalent to those experienced by an observer in a system in a constant-acceleration motion. To illustrate this point the following thought experiment is proposed (Einstein & Infeld, 1938). Assume that an elevator is pulled upwards with the constant force and, thus it moves with acceleration for an outside observer. The observer inside the elevator wouldn't notice the motion, but would attribute the downward pull to gravity. Now, imagine a ray of light that enters through a hole on one side of the elevator and reaches the opposite side. Since light has a finite speed, it would cover the distance from one side to another in some period of time. By then the elevator would have moved up a bit, and thus the light would hit the opposite side at a somewhat lower point relative to the side through which it had entered. Thus, the light would be "bent." An outside observer would attribute this bending to the accelerated movement, while the observer inside the elevator would equivalently well attribute it to the effects of gravity.

As valuable as they are, the thought experiments should be approached carefully not to lead to the wrong conclusions. Newton believed that all motion could be considered with the reference to "absolute space." In order to prove the existence of the absolute space he had designed a thought experiment. In this experiment Newton proposed a setup where a bucket with water was hung on a rope which is initially twisted. As the rope begins to untwist, the bucket starts its circular motion, while the surface of the water remains flat initially. As the bucket spins further the water starts following the motion, and its surface starts taking a concave shape. At some point the water twists with the same speed as the bucket, and so there is no motion of the water relative to the edge of the bucket. Now, if an observer could be imagined to be gazing at water from the edge of the bucket, he or she would see the water as standing still, and yet, for some reason assuming a concave shape. Newton had argued that the appearance of this shape is due to the existence of the absolute space. This conclusion was criticized by Mach, who noted that the water and the bucket are not the only components of the system, one should also factor in the gravitational pull of the earth and other celestial bodies (Davis & Gribbin, 2007).

Another example concerns "Maxwell's demon" (Leff & Rex, 2002). In order to invalidate the second law of thermodynamics (claiming that the entropy of a closed system does not decrease) Maxwell has proposed to think of a chamber separated into two parts by a wall. Then, he envisages a demon that is capable of opening and closing a door between the compartments letting the energetic molecules in one, and the less energetic ones in the other. Therefore, with time on of the compartments will become hotter and the other one colder, thus violating the law. However, it was shown later that the demon is also part of the system and it would actually produce more entropy than he would try to decrease.

Thought experiments are not solely limited in their applicability to the realm of physical sciences. For example, the famous "Chinese room" metaphor was introduced by John Searle to argue against the strong view of "Artificial Intelligence" (which suggests that computers could, indeed be built to think and understand) (Searle, 1980). Searle invites to view the situation, where a person is booked in a room with Chinese symbols and rules for correlating them. The person would get a question in Chinese, and then follow the rules to match these symbols with the ones available at his/her disposal to compose an answer. To an outside observer it would seem that whoever is in Chinese room indeed understands Chinese, whereas all that is being done is symbol manipulation.

NATURE OF A THEORY

Theory is perhaps one of the most vaguely defined, and yet the most important component of scientific inquiries. Popper views theories as "nets cast to catch what we call 'the world': to rationalize, to explain, and to master it" (Popper, 1968, p. 59). In empirical sciences theories can be expressed as a set of statements, expressing general laws, claims, and facts (Kline, 1998). Theories are the ultimate vehicles of science developed to explain and predict the multitude of phenomena within a given scientific domain. Thus, theories must have a power to go beyond particular sense-perceptions and express the inner workings of the hidden mechanisms behind the observed objects, events, and processes. Such mechanisms represent the result of "reverse engineering" the natural processes and may rely on components, which are largely hypothetical in nature.

In this respect it is worthwhile revisiting ancient Greek philosophy, namely Anaximander of Miletus. Just like Thales, he sought for the ultimate primary element of the material world. He suggested that such an element could not be any particular substance, and is not detectable directly (Copleston, 1993). Actual material things derive from this infinite and ageless mysterious element. Thus, Anaximander had an unobservable hypothetical component at the core of his theory about the world.

In the context of physical sciences, Carnap distinguished empirical laws from the theoretical ones (Carnap, 1966) (also reprinted in (Klemke, Hollinger, Rudge, & Kline, 1998)). The empirical laws express the relationships between the entities which are observable. For example, a gas expands when it's heated. Massive objects fall down with the same speed. Here, references are made to the observables quantities, such as temperature and mass. These "laws" apply to any gases or objects, thus enjoying a degree of generality. Theoretical laws involve statements that make references to the unobservable variables, such as "electron," "force," or "field." The scientist's job is then to explain as many phenomena as possible involving the variety of the observable variables by putting forward a mechanism that is based on few unobservable components. Carnap had further suggested that the unobservable entities should be linked to the observable ones through "correspondence rules." For example, the intensity of molecular movement can be translated into the temperature of the matter. While molecules and atoms are not directly observable, temperature is measurable. Using the theoretical laws with unobservable elements it would be possible to deduce many empirical rules (Figure 6), which could, in turn be used to predict or explain a multitude of concrete observations. Carnap stressed, thus while

the empirical laws can be tested directly, the theoretical one are confirmed or falsified indirectly.

One issue related to the nature of unobservables is their ontological status. Xenophanes of Colphon was among the first thinkers to suggest that while a humans may make a progress in getting to know the world, they will never know it fully (Stanford, 2008). One school of thought follows a straightforward thinking by positing that the scientific theories are either true or not. At least some of the unobservable entities do indeed exist and are a part of reality that the science looks to uncover. This is the view known as realism (see, e.g. Maxwell, 1962; also reprinted in Klemke, Hollinger, Rudge, & Kline, 1998).

An alternative view suggests that we do not have the right to ascribe ontological status to the elements of our theories. The theories are, after all artifacts. They do not have a truth value. Entities like fields, forces, and electrons are simply invented things that help us better build our predictive tools, called theories (see e.g. Stace, 1967; Toulmin, 1953; also reprinted in Klemke, Hollinger, Rudge, & Kline, 1998). There is no justification to the practice of assuming that the hypothetical components actually exist, other than in mathematical formulas. This position is known as "instrumentalism," and it views theories (and thus, much of the scientific knowledge) as nothing more than useful tools. Thus, according to instrumentalism theories are artifacts, and the job of the scientist is to design a good artifact that could be used to predict natural phenomena, rather than uncover the hidden truths.

FALSIFICATION AND THEORETICAL PLURALISM

One of the nagging questions in philosophy of science is distinguishing between what is and what is not to be considered a science. As noted earlier, science constitutes only part of all human knowledge. Religion and pseudosciences also arguably

Figure 6. Theoretical and empirical laws

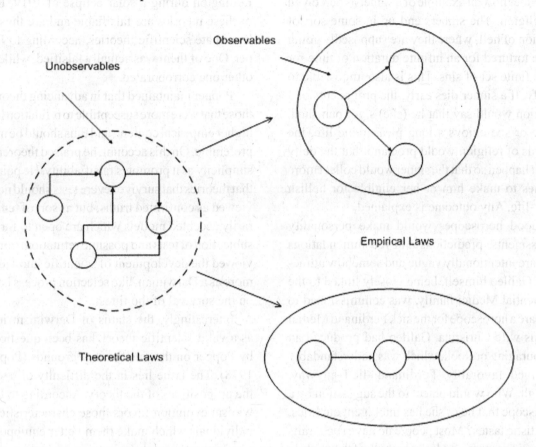

contain bodies of (non-scientific) knowledge. Then the important question is: where are the boundaries of science? The problem of demarcation was first addressed by Aristotle, who sought to distinguish between empirical science and pure mathematics. According to Aristotle, the subject matter of empirical sciences is change, while that of mathematics is form (Losee, 1972). Galileo in drawing the boundaries between empirical scientific and non-scientific statements distinguished between the primary qualities of objects, such as extension and mass, and the secondary ones, such as taste and color. He proposed that scientific propositions should hypothesize about the primary qualities, and not the secondary, perceptual ones.

Probably the most influential thought on demarcation of empirical sciences have been ad-

vanced by Sir Karl Popper. Discarding the idea of induction as the source of knowledge Popper proposed that scientific theories must make definitive claims that could be tested empirically (Popper, 1969). He noted that the areas of knowledge, such as psycho-analysis do not qualify as sciences as they fail to make such claims.

A non-scientific approach would be able to explain any observation, or an outcome of an experiment. For example, it is common in many cultures to use the notion of "fate" to assess events of people's lives. Any possible realization of a person's life would be "explained" as a fate that couldn't be possibly circumvented. Such statements are not testable, as one cannot re-run his or her "life" experiment to see if they would wind up having gone through these "fate" check-points.

Consider now an example of a sinner as perceived in religion. The sinners end up in some sort of version of hell, where they are supposedly going to be tortured for an infinite duration of time for their finite set of sins. This is also impossible to verify. If a sinner dies early, the proponents of a religion would say that he (she)'s got punished. If he or she enjoys a long pleasurable life, the guards of religion would proclaim that the deity lets it happen so that the sinner would collect more crimes to make him or her eligible for hellish after-life. Any outcome is explained.

Good horoscopes would make personality assessments, predictions and recommendations that are intentionally vague and somehow attractive. Galileo himself, being closely linked to the influential Medici family, was commissioned to prepare a horoscope for the sick Ferdinand Medici by his wife Christina. Galileo had produced an encouraging outlook, which was understandably received favorably. Ferdinand died anyway, though. Who would object to the suggestion by a horoscope that he or she has intelligent qualities, or artistic tastes? Most people do have such traits to varying extents, or desire to think of themselves as having them.

Popper thus argued that the defining characteristic of empirical science is its ability to make statements that can be falsified. A good scientific theory, thus should allow for derivation of hypotheses which are exposed to potential refutation. This is in line with the view of science as a self-critical self-correcting enterprise. Thus, for example, before Einstein in the 19th century it was proposed that light travels through the Ether, a hypothetical medium. The consequence of positing such a medium implies that there must be the "ether wind" since the earth was in motion. The famous Michelson-Morley experiments failed to demonstrate that this was the case. Another famous example is testing of Einstein's general relativity theory. It predicted that a light passing by a massive object should be bent – the expectation that was confirmed by the observation by Sir Arthur Eddington during a solar eclipse of 1919. Both of these theories are falsifiable and are thus the legitimate scientific theories, according to Popper. One of them was actually falsified, while the other one corroborated.

Popper maintained that in advancing theories, those that were more susceptible to refutation have higher empirical content, and thus should be more preferable. On this account, he praised theoretical simplicity as it promotes falsifiability. He pointed that theories that survive severe tests should not be viewed as confirmed truths, but as sort of temporarily accepted models which are open to further subjection of tests and possible refutation. Popper viewed the development of scientific knowledge more as a Darwinian-like selection process based on the survival of the fittest.

Interestingly, the status of Darwinism itself as a valid scientific theory has been questioned by Popper on the falsifiability grounds (Popper, 1978). The issue lies in the difficulty of testing the propositions of the theory. According to Darwinism evolution favors those characteristics in individuals which make them better equipped to survive and reproduce in their respective environments. In reality, however making definitive predictions (or rather "postdictions") about the form and behavior of the representatives of a given species is not so straightforward. There are many factors influencing the selective pressures, some of which try to drag the evolution process in opposite directions. (This is also what Alexander pointed in regard to the synthesis of the form). Dawkins brings an example of the African long-tailed widow bird, where natural and sexual selection pressures come into interplay. The long tale of a bird is a costly structure that impedes their ability for efficient flight, so one could conclude that it shouldn't have been favored in the first place. Nevertheless, it plays an important role in males finding a mate as the females appear to prefer the long-tailed representatives. One explanation is that females are much scarcer than males in these birds, and the preference for a long tale just happened to gain preference, since it just happened that there were more females with such a preference at some point in the past. Once the preference has got the foothold, it acted as a positive feedback to reinforce itself (for details see (Dawkins, 2006)). Traditionally the philosophers of science have relied heavily on Physics as a model of a science. Biology however is a different kind of science, where the complexity of interactions between different forces and influences could lead to alternative forms. Evolution processes may have characteristics similar to those in chaotic systems, where small variations in the inputs (e.g. in the initial distribution of mating preferences) may lead to drastically different forms. Perhaps the falsifiability is not as readily applicable to biology-type disciplines in a straightforward manner.

To return the consequences of adopting falsificationist view, they imply presence of alternative theories to facilitate growth of the body of scientific knowledge. In other words, theoretical rivalry demands some degree of pluralism, and the existence of alternative theories. Like Popper, Imre Lakatos had also argued in favor of diversity in scientific communities. However, he had cautioned against too hastily rejection of theoretical cores. He introduced the notion of the "protective belt" of auxiliary hypotheses around the "hard core" of research programs (Lakatos, 1981). The function of the belt is to separate the "softer" part of theoretical conjectures from the essential part and allow for changing the contents of the belt in order to keep the core intact. This recommendation is very similar to the concept of "core constructs" which are immune to change in the personal construct theory mentioned in the beginning of the chapter. Furthermore, going back to the analogy with the systems development, it is similar to changing some detailed design decisions before rejecting the entire design concept in face of the unfavorable observation.

Perhaps nobody spoke in favor of pluralism in science as forcefully as Feyerabend (1975). He had argued against any prescriptive principles and guidelines that the philosophers would attempt to impose on the scientific communities. His position represents an interesting case where the philosopher of science tries to convince the audience not to listen to the philosophers of science. Really he stresses "anything goes" attitude when it comes to scientific progress. Feyerabend, for example argues against the requirement that the new theories should be compatible with the older ones, for in this case the older theories are invariably favored over newer ones. He further notes that even interpretation of observations should not be contaminated by the older theoretical framework. He uses an example of Galileo in relation to the "tower" problem. The traditional argument went that if the earth is moving, then the objects falling from a tower should land further away from the vertical trajectory. Since this was not observed, the earth must be stationary. Galileo had to invent temporary working hypotheses before proceeding with the development of new theoretical insights about momentum and relative motion. "Inventing" more diverse hypotheses without the burden of older theories is the common advice that Feyerabend is trying to convey. His position to the development of scientific knowledge is regarded as somewhat anarchistic.

As opposed to pluralistic view of scientific communities, Thomas Kuhn had introduced the paradigmic (monistic) perspective (Kuhn, 1962). Kuhn maintains that among the alternative competing scientific systems in a given area a model that attracts a sufficient number of followers and provides sufficient amount of questions for further investigation comes to dominate that community while eliminating other rivals. The paradigm settles in and the period of "normal science" begins. During this period the scientists act as efficient "puzzle solvers" to fit in the pieces within the framework provided by a paradigm. He brings the historical examples of paradigms, such as Ptolemaic astronomy, or Newtonian dynamics. During the periods of normal science the anomalies (observations and conclusions incompatible with the accepted paradigm) may accrue pointing at the need to change, which the paradigm resists. With the accumulation of anomalies the old paradigm is discarded by a scientific revolution, and new models are proposed. Soon, one of these models gains acceptance and crystallizes into a new paradigm.

Thus, Kuhn sees a different pattern in the evolution of scientific research from that of proponents of pluralism and steady progress of sciences. Interestingly, in the study of biological evolution there are similar suggestions of process patterns. The conventional gradualism views the nature evolving gradually by taking small steps which over longer periods of time lead to major changes in biological forms and speciation. The punctuated equilibrium theory posits that for extended periods of time little change occurs in populations (Eldredge & Gould, 1972). Thus populations are in the state of stasis, and actually resist the change. Then speciation and branching takes place rather rapidly, before the new species settle in a stasis again.

REFERENCES

Aaboe, A. (1964). *Episodes from the early history of mathematics*. New York: L. W. Singer.

Bacon, F. (2000). *The new organon*. Cambridge, UK: Cambridge University Press.

Battistini, M. (2007). *Astrology, magic, and alchemy*. Los Angeles, CA: J. Paul Getty Museum.

Berry, A. (1961). *A short history of astronomy: From earliest times through the nineteenth century*. New York: Dover Publications.

Boose, J. H., & Bradshaw, J. M. (1987). Expertise transfer and complex problems: Using Aquinas as a knowledge-acquisition workbench for knowledge-based systems. *International Journal of Man-Machine Studies, 26*, 3–28. doi:10.1016/S0020-7373(87)80032-9

Brown, J. R. (1993). *The laboratory of the mind: Thought experiments in the natural sciences*. New York: Routledge.

Bruner, J., Goodnow, J. J., & Austin, G. A. (1967). *A study of thinking*. New York: Science Editions.

Bunge, M. (1984). What is pseudoscience? *The Sceptical Inquirer, 9*(1), 36–46.

Cambridge. (1997). *The Cambridge illustrated history of astronomy*. Cambridge, NY: Cambridge University Press.

Carnap, R. (1966). The nature of theories. In Carnap, R., & Gardner, M. (Eds.), *Philosophical Foundations of Physics: An Introduction to the Philosophy of Science* (pp. 316–332). New York, NY: Basic Books.

Copleston, F. (1993). *A history of philosophy: Greece and Rome* (*Vol. 1*). New York: Doubleday.

Coren, S., Ward, L. M., & Enns, J. T. (1999). *Sensation & perception* (6th ed.). Hoboken, NJ: John Wiley & Sons.

Davis, P., & Gribbin, J. (2007). *The matter myth: Dramatic discoveries that challenge our understanding of physical reality*. New York, NY: Simon & Schuster.

Dawkins, R. (1976). *The selfish gene*. New York: Oxford University Press.

Dawkins, R. (2006). *The blind watchmaker*. London: Penguin.

Dennett, D. C. (1987). *The intentional stance*. Cambridge, MA: MIT Press.

Dennett, D. C. (1995). *Darwin's dangerous idea: Evolution and the meanings of life*. New York: Simon & Schuster.

Descartes, R. (1996). *Discourse on method and meditations on first philosophy*. New Haven, CT: Yale University Press.

Dorst, K. (2006). *Understanding design: 175 reflections on being a designer.* Amsterdam, The Netherlands: BIS Publishers.

Dudley, U. (1997). *Numerology, or, what Pythagoras wrought.* Washington, DC: Mathematical Association of America.

Einstein, A., & Infeld, L. (1938). *The evolution of physics: The growth of ideas from early concepts to relativity and quanta.* New York, NY: Simon and Schuster.

Eldredge, N., & Gould, S. J. (1972). Punctuated equilibria: An alternative to phyletic gradualism. In Schopf, T. J. M. (Ed.), *Models in Paleobiology* (pp. 82–115). San Francisco, CA: Freeman Cooper.

Feyerabend, P. K. (1975). *Against method: Outline of an anarchistic theory of knowledge.* London, UK: NLB.

Gaines, B. R., & Shaw, M. L. G. (1993). Knowledge acquisition tools based on person construct psychology. *The Knowledge Engineering Review, 8*(1), 49–85. doi:10.1017/S0269888900000060

Gower, B. (1997). *Scientific method: An historical and philosophical introduction.* London, UK: Routledge.

Grant, E. (2007). *A history of natural philosophy: From the ancient world to the nineteenth century.* Cambridge, UK: Cambridge University Press.

Kant, I. (1987). *Critique of judgment.* Indianapolis, IN: Hackett.

Kant, I. (1999). *Critique of pure reason.* Cambridge, UK: Cambridge University Press.

Kelly, G. A. (1955). *The psychology of personal constructs.* New York: Norton.

Klemke, E. D., Hollinger, R., Rudge, D. W., & Kline, A. D. (Eds.). (1998). *Introductory readings in the philosophy of science* (3rd ed.). Amherst, NY: Prometheus Books.

Kline, A. D. (1998). Theory and observation: Introduction. In Klemke, E. D., Hollinger, R., Rudge, D. W., & Kline, A. D. (Eds.), *Introductory Readings in the Philosophy of Science* (3rd ed., pp. 309–315). Amherst, NY: Prometheus Books.

Kuhn, T. S. (1962). *The structure of scientific revolutions.* Chicago, IL: University of Chicago Press.

Lakatos, I. (1981). Falsification and the methodology of scientific research programmes. In Worrall, J., & Currie, G. (Eds.), *The Methodology of Scientific Research Programmes* (pp. 8–101). Cambridge, UK: Cambridge University Press. doi:10.1007/978-94-010-1863-0_14

Le Sage, A.-R. (1972). *The history and adventures of Gil Blas of Santillane.* New York, NY: Garland Pub.

Leff, H. S., & Rex, A. F. (2002). *Maxwell's demon 2: Entropy, classical and quantum information, computing.* New York, NY: CRC Press.

Losee, J. (1972). *A historical introduction to the philosophy of science.* Oxford, UK: Oxford University Press.

Mankiewicz, R. (2000). *The story of mathematics.* London, UK: Cassel & Co.

Maxwell, G. (1962). The ontological status of theoretical entities. In Feigl, H., & Maxwell, G. (Eds.), *Minnesota Studies in the Philosophy of Science* (*Vol. 3*, pp. 3–14). Minneapolis, MN: University of Minnesota Press.

Miner, J. B. (2006). *Organizational behavior 3: Historical origins, theoretical foundations, and the future.* Armonk, NY: M.E. Sharpe.

Nagel, E. (1961). *The structure of science: Problems in the logic of scientific explanation.* New York, NY: Harcourt, Brace & World.

Nissen, H. J., Damerow, P., & Englund, R. (1993). *Archaic bookkeeping: Early writing and techniques of the economic administration in the ancient Near East*. Chicago, IL: University of Chicago Press.

Plato,. (1973). *Theaetetus*. Oxford, UK: Clarendon Press.

Popper, K. R. (1968). *The logic of scientific discovery*. London: Hutchinson.

Popper, K. R. (1969). *Conjectures and refutations: The growth of scientific knowledge*. London: Routledge & K. Paul.

Popper, K. R. (1978). Natural selection and the emergence of mind. *Dialectica, 32*, 339–355. doi:10.1111/j.1746-8361.1978.tb01321.x

Roger, N. S. (2007). The genetic basis of human scientific knowledge. In G. R. Bock & G. Cardew (Eds.), *Ciba Foundation Symposium 208 - Characterizing Human Psychological Adaptations,* (pp. 23-38). Chichester, NY: John Wiley & Sons.

Ronan, C. A. (1982). *Science, its history and development among the world's cultures*. New York, NY: Facts on File.

Sagan, C. (1996). *The demon-haunted world: Science as a candle in the dark*. New York: Random House.

Searle, J. (1980). Minds, brains and programs. *The Behavioral and Brain Sciences, 3*, 417–457. doi:10.1017/S0140525X00005756

Stace, W. T. (1967). *Man against darkness, and other essays*. Pittsburgh, PA: University of Pittsburgh Press.

Stanford. (2008). *Encyclopedia of philosophy*. Palo Alto, CA: Stanford University Press.

Strahler, A. N. (1992). *Understanding science: An introduction to concepts and issues*. Buffalo, NY: Prometheus Books.

Toulmin, S. (1953). Do submicroscopic entities exist? In *The Philosophy of Science: An Introduction* (pp. 134–139). London, UK: The Hutchinson Publishing Group.

Whewell, W. (1967). *The philosophy of the inductive sciences*. London: Cass.

ENDNOTE

[1] All website references valid at the time of writing

Chapter 3
Research in Information Systems

ABSTRACT

Information Systems (IS) are complex artifacts which could be viewed as playing the role of an inter-face between the organizational structure and processes and the technological capabilities. IS design is influenced by—and has an influence on—its outer environment: organizational context. Much of past research in IS is of explanatory nature and has largely focused on the processes and functions of outer environment, including organizations and individuals. There is not sufficient theoretical elaboration on the organizational and technological connections of the IS artifacts. Some of the most prominent theo-retical models of IS do not incorporate the very nature of information systems to a substantial extent. The information content of these models is also questionable. IS research has been criticized by some members of the research community for lack of identity and lack of relevance.

INFORMATION SYSTEMS

The term "Information Systems" (IS) unfortu-nately is not always as readily recognized outside the academe by common business professionals and prospective students as compared to the terms related to such areas as Finance or Marketing. Recent downward trends in the student enrollment in the IS programs poses a serious problem for the respective academic departments in educational institutions (George, Valacich, & Valor, 2005). It has prompted many IS faculties to reach out to the bodies of potential students with the purpose of explaining the kind of professional profiles the discipline is targeting. We, the teachers of IS are often involved with visiting colleges and partici-pating in "open house" events just to convey the

DOI: 10.4018/978-1-4666-0131-4.ch003

message about the very nature of IS education. Many people, in general, have no difficulty with recognizing such disciplines as "Management" or "Computer Science," while they seem to struggle trying to comprehend the *Raison d'être* for IS discipline.

An information system is commonly defined as a composition of software, hardware, data resources, and people that has a purpose of supporting business functions within organizations. IS, thus can be viewed as part of the intra- and inter-organizational infrastructure designed to enable a variety of transactional and decision making processes within organizations. The infrastructure view of IS may suggest that its role, however important, will sort of "sink" in the organizational background (Carr, 2003). However, reducing IS to a simplistic notion of common infrastructure (such as elevators or power lines) is hardly justifiable due to the following critical reasons. First, the value of information and information processing practices within organization has a direct impact on the effectiveness and efficiency with which a firm interacts with its customers and business partners. Therefore, the design of IS may have a huge impact on the way a firm fulfills its obligations and adheres to its business principles, tactical *modus operandi*, and strategic mission and vision. Second, the revolutionary expansion of the capabilities of Information Technology (IT), its proliferation throughout numerous aspects of the economic and social environments continuously poses new challenges for organizational decision makers in terms of emerging opportunities and threats. These factors considerably complicate the wicked problem of managing IS portfolios within firms.

Conceptually, IS can be viewed as a "bridge" between the information technology and organizational structure (Figure 1). The problem of adequate design of IS involves finding the right arrangement and orchestration of IT components to meet the demands of organizational processes. In Alexander's terms this can be expressed as shaping the form using the IT capabilities to find a proper fit with the context produced by the field arising from an organization's information demands. In light of the above challenges, the process of IS design can be viewed as being ultimately "self-conscious." Revisiting Alexander, we could note that such design processes are especially challenging because the "misfits" – the critical measures of the goodness of a form – are difficult to spot. As a result, one could predict creation of multiple poor forms. It is hardly surprising, then that the failure rate (in terms of expectations, time, and money) of IS projects is so high. For example, in (Armour, 2007) it is estimated that 80% of IT projects are doomed for failure.

An organization itself can be viewed as a form that had emerged to fit in the context of its relationships with its key stakeholders, competitors, and legal environment. Thus, IS development for an organization can be viewed, in a sense, as an attempt to fit a form to a form. Hence, there is a possibility for an intriguing interaction and co-

Figure 1. IS and its context

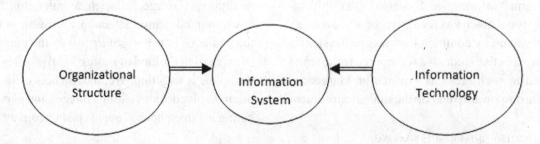

adaptation of the organization-form with the IS-form. For example, as noted earlier, enterprise systems often demanded the change of existing organizational practices to fit the logic of the software package. Lee notes that the IS structure often has an impact on the organizational structure, and the resulting change in the latter demands new adaptation on the technology side. This co-adaptation leads to the view of IS as emerging structures (Lee, 2004). This co-evolution view of problem-solution pair has been mentioned in previous chapters and it seems to be a necessary evil for self-conscious design processes.

IS organization is an intriguing topic for the creative designer minds precisely because it is so challenging. The core disciplines within IS educational programs center around the analysis and design of systems and proper project management practices. The students of IS are expected to be, above all, good problem solvers equipped with proper analytical skills. Typically, the profile of a student in the IS program does not emphasize strong technical skills, such as programming, although some familiarity is essential. This does not imply that creative problem solving skills are not required at the technical development level. The IT artifact must be implemented and built to fit the system design specifications, and undoubtedly, the capabilities and limitations of technology influence the manner in which IS design is conceptualized. Technical development also constitutes a process of finding the appropriate form to fit the IS design as its context.

Thus, an information system on one hand influences and is influenced by the organization-form, and on the other it has the same type of reciprocal dependencies with the technology-form. An IS is a form sandwiched between two other forms in a sort of complex and, well, exciting pattern of interactions. The difficulty of the IS design problem is thus doubled (or squared?) as compared to other problems where either the context or the toolbox is relatively stable and well-understood.

INFORMATION SYSTEMS RESEARCH

Let us imagine that there hasn't been any research tradition in the area of Information Systems. Let's entertain this luxury of conceiving the possible avenues for conducting scientific inquiries into the nature of IS. The "double-wicked" nature of IS suggests the possibilities of venturing into its core as well as into its "connects" with the outer (organizational) and inner (technological) environments. Figure 2 displays the form (structure) and process (behavior) aspects of an information system artifact together with its "connects." The IS artifact as an "interface" looks to fulfill organizational demands by employing the capabilities of technology.

It would not perhaps be too bold of a suggestion that the core subject-matter of the IS research should be, well, the IS. Since it cannot exist in isolation from its inner and outer environments (it is, in fact largely defined by them), a good deal of attention needs to be paid to the organizational and technological sides. In terms of researching the outer environment one could fancy investigating the adequate IS/Organization links. In accordance with the "interface" view only those aspects of organizational environment would be included that matter to the definition of the shape of the system. One could, thus, set out to investigate, say which processes and structures should an information system support to better fit the organization context? Or, which characteristics of the system would facilitate its adoption by an organization, and its success? In doing this, a scholar of IS would have to abstract from particular organizational settings to obtain general knowledge that would be ideally transferrable to the IS professionals and managers.

In researching the links with the inner environment a researcher would perhaps try to find the adequate technological structures and methods to better fit the system context. Here, the emphasis is on the application of relatively generic tools to

Figure 2. IS and its connects

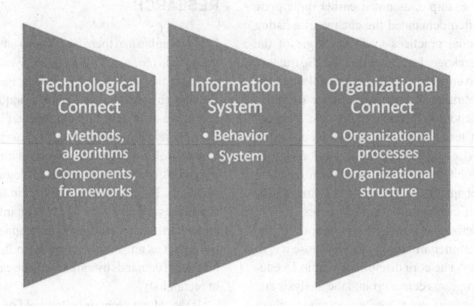

develop the functionality of the system (and not on the invention of innovative generic tools). IS itself is a meeting place of the technological capabilities and organizational needs. For example, business analytics could be a capability required by the companies to help with better situation assessment and perform adequate tactical or strategic decision-making. One example requirement could be the need to recognize patterns in customer buying behavior. This is essentially an instance of the organizational connect. A researcher might be interested in answering the question of whether such a need indeed exists, and to what extent it is present, if it does. Another question focusing on the IS design per se could be what overall structure and behavior should the system have in order to fulfill the required analytics. On the technological side, one could further investigate which technology is best suitable for fulfilling the pattern-recognition function required by the system.

Figure 3 shows schematically the idea of fit of the information system to fill in the features required by the organizational environment. On the other hand, technological environment provides tools that could be configured into the shape required by the system context. IS concept itself serves as a nexus, a junction that need to be properly designed to fulfill its role. Since research is about knowledge which is applicable to classes of processes and objects, by the IS concept here we refer to more or less general notion of a type of information system with salient properties and behaviors aimed at supporting common organizational requirements. The process of developing a particular system relies much on the type of the system to be developed. System development methods thus depend on a class of the system and the corresponding nature of requirements.

Thus, if one were to ignore the history of research in IS for a moment and do a creativity exercise in proposing the categories of topics for such research, then, it seems that one could legitimately come up with at least four major categories:

- Organizational connect (outer environment: types of common requirements)
- Technological connect (inner environment: technological basis for supporting the system concept)

Figure 3. Fitting of IS

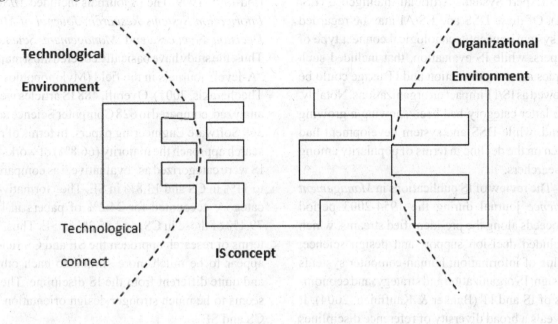

- Information system concept (interface: typology, design)
- Development methodology (proper development method for a given type of IS)

With this post-diction of the major research areas, we can now review the IS research tradition to see how it fits with the "artifact as an interface" model. Research in Information Systems goes back to over fifty years (Banker & Kauffman, 2004). The premier outlets for publishing the findings in the field include such journals as *Management Information Systems (MIS) Quarterly*, *Information Systems Research*, *Journal of MIS*, *Management Science*, *Decision Sciences*, and others.

In (Lee, Gosain, & Im, 1999) an analysis of topics of interest for the period from 1991 to 1995 was presented based on publications in academic journals. Particular publications were categorized into a set of 48 topic categories representing research themes in IS. The four journals adopted for the study showed a considerable diversity in the frequency of topics. Arguably, the top journal intrinsic to the area *MIS Quarterly (MISQ)* had the following most frequent five categories of

topics: IT usage and user modeling/adoption; user satisfaction, involvement; IS function issues; system design, development; and IS personnel issues. It is not easy to tell how exactly the papers were categorized and what the categories refer to precisely. Still, one could see much emphasis on the organizational side, and specifically the usage of the instantiated systems in organizations. It is not evident that the papers have addressed the organizational connect in the sense proposed above. The technological connect seems to be missing altogether from the list of frequent topics (although it does seem to appear in a journal like *Communications of the ACM*, which is more of a general computing discipline outlet). There has also been some work addressing system development methodology.

In (Claver, Gonzales, & Llopis, 2000) a study of publications in two IS journals: *MISQ* and *Information and Management* covering the period from 1981 to 1997 has been presented. The papers from the latter outlet were more than twice in number than those from *MISQ*. The most popular topics from those years included IS development; Decision Support Systems (DSS); IS evaluation;

and Expert Systems/Artificial Intelligence (ES/AI). Of these DSS and ES/AI may be regarded as system concept/technological connect type of papers, while IS evaluation, that included such topics as user satisfaction and IT usage could be viewed as IS/IT impact on organizations. Notably, the latter category had been showing a growing trend, while DSS and system development had been on the decline in terms of popularity among researchers.

The review of IS publications in *Management Science* journal during the 1954-2003 period proceeds along the pre-identified streams, which included decision support and design science; value of information; human-computer systems design; IS organization and strategy; and economics of IS and IT (Banker & Kauffman, 2004). It reveals a broad diversity of reference disciplines involved in building IS theories, including computer science; operations research, marketing; strategic management; cognitive psychology; social psychology; organizational theory; economics, and others. While the paper proceeds to discuss various significant contributions along these strings, it does not provide the quantitative information on the dynamics of the number of publications in these streams.

Recently, a semantic analysis of a substantial set of research publications in three top pure IS journals, including *MISQ, Information Systems Research*, and *Journal of MIS* has been presented (Sidorova, 2008). Five research areas have been identified, including IT and organizations, IS development, IT and individuals, IT and markets, and IT and groups. The analysis suggests that IS development topic has been on the decline among the published papers, while IT and markets and IT and individuals have been on the rise in recent years.

Glass et al. (2004) conducted an analysis of research topics in computing disciplines, including Computer Science (CS), Software Engineering (SE), and Information Systems covering the pe-

riod 1995-1999. The IS journals included *MISQ, Information Systems Research, Journal of MIS, Decision Sciences*, and *Management Science*. Thus, the study have basically covered most major "A-level" journals in the field (Mylonopoulos & Theoharakis, 2001). Overall, 488 IS articles were analyzed, compared to 628 Computer Science and 369 Software Engineering papers. In terms of research approach the majority (66.8%) of works in IS were categorized as "evaluative," as compared to 11% in CS and 13.8% in SE. The "formative" category accounted for 24.2% of papers in IS, 79.1% of those in CS, and 55.3% in SE. Thus, in terms of research approach the SE and CS fields appear to be much more similar to each other and quite different from the IS discipline. There seems to be much stronger design orientation in CS and SE.

The topic categories used in the analysis included problem-solving concepts; computer concepts; system/software concepts; data/information concepts; problem domain-specific concepts; system/software management concepts; organizational concepts; societal concepts; and disciplinary issues. The vast majority of IS papers (65.5%) were found to focus on organizational concepts, which included such topics as organizational structure, strategy, alignment, organizational learning/knowledge management, technology transfer, IT usage, IT impact, and the like. Systems/software, data/information, and problem-solving concepts together accounted only for 15.3% of papers in IS, as contrasted to 49.2% in CS, and 68.3 in SE.

The analysis suggests that the organizational emphasis is truly predominant in IS research with much less attention paid to the other facets of information systems. Indeed the IS research tradition does not seem to properly fit the description of a computing discipline. And yet, Information Systems are the computing artifacts, the class of systems primarily targeting support of business processes. Such a drastic deviation of IS from its sister IT disciplines does seem somewhat bewildering. The central topic of the IS undergraduate programs is, most commonly, system development, including systems analysis, design, and, to a lesser extent, implementation. Most of the organizational topics are adequately covered by the Management departments of business schools. Issues such as IT adoption, usage, strategy, knowledge management and the like are typically introduced at the graduate level, where students are prepared for making their research contributions in form of theses, with the prospects of publishing in scholarly outlets.

Thus, one can sense the significant deviation of IS research in terms of topics, not only from other (design-centric) computing disciplines, but also from its own undergraduate curricula. Undergraduate programs are the workhorses preparing students for the industry, where the objective is equipping the students with relevant knowledge and skills to enter the workplace. The significant mismatch between what IS programs teach and what the faculty members choose to do research on could suggest the potential relevance problems: the issue discussed later in the chapter.

On the other hand, the organizational connect is an important issue in the proper design and subsequent adoption and usage of information systems. Thus, organizational studies may be important in clarifying the kind of the IS form that would properly fit in an organizational context. Nonetheless, the overly emphasis on a non-system side may put the research in danger of moving away from the Simonian "interface" deep into the study of organizational phenomena that have weak links with the IS form. The organizational orientation sets the stage for the evolutionary tree of IS research that may grow deep and bushy in the direction of the original momentum. The established research paradigm demands the efficient IS researchers to engage in puzzle-solving, if they are to obtain the access to premier outlets. But are they solving the right puzzle?

The studies of literature show the birds-eye view of the research tradition in Information Sys-

tems. To get a better insight into its nature and to appreciate its coverage of the IS artifact together with its connects, perhaps it is worthwhile to examine some of the prominent theories in the field.

SOME INFLUENTIAL THEORETICAL MODELS IN INFORMATION SYSTEMS RESEARCH

Nature of Theories in IS

In a recent essay Gregor has looked into the nature of theories in Information Systems research (Gregor, 2006). The questions pertaining to outlining the framework for theoretical developments in the field, according to her include: domain questions (e.g. what are phenomena of interest? What are core problems and boundaries of the field?); structural or ontological questions (e.g. what is theory? How is it expressed?); epistemological questions (e.g. how scientific knowledge is acquired? How theory is constructed?); and socio-political questions (e.g. who are the stakeholders? How theories are applied?).

It has been stressed that what makes the IS discipline distinct, is the involvement of artifacts, thus representing the intersection of knowledge and properties of physical objects and knowledge of human behavior. IS theories need to link the natural, social, and artificial worlds. Five theory types have been outlined. Analysis-type knowledge does not consider causal knowledge, but is concerned with description, classification schemes, and taxonomies. Alter's early work on outlining seven types of decision support systems represents an example of analysis-type theory. Explanation-oriented theories answer the questions of what, how, why, when, and where. The author provides an example of structurational model of technology by Orlikowski as an instance of such a theory. Prediction-type theories answer the questions of what is and what will be. Moore's law is provided as an example. Explanation and prediction theories combine the elements of both, with the example being the Technology Acceptance Model. Design and action theories are concerned with the development of novel methods, techniques, and tools.

A review of *MISQ* and *Information Systems Research* publications from March of 2003 to June of 2004 the majority of them (33 out of 50, or 66%) were of the explanation and prediction type, while only 9 (18%) related to design and action. Thus, in light of the "ABCDE" view of sciences introduced in the previous chapter, much of theoretical development in IS falls into "E" category. This might sound surprising, as the "E" sciences aim at explaining what already exists. They are not innovation or design-oriented. Theories are further defined as grand theories: those that apply to broadest classes of IT-related phenomena, and mid-range theories, which are moderately abstract, are capable of producing better testable hypotheses, and whose scope is limited. In the remainder of this section we will review some of the grand IS theories in a moderate detail. The isworld.org website has a concise description of a substantial set of IS-related theories, and the reader is referred to it for further information regarding theoretical models in IS.

Technology Acceptance Model

Probably the most celebrated theoretical model in the area of Information Systems is the Technology Acceptance Model (TAM) (Davis, Bagozzi, & Warshaw, 1989). Nowadays IT and IS have become ubiquitous in a variety of organizational contexts and the mastering of key computer usage concepts is regarded as the question of basic literacy. In the past, however, introduction of computer-based systems at various levels in organizations was not always a painless process. The question of the determinants of the system acceptance by the prospective user base was of considerable importance. Even presently, while judging the adoption of a new type of a system by the business users

and customers is of critical importance, as it could result in saving significant funds in purchasing, or developing software solutions.

The motivation behind introduction of the TAM had been exactly this concern: to investigate factors that could help explain and predict the usage of the new system solution for addressing a given organizational need. To propose a theoretical explanation a model originating from social psychology known as Theory of Reasoned Action was taken as the basis. The model suggests that a person's behavior is determined by his/or her behavioral intention, which is influenced by the person's attitude towards that behavior and the pertinent social norms. The attitude, in turn, is influenced by that person's beliefs regarding the results of the behavior in question. Thus, to summarize, in actuating a given behavior a person is guided by his or her intentions, influenced by attitudes, determined by the person's beliefs.

In the IS context the actual behavior in question is the usage of the system, i.e. whether or not the person will actually tend to use it. The refinement of the other mental categories to the case of IS usage resulted in the specification of TAM (Figure 4) (Davis, Bagozzi, & Warshaw, 1989).

According to TAM the intention to use a system is influenced by a person's attitude towards the system. The favorable attitude would contribute towards forming an intention towards usage, while the unfavorable one could lead to the rejection of system. The attitude is formed as a result of user's beliefs about the system. The relevant beliefs relate to whether a person believes that use of the system could help him or her to do the job that the system is designed to support better (effectively-perceived usefulness) in some sense, and whether he or she thinks that they could get the system to do what it's supposed to do with a relatively low level of effort (efficiently-perceived ease of use). Additionally, the perceived usefulness is influenced by the perceived ease of use of the system. These beliefs are formed as a result of interaction with the system, with the system

Figure 4. Technology acceptance model

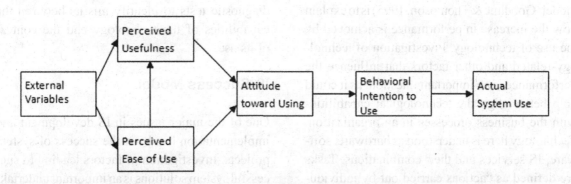

features appearing as part of the "external variables" in the model.

The TAM has been tested empirically through a questionnaire which was thoroughly validated, with the attitude and intention constructs measurements borrowed directly from the previous work on the original theory of reasoned action. System usage was measured by the self-reported frequency of usage on part of the respondents. The perceived usefulness was measured by the questions, including the following generic scheme: "Using S would improve my performance in J"; "Using S in J would improve my productivity"; "Using S would improve my effectiveness in J"; "I would find S useful in the J." Here S and J should be substituted by the respective system and job references. In the original study word processing software was playing the role of S, while MBA program appeared in place of J. Ease of use was measured by the questions of the following type: "Learning to operate S would be easy for me"; "I would find it easy to get S to do what I want it to do"; "It would be easy for me to be skillful in using S"; "I would find S easy to use."

TAM has been introduced as a predictive model that could help foresee the future usage of a system under consideration by the user group. Practical implications, as indicated by the authors include being able to predict system acceptance by the users; diagnose why system may not be acceptable; and take corrective actions to promote the accept-

ability of the system. In particular, in regards to diagnosis it has been mentioned that "...although ease of use is clearly important, the usefulness of the system is even more important and should not be overlooked...Diagnostic measurements of the kind we're proposing should augment designers' intuition, and help them identify and evaluate strategies for enhancing user acceptance" (Davis, Bagozzi, & Warshaw, 1989).

TAM has been applied extensively in many settings and it's been extended and refined in multiple ways in many publications, the discussion of which is beyond the scope of this book.

Task-Technology Fit Model

Technology in organizations is employed with the purpose of supporting and improving organizational processes, in particular its aim is to improve the performance of the individuals working within a business. Employees in a typical organization perform a variety of operational tasks, such as order processing, customer support, accounting, and others. Some of these tasks demand efficient data entry and retrieval capabilities of IT. Other types of tasks require the capabilities to support the activities like analytics, operational, tactical, and strategic decision-making, and negotiations. Different tasks have different performance implications.

The purpose of Task-Technology Fit (TTF) model (Goodhue & Thompson, 1995) is to explain how the increase in performance is achieved by the use of technology. Investigation of technology-related and other factors that influence the performance is an important question, as it could help better align the technological capabilities with the business processes in an organization. Technology here is understood as hardware, software, IS services and their combinations. Tasks are defined as "actions carried out by individuals in turning inputs into outputs" (Goodhue & Thompson, 1995).

The Task-Technology Fit (TTF) model posits that individual performance depends on the fit between the task a user needs to undertake and the technology (information system) used for this task. The better the fit is the higher user performance and thus value of the technology. The characteristics of an individual using technology in carrying out a given task may also have an effect on the assessment of fit. The fit is understood as "the degree to which a technology assists an individual in performing his or her portfolio of tasks" (Goodhue & Thompson, 1995).

The fit was originally defined along 14 different dimensions. In Goodhue & Thompson (1995) the TTF was combined with the "utilization" variable and eight dimensions of fit were retained, including: data quality; locatability of data; authorization to access data; data compatibility; training and ease of use; production timeliness; systems reliability; and IS relationship with users. In the empirical study the tasks were characterized by their non-routineness and interdependence. Technology was encoded as dummy variables representing systems used at the departments where the study was undertaken. Performance impacts were self-reported. Overall, the model found statistical support.

The authors suggest that "when users understanding the business task are involved in systems design, it is more likely that resulting system will fit the task need." They further argue that the TTF model could be taken as a basis for designing diagnostic tests to identify misfits between the capabilities of the technology and the context of its use.

IS Success Model

One of the major issues in IS development and implementation has been the success of system projects. Investigation of factors leading to successful system solutions is an important undertaking that could help explain why certain systems have a positive impact on the organizational performance, while others do not. DeLone and McLean had analyzed an impressive body of IS literature to produce a set of dimensions of success (DeLone & McLean, 1992). They have identified the following categories: information quality; system quality; use; user satisfaction; individual impact; and organizational impact. The model aims at predicting the individual and organizational impact of the system based on the attitudes formed by its users. The key factor conveying the attitude is user satisfaction. According to the model user satisfaction is influenced by the two essential quality-related factors of the system. Satisfaction has a significant impact on the actual system use, and the latter reciprocally affects the level of user satisfaction. Both of these constructs (use and satisfaction) affect the construct of individual impact, which in turn has an influence on the organizational impact.

The dimensions included in the model incorporate multiple measures, which assess many concrete aspects of IS success. System quality includes such measures as data accuracy and currency, ease of use, ease of learning, usefulness of system features and functions, system flexibility, reliability, efficiency, sophistication, and others. Information quality is understood such terms as information importance, relevance, usefulness, informativeness, usableness, readability, clarity, completeness, timeliness, etc. Use is measured through amount of use, number of inquiries, number of functions used, frequency of access and the like. Satisfaction involves overall satisfaction, information satisfaction, enjoyment, software satisfaction and others. Individual impact includes information understanding, learning, information awareness, decision effectiveness, etc. Organizational impact is exemplified by such issues as application portfolio, cost reduction, productivity gains, increased revenues, return on investment, and the like. The authors point that the model organizes the many measures of IS success by providing its major categories and their interrelationships.

THE ISSUE OF IDENTITY IN INFORMATION SYSTEMS RESEARCH

A brief overview of research in Information Systems has revealed the tendency of gravitating more towards organizational and individual side in an explanatory mode. Excessive investigations of an outer environment without anchoring on the system artifact as an interface though, may propel the research into outer spaces, i.e. delving into theoretical explorations of little importance to IS. The repeated promenades into such areas as psychology, organizational science, economics and the like could endanger the very identity of the discipline.

The issue of identity of the field of Information Systems had been raised in the past (Banville & Landry, 1989; Nolan & Wetherbe, 1980; Nunamaker, Chen, & Purdin, 1991; Walls, Widmeyer, & El Sawy, 1992) and has arguably become even more pronounced in recent years (Alter, 2003; Izak Benbasat & Weber, 1996; Izak Benbasat & Zmud, 2003; Changchien, Lee, & Hsu, 2004; Dufner, 2003; Gorla & Paulraj, 1999; Gray, 2003; Khazanchi & Munkvold, 2000; Livari, 2003; Lucas, 1999; Orlikowski & Iacono, 2001; Robey, 1996; Weber, 2003a, 2003b; Whinston & Geng, 2004). In their influential paper published in *MISQ* Ben-

basat and Zmud distinctly articulate the problem: "We are worried that the IS research community is making the discipline's central identity even more ambiguous by, all too frequently, under-investigating phenomena intimately associated with IT-based systems and over-investigating phenomena distantly associated with IT-based systems" (Benbasat & Zmud, 2003).

One of the major concerns that surface in conjunction with this "identity crisis" is the presence of diversity in IS research (Banville & Landry, 1989; Benbasat & Weber, 1996; Benbasat & Zmud, 2003; Changchien, Lee, & Hsu, 2004; Nolan & Wetherbe, 1980; Robey, 1996). In the already mentioned paper, Glass et al. have found that only 27.2% of cited work in published papers in the IS discipline come from the IS sources. So, about 73% of citations come from other fields, such as cognitive psychology, management, economics, and others (Glass, 2004). Compare this figure with the finding that 89.3% and 98.1% of citations in computer science and software engineering respectively come from their own disciplines.

On the positive side, the value of "reference disciplines" in the development of IS as a field had been recognized in the earlier years (Keen & Morton, 1978). Banville & Landry have advocated an anti-Kuhnian view for MIS characterizing it as "fragmented adhocracy" (Banville & Landry, 1989). Robey has argued in favor of diversity pointing to its intrinsic advantages that included: expansion of foundation upon which the knowledge claims are based; attraction of highly qualified researchers to the field; fostering creativity; and enabling the academic freedom (Robey, 1996). He has further stressed the importance of "disciplined" approach to diversity and collaborative attitude among colleagues involved with different approaches to and views on research in Information systems (e.g. "techies" vs. "behaviorists"). Whinston & Geng have described what they call "the gray area" in the IS discipline and advocated the policy of strategic ambiguity for deliberately suspending judgment on the relevance of research topics (Whinston & Geng, 2004). They believe that such "fuzzifying" of the boundaries of the discipline would foster innovative work in the field.

The separation of IS research from foundational base that included such areas as Computer Science, Management Science, and Organizational Science and its solidification as a distinct discipline was investigated in the Eighties based on the citation studies (Culnan, 1987; Culnan & Swanson, 1986). It was concluded then, that while there had still been considerable reliance on the reference disciplines, there also had been a shift towards more organizational and managerial focus and hopes of the eventual evolution towards maturity. In fact, Baskerville and Myers have recently suggested that IS has matured to the point that it should move beyond the conventional position of the "end of food chain" (S-apply chain) to serve as a reference discipline for other related fields (Baskerville & Myers, 2002). In particular, they argued that the sheer ubiquity of information systems in organizations supports this view. Building on this theme, Nambisan has proposed that the IS field could serve as a reference discipline for new product development support (Nambisan, 2003). A good portion of these potential contributions relate to system development research (e.g. software development process, theories of collaborative IS development) and research in design of IS (DSS/GDSS).

Recent citation studies of IS academic literature, however present serious challenges to the claims of the maturity of the field. Farhoomand and Drury have found that the proportion of cited sources in IS papers published in eight leading journals and the ICIS Proceedings in the 12-year period between 1985-1996 that rely on reference disciplines had increased to two-thirds (Farhoomand & Drury, 1999). Gorla and Paulraj have found that the percentage of references has shifted from MIS to the allied fields over the same period (Gorla & Paulraj, 1999). These findings, along with the concerns of over-dependence on other disciplines (Benbasat & Zmud, 2003) cast

a serious doubt on the maturity of the discipline in terms of reliance on the endogenously generated theories. In fact, there are even claims that the technology acceptance model is almost the only own theory that IS has to propose (Järvinen, 2004). If the scarcity of endogenously generated content is actually the case, then the manner in which IS could serve as a reference discipline could be characterized as predominantly *transitive*, or *intermediary* mode, whereby the referring discipline would borrow theories which are in turn borrowed from other fields.

Benbasat and Weber warned about the potential dangers of promoting diversity and the need for managing pluralism (Benbasat, 1996). They have identified three aspects of diversity including: the problems addressed within the discipline; the theoretical foundations and reference disciplines that guide information systems research; and the methods used to collect, analyze, and interpret data (Benbasat, 2001; Benbasat & Weber, 1996). The methodological diversity relates to the ways IS phenomena are studied, including, for example, positivist, interpretive, critical (Orlikowski & Baroudi, 1991), historical (Mason, McKenney, & Copeland, 1997), system development (Nunamaker, Chen, & Purdin, 1991), or pluralistic (Mingers, 2001) approaches. It is the diversity in reference disciplines and theoretical foundations that Benbasat and Weber are particularly worried about, pointing among the downsides the distraction of researchers from the focus on the core of the discipline, and possibilities of hostile takeover from within and outside. Concerned about the "confused state" of IS Khazanchi and Munkvold warned that it could be absorbed by other departments (Khazanchi & Munkvold, 2000).

The discussion of diversity vs. identity naturally leads to the questions of the core of the discipline. In an already mentioned publication Sidorova et al. have conducted an extensive analysis of the IS literature with the purpose of uncovering its core (Sidorova, 2008). The "IT and ..." pattern has then been used to describe different clusters, like individuals, organizations and markets. The conclusion is that the core over time had stayed stable. Now, when researchers in a discipline *do not know* what their discipline is about and have to *uncover* the core by looking at what has been published, it does seem to be a very serious symptom. The conclusion that the core is stable does not really help answering the question of identity. If one *consistently* over-hits the intended target one could not consider him- or her-self a successful shooter. But, then they *could* say, that they have "uncovered" the new target, it's right at the center of the cluster of misses. Furthermore, the general words like "IT and markets" do not really help understanding to what extent the link between the markets and technological capabilities have been elaborated in the works. IS is a form, and research should help discover that form.

Another "inductive" approach to uncover the core has been attempted in (Lim, 2007). The authors claim that such an inductive process is legitimate, from the view of the field as an artifact of social construction. They have used content analysis software to find the most frequent terms appearing in IS publications. These included information, organization, system, model, process, management, data, decision, user, development, and strategy. From this collection the authors then synthesized the core: "the core of IS research focuses on data and information systems, their development(modeling), management and strategy, and how they are related to organizations, processes, decisions and users." Now, as we have seen in a previous chapter induction has been largely downgraded in modern scientific thinking as a reliable source of knowledge. The problem with using induction to uncover the core is that it *cannot fail*. Some sort of core will appear eventually, and the researcher undertaking such a study is doomed for success.

To finish with the topic of inductive approaches, it is worthwhile mentioning the paper by Neufeld et al. (Neufeld, 2006). They have argued that: "It is more pragmatic and inclusive in the

sense that our identity is determined not by *a priori* principles (as with the normative approach), but rather by the sum total of whatever the body of IS scholars chooses to investigate, however focused or diverse." Here "whatever" seems to be the keyword. They have analyzed past publications in order to establish the field's identity in terms of central character, temporal continuity, and distinctiveness. In particular, distinctiveness was established through a chi-square test comparing the various categories of IS-related topics. Thus, if there is any difference at all between the frequencies of keywords appearing in different categories between the IS and non-IS publications, this was deemed to indicate the distinct character of the field. The authors conclusion is that the field has a distinct "shifting" identity. This shifting is considered to be an indication of responsiveness of IS researchers to the calls for change. However, couldn't this also be considered as a search for an identity by a field that *lacks* one? What is peculiar, in the summary, the authors note: "Our study adds empirical evidence to the normative/descriptive debate." Normative or descriptive (deductive vs. inductive) debate is about whether the identity of the field should be set a-priori or a-posteriori and this is a "meta" question. How could the results produced by the study provide evidence that could help resolve the "meta" issues?

Benbasat & Zmud's treatment of identity crisis and their recommendation to re-focus on the IT artifact as the core subject has been challenged by many, for example by Agarwal et al. (Agarwal, 2005). The authors argued that the focus of IS research should be more on a macro- level, rather than micro- level (to which they argue the IT artifact view relates). What is this macro- view according to the authors? They argue in favor of investigating the transformational role of IT. As an example they provide a research question of how internet has changed the music industry. Now, apparently the authors firmly believe in an explanatory role of research in IS. The IS as a field, it appears should not engage in the discovery of the forms. It should help explain things that already happened. But then, is there really an important need for such explanations? Is IS research in the same category as historical science? Technology is a result of looking forward, and why in IS, sensibly a very much technology-related field, we should be looking backwards? Who would benefit from such an after-talk? IT professionals? Businesses? Individuals?

Weber has stated that the phenomena studied by IS researchers must be believed to be "special" in some way (Weber, 2003a). Benbasat and Zmud have proposed the concept of nomological net for outlining what constitutes legitimate research in Information Systems (Benbasat & Zmud, 2003). They even proposed metrics (nomological density, degrees of separation) to evaluate the relevance of contributions and their distance from the core of the discipline represented by an IT artifact. Orlikowski and Iacano pointed that IS research "has not deeply engaged in core subject of the matter," which is, according to them, the IT artifact. They figuratively noted that IT artifact "dissipates into the atmosphere around us" and voiced the call for the theories of the IT artifact (Orlikowski & Iacono, 2001). Similar concerns regarding "factoring in" IT artifacts in IS research projects have been raised by Weber (2003a) and Benbasat (2001).

To assess the maturity of the field Karuga et al. have collected over 19,000 citations of papers published in premier IS journals by the researchers in other related disciplines for the 1982-2004 period (Karuga, 2006). They note that the number of IS references cited by the IS papers have increased, though this increase is not statistically significant (from 26.9 in the 1993-1996 time period to 28.8 percent in the most period from 2001-2004: less than 2%). The authors speculate that "a stable mix" of IS and non-IS citations, as well as the increase in the sheer number of overall citations may be an indicator of the maturity of the field. This is, arguably, a questionable conclusion.

The authors did discover, though, a significant increase of IS citations by the authors in other disciplines. However, the number of IS paper citations dealing *directly with IT artifact* was significantly higher than those remotely related to it. So, researchers in the related disciplines appear to have significantly more interest in those IS publications that address the IT artifact. The authors conclude "This seems to be consistent with Benbasat and Zmud's arguments that the most influential articles would be those that directly address the IT artifact. To reiterate, the citation impact seems to be greater both inside and outside the IS discipline as evidenced by the higher IS and non-IS citations for articles that directly address the IT artifact versus those that do not" (Karuga, 2006).

Summarizing the above discussion one can conclude that the identity crisis is a critical issue in the field. The sheer extensity of the waves Benbasat & Zmud's publication had generated throughout the IS community is very much telling. The identity crisis could be characterized as *endogenous*, since it pertains to the very core of the discipline.

THE ISSUE OF RELEVANCE OF INFORMATION SYSTEMS RESEARCH

A philosopher Ingvar Johansson, while discussing the nature of competition in scientific communities makes a distinction between public-oriented and actor-oriented disciplines (Johansson, 1991). In actor-oriented disciplines the actors, i.e. the members of the community, and not the public are deciding about the prizes and rewards. Such competition, akin to that among avant-garde poets, best suits the characterization of basic research. In public-oriented domains, where applied sciences belong, the public decides on rewards. Therefore, the outcome of such research (at the end of the S-apply chain), ideally oriented towards relevant practitioner communities must be "consumable" in some sense (Robey & Markus, 1998).

Cooper & McAlister, discussing research in business schools in general note that according to one of the AACSB reports much research in universities lacks relevance to the industry (Cooper & McAlister, 1999). They stress that applied research should be directed to practical use, rather than pure understanding. The authors advocate the concept of application-driven theories, arguing that: "research (in a professional school) should be initiated … around a concrete problem," and then generalization beyond concrete application should be sought. It is through this sort of combination of rigor and relevance the long-term survival of research in business school can be achieved, according to the authors.

The issue of rigor vs. relevance have also been one of the major topics of discussion in IS literature in recent years (Davenport & Markus, 1999; Gosain, Lee, & Im, 1997; Jani, 2001; Lyytinen, 1999; Mandviwalla & Gray, 1998; Moody, 2000; Nunamaker, Chen, & Purdin, 1991; Orlikowski & Iacono, 2001; Robey & Markus, 1998; Saunders, 1998; Senn, 1998; Todd & Benbasat, 1999; Weber, 2003a). Information systems research is criticized for its inability of contributing towards solving day-to-day problems faced by businesses (Saunders, 1998).

The "Memorandum" mentioned earlier in the preface (Österle, et al., 2011) gets straight to the point with the question: "Is information Systems (IS) research supposed to be beneficial for society and business?" They then go on to note that in the predominantly design-oriented European IS community the answer so far has been definitely positive. However, the authors have expressed their concerns about the possible shift among the young researchers towards the heavily behaviorist-oriented perspective as a result of encountering difficulties with publishing their work in what are considered the "top outlets." They note: "If we seek the cause for this *quite questionable trend* (both from a societal and a business perspective),

the discipline itself needs to be put under scrutiny" (italics added).

Noting that IS research has to be of the applied nature, Moody pointed at the disconnect between research and practice (Moody, 2000). Arguing that the real audience for IS research comprises other researchers, he cited Keen's comment that "IS research is in danger of talking about itself to itself." Supporting this claim are the findings of the analysis of academic vs. practitioner literature suggesting a wide gap between topics of interest (Gosain, Lee, & Im, 1997). Therefore, it seems that IS research has grown to become more actor-oriented, rather than public-oriented (Johansson, 1991).

As possible causes of lack of relevance to practice of IS academic literature Benbasat and Zmud mention the following issues: emphasis on rigor over practical relevance; lack of a cumulative research tradition; rapid and continuous change in information technology; limited extent of academicians' exposure to business and technological contexts; and institutional and environmental constraints within academia (Todd & Benbasat, 1999). They encourage the community to rethink the pertinent topics in IS research; the implementability of the implications; and the style and tone of presentation. One of their recommendations reads: "In order for IS research to be more relevant, it is important that authors develop frames of reference which are intuitively meaningful to practitioners to organize complex phenomena and to provide contingency approaches to action."

Robey and Markus argue that there is no inherent conflict between rigor and relevance in research (Robey & Markus, 1998). The primary barrier to achieving the relevance is the predominant practice of targeting academic outlets by the researchers. Moreover, the rate of technological change could be responsible for outdatedness of rigorous research projects. They proposed that IS research must be made more "consumable" through seeking for practitioner sponsorship; adopting new models of research (applied theory, evaluation research, etc.); producing consumable reports; and exploiting non-traditional publication channels.

Davenport and Markus noted that improving the relevance is crucial to the survival of the field (Davenport & Markus, 1999). However, increasing relevance cannot be done without revisiting fundamental core academic values. Similar to Robey & Markus they stressed the importance of utilizing practitioner outlets and fostering respect to consulting (they refer to medicine and law as fields where the researchers are also practitioners).

Speaking in the context of Group Support Systems with implications stretching to IS research in general, Mandiviwalla and Gray noted that IS research should not be limited to what already exists (Mandviwalla & Gray, 1998). Their position is that GSS research should encourage theory-based systems development research projects and methodologies. Lyytinen contended that researchers lack sufficient understanding of technical matters and associated practical problems (Lyytinen, 1999). In particular, he noted that development research, which combines both constructive and empirical elements, is largely missing from the field.

Recently a method based on "applicability checks" have been proposed in (Rosemann & Vessey, 2008). The idea is in repeated assessment of the applicability of research questions and findings as research projects progress. The authors propose a series of steps in preparing and conducting such checks, including: plan applicability check; select the moderator; ensure the familiarity of the participants with research questions; design interview guide; establish environment for check; conduct the check; and analyze the data. The checks can be applied in connection with the research lifecycle moving from researching problem, theory development, and all the way to communicating results. It is as if a researcher would ask practitioners every now and then: "does what we do and what we find

matter to you?" The very idea of using such "applicability" checks is an indication of the major relevance problem in the discipline.

Summarizing the above opinions and findings one is lead to conclusion that the issue of relevance is one of the most troubling concerns to the IS research community. It can be characterized as an *exogenous* issue, since it relates to the question of what value does the field provide to the relevant (outside) practitioner communities.

BLACK HOLES AND BLACK BOXES

In light of the above discussion, a worrisome impression about the IS discipline could be that the state of affairs is unsatisfactory on both endogenous as well as exogenous accounts. Interestingly, it is exactly where the field must strive for endogeneity (the identity crisis) it seems to be exogenous (reliance on other disciplines); and where exogeneity must be sought (the relevance crisis) it leans towards endogenous side (the actor-oriented perspective). In other words, it adopts theories developed in other disciplines as an input and produces little relevant output to its target audience (according to some aforementioned authors). A proper metaphor that best suits such a description is that of a black hole. In the absence of a solid core, the field has to rely on other transient sources of support, such as lobbying (Weber, 2003a), or healthy student enrollment (Robey, 1996), which has been waning in recent years.

While the suggestions made by the prominent scholars in the field that included managing diversity and building better communication channels with the practice of IS undoubtedly point at the crucial directions on improving the situation, one is left to wonder if there is one common "higher-order factor" that causes both the concerns of identity and relevance. If such a factor indeed exists, there is a chance that identifying and properly approaching its treatment could have a positive impact in both of the above dimensions.

One central topic that surfaces while analyzing the discussion along the two issues is that of representing information systems (or "IT artifact" according to some authors) (Benbasat, 2001; Benbasat & Zmud, 2003; Lyytinen, 1999; Orlikowski & Iacono, 2001; Orlikowski & Barley, 2001; Weber, 2003a, 2003b). Orlikowski and Barley claimed that IT and organizational studies can learn much from each other, but the latter can benefit even more if taking the material properties of technology into account (Orlikowski & Barley, 2001). They further note that changes occurring in the nature of work and organizing cannot be understood without considering changes in IT. Lee stressed that IS and organizational context have a transformational effect on each other as re-agents, thus being reactive and inextricable elements (Lee, 1999). Along the same lines, commenting on the view of human artifacts (in general) from the socio-technical perspective, Ropohl noted that there is no invention which would not lead to a novel pattern of human action at the same time (Ropohl, 1999). He stated bluntly: "every invention is an intervention."

It thus, seems legitimate to conclude that the inseparability of information systems from the relevant human and organizational contexts should lay as a fundamental principle of all research in Information Systems. The question is whether satisfactory conceptualizations have been adopted in the practice of IS research. In an article aptly titled "Desperately Seeking the 'IT'" in *IT Research - A Call to Theorizing the IT Artifact*, Orlikowski and Iacano have proposed a scheme for technology conceptualization metacategories, including: tool view; proxy view; ensemble view; and computational view (Orlikowski & Iacono, 2001). While the first two (meta-)categories tend to largely reduce the IT artifact to "black box" representation, and the fourth one largely ignores the organizational context, the seemingly most ap-

propriate (for IS research) ensemble view promises to adequately integrate both organizational as well as technological contexts. Incidentally, it is also the least popular category among IS researchers according to the authors. In editorial notes in the ISR journal Benbasat shared similar sentiments (Benbasat, 2001), while Weber had repeatedly stressed the same issue calling for the appropriate ontology of IT artifacts (Weber, 2003a, 2003b).

In light of the above concerns, it is only natural to ask whether the "black box" view of the artifact jeopardizes the relevance of IS research. (Actually, in many instances even the black box is not there. A black box view can provide some insights into the nature of interactions between humans and IT. In many theoretical models, there is simply no box. Information system is "an external variable"). If the human-technology inseparability principle is (either implicitly or explicitly) agreed upon, then how could the relevant insights be produced without taking the nature of the information systems into consideration through some *appropriate representational framework*? How could the *epitechnical* phenomena be investigated while the salient characteristics of systems are missing from the investigation? Blackboxing effectively reduces the competency requirements for a researcher. Weber notes that the IS researchers must believe the phenomena they study are *special* in some way, to establish the *ownership* of the theories (Weber, 2003a). However, if a researcher from any other discipline is competent in conducting IS research (through the blackboxing trick), the crisis of identity could, in principle, be predicted *a priori* (and has become manifest a posteriori).

Thus, one possible conclusion is that the "black box" treatment of information systems is one of the major culprits in contributing to the "black hole" state of the discipline. Perhaps the momentum acquired by the field in moving away from technocracy has been strong enough to result in the almost complete abandonment of technological views.

THE WORST POSSIBLE QUESTION

In a recent editorial the Editor of the *ACM Transactions on MIS* wrote (Chen, 2011): "I am afraid that the perception and reality remain the same: there is a strong bias towards the behavioral paradigm in MIS that has developed over the years. I don't believe there is purposeful manipulation. It reflects mostly the *historically larger composition* of behavioral scholars in the MIS field at the early stage of our discipline. However, the IT and MIS landscape has changed dramatically over the past decade. There have been tremendous developments and opportunities for performing high-impact, macro-level … design-oriented research" (italics added). And further: "I often fear that there is not much tangible societal impact that our MIS community has collectively made over the past 30 years. Although many attempts have been made that call for high-visibility and high-impact MIS research …, the results have been less than stellar." The sheer disbalance between the presence of behavioural vs. design-oriented perspectives in the community, thus, may be one of the culprits leading to the relevance crisis in the field.

Modern system testing practices adopt a critical view of the system artifacts under development. The purpose of testing is to uncover important hidden defects in any given system. Thus, the objective of a tester is to show that the developed artifact does not work as intended. To this end often tests are designed to see how the system would respond to unusual situations, such as the use by a non-trained user. This destructive attitude in the testing phase helps to ultimately produce good quality system solutions. As scientific body of knowledge is also a (special) type of an artifact, the critical attitude should help ultimately play a positive role in its development. Science espouses criticism.

Let us take as examples the theoretical models introduced earlier, and examine them from a somewhat vulgar (non-trained "user") perspective. TAM, for example, posits that perceived usefulness and perceived ease of use affects the attitude towards usage, which affects intention to use, which affects the usage. In other (agreeably layperson's) words, if you see the thing is useful and easy to handle, you would want to use it, you will decide to use it, and you will use it. This sounds simplified, but nonetheless, much more communicable to a greater audience. After all were there not recommendations to improve communicability of theoretical developments in IS to non-academic audiences? The academic outlets are not "easy to use" for non-academicians, neither they show a great deal of "cognitive fit" with the characteristics (background and training) of IT professionals.

Let me really push this criticality to the limit, and re-state TAM (as I would have to explain it to my imaginary non-academic drinking buddy in a bar) in following terms: "useful things will be used. Of things that are useful, the ones that are easier to use will be used even more." There is a difference here now. TAM uses the keyword "perceived," which is not the same as bare usefulness and ease. This "perceived" part is perhaps where the "predictive power" of TAM comes from. One could say everything is perceived for that matter. There is a possibility that something is not useful, while it is perceived as useful. People would adopt it and use it, while it is not getting the job done right. This sounds like a case of illusion, almost like failing to perceive the reality under the influence of a drug. The same applies to the opposite situation. Why there should be a mismatch at all between what is perceived and what is, for that matter?

So, let's say if one sees something is useful, he or she will eventually use it. Theories are developed to advance the knowledge – the ultimate form of information. Theories should inform. What is then the information content of models like TAM? Well, in Shannon's formula for enthropy, the information content of a particular outcome is measured as:

$$I = -\log(p(m)),$$

where p(m) is the probability of that outcome. Suppose an outcome is a message summarizing a research finding. In other words, the information content decreases as the "surprise" value, of say, a message decreases. Now, I haven't done a survey, but how much surprised would one be if he or she would get a message like "if you see something is useful, you will use it, whatever you need to use it for"? Not surprised at all, I dare say. Or, in other words the probability of getting such a message would be quite close to one. Then, according to the formula above, what would be the informational content of such a message? Close to zero.

Consider, briefly the TTF model. In a nutshell it says that perceived fit between a task and a tool to tackle the task impacts the performance. Again, in layperson's terms: "if you think the tool you have fits the job you've got to do, better than, say an older tool, then you'll do the job better." What is the information content of this message?

Or let's go back to a suggestion of focusing on a "macro" level theories, and consider the research question provided as an example "how has internet changed the music industry"? The consuming public of such research would be, I presume, the companies that produce music items, and the consumers that consume them. Now do not the businesses already know that their businesses had been affected dramatically by the Internet. If the research finding suggests that "much music nowadays is downloaded as compared to the pre-internet era," how surprised these companies would be? What would be the information content of this message?

Let's re-visit Alexander's form and its context. It is taken as a *given* that the form must ideally fit the context. Fitting in the case of IT and organizations means that a particular IT solution must fit organizational practices and structures. The TTF model, basically re-states it linking the fit to the performance. The TAM model states that IT form should be useful and easy to use for the context, which in essence is the same notion of fit in form-context terms. The IS success model states that the quality of information and that of a system impacts individual and organizational performance. Now, information quality could be largely related to functional requirements, while system quality has a lot to do with non-functional (operational) requirements. Requirements are essentially the forces that shape the context. Again, we can reduce it to the idea of form-context fit. Why that, which is obvious to design researchers and taken as a given as an ultimate purpose of design requires extensive empirical studies?

Agreeably, one could argue that the empirical studies could overthrow the latent strongly held beliefs. After all, one could discover that people start using things that they don't see as useful, or their perception of usefulness does not influence the actual usage. This would be a very strange finding indeed, with huge information content. However, do these models really deserve being amongst the most espoused theoretical developments in the field?

To reiterate, I largely accepted the layperson's critical attitude in this criticism. But then, a haunting vision of IS research arises: that of the emperor's new clothes. A rather wild speculation leads one to wonder whether the disguise of rigor is necessary to conceal the lack of relevance?

To think about it, the ideas of usefulness and fit are applicable well beyond IS and IT – to any tools, really. Our remote ancestors some 3.5 million years ago saw a potential usefulness of chopper tools and developed the Oldowan industry. Presumably, they also had some sense of a fit as well. Later on, they had discovered that more refined Acheulean tools were even more useful, easier to use, and also fitful to go about improving their daily lives. These perceptions must have

Figure 5. IS core and related disciplines

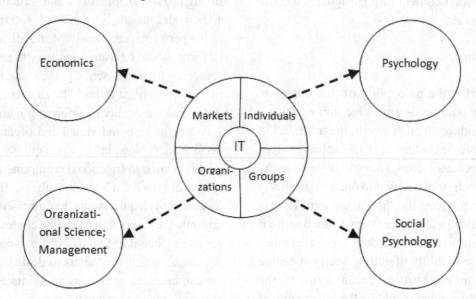

led to more usage and impacts to their individual and tribe performances. And yet, there is nothing especially IS-ish or IT-ish about either Oldowan or Acheulean industries.

A colleague of mine once related me a story about a conference presentation he attended. The presenter was sharing his work that involved yet-another extension/confirmation of TAM. The conference itself had a somewhat technical/computer science flavor. After the talk was over the speaker had asked if anyone had questions. There was a minute of silence, and then, one of the attendants asked the *worst possible question*. He asked: "*Why* are you doing this?" No, really, why?

DESPERATE FOR THE HOOKS

The title of this section is inspired by Orlikowski & Iacano's article "Desparately seeking the IT in IT Research" (Orlikowski & Iacono, 2001). The identity and relevance concerns are (or, at least, should be) truly troublesome for the entire IS community. Inevitably, the question of the core subject matter arises in this regard. Let us revisit one of

the empirical studies aimed at the discovering the "as-is" core of the predominant paradigm in IS research (Sidorova, Evangelopoulos, & Valacich, 2008). Apart from systems development, all of the other facets of IS research follow the "IT and X" pattern. Now, what stands for X is organizations, groups, individuals, and markets. Each of these elements have their own largely developed fields, which, apparently do have their respective established identities. These fields necessarily have an impact on IS research directed to study a particular intersection of IT with them. We can represent this graphically on Figure 5.

Now, the influence of the field, rather metaphorically, can be viewed as a gravitational pool that tries to attract its own share of the "IT and …" pie. This implies that there is always a danger that the total gravitational pool of the related disciplines would tear the "IT and …" core apart (Figure 6). Where would the IT core go? Some of the above-mentioned authors seem to suggest it was not there after all. Or it dissipated into the air. What is lacking there to keep the field together is the hooks. There seem to be little appreciation of the hooks, in a form-context sense.

Figure 6. A possible scenario

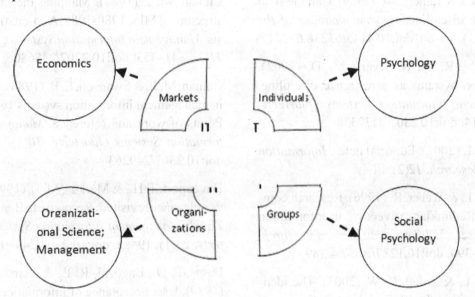

IT must have hooks to ensure the strong "AND" with its various outer environments. The structures and processes of the systems must be related to those of these environments. The IS field is apparently in a desperate need for the hooks.

And it's tempting to say: "let's just continue doing whatever we've been doing." It's possible to do laborious citation studies and proudly announce: "Yes, we have an identity." But this hardly settles the issue.

There was a funny joke that went around in USSR during the times of economic stagnation under Brezhnev's rule. I'll relate it partially here. Once Stalin, Khrushev, and Brezhnev were travelling on the train that suddenly came across a large tree trunk lying on the tracks. Stalin pulled out a gun and threatened to shoot everybody if they do not remove the trunk. They went on further until they came across another fallen tree on the tracks. Now Khrushev ordered everybody to lift the entire train and carry it over the tree, and put it back on the tracks on the other side of the tree. (This illustrates the irrational character of some of Khrushev's major decisions). When they encountered another tree on their way, it was Brezhnev's turn to offer a solution. And he suggested "Let's just all get back in the train and think that we are moving."

We can think all we want, but this does not mean that we are making any progress in regards to improving the identity or the relevance of research in information systems.

REFERENCES

Alter, S. (2003). 18 reasons why IT-reliant work systems should replace "the it artifact" as the core subject matter of the IS fiel. *Communications of the Association for Information Systems, 12*(23), 366–395.

Armour, P. G. (2007). Twenty percent: Planning to fail on software projects. *Communications of the ACM, 50*(6), 21–23. doi:10.1145/1247001.1247020

Banker, R. D., & Kauffman, R. J. (2004). The evolution of research on information systems: A fiftieth-year survey of the literature in management science. *Management Science, 50*(3), 281–298. doi:10.1287/mnsc.1040.0206

Banville, C., & Landry, M. (1989). Can the field of MIS be disciplined. *Communications of the ACM, 32*(1), 48–60. doi:10.1145/63238.63241

Baskerville, R. L., & Myers, M. D. (2002). Information systems as a reference discipline. *Management Information Systems Quarterly, 26*(1), 1–14. doi:10.2307/4132338

Benbasat, I. (2001). Editorial notes. *Information Systems Research, 12*(2), iii–iv.

Benbasat, I., & Weber, R. (1996). Research commentary: Rethinking "diversity" in information systems research. *Information Systems Research, 7*(4), 389–399. doi:10.1287/isre.7.4.389

Benbasat, I., & Zmud, R. W. (2003). The identity crisis within the IS discipline: Defining and communicating the discipline's core properties. *Management Information Systems Quarterly, 27*(2), 183–194.

Carr, N. (2003). IT doesn't matter. *Harvard Business Review, 81*(5), 41.

Changchien, S. W., Lee, C. F., & Hsu, Y.-J. (2004). On-line personilized sales promotion in electronic commerce. *Expert Systems with Applications, 27,* 35–52. doi:10.1016/j.eswa.2003.12.017

Chen, H. (2011). Editorial: Design science, grand challenges, and societal impacts. *ACM Transactions on Management Information Systems, 2*(1), 1–10. doi:10.1145/2037661.2037663

Claver, E., Gonzales, R., & Llopis, J. (2000). An analysis of research in information systems (1981-1997). *Information & Management, 37,* 181–195. doi:10.1016/S0378-7206(99)00043-9

Cooper, W. W., & McAlister, L. (1999). Can research be basic and applied? You bet: It better be for B-schools! *Socio-Economic Planning Sciences, 33,* 257–276. doi:10.1016/S0038-0121(99)00017-8

Culnan, M. J. (1987). Mapping the intellectual structure of MIS, 1980-1985: A co-citation analysis. *Management Information Systems Quarterly, 11*(3), 341–353. doi:10.2307/248680

Culnan, M. J., & Swanson, E. B. (1986). Research in management information systems 1980-1984: Points of work and reference. *Management Information Systems Quarterly, 10*(3), 289–302. doi:10.2307/249263

Davenport, T. H., & Markus, M. L. (1999). Rigor vs. relevance revisited: Response to Benbasat and Zmud. *Management Information Systems Quarterly, 23*(1), 19–23. doi:10.2307/249405

Davis, F. D., Bagozzi, R. P., & Warshaw, P. R. (1989). User acceptance of information technology: A comparison of two theoretical models. *Management Science, 35*(8), 982–1003. doi:10.1287/mnsc.35.8.982

DeLone, W. H., & McLean, E. R. (1992). Information systems success: The quest for the dependent variable. *Information Systems Research, 3*(1), 60–95. doi:10.1287/isre.3.1.60

Dufner, D. (2003). The IS core-I. *Economic and systems engineering approaches to IS identity, 12*(31), 527-538.

Farhoomand, A., & Drury, D. H. (1999). A historiographical examination of information systems. *Communications of the AIS, 1*(19), 1–20.

George, J. F., Valacich, J. S., & Valor, J. (2005). Does information systems still matter? Lessons for a maturing discipline. *Communications of the Association for Information Systems, 16,* 219–232.

Glass, R. L., Ramesh, V., & Vessey, I. (2004). An analysis of research in computing disciplines. *Communications of the ACM, 47*(6), 89–94. doi:10.1145/990680.990686

Goodhue, D. L., & Thompson, R. L. (1995). Task-technology fit and individual performance. *Management Information Systems Quarterly*, *19*(2), 213–236. doi:10.2307/249689

Gorla, N., & Paulraj, A. (1999). *On the maturity of the MIS research field*. Paper presented at the Americas Conference on Information Systems. Milwaukee, WI.

Gosain, S., Lee, Z., & Im, I. (1997). *Topics of interest in IS: Comparing academic journals with the practitioner press*. Paper presented at the Eighteenth International Conference on Information systems. Atlanta, GA.

Gray, P. (2003). Introduction to the debate on the core of the information systems field. *Communications of the Association for Information Systems*, *12*(42).

Jani, A. Y. (2001). *IS research relevance: A perspective from the design science and the philosophy of technology*. Paper presented at the Seventh Americas Conference on Information Systems, Boston, MA.

Järvinen, P. (2004). *Supplementing Ron Weber's view on a theory building*. Paper presented at the Information Systems Research in Scandinavia (IRIS 27). Falkenberg, Sweden.

Johansson, I. (1991). Pluralism and rationality in the social sciences. *Philosophy of the Social Sciences*, *21*(4), 427–443. doi:10.1177/004839319102100401

Keen, P. G. W., & Morton, M. S. S. (1978). *DSS: An organizational perspective*. Reading, MA: Addison-Wesley.

Khazanchi, D., & Munkvold, B. E. (2000). Is information system a science? An inquiry into the nature of the information systems discipline. *ACM SIGMIS Database*, *31*(3), 24–42. doi:10.1145/381823.381834

Lee, A. S. (1999). Researching MIS. In Currie, W. L., & Galliers, R. D. (Eds.), *Rethinking Management Information Systems: An Interdisciplinary Perspective* (pp. 7–27). Oxford, UK: Oxford University Press.

Lee, A. S. (2004). Thinking about social theory and philosophy for information systems. In Mingers, J., & Willcocks, L. (Eds.), *Social Theory and Philosophy for Information Systems* (pp. 1–26). Chichester, UK: John Wiley and Sons.

Lee, Z., Gosain, S., & Im, I. (1999). Topics of interest in IS: Evolution of themes and differences between research and practice. *Information & Management*, *36*, 233–246. doi:10.1016/S0378-7206(99)00022-1

Livari, J. (2003). The IS core – VII: Towards information systems as a science of meta-artifacts. *Communications of the Association for Information Systems*, *12*(37), 568–581.

Lucas, H. C. (1999). The state of the information systems field. *Communications of the AIS*, *1*, 1–5.

Lyytinen, K. (1999). Empirical research in information systems: On the relevance of practice in thinking of IS research. *Management Information Systems Quarterly*, *23*(1), 25–28. doi:10.2307/249406

Mandviwalla, M., & Gray, P. (1998). Is IS research on GSS relevant? *Information Resources Management Journal*, *11*(2), 29–37.

Mason, R. O., McKenney, J. L., & Copeland, D. G. (1997). An historical method for MIS research: Steps and assumptions. *Management Information Systems Quarterly*, *21*(3), 307–320. doi:10.2307/249499

Mingers, J. (2001). Combining IS research methods: Towards a pluralist methodology. *Information Systems Research*, *12*(3), 240–259. doi:10.1287/isre.12.3.240.9709

Moody, D. L. (2000). *Building links between IS research and professional practice: Improving the relevance and impact of IS research.* Paper presented at the Twenty First International Conference on Information Systems. Brisbane, Australia.

Mylonopoulos, N. A., & Theoharakis, V. (2001). On site: Global perceptions of IS journals. *Communications of the ACM, 44*(9), 29–33. doi:10.1145/383694.383701

Nambisan, S. (2003). Information systems as a reference discipline for new product development. *Management Information Systems Quarterly, 27*(1), 1–18.

Nolan, R. L., & Wetherbe, J. C. (1980). Toward a comprehensive framework for MIS research. *Management Information Systems Quarterly, 4*(2), 1–19. doi:10.2307/249333

Nunamaker, J. F. J., Chen, M., & Purdin, T. D. M. (1991). Systems development in information systems research. *Journal of Management Information Systems, 7*(3), 89–106.

Orlikowski, W., & Iacono, C. (2001). Desperately seeking the "IT" in IT research - A call to theorizing the IT artifact. *Information Systems Research, 12*(2), 121–134. doi:10.1287/isre.12.2.121.9700

Orlikowski, W. J., & Barley, S. R. (2001). Technology and institutions: What can research on information technology and research on organizations learn from each other? *Management Information Systems Quarterly, 25*(2), 145–165. doi:10.2307/3250927

Orlikowski, W. J., & Baroudi, J. J. (1991). Studying information technology in organizations: research approaches and assumptions. *Information Systems Research, 2*(1), 1–28. doi:10.1287/isre.2.1.1

Österle, H., Becker, J., Frank, U., Hess, T., Karagiannis, D., & Krcmar, H. (2011). Memorandum on design-oriented information systems research. *European Journal of Information Systems, 20*, 7–10. doi:10.1057/ejis.2010.55

Robey, D. (1996). Research commentary: Diversity in information systems research: Threat, promise, and responsibility. *Information Systems Research, 7*(4), 400–408. doi:10.1287/isre.7.4.400

Robey, D., & Markus, M. L. (1998). Beyond rigor and relevance: Producing consumable research about information systems. *Information Resources Management Journal, 11*(1), 7–15.

Ropohl, G. (1999). Philosophy of socio-technical systems. *Philosophy & Technology, 4*(3), 59–71.

Rosemann, M., & Vessey, I. (2008). Toward improving the relevance of information systems research to practice: The role of applicability checks. *Management Information Systems Quarterly, 32*(1), 1–22.

Saunders, C. (1998). Editorial preface: The role of business in IT research. *Information Resources Management Journal, 11*(1), 4–8.

Senn, J. (1998). The challenge of relating IS research to practice. *Information Resources Management Journal, 11*(1), 23–28.

Sidorova, A., Evangelopoulos, N., & Valacich, J. (2008). Uncovering the intellectual core of the information systems discipline. *Management Information Systems Quarterly, 32*(3), 467–482.

Todd, P., & Benbasat, I. (1999). Evaluating the impact of DSS, cognitive effort, and incentives on strategy selection. *Information Systems Research, 10*(4), 356–374. doi:10.1287/isre.10.4.356

Walls, J. G., Widmeyer, G. R., & El Sawy, O. A. (1992). Building an information system design theory for vigilant EIS. *Information Systems Research, 3*(1), 36–59. doi:10.1287/isre.3.1.36

Weber, R. (2003a). Editor's comments: Still desperately seeking the IT artifact. *Management Information Systems Quarterly, 27*(2), iii–xi.

Weber, R. (2003b). Editor's comments: Theoretically speaking. *Management Information Systems Quarterly, 27*(3), iii–xii.

Whinston, A. B., & Geng, X. (2004). Operationalizing the essential role of the information technology artifact in information systems research: Gray area, pitfalls, and the importance of strategic ambiguity. *Management Information Systems Quarterly, 28*(2), 149–159.

Chapter 4
Traditional Science vs. Design–Type Research

ABSTRACT

Is science fundamentally different from the design of novel artifact concepts? This chapter aims to examine if there are essential differences between traditional science and design-type research. Human capacities allow us to perceive and understand the world as well as act on it to make changes in a purposeful fashion. As the subjects of knowledge and creation grow increasingly abstract, the differences between creating and understanding tend to fade away. While science studies natural phenomena, the focus of design is on artifacts. Could this be the definitive dividing line between design and science? Regarding the ontological status of the artifacts the opinions are split, some suggesting that they are distinct from natural objects, while others seeing continuity, the position which is defended in this chapter. Other possible differentiation criteria (e.g. design is application of science) are also discussed and it is argued that none of these makes design essentially distinct from science.

RESEARCH AND DESIGN: FUSION

Chapter 2 mentioned the "Tower of Generate-and-Test" introduced by Dennet, in which he placed different types of living organisms on different levels with respect to their "perceive-and-act" cycles. According to this model, The Popperian creatures have a capability to model relevant aspects of reality with the purpose of making their choices before committing to an action. Simple creatures come with the pre-wired perception-action circuitry. Humans are Popperian creatures. We have the capacity to perceive the environment, and also, as a result of such perception to build knowledge about its workings. This knowledge

DOI: 10.4018/978-1-4666-0131-4.ch004

then helps us to plan actions and modify the environment that we live in according to our needs and desires.

Let's take a closer look at different levels of the perception and action sides. On the perception side, as humans come equipped with the capacities for pattern-recognition, analysis and synthesis, they are able to notice similarities among the various phenomena they encounter while ignoring irrelevant details. We have this categorization capacity, which, in conjunction with the synthetic abilities helps us to model the outer world in a meaningful way. Thus we develop knowledge that simplifies our lives by relating new phenomena with the mental models we have about similar cases. The previously mentioned personal construct theory posits that individuals develop their private theories about the world around them throughout their lives.

On the action side we can design plans in order to achieve the desired objectives. We can also modify the environment so that it fits better with our survival and quality of life objectives. Having recognized a particular situation we could refer to previous cases and produce a plan to change the present state of affairs into a desired condition. A good portion of these actions involve creating new objects that we think are going to bring us to the desired states. These are called artifacts (henceforth we will imply technical artifacts, rather than, say works of art), as the nature does not provide us with them readily made. The artifacts made for any given purpose also share profound similarities both in structure and workings. This presence of common forms in artifacts could be also regarded as a sort of knowledge. The "artifact-making" knowledge.

Humans historically lived in various forms of society, and some of the interactions among the individuals related to explicating and sharing their private theories. This process led to collective knowledge and the birth of proto-sciences (see Chapter 2). Later developments led to the realization of the need for systematicity in conducting inquiries for knowledge. The advance of the scientific method has led to the higher level organization of knowledge, which we presently refer to as Science.

So, a traditional notion of science involves a higher-level perception organized as knowledge artifacts of different fields obtained in a systematic fashion. The action side led to the development of design and technology. But here one could sense some sort of a misbalance. Apparently, there is little appreciation by us, that the design side could also have a counter-part to the Science of the perception side. It is not a commonly accepted view (apart from those researchers who are in the design-related disciplines) that design could be regarded as a Science as well. Researchers in traditional scientific disciplines are considered to be somewhat more "scholarly" than their colleagues in the various fields related to design. There is hardly something like a scientific method for design oriented sciences. There is not nearly such a sizable body of literature on the philosophy of design-kind of sciences as there is on the traditional philosophy of science.

The fact that philosophy of science has a millennia-long tradition, while the philosophy of design science may be just making its appearance is not surprising per se. When humans started studying the world around them, its objects and processes were present as they are nowadays, and their workings were far from transparent and trivial. In contrast, the human-made objects and the corresponding needs of the ancients were much simpler. There was no need for elevating design to the level of science. Nowadays, however, the technology has grown tremendously in complexity, and our needs are progressing in a somewhat dynamic and non-obvious fashion. This might be the right time for the promotion of design knowledge to the status of a science. After all, action comes after perception. The perception-based science made its appearance before the action-based science.

If we call the perception side, which hosts all sorts of theoretical models about classes of phenomena "the Science," then why a legitimate counter-part of it cannot exist on the action side? Why not call higher-level abstraction design products also a Science? Design-type Science. In essence, the traditional Science, as it has been argued earlier, is a type of reverse engineering of existing phenomena. Design Science is a forward engineering. They are both valuable for human-kind. And they both should be duly recognized as being at par. The only difference is in the long history that the traditional science enjoyed and the related conventional opinion of what a Science ought to be like. Design science is relatively new. But since they both aim at knowledge about classes of objects and phenomena, one could think about learning from the philosophy of the traditional science with the purpose of applying scientific method and principles to the design-type science.

To add some "color" in conveying the point one could invoke a metaphorical reasoning. Physics is the science that studies the forces of nature. There are four fundamental forces: electromagnetic, weak nuclear, strong nuclear, and gravitational. Energy is the fundamental notion in Physics, which defies precise definition. The Grand Unification Theory in physics states that when energy rises to a certain level (about 10^{15} GeV) there will be a point at which the distinction between the first three listed forces will disappear. Such a convergence has already been demonstrated for the electromagnetic and weak forces (the "electroweak" force). Theory of Everything expects that at higher energy level (Plank energy) all four forces will fuse into one.

Let's now, admittedly somewhat whimsically carry over the same schema from a physical world into the world of mental. In human perception and action, there is a role for intellect that helps us understand the world, and shape it through actions. What if we try to raise the intellectual analog of "energy"? One could suggest abstraction as an analog of energy, as it relates to the true intellectual power, the ability to see the common patterns in concrete objects. When we raise the abstraction

level, we could progress from simple perception-action to knowledge level of the experts (on perception side) and craftspeople (on action side). When we raise level of intellectual "energy" even higher, we arrive at the science – design-type science pair. At this level there is a distinction between studying existing things and conceptualizing new things. If we raise the abstraction level to the maximum possible, we will eventually end up with purely abstract objects (Figure 1). No longer will we be able to see whether these abstractions refer to the phenomena of nature or the artifacts. We arrived at pure mathematics, where we can't even tell if its objects are results of discoveries or inventions. We arrived at the fusion point. Therefore, science and design-type science are not completely different animals, but are probably sharing a good deal of similarities. And they must be viewed at par in respect to each other. Design-type sciences are not mere "applications" of traditional sciences (as it will be discussed further), but represent legitimate bodies of scholarly knowledge.

DESIGN-TYPE RESEARCH

In Chapter 1 we have reviewed some of the prominent ideas emanating from the studies in "design science." The terms "design science" and "science of design" refer to the scientific investigation of design-related principles, rules and activities. Cross defines design science as "an explicitly organized, rational, and wholly systematic approach to design, not just the utilization of scientific knowledge of artifacts, but design in some sense as a scientific activity itself" (Cross, 2001). He identifies the term "science of design" with design methodology, defined as "the study of how designers work and think, the establishment of appropriate structures and design processes, the development and application of new design methods, techniques and procedures, and reflection on the nature and extent of design knowledge and its application to design problems" (Cross, 1984).

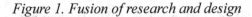

Figure 1. Fusion of research and design

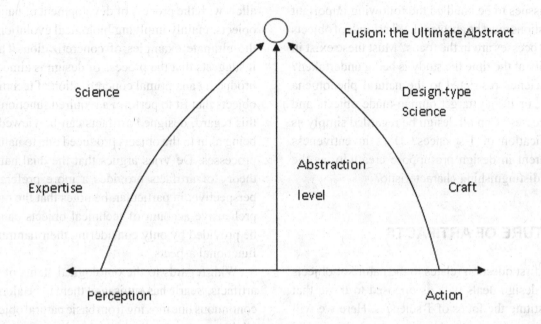

The process of design of artifacts involves movement from abstract concepts to concrete specifications for that artifact. This is what the designers do in their respective workplaces. Through this process the designers produce new concrete products, tools, and processes. The aims of the design science (as well as science of design) appear to be helping the designers to improve various aspects of the process through providing them with the scientifically derived systematic knowledge.

An intriguing question, which is the central topic of the book, is: can design process itself be characterized as scientific research? Can invention of new forms be regarded as a science in itself, or, at least something akin to the traditional conception of science? There are academic departments with members engaging primarily in design-sort activities, rather than traditional kind of science. By traditional (T-science) science here we refer to all types of sciences in the ABCDE framework (Chapter 3), except for the "C" category. There are major areas, such as computer science, engineering, and operations research along with

their branches, in which new types of objects and methods (i.e., artifacts) are being invented, and their respective memberships are regarded as scientific communities. Researchers in those areas conduct research experiments, publish papers in their scholarly journals, present their work at academic conferences, obtain research grants from the governments and businesses, in short do what any scientific community would normally do. And yet, their primary preoccupation is invention. These are predominantly creation – oriented disciplines. Their outputs are artifacts, like expert system models, new types of data structures, and new optimization algorithms.

Therefore, since the design-centric disciplines and their respective communities have these essential attributes of T-scientific fields, it may be suggesting that they also can be regarded as Science, or something similar to Science. It would be too simplistic and premature to accept this reasoning as a firm conclusion, though. Issues related to the characteristics of T-sciences have to be compared with those of the C-sciences. This comparison cannot be done within some framework developed for the description of T-sciences alone. Among the issues to be handled the following important questions must be answered. What kinds of objects or processes are in the focus? Must these exist in reality at the time the study is being undertaken? Is Science restricted to the natural phenomena only, or it may target human-made objects and processes? Can all design be regarded simply as application of T-sciences? Does inventiveness inherent in design presuppose creativity as the key distinguishing characteristic?

NATURE OF ARTIFACTS

The first question relates to the nature of objects that design deals with as opposed to those that constitute the focus of T-sciences. Here we will concentrate on natural sciences, as the formal sciences are concerned with purely abstract entities, where the distinction between invention and discovery disappears. The question raised here relates to the essential differences between the natural and artificial objects. The fact that artifacts are different from naturally-produced things in many respects is hardly a questionable conjecture. It is rather a question of the ontological status of the artifacts that we are concerned with, as this helps partly clarifying the question of whether some designed artifacts can be placed at the same level as scientifically derived knowledge.

As noted earlier, some design scientists stressed the dual nature of technical objects: on one hand they are physical objects (although, say software can hardly be seen as a physical object), while on the other they perform functions to serve the needs of humans. This essentially translates into re-invoking the final cause of Aristotle in a descriptive framework of objects of the reality. In this respect, de Vries compares the dual view of artifacts with those suggested in an early work by Simondon (de Vries, 2008). Simondon regarded the process of design as that of concretization by which the abstract artifacts turn into the concrete

objects of reality (Simondon, 1989). He drew parallels with the process of development of natural objects, mainly implying biological evolution as the ultimate examples of concretization. Thus, it suggests that the process of design is aimed at producing an optimal concretization of technical objects that fit to perform a required function. In this regard, designed artifacts can be viewed as being akin to the objects produced due to natural processes. De Vries argues that the dual nature theory of artifacts provides a more preferable perspective; in particular, he notes that the comprehensive account of technical objects cannot be provided by only considering their natural or functional aspects.

With regards to the ontological status of the artifacts, Searle has envisaged them to be along a continuous line moving from basic natural objects all the way to socially created realities. Thus, according to Searle, artifacts do not constitute an ontologically distinct category as compared to, say, atoms, mountain ranges, or organisms (Searle, 1995). There is, however a difference between the artifacts and the objects of the natural world, since the former are crafted to perform certain functions, while the latter do not have any naturally generated functions. Searle introduces a distinction between the intrinsic and observer-relative features of the artifacts. Functions, he argues, are always assigned from the outside and are never a part of the intrinsic structures of the objects. He further notes that since functions are assigned intentionally, and the intentionality itself is an intrinsic feature of the world, therefore, functional aspects of the artifacts can also be linked to the basic ontology. Kroes has criticized Searle's views on the grounds of incompleteness of the assignment of the causal agentive functions (Kroes, 2003). He pointed that Searle failed to provide a sufficient condition for an entity to be characterized as a functional object.

The observer-dependent aspects of the artifacts highlight their relational nature. Lawson notes that technical objects are irreducibly social (Lawson, 2008). Meijers distinguishes between the intrinsic, context-dependent, and relational properties of artifacts (Meijers, 2000). He argues that function is a relational property, and that the relational aspects cannot be reduced to the intrinsic properties: " ... the issue of what constitutes an artifact cannot be answered independently and separately from its wider context" (p. 88). Function of an artifact is a result of intentional design exercised by a human designer. Functions can be analyzed in terms of beliefs, desires and intentions of those who bring the artifacts into existence. According to Meijers, artifact creation is not simply a causal, mechanical process as compared to biological evolution. They are the result of rational intentional planning.

In connection with the ontology of technical artifacts, Ladrière introduced the idea of a world comprising technical objects. He notes that as the technical world becomes more interconnected and, in some sense, growingly autonomous, one would be justified in drawing the analogy with the natural world, in particular with its biological domain. With regards to the process of invention, which can be viewed as generating novel configurations, he notes that this could take place outside conscious activities, and relates it to the capability of human brains to recognize these configurations as providing solutions to the problems articulated previously.

Artifacts, according to Ladrière in their abstract representation are reduced to pure structure and behavior, or a form. Their materialization hinges upon the notion of objective possibility. "The possible thus, so to say, reduplicates itself in itself: it is an admissible and even expected determination, wrapped in the present as the reality of the virtual; it is the possibility of the actualization of a determination. ... And as oriented toward its occurring, that possibility introduces within Being an internal movement, which is the tension in which the possible relates, in virtue of its constitution, to its realization. And if the presence, in finite being, of the dimension of the "real possible" must be admitted as essential, then the tension interior to Being, between the virtual and the real, must be

seen as a really constitutive feature—and thus as an ontological disposition." (Ladrière, 1998, p.85). Thus, the world ("Being") is seen as unfolding itself towards material realization of the "really possible."

THE RENAISSANCE OF THE "ΤΗΛΟΣ"?

The brief review of some pertinent views on the nature of artifacts, emanating largely from the philosophy of technology reveals some major issues on which opinions are split. The two interlinked issues include the necessity of treating artifacts as objects possessing dual nature, and the relational character of artificial objects. The dual nature position essentially looks to revive the Aristotelian fourth cause, e.g. the final cause as a legitimate account for the existence of a given object. The argument states that it is not sufficient to rely solely on intrinsic features to explain the function of an object. The intentionality and rationality of human designers must be factored in. Conversely, the so-called etiological theories attempt to provide an account for the functions in terms of causal chains (Neander, 1991a, 1991b; Preston, 1998). These theories are naturally referring to biological organisms, which obviously exhibit features of design, in particular, emergence of functions generated by a process of natural evolution. Thus, there appears to be a natural extension into the world of human-made objects (Neander, 1991b). For example, Preston notes that the difference between changes in driving the evolution of biological and technical objects is that of a degree, not a kind. Vermaas & Houkes criticize the etiological approaches for failing to meet requirements for the account of technical objects (Vermaas & Houkes, 2003). In particular, they note that ascription of proper functions (i.e. those functions that the object primarily fulfills) to accidental ones is not handled by etiological views. According to them accidental functions in biological evolution become deviations, and thus never become proper. Human inventors, on the other hand, can recognize new functions as fulfilling certain requirements and those turn them into proper functions.

The evolutionary approach to study of the development of technology has been elaborated in (Basalla, 1988). Biological realm includes a huge diversity of various living forms, each occupying a particular niche in the environment, including living in particularly harsh conditions. In the presence of some context that allows for survival and reproduction in one way or the other the evolutionary process will most likely generate some form to exploit that niche. The diversity of the forms is the footprint of evolution at work, as is the presence of continuity in the course of form development. In this respect Basalla compares the diversity of biological world, which includes some 1.5 million species with that of technological artifacts. As a very rough estimate he cites 4.5 million patents issued by the time of the publication of the book (1988) in the U.S. since the end of the 1790. One is left to wonder how many other kinds of artifact forms exist in the world, in particular those generated in the computing realm. How many different software and hardware types had appeared within the past two decades or so? In any case, the technological diversity is by far richer than the biological one. This speaks in favor of evolution being at work in the world of artificial.

Basalla also discusses two opposing schools of thought in the study of the development of technology. One espouses gradual transition between artifact forms, thus diminishing the contribution of any given inventor in the course of progress. The other cherishes the idea of "hero" inventors who produce drastic interventions, which are very weakly connected with the pre-existing artifact forms. In evolutionary view, changes to forms, however large, can be accommodated by the grand process. Compared to the biological evolution, the technological one is more difficult to study.

Biological evolution works with macromolecules, the technological one has to deal with the capacities of human minds. Large jumps are possible in the evolution of the artifact forms. Furthermore, in biology members of two species cannot interbreed, or if they do, their offspring is sterile (for example, mules). This leads to a nice hierarchical organization of the typology of organisms. In the realm of the artificial, this is not the case. Many different parent forms could give rise to a single child form. This is why it is difficult to arrive at a classification scheme for the artificial objects that would uniquely identify each type employing major class—subclass - ....sub- sub- ... class. Consider, for example the case of an ordinary pencil form, which is most common nowadays. The idea of merging a pencil with an eraser belongs to Hymen L. Lipman, who had patented it back in 1858 (Petroski, 1990). Both artifact components served a single task: that of writing. The new form had introduced the convenience of using the same device for writing as well as making corrections, though it derived from two different "species," at least in terms of chemical composition. Interestingly, the patent was later revoked as it was judged as the artifact was simply a combination of two pre-existing types. One would think that this judgment was rather unjust, as many artifacts combine the components derived earlier.

The new forms change the environment, the context, which in turn, creates the needs and opportunities to still newer forms, making the criteria for survivability very dynamic and complex. Let's say that somebody in the Fifties or Sixties (or even later) came up with an idea of the design of an artifact which combined a telephone with a photo camera. Would it sell? Perhaps, back then the idea would be considered to be odd, to say the least. A telephone was pretty much a static device, while a camera implied a good degree of mobility. While combine the two? What if a super-combo device was proposed that integrated a telephone, a camera, and an LP record player? Yet, nowadays, virtually any cell phone incorporates music playing, picture taking and video filming, and other capacities. The environment has changed, phones are no longer static, and they have become radically new types of devices inheriting from many parent concepts.

However different the biological and technological development processes may be, it is difficult not to see the basic similarities underlying the two forms of evolutions. The most obvious differences between the two are their respective paces and the magnitude of changes. In Lyytinen & Newman (2008) the authors propose a "punctuated" model for describing information systems changes. A change is defined as "generation, implementation, and adoption of new elements in an organization's social and technical subsystems that store, transfer, manipulate, process, and utilize information." They note that the traditional view of IS change (and change is what drives evolution) has been that of a linear "Darwinian"-like process. They argue that adopting a "white-box" view on the process of introducing innovative elements in IS reveals relatively extended periods of stasis interrupted by the periods of revolutionary change that upsets the equilibrium. The period of stasis is maintained by exerting resistance to the change. The authors note that the change is not necessarily a progressive one.

It is curious that the authors did not make a single reference to Eldredge & Gould' model of "punctuated equilibrium" proposed to describe the appearance of the species in the animate world (the model has been especially popularized by Stephen J. Gould) (Eldredge & Gould, 1972). The similarities between the socio-technical and biological "punk eeks" are evident. But Eldredge & Gould's model (also a target for criticism, see e.g. Dennett, 1995) does not negate Darwinism per se. Thus, one can see the traditional "gradualist" models and the newer "punctuated" ones proposed to describe the emergence of new living forms as well as of novel artifacts. These similarities suggest that perhaps it is legitimate to draw analogies between the technological progress and the growing tree of life.

The question that is raised in this chapter regarding the possibility of design as a science relates in a major way to the nature of objects involved in design. Do these objects fit however subtly in the fabric of the natural world, or do they have a distinct ontological domain? As pointed earlier, it is of little doubt that there is a difference between artifacts and the things readily observed in the nature. In this respect it is unquestionably convenient to invoke the final cause in a given design context. As mentioned previously, Dennett had proposed adopting different stances (physical, design, intentional) for domains studying phenomena of various degrees of complexity to make analysis and prediction easier. Function and its context would greatly simplify the description of the structure of an artifact and its *raison-d-être*. But could the artifacts, in principle, be viewed as a product of the efficient cause?

The very nature of causality has been revised by the findings of physical science in the 20th century. In quantum world, no longer one could predict an outcome of a single experiment with absolute certainty. The efficient cause, as appears, works in subtle ways at the particle level. Randomness is inherent part of the Nature. It is true, though that the probabilities of different outcomes of quantum experiments can be predicted quite accurately. Moving from the physical realm to the biological one, the randomness in the pattern of cosmic rays influences the gene copying machines of various organisms, which leads to mutations. Mutations are the workhorse of the evolution, as they lead to the emergence of new forms (though the predominant majority of these mutations are harmful). Whether these forms are more fit to survive is determined by the complex network of interactions with the environment, other species (e.g. predator-prey relationships), or individuals within the species (e.g. mating relationships). Biological forms co-evolve and many random factors play a role in determining the fitness of a given form.

Unlike in physics, where experiments involving a huge number of particles can, in principle be conducted repeatedly, biological evolution takes the shape of one single realization. Could life have evolved in a somewhat different fashion? If we could re-run the evolution "experiment" large number of times, we could, in principle, collect some statistics, which could help us estimate the probabilities of this or that form making its appearance. More, likely, there would be probabilities assigned to different form clusters including co-evolving members. Then, it is hypothetically imaginable, just like in physics, that one could estimate the probabilities of the different outcomes of the "evolution" experiment. The efficient cause works in subtle ways.

Now, moving on to the objects produced by humans, could we apply similar reasoning? The difference between artifact-making and the natural evolution is that the latter works by trial-and-error, while the former relies on the synthetic abilities of Popperian creatures to take shortcuts and introduce large changes to the structure of the existing artifacts. These changes can essentially be viewed as "macro-mutations," which are not characteristic of a biological evolution. The difference is, in essence, that the biological evolution takes random gradual steps (and thus can only generate certain living forms accessible from the initial form in small steps), while the latter is more directed and could involve "jumps" ("saltations"). Does this imply a distinct nature of the technical objects? As with biology, we could imagine re-running the technical evolution "experiment" a large number of times to collect the statistics on the emergence of certain forms and their clusters. Some forms would have a high probability of turning up, e.g. the wheel. A screwdriver would also have a high chance of making the list. At some point there would be a need to connect two objects (e.g. two planes) firmly, and the shape of a screw would naturally be produced by our synthetic minds. There would be a need for something to turn the screw, and thus, the characteristic shapes of the screw

hat and the screwdriver tip would appear. Other objects would have a smaller chance of appearing and persisting. There are books and websites that abound with the examples of "not-so-smart" inventions. For example one website presents as a joke a sort of anti-flatulence underwear with a built-in gas filter (www.purpleslinky.com).

One of Dennett's ingenious philosophical models is what he refers to as a "cosmic pyramid," where different layers include Nothing, Chaos, Order, Design, Mind, and God (Dennett, 1995). He defends the idea of the pervasiveness of the Darwinian evolution that stretches beyond the biological realm. The hypothetical "universal acid" that can dissolve anything is used metaphorically to signify the ubiquity of evolutionary processes. He points that given the order the design will appear as a result of evolution. In this regard, he notes that the Aristotelian final cause, the "telos" was no longer needed after Darwin's work, as the "design" of living forms could be explained by the efficient cause alone.

The complexity of biological forms was initiated (in some way) by the replicator molecules that got their structures copied. Replicators that were doing a better job naturally grew in numbers. Gradually through random variation the replicators proceeded in building the machinery that helped them being better at survival and copying. These "survival machines" (Dawkins, 1976) appeared as a product of random mutation, crossover, and natural selection, produced completely due to the efficient cause, yet they possess what we ordinarily refer to as functions. The "telos" here in analyzing a given function is a convenience vehicle, not a "cause."

Genes encode the design of the survival machines that help them to copy themselves effectively. But this encoding stretches beyond the boundaries of the machines. This point is well articulated by Dawkins as action at a distance in "The Extended Phenotype" (Dawkins, 1982). Phenotype refers to an external manifestation of the genotype: a genetic composition of a given type of an animal. One of the examples includes the beaver dam. The genetic encodings of beavers dictates them to build impressive dams to create "artificial lakes" which could extend to miles. What would be the ontological status of such lakes, one would wonder? Are they a part of nature, or have a "dual" twist to them?

The dam-building behavior of the beavers is sort of "hardcoded" in their genotype. The nest-building behavior of birds is also hard-coded. One could think about these behaviors as algorithms wired into the animal "hardware." A specific type of an organism that has in its "hardware" the specifications for a unit capable of synthesizing "software," thus the capability of flexibly generating algorithms to help its survival is a biological possibility, and, in fact, the naturalized reality. Humans have in their genotype a lucky twist that allows them to extend their phenotypes far, far beyond the boundaries of their bodies. Our artifacts are, in essence, our extended phenotypes. How far does a human extended phenotype stretch? The Pioneer and Voyager spacecrafts by now have "stretched" it beyond the limits of the solar system.

It is true that our extended "phenotype" is not directly encoded in our genes. And yet, the genes dictate the building of the arena for the other types of units of evolution. According to Dawkins, our brains are inhabited by "memes" (Dawkins, 1976), the units that partake in defining human cultures. These memes undergo evolution and are subject to the selective pressure, just like the genes. Part of our culture is the design tradition, and, arguably, our technical progress can be viewed through the prism of the evolution of "design" memes. So, unlike the animal-world schema "genes – extended phenotype," in the case of humans we have a longer chain "genes – human brain – memes – extended phenotype (technology)." The genes act as, in Dennett's words "cranes for building cranes" (Dennett, 1995).

The point that technical artifacts are relational objects also fails to distinctly separate them from the Mother Nature. Chromosomes per se are *mean-*

ingless unless there is machinery for reading and interpreting them. Chromosomes have a relational aspect, then. And a dual nature. On one hand they are long carbon-bound chemical molecules, and on the other, they are information, or specification carriers. Various parasites living in animal intestinal tracts have much simplified survival mechanisms; in particular, their digestive system is primitive. (Gould used this point to demystify the view of evolution as that of a steady progress [Gould, 1996]). Such a parasite can barely be suitably described without its "relational" aspects towards its host.

To summarize, adopting the "telos" helps tremendously in understanding and creating the technological world. However, to seriously suggest that the artifacts are distinct forms that do not fit the natural-world description context seems to be an extremity. The revival of the "telos" as a defining factor in providing an ontological description, is in essence a return to Aristotelian times. We might as well accept that heavy objects have their "natural" place located at the center of the Earth, towards which they have inherent aspirations.

SCIENCE AND DESIGN: DIFFERENCES?

The previous section has defended the view that there is no gaping discontinuity between the objects of nature (the target of traditional sciences) and technological objects (the focus of design-type research). This section discusses other apparent differences between science and design. It argues that the distinction humans make between science and design is rather a matter of convenience. The nature of work in the two human traditions and the kind of products generated share deep similarities.

First, let's consider a widely accepted (mis-) conception of design as application of scientific knowledge. In this view, scientists discover laws and formulate theories to explain various phenomena, and the designers "merely" apply that knowledge to produce concrete artifacts. Poser notes that this view is "historically and systematically misleading" (Poser, 1998). Human artifacts have appeared long before anything comparable to scientific knowledge had been produced. As mentioned in chapter 2, design has been the first human tradition (Nelson & Stolterman, 2003). Human-made tools date back to millions of years ago, whereas early sciences had emerged a few thousand years back. Thus, the existence of scientific knowledge does not seem to be a prerequisite for the design activity.

The conception of technology as applied science has come under criticism (de Vries, 1996). Poser notes that the industrial revolution was carried out by craftsmen's tradition with no apparent link to the scientific body of knowledge of the time. He points out that the only two noticeable examples of scientific conceptions realized directly in artifacts are the Huygen's perpendicular clock and Leibnizian calculator (Poser, 1998). Undoubtedly, science discovers laws which help the engineering discipline. Yet, design as an activity should not be viewed as a sort of "mechanical" application of scientific discoveries.

The adoption of the "applied" vs. "pure" criterion to differentiate between science and design becomes especially questionable when considering such a discipline as Computer Science (Clark, 2003; Tedre, 2007). The discipline definitely is design or "construction" - oriented as it generates useful abstract artifacts, such as algorithms, methods, and computing structures, some of which become part of the real-world technology. If it is an applied science then the natural question would be what science it is an application of? Mathematics, perhaps? But Mathematics provides tools which could be used by any science. Could Physics be regarded as an application of Mathematics? Would Einstein's general relativity theory count as a successful application of Riemann geometry?

Second, the evident difference between design and science is that the latter studies natural phe-

nomena, while the subject matter of the former are artificial objects. However, there are traditional sciences whose subject matter is "contaminated" by the creeping in of the human-made or, at least human-influenced entities. The synthetic elements, such as Plutonium or Einsteinium did not exist on Earth (although they might have been produced elsewhere under suitable conditions), but were generated by nuclear reactions. Would this fact be sufficient to send them into an "exile" from the domain of physics? Synthetic polymers were also produced as a result of human activity. Does this mean that chemistry is not appropriate to study their properties?

Consider now Biology, the science to which admittedly extensive reference is made here (precisely because it somewhat "fuzzifies" the difference between science and design). By the time it had matured into a scientific discipline many species have taken their present-day form as a result of artificial (human-directed) selection. Our crops, cattle and pets are the most vivid examples. Somewhat less obvious cases include the evolutionary split between the head and body lice species as a result of humans starting to wear clothes. In fact, many species have influences on each other. Thus, to really stretch the point one could dare say that bees had "designed" many flowers in their present form. Of cause, in case of other animals there is no foresight involved in reshaping other species. But in case of humans orchestrating the selective pressures, could anybody definitively state that the particular change being initiated was more rational or more "blind"? While it is doubtful that any of our ancestors saw a clear picture of the "specifications" of the target animal form to be produced, the selection process did involve the human abilities to recognize the desirable characteristics and act accordingly.

Furthermore, the socially-oriented sciences, such as Organizational Science and Economics deal directly with human-formed structures and processes. Economics, for example studies the workings of the processes supporting different forms of human exchanges. In one model a market mechanism design features as the central element that influences the allocation of items being exchanged and their prices (Smith, 1982). Thus, the fact that the subject matter of a discipline contains artificial (explicitly designed or produced by selection) objects does not necessarily make it "non-scientific" in character.

Third, let's tackle the issue of whether the objects of subject matter must exist at the time of the study. In some traditional disciplines indeed the studies are directed towards forms and processes that are not contemporary with the time the research is being undertaken. The historical sciences and paleontology are the prime examples. Here the flows of events and past forms are sort of re-engineered based on sources that reflect their historical tracks. But one could argue that these areas look into the past, whereas design is future-oriented.

The question is discussed at length by Galle (2008). He observes that the capability to predict is a necessity for a design process. The prediction statements then would refer to the properties of the objects being designed. However, how could a reference be made to something that does not exist yet? Galle calls this philosophically puzzling question a "dilemma of reference." He provides the ways of its resolution from both nominalist and realist perspectives, some of which will be only briefly outlined here. Adopting a second-order predictions stance he distinguishes between the design prediction per se (the form of the future artifact) P, and its estimation (or expectation) E. While P does not have a truth value, $E(P)$ does, and, hence this resolves the reference issue from a nominalist perspective. He figuratively notes "… using E as a crutch, P limps along and eventually manages to fulfill its purpose of guiding rational decision-making."

Adopting the realist perspective then Galle discusses, in particular the ideas of eternalism and possible artifacts. In the eternalist view the importance of time as a defining criterion is disregarded.

This vantage point has much in common with the standard four-dimensional view of space-time in Physics. Therefore, according to this perspective, time is akin to the three spatial dimensions. Just like science could examine distant objects, one could similarly treat the objects located further along the fourth dimension. The four-dimensional model in physics had been advanced by the Einstein's relativist theories.

Another realist approach proposes a "possible artifacts" model, according to which alternative artifact forms exist in different multiple worlds. We simply happen to inhabit one of these worlds. Again, there is an evident similarity in this conception to one of the interpretations of indeterminate quantum effects, known as a multiple-worlds model. It is curious to note, that the above two perspectives are related to the relativity theories and quantum physics, the two areas that apparently defy unification at the present time. The analysis of the issues related to prediction and existence as applied to artifacts seems to lead to conclusion that objects that do not exist at the time can legitimately be studied by a science.

Finally, design or invention is often associated with creativity and ingenuity. Could this serve as a distinguishing feature of engineering as compared to science? In this regard Poser rejects the idea of creativity serving as a useful discriminator (Poser, 1998). He notes that the design process can be systematized to limit the need for totally creative solutions. This point has much in common with the systematic and reflective views on design mentioned earlier. Furthermore, he notes that creativity plays an important role in scientific research as well. The idea to fix the speed of light was truly a creative step. So was the mental experiment of Galileo that suggested that objects with different weights travel with the same speed.

Thus, we arrive at the conclusion that design cannot be decisively differentiated in general from science based on ontology and nature of objects and their temporal status. The applied vs. pure categorization and the need for creativity also fail to provide clear-cut discriminating criteria. At a deeper level there does not appear to be discontinuity between the two practices. Design can be viewed as type of science, although admittedly not all design. (Similarly not all research would necessarily count as scientific). What would be then the nature of knowledge produced by the design-type research? We will return to this question later.

CRITERION OF TRUTH

Scientific research is conventionally understood as a search for truth. The laws of physics, for example express properties and behavior of natural objects and their relationships. These laws therefore could be regarded as true generic statements reflecting the essence of those properties, behaviors and relationships. The task of science is to uncover the truth. The task of design is to produce an artifact. There is, apparently, a very clear-cut difference, a true gap between design of any form and traditional science. Or is there?

First, the very vision of science uncovering truths about the nature had been criticized since the times of ancient Greek thinkers. A pre-Socratic philosopher Xenophanes of Colophon had contended that humans may not be able to uncover the whole truth, but rather approach it indefinitely in their inquiries (Vamvacas, 2009). The famous scientific revolutions in various sciences (e.g. Astronomy and Physics) have demonstrated that what was a firm belief, an uncovered "truth" yesterday may be replaced by the alternative stronger "truth" of tomorrow.

Apart from the question of chasing the "truth," in comparing science and design one would inevitably run into the issue of what is understood by truth. There is a number of theories of truth (Kirkham, 1992) advanced by different schools of thought, some of which will be reviewed here briefly. Intuitively, truthfulness of a statement can be judged by the relationship of its content

to the actual state of things, which the statement attempts to address. In other words, a given statement about phenomena must correspond to the actual state of things, i.e. the objective reality comprising those phenomena. Accordingly, such a view of truth has been accommodated under the name of correspondence theory. Straightforwardly, in layperson's terms if someone states that the weather is cold, the truthfulness of the statement is established by relating it with the actual state of the weather. Note that linguistic characterizations of the objective reality bring in vagueness to the very essence of truthfulness.

Could design be differentiated from science under the correspondence theory of truth? Design efforts address certain needs, which the designer assumes are present in the target user groups. Therefore, a statement that a certain type of needs is present can be judged by validating this claim to ascertain the presence of such a need. The statement may or may not correspond to the actual need in target user groups, but, nevertheless design in this respect, just like traditional science is in pursuit of truth. Subsequent to the identification of need a designer, by producing artifact design, in essence makes a prediction about the form, which would appear to target a given type of need. Again, this prediction can be checked against the reality to verify the emergence of the predicted form. Thus, adopting correspondence theory of truth does not lead to separation between design science vs. the traditional one.

The peculiarities of the linguistic aspects regarding correspondence theory have prompted alternative views on what constitutes truth. The most rigorous and formal way of reasoning claiming to affirm absolute truths is characteristic of mathematical sciences. Some great philosophers, including Plato, Aristotle, DesCartes, and Spinoza, to name a few, have cherished mathematical way of thinking as the method to arrive at true conclusions. In mathematical or formal approaches, a set of statements is judged to be true if it does not contain contradictions within itself. Given a set of basic propositions, or axioms, every statement (a theorem) can be checked for its coherence with the other statements. Such view on the nature of truth, not surprisingly has been called a coherence theory. In fact Logic as a mathematical field, is often defined as a study of methods for establishing validity of statements with respect to accepted axioms. Five postulates of Euclid provide a framework within which any other statement on geometrical properties of shapes on a plain can be validated (let's leave out Gödel's incompleteness for now). That is, provided the world has no curvatures, any statement about its geometrical properties can be shown to be true or not in terms of its consistencies with the system of known coherent statements.

The coherence theory could also be made intuitive from the layperson's perspective. It is difficult to come up with a solid lie. The false statement has to be coherent with the set of known other statements and facts. Any lie has to be "well-designed," so to speak. In any case, the coherence theory of truth has direct correspondence with design. Formal methods in computer science, such as Petri nets and Z-specifications look to establish the coherence of computing artifacts. In general, provided with the set of basic design principles, a designer looks to make decisions coherent with the principles. There are larger design paradigms, which guide the design communities in devising new artifact forms, which could be judged to be "true" or "false" in light of the compliance with basic common design principles. "Loose coupling" is one such principle in software engineering, and any architecture that defies it would not be coherent with the design paradigm. Thus, truth cannot serve as a separating criterion for distinguishing science from design on the account of coherence.

The further we delve in the theories of truth, the easier to erase the lines between science and design. In respect with societies and cultures, the truth itself becomes subject of evolution and construction. Different cultures have different opinions on what is to be considered true, and what is not. The truth is shaped by the societies in the course of their development in interaction with other societies. The truth is *constructed*. Constructivist theory of truth holds that truth is an artifact produced by members of any given societies. So, the truth is an artifact, and as such it is designed by humans. Arguably, it is not designed by a single designer in an act of purposeful design act, but rather emerges out of the collective, however semi-conscious design process. Yet the design of complex artifacts is also a largely collective effort. The view that the truth is designed fits rather well with the idea of construction of "true" artifacts.

The pragmatic school of thought, including the likes of Peirce and Dewey, espouses usefulness and practicality as the characteristics of truth. It is of no surprise that pragmatism had emerged in North America, the New World: a practically oriented society. It had risen somewhat opposed to the philosophy of Europe. It is curious to note that nowadays, in the field of information systems, the rigor has gotten an upper hand over the relevance, the practicality in research. IS research in Europe is much more design- and practice- oriented than it is in North America. Pragmatism explicitly places emphasis on utility, above all, and in this respect design kind of science acquires a more heightened status in the quest for truth and knowledge, than the traditional science.

The brief review of the truth theories does not indicate that design is not about discovering the truth. But is truth in itself an indisputable major criterion for judging the importance of human inquiries? In attempting to define what constitutes a design science Bartneck considers design as a meeting place between the artifacts and humans (Bartneck, 2009). He contends that neither the artifacts, nor the human side could be the subject of design science research, as the former is for a large part a topic for the underlying disciplines, such as physics, and the latter is the target for other areas, such as psychology and sociology. In search of the definition of the subject matter of design science Bartneck refers to the so-called metaphysics of quality advanced by Pirsig (1974). Quality, described by Pirsig as "the continuing stimulus which our environment puts upon us to create the world in which we live" is the primary driving source of all kinds of human inquiries, according to Bartneck. He further notes, that there is no reason to place the criterion of truth above that of the value (the "good"). Referring to the scientific mode of search for truth, he writes: "preferring to know about the world is already a value judgment. Therefore, science can never be free of values and values are above the truth." Thus, he challenges the view that the truth in itself constitutes the most dignified criterion. He positions the truth as serving the values. Values rule, truth serves.

TECHNOLOGY AS KNOWLEDGE: HEIDEGGER'S ACCOUNT

The relationship between technology and knowledge and discovery had been treated by Martin Heidegger in an intriguing fashion (Heidegger, 1971, 1977). His views are well worthwhile a brief overview here, especially in the context of the present chapter. The presentation of Heidegger's ideas on technology here will be based on the secondary sources that elaborate them in detail (Pattisson, 2000; Rojcewicz, 2006).

Referring to the origins of the word "technology," Heidegger discusses the meaning of "technē." Traditional aesthetic paradigms tended to regard the works of art as higher-level human endeavors, which have a closer relationship with the morality and truth, than production (and, implicitly, design) of useful (non-artistic) artifacts. Heidegger notes however, that the Greeks tended to call both fine arts as well as mechanical ones using the same term: "technē." Thus, Heidegger

believed that "technē" actually means knowledge (Rojcewicz, 2006), or a way of knowing (Pattisson, 2000). It is tempting to draw the analogies with the concept of "designerly way of knowing" mentioned earlier (Cross, 2006).

Continuing in an etymological fashion, Heidegger also points at the meaning of the word "truth": "alētheia." He notes that this term comes from the original composition of words that meant "unconcealment." Thus, truth is something that is unconcealed or uncovered (discovered, as we say today). Linking these two lines of thought, since knowing is related to truth, technē should be also linked to alētheia. Therefore, the creation of the works of art as a kind of technē is an act of bringing-forth out of unconcealement (Pattisson, 2000).

Moving on the focus to technology as a form of technē, Heidegger stresses that technology "is a mode of revealing. Technology comes to presence in the realm where revealing and unconcealement takes place, where alētheia, truth, happens (Heidegger, 1977, p. 13) (also cited in (Pattisson, 2000, p. 53)). The essence of technology is, then, knowledge. Designing and producing artifacts should be regarded as a process of unconcealement, or *discovery*. Things are not made, but discovered, "unwrapped" (Rojcewicz, 2006). Thus, for Heidegger "the philosophy of technology is equivalent to first philosophy... technology is nothing else than what it means to be in general" (Rojcewicz, 2006, p. 9). Technology is not seen as the application of some basic knowledge, but as the most basic knowledge, "the understanding of what it means to be at all" (Rojcewicz, 2006, p. 9).

Heidegger's perspectives can be related to the discussion of the differences between science and design. It suits well with the evolutionary view of the development of the artifacts as a process in the course of which the latter are seen as being revealed (unconcealed). This thought coupled with the Heidegger's very notion of truth as unconcealement seems to suggest that design could be viewed as a truth-seeking activity, rather than trivial "application." But if design is seen as truth-seeking then at least some form of it could be viewed as a science. In the sections below we will discuss the development of "design-as-a-science" notion in the area of Information Systems.

SCIENCE AS TYPE OF DESIGN

The second-rate attitude towards researchers working in fundamentally design-oriented disciplines has been justifiably irritating for the members of design-minded communities. Glanville notes in this respect the past attempts to make design "more scientific" (Glanville, 1999). He writes sarcastically: "Research was science. In shameful contrast, design was not scientific. Design should be "scientific." Design, therefore, needed research. Since research should be scientific, design research should be scientific."

Glanville sets out to critically reconsider what is regarded as research. Research, he contends, is conducted in two modes: through advancing theories and experimentation. He notes that Popper's depiction of scientific research is an idealization, rarely reflecting the way the researchers work in practice. Experimentation has to do with repetition. The conditions in the experiments are changed in a manner similar to the trial-and-error: a signature of the design process. Circularities of repetition present in the experimental studies make the experimenter, i.e. the scientist, a part of the investigation. This flies in the face of the notion of an independent subject, i.e. the scientist passively studying the unfolding phenomena of the nature, i.e. the object. The scientist is actively involved. The scientist is the designer.

In building theories scientists invoke Ockham's razor to choose between competing alternative explanations. However, Glanville notes that there is no truth in simplicity. Simpler models are more convenient than the more complex alternatives,

and they are easier to test for coherence (note, that the coherence theory of truth would tend to favor simpler theoretical constructions as the latter promote coherence). Glanville writes: "Occam's criterion can never be proved … nor properly tested" (Glanville, 1999). The natural tendencies of humans to simplify in order to understand the world around them have a lot in common with the design processes, where simpler artifacts are preferred to more complex ones. Tradeoffs between simplicity and performance are well-known to designers.

Referring to the deductive mode of theory development, Glanville points that building a theory from and of theory is a self-referential process "…and self-reference is, necessarily circular." Then further: "this circular process is, I argue a design process of continuous modification and unification, the inclusion of more and more in a coherent whole; occasional restart, extension and revolution…" (p. 87).

So what is the whole point here? There have been calls to make design more of a scientific discipline, in particular, to impose the principles and methods of conducting science to all design. However, according to Glanville science itself is a subset of design. Then why the principles and methods of the subclass of design problems should be forced upon the entire domain of design? Why stretch that what suites the particular to the whole?

Now, consider the case of design-type research in light of Glanville's conclusions. The object of such design/research is to produce classes of artifacts, rather than particular solutions. Therefore, design-type research is also a subclass within the ocean of design problems and situations. This subclass has much in common with science in general. Therefore, it may be beneficial to adopt the apparatus of the scientific method to design kind of sciences after all. In fact, a chapter further in this book will discuss application of different scientific principles to design-type research.

REFERENCES

Bartneck, C. (2009). *Using the metaphysics of quality to define design science*. Paper presented at the Fourth International Conference on Design Science Research in Information Systems and Technology. Malvern, PA.

Basalla, G. (1988). *The evolution of technology*. Cambridge, NY: Cambridge University Press.

Clark, M. (2003). Computer science: A hard-applied discipline? *Teaching in Higher Education*, *8*(1), 71–87. doi:10.1080/1356251032000052339

Cross, N. (1984). *Developments in design methodology*. Chichester, UK: Wiley.

Cross, N. (2001). Designerly ways of knowing: Design discipline versus design science. *Design Issues*, *17*(3), 49–55. doi:10.1162/074793601750357196

Cross, N. (2006). *Designerly ways of knowing*. London: Springer-Verlag.

Dawkins, R. (1976). *The selfish gene*. New York: Oxford University Press.

Dawkins, R. (1982). *The extended phenotype: The gene as the unit of selection*. Oxford: Freeman.

de Vries, M. J. (1996). Technology education: Beyond the "technology is applied science" paradigm. *Journal of Technology Education*, *8*(1), 7–15.

de Vries, M. J. (2008). Gilbert Simondon and the dual nature of technical artifacts. *Techné: Research in Philosophy and Technology*, *12*(1), 23–35.

Dennett, D. C. (1995). *Darwin's dangerous idea: Evolution and the meanings of life*. New York: Simon & Schuster.

Eldredge, N., & Gould, S. J. (1972). Punctuated equilibria: An alternative to phyletic gradualism. In Schopf, T. J. M. (Ed.), *Models in Paleobiology* (pp. 82–115). San Francisco, CA: Freeman Cooper.

Galle, P. (2008). Candidate worldviews for design theory. *Design Studies*, *29*, 267–303. doi:10.1016/j.destud.2008.02.001

Glanville, R. (1999). Researching design and designing research. *Design Issues*, *15*(2), 80–91. doi:10.2307/1511844

Gould, S. J. (1996). *Full house: The spread of excellence from Plato to Darwin*. New York: Harmony Books.

Heidegger, M. (1971). *Poetry, language, thought*. New York: Harper & Raw.

Heidegger, M. (1977). *The question concerning technology and other essays*. New York: Harper & Raw.

Kirkham, R. L. (1992). *Theories of truth: A critical introduction*. Cambridge, MA: MIT Press.

Kroes, P. (2003). Screwdriver philosophy: Searle's analysis of technical functions. *Techné: Research in Philosophy and Technology*, *6*(3), 22–35.

Ladrière, J. (1998). The technical universe in an ontological perspective. *Philosophy and Technology*, *4*(1), 66–91.

Lawson, C. (2008). An ontology of technology: Artefacts, relations and functions. *Techné: Research in Philosophy and Technology*, *12*(1), 48–64.

Lyytinen, K., & Newman, M. (2008). Explaining information systems change: A punctuated socio-technical change model. *European Journal of Information Systems*, *17*, 589–613. doi:10.1057/ejis.2008.50

Meijers, A. (2000). The relational ontology of technical artifacts. In Kroes, P., & Meijers, A. (Eds.), *The Empirical Turn in the Philosophy of Technology* (*Vol. 20*, pp. 81–96). New York: JAI Press.

Neander, K. (1991a). Function as selected effects: The conceptual analyst's defence. *Philosophy of Science*, *58*, 168–184. doi:10.1086/289610

Neander, K. (1991b). The teleological notion of function. *Australasian Journal of Philosophy, 69*, 454–468. doi:10.1080/00048409112344881

Nelson, H. G., & Stolterman, E. (2003). *The design way: Intentional change in an unpredictable world: Foundations and fundamentals of design competence.* Englewood Cliffs, NJ: Educational Technology Publications.

Pattisson, G. (2000). *The later heidegger.* London, UK: Routledge.

Petroski, H. (1990). *The pencil: A history of design and circumstance.* New York, NY: Alfred A. Knopf.

Pirsig, R. M. (1974). *Zen and the art of motorcycle maintenance: An inquiry into values.* New York, NY: Morrow.

Poser, H. (1998). On structural differences between science and engineering. *Philosophy and Technology, 4*(2), 81–93.

Preston, B. (1998). Why is a wing like a spoon: A pluralist theory of function. *The Journal of Philosophy, 95*, 215–254. doi:10.2307/2564689

Rojcewicz, R. (2006). *The Gods and technology: A reading of Heidegger.* Albany, NY: State University of New York Press.

Searle, J. R. (1995). *The construction of social reality.* London: Penguin Books.

Simondon, G. (1989). *Du mode d'existence des objets techniques* (2nd ed.). Paris: Aubier.

Smith, V. (1982). Microeconomic systems as an experimental science. *The American Economic Review, 72*(5), 923–955.

Tedre, M. (2007). Know your discipline: Teaching the philosophy of computer science. *Journal of Information Technology Education, 6*, 105–122.

Vamvacas, C. J. (2009). Xenophanes of Colophon. In *The Founders of Western Thought – The Presocratics* (pp. 85–99). New York: Springer. doi:10.1007/978-1-4020-9791-1_8

Vermaas, P. E., & Houkes, W. (2003). Ascribing functions to technical artefacts: A challenge to etiological accounts of functions. *The British Journal for the Philosophy of Science, 54*(2), 261–289. doi:10.1093/bjps/54.2.261

Chapter 5
Design–Type Research in Information Systems

ABSTRACT

Information systems are socio-technical artifacts whose design should fit to serve the needs of organizations as well as the individuals who employ them. The central purpose of this chapter is to argue that design of new IS concepts can be regarded as a scientific research activity. To this end, several important questions need to be tackled, including the following ones: What is the meaning of observation in design-type research? Is there a notion of a theory in design-type research that corresponds to that in traditional science? If so, what are its building blocks? How does design-type research relate to the issues of truth and discovery? This chapter makes an attempt to provide the answers to these and other related questions.

THE RISE OF DESIGN-TYPE RESEARCH IN INFORMATION SYSTEMS

Chapter 3 discussed the alarming issues concerning the identity and relevance of research in Information Systems. Apparently, IS as a scientific applied discipline has a weak impact on practice in the related professional communities. The overly emphasis on rigor in the empirical studies of IS while promoting the quality in disseminating scientific outputs seems to jeopardize the very content of these outputs in terms of their interest to the practitioner.

Perhaps, it wouldn't be a shocking presumption to suggest that information systems viewed as an interface between the information technology and the organizational environments should be in the focus of research in the corresponding scientific field. Understandably, the inner and

DOI: 10.4018/978-1-4666-0131-4.ch005

outer environments of IS also represent important possibilities for research in their relation to the IS. However, the literature analysis suggests that the center of gravity of scientific interest in the field had shifted much into the outer environment (individuals, organizations, markets, etc.). This loss of the focus had led to the identity problem and it threatens to lead to the disintegration of the discipline. In light of the above concerns, some researchers have proposed that design-type of research can contribute towards improving the identity of the field (Iivari, 2007), as well as the relevance of its findings to its target professional domains (Carlsson, 2005; Cole, Purao, Rossi, & Sein, 2005).

Here, it is important to avoid the possible confusion in regard with the terminology used to refer to the design kind of activities, which would at the same time qualify as research. The terms such as "design science," "design research," and "design science research" are used to refer to somewhat different traditions by various researchers (Cole, et al., 2005; Piirainen, Gonzalez, & Kolfschoten, 2010). This could potentially perplex the newcomers to the design-oriented research community, the IS research community at large, the members of the allied disciplines, as well as the practitioners and the students of the field.

Cole et al. note that the terms such as "design research" and "design science" have long been adopted by the scientific community whose purpose is studying the principles of design. This community had produced valuable insights into the nature, process, and outputs of design in general, which were discussed earlier in the book. Thus, a distinction needs to be made between studying design and doing design. Cole et al. note that design research in IS and IT means design as research, i.e. doing design (Purao, et al., 2008). Design as research is concerned with the creation of innovative artifacts. It is different from researching design in several respects, notably due to the former placing emphasis on the domain where design is carried out, while the latter focuses on

designing in general, largely disregarding the domain of design activity.

Vaishnavi & Kuechler have also used the term "improvement research" to stress that it is always directed towards introducing improvements through novel artifact concepts (Vaishnavi & Kuechler Jr., 2008). The term however is not currently widely adopted. Occasionally the expression "constructive research" is also used to refer to the very nature of the kind of work done by the researchers (Iivari, 2008; Kasanen, Lukha, & Siitonen, 1993). In this book the term "design-type research" is preferred to distinguish it from the efforts in design studies. However, the other forms of expression will also be used as they are more readily recognizable by the design-oriented community in IS.

Thus, design research (in IS and IT) is about creating new and innovative artifacts. More precisely, it refers to the "activities concerned with the construction and evaluation of technology artifacts to meet organizational needs as well as the development of their associated theories" (Carlsson, 2005). The purpose of design research in IS is the development of practical knowledge for the design and implementation of "IS initiatives," according to Carlsson et al. An initiative is interpreted as an intervention in a socio-technical system a core component of which (intervention) is an information system. Design research should be oriented towards practitioners as its key target audience.

Iivari points that much of early IS research was of design type, however, in last twenty-five years its presence as an academic practice have considerably faded away (Iivari, 2007). The design tradition was kept relatively alive in Europe (Winter, 2008). The authors of the already-cited "memorandum" (Österle, et al., 2011) write: "The most prominent objective of European IS research has basically been to produce practically beneficial, business relevant results. Adoption of these results by business (i.e. economic payoff) has often been considered more important in terms of providing evidence of the correctness of results than transparent, well-documented scientific development of results following generally accepted criteria (i.e. scientific rigor)." And further: "European IS research has an excellent opportunity to build upon its strengths in terms of design orientation and at the same time demonstrate its scientific rigor through the use of generally accepted methods and techniques for acquiring knowledge."

Provided that information systems are artifacts one is left to wonder why the design attitude towards research in IS has started gaining popularity only recently? To answer this question one has to accept that conventionally science has been viewed as having a somewhat privileged status when compared to "mere" design (March & Smith, 1995; Poser, 1998; Simon, 1996). Then what about the inherently construction-oriented disciplines, like computer science and operations research? Are they in some way inferior to the traditional explanation- and description- centric science?

The point is, in those constructive disciplines the question never arises as all members of the communities have shared perspectives on what their respective projects entail. The communities are not mixed. To clarify the issue, consider Owen's categorization of sciences through the introduction of the dimensions "Symbolic vs. Real" and "Analytic vs. Synthetic" (Owen, 1997). For example, mathematics would be placed more in the "symbolic/analytic" quadrant, with some overlap with the "synthetic" category. (As mentioned earlier this positioning of mathematics is somewhat questionable as it is not clear whether mathematical objects are inventions or exist in some sort of platonic reality. In our view, the lines blur, as the phenomena investigated grow more abstract). Owen further noted that engineering science is on the analytic side, while engineering design is on the synthetic side of this framework. He indicated that both traditional and engineering research can be pictured in form of general relationship between knowledge and works. However, while in discovery-focused inquiries knowledge

generates proposals by means of a theory, in design context knowledge produces work by means of principles.

Now, the research in IS apparently would not fit distinctly in any of the quadrants, but will most likely be present in all of them. First, since IS is an artifact, its design in a broader sense implies both analysis and synthesis. Second, much of the behavioral research in IS has been conducted using instantiated (i.e. real) systems. Somewhat along the same lines it has been argued that design-type research is an approach that cannot be separated as a distinct paradigm (Weber, 2010). The design-type researcher's interest however should be primarily, as it will be argued later, on classes of artifacts, i.e. abstract, or symbolic objects.

IS discipline interacts with the its "allied" disciplines, including organizational sciences, Economics, and others on one hand, and the ones like software engineering and computer science on the other (Purao, et al., 2008). Naturally, the field of IS is not, and probably cannot be viewed as purely synthetic or analytical. The analytical-synthetic duality of the subject matter had led to the split between the behavioral and design-type camps. In our view, the decrease in the presence of design-type research initiatives in IS have been prompted by a) the conventional view of traditional scientific attitude as being superior to that of design stance; and b) the lack of the equivalents of the philosophy and methodology of science as applied to design-type research.

In view of the somewhat disappointing impact of the IS research on the professional audiences, the rise of design-oriented research is hoped by many to bring about improvements in terms of the relevance of its findings. In (Chen, 2011) the author writes: "Design-oriented MIS research targeting actual high-visibility, high-impact macro-IT applications (i.e., "macrodesign science") would bring significant attention and rewards to our community, from healthcare informatics to security applications, and from business intelligence to global supply-chain. Instead of adopting the micro approach (focusing on specific techniques and algorithms) often used by the Computer Science community, the MIS community can potentially offer more holistic, multidisciplinary, application-driven, and business-centric approaches and solutions for many emerging, high-impact organizational and societal problems. This kind of research calls for collaborative, multidisciplinary teams of design, modeling, and behavior researchers. Instead of studying only what other IT researchers and practitioners have designed and developed (a traditional behavioral paradigm), we should become a leading force in bringing unique innovations, solutions, and knowledge to society."

A design researcher is a sort of a problem-solver. This problem-orientation would ideally help to uncover the current common business needs (design contexts) to be addressed by generic solution concepts. As such the role of a design-type research would be in effectively facilitating the discovery and communication of the common problem-solution forms to the large practitioner audiences. Therefore, there has been the rise of interest in the role of design in information systems research. Apart from the classical book by Simon (1996), several influential papers had appeared in respected academic outlets that significantly improved the awareness of the design-oriented paradigm among IS researchers and students starting from the early Nineties (Hevner, March, Park, & Ram, 2004; March & Smith, 1995; Walls, Widmeyer, & El Sawy, 1992).

Amongst the recent publications, perhaps the one that had the biggest impact was that by Hevner et al. In a recent citation analysis Piiranen et al. have reported a sharp rise in design science related works, which was most noticeable shortly after the above paper had appeared in MIS Quarterly in 2004 (Piirainen, et al., 2010). Moreover, their co-citation analysis had shown that the largest portion of the papers on design science was within the domain of Information Systems (37%), as compared to other domains, e.g. Engineering and Management Science. These results clearly indicate the rise of interest in design-type research in IS. The paper by Hevner et al. may have triggered this explosion of interest that must have been incubating in the design-oriented community within the IS field.

Hevner et al. had argued that "application-driven technology-oriented research is critically needed to meet challenges of globalization, interactivity, high productivity, and rapid adaptation faced by businesses" (Hevner, et al., 2004). They noted that IS researchers are uniquely positioned to perform such research that relies both on organizational science and technology. There have been special issue announcements on design research in top academic journals (e.g. MIS Quarterly) and special sessions introduced at premier forums (e.g. International Conference on Information Systems - ICIS). The first conference on Design Science Research in Information Systems and Technology (DESRIST) was organized in 2006 and is held on an annual basis.

Prior to the appearance of this, by now seminal work, few papers were published to advance the design-centric perspectives in the area. Walls et al. have introduced the notion of a design theory in information systems (Walls, et al., 1992). March and Smith pointed at the necessity to reconcile the descriptive and prescriptive perspectives in IS research under the wide broad notion of Science (March & Smith, 1995). They showed how these two kinds of research could interact and mutually enrich each other.

Despite these positive developments, the researchers feel that there is a need to establish a legitimacy of design-type research as a scientific practice (Gregg, Kulkarni, & Vinze´, 2001; Purao, 2002). This largely relates to the fear of the possibility of de-emphasizing rigor as a result of searching to improve relevance. Design-type research, then should be both practical (since it is design) and theoretical (since it is research) (Cole, et al., 2005). This seemingly paradoxical view should be resolved by methodological groundings for conducting design-type research.

In this respect, Iivari had recently put forward twelve theses, which address disciplinary, ontological, epistemological, and methodological perspectives (Iivari, 2008). These include:

- Disciplinary
  - IS is ultimately an applied discipline;
  - Prescriptive research is an essential part of IS as an applied discipline;
  - Design science activity of building IT artifacts is an important part of prescriptive research in IS.
- Ontological
  - The primary interest of IS is in IT applications, thus IS as a design science should be based on sound ontology of applications;
  - IS as a design science builds IT meta-artifacts that supports the development of concrete IT artifacts.
- Epistemological
  - Prescriptive knowledge of IT artifacts forms a knowledge area of its own, and cannot be reduced to the descriptive knowledge of theories;
  - The resulting IT meta-artifacts entail design product and process knowledge;
  - The term "design theory" should be used only when it is based on a sound kernel theory.
- Methodological
  - Constructive research methods should make the process of building IT meta-artifacts disciplined, rigorous and transparent
  - Explication of practical problems, existing artifacts needing an improvement, metaphors and analogies, and relevant kernel theories help in achieving the above,

- Ethical
  - IS as a design science cannot be value-free, but it may reflect means-end, interpretative or critical orientation;
  - The values of design science research should be made as explicit as possible.

Two of above theses make use of the term "kernel theories," which will be introduced later in this chapter. These theses essentially could be used as guidelines in making a decision as to whether a particular design project constitutes research, or plain design.

The attempts to legitimize design as research have been treated in a somewhat critical fashion by Stahl (Stahl, 2008). He noted that while there is no apparent problem with emphasizing "practice and production," nonetheless the consequences of such a paradigm could be troublesome. Based on a critical theory he pointed at the dangers of reification (the artifact becomes of central importance), commodification (the object becomes commodity that could be traded), ideology, and fetishism. Answering these criticisms is the subject of the emerging design-type research methodology and philosophy.

In (Rohde, Stevens, Brödner, & Wulf, 2009) the authors have proposed a social practice perspective on describing design-oriented research. They critiqued some of the existing views on the subject and aimed at reconciling the behavioral and technical perspectives on IS. Their view is based on the "double hermeneutics" approach to viewing the process of acquiring knowledge on social practices in organizations. They reject the notion of pre-existing social reality as an object, which is studied by a subject through the act of non-intrusive observation. Rather they adopt the constructivist view, according to which such a reality is constructed rather than discovered. The process is self-referential as the study of social practices actually changes these practices, which in turn leads to a need for a new stage, which again implies a change. IS artifacts are embedded in the fulfillment of social processes, and therefore, they are an integral part of their on-going evolution. These artifacts, therefore, should be defined in a flexible fashion, i.e. leaving some room for contextualization and recontextualization. Thus, they advocate an evolutionary approach as a method for IS artifact design. Although the paper appears to address the issues related to research into design, rather than design as research, the view of IS artifacts as being an integral part of (and enablers of) social practices would definitely serve the purpose of closing the conceptual gap between the social vs. technical oriented perspectives.

Hevner & Chatterjee define design science research as "a research paradigm in which a designer answers questions relevant to human problems via the creation of innovative artifacts, thereby contributing new knowledge to the body of scientific evidence. The designed artifacts are both useful and fundamental in understanding the problem" (Hevner & Chatterjee, 2010). Although we will be mostly concentrating on IS/IT artifacts, it is important to realize that design also applies to processes. For example, in a recent publication, Carlsson et al. have argued that from a socio-technical perspective design-type research can also be applied to IS management and governance (Carlsson, Henningsson, Hrastinski, & Keller, 2011).

The scientific grounding of design work needs revisiting some of the concepts intimately linked with the very concept of science. The relevant questions include: in a design-type research what is an observation? What is a theory? Is the notion of truth applicable to design? What is the method of design-type science? What makes it different from plain design? These questions will be discussed in the remainder of this chapter.

OBSERVATION

While theories constitute the core of traditional sciences, observations are essential in conceiving the theories and testing theoretical hypotheses against the reality of phenomena. What would be an equivalent of an observation in design-type research? Based on the IS as an interface view, one could suggest that the key type of observation is a particular instantiated system, along with its structural and dynamic aspects. However, here we arrive at the seemingly unusual relationship between theory and observation. If the raison d'être for design-type research is producing novel solutions, then it appears that such observations cannot exist before the design research project is undertaken. Furthermore, if any sort of theoretical knowledge is expected as a result of the project, then it appears that an observation cannot be produced until the theory is devised. In other words the theory is developed to describe non-existing observations.

This somewhat counter-intuitive conclusion can be handled in three different ways. First, an observation (a system) may exist prior to the development of a theory, but it does not reflect a theory in its pure form. A particular instantiated system contains many details that are appropriate specifically to the given context. Extraction of a pure artifact form could be a topic for a project. Thus, innovation should not be understood in a literal form, meaning that no similar features of the design research artifact existed in the multitude of instantiated systems. It should be understood in a way that no prior research work has produced the artifact as a theory, the system concept in its pure, abstract form. In this regard the rise of the concept-artifact "autonomous agent" and the related design research does not mean that agent-like features never existed in any of the instantiated systems.

Second, the observation could be produced at the same time as a theory. In this mode, a truly innovative solution is developed in form of the instantiated artifact, and at roughly the same time its essential structure and behavior are being conceptualized at the theoretical level. Third, observations do not necessarily refer to the systems, but also to the inner and outer environments. The range of particular needs sharing significant commonalities in various organizational contexts and also developments of new technological capabilities may well serve as observations (the potentialities). These are sort of inverted system observations as they characterize the new system concept from outside and inside. One could refer to the case of pre-existing systems as positive observations, and to the case of pre-existing potentialities as negative ones. In this regard Iivari indicates that the sources of ideas for design research include practical problems and opportunities (negative observations) as well as existing artifacts (positive observations) among other possibilities (Iivari, 2007)

Let's first consider positive cases. The two possibilities here are that a particular system existed before something theoretical about it has been conceptualized, or it comes into existence concurrently with the theoretical elaboration. In the first case a system was in place and was probably developed without design researcher's participation. Then the task of a researcher would be in analyzing the features of such an instantiated artifact with the purpose of filtering out the particularities of a specific context from truly generic structures. The design researcher may then develop a conceptual generic system solution that would amount to a theoretical sort of contribution. One research method that fits such a path is a case study, and it has been recommended as beneficial in design research projects (Becker, Niehaves, & Pfeiffer, 2008) based on its fit with the guidelines for design research suggested by Hevner et al. (Hevner, et al., 2004). A case study is a passive approach in generating positive observations as it does not require the involvement of the researcher in introducing a real-world intervention.

Positive observations can also imply a sort of co-emergence of the IS artifact-observation and the IS artifact-theory. In this active approach, the researcher will more likely take some part in the development of the concrete system. The research method that nicely fits this mode is action research. Action research has been suggested as a way of improving the relevance of the IS research outputs (Baskerville & Myers, 2004). Burstein and Gregor have argued that IS development can be one way to conduct action research (Burstein & Gregor, 1999). Action research is a well-established research method aimed at generating change and at the same time producing knowledge about change. The method had been originally proposed by Kurt Lewin (the term first appeared in Lewin [1946]). Based on Davison, Martinsons, & Kock (2004), Cole et al. mention the following principles of action research: principle of researcher-client agreement (mutual commitment and expectations); principle of cyclical process model that includes diagnosing, action planning, action taking, evaluating, and specifying learning; principle of theory (theory must play a central role); principle of change through action (action and change are indivisible); and principle of learning through reflection (reflection to make practical and theoretical contribution) (Cole, et al., 2005).

Negative observations should ideally lead to the detection of potentialities present in the possibilities of matching common business needs and the capabilities of the technology. Such potentialities are rarely based on studying needs within a specific organization, as the immediate value of such study is not readily perceived by the organizational decision makers (if it is, then this would typically imply a development project, which would count as an action research, i.e. a positive observation). Thus, surveying those needs (e.g. through business and scholarly publications) in a detached mode with consequent generalization and the development of system prototypes (also kind of observations) is probably a more appropriate approach for design researchers. While acknowledging the value of action research and its similarity to design research, Iivari warns, that nonetheless they are different in certain relevant aspects. He points that much design work is taking place in labs, away from practice (Iivari, 2007). Nunamaker et al. had encouraged researchers to develop prototypes as means of better understanding the research domain, thus emphasizing the *instrumental* role of artifacts (i.e., the means) in IS research. Therefore, a good portion of negative observations would lead to the development of positive ones in form of artifact prototypes and their consequent testing against a set of expected improvements.

UTILITY OR TRUTH? INVENTION VS. DISCOVERY

An earlier chapter had discussed search for truth as a major defining characteristic of the traditional science. In this respect a number of theories of truth had been briefly described. It further tried to defend an argument that design-type research also can be viewed as targeting truth in light of its different theories. The issue of truth is an important one and it is revisited in this chapter within the context of its relationships with the concepts of utility, discovery, and invention.

Scientific research as a major human enterprise has been traditionally targeting the truth, although there is a common understanding that the quest for truth may not necessarily lead to its attainment. The issue of truth then is central to the very identity of the notion of science and, one could argue, for any undertaking to be counted as scientific research, it should have truth as an ultimate criterion. In case of design-type research, however, the relationship between research initiatives and truth as a target is quite subtle and far from the obvious.

There is little doubt that the goal of design science research is improvement, essentially the increase in utility that the instantiated artifacts deliver (Hevner, et al., 2004; March & Smith, 1995; Vaishnavi & Kuechler, Jr., 2008). In this respect Purao notes that the goal of design research projects is invention of virtual artifacts, not truth per se. Design research projects aim at supporting and improving real-world phenomena. And yet, though the truth is not out there, design researchers "facilitate its enactment" (Purao, 2002).

Venable notes in this respect that explanations (one of the key deliverables of much of the traditional science) of how things work are interesting but not so important (Venable, 2006). He also points that the use of the term "prescriptive" does not seem appropriate in design research context as it implies optimality of the recommended solution. In other words the term "prescriptive theory" means to him that the best possible solution should be provided for a given context. As this is not the case with the majority of design projects, he proposes instead the concept of utility theories, i.e. those where the ultimate criterion is utility, not truth. He suggests several forms of utility theories:

- (new) technology X will help effectively solve problems of type Y;
- (new) technology X will efficiently provide improvements of type Y;
- technology X is more effective than technology Z (Venable, 2006).

These schemas are indeed very reminiscent of typical hypotheses tested in design research projects. For example, "customers using a (particular form of) collaborative-filtering system would find products of higher interest to them, than those using catalogs and simple search engines." It should be noted, though, that theories are not synonymous with hypotheses. The latter are testable statements deduced from the core statements of theories.

Here, one could again refer to Heidegger's view of truth as unconcealement, and design research as essentially aimed at producing such a result, i.e. aimed at truth. We should note however that there is a common realization that scientific theories are also kinds of artifacts, which are devised to explain a set of phenomena, and in this respect have a certain utility aspect to them. Instrumentalist views on science, briefly mentioned in Chapter 3 deny the truth value in scientific statements, but regard them as instruments (artifacts) that are useful (have utility) in predicting observations. In science in general a theory that makes better predictions than its traditional rival (e.g. Einsteinian vs. Newtonian mechanics) would normally replace the older one as it does a better job, i.e. has higher utility. The area of quantum physics has introduced many peculiar, unexpected, barely comprehensible models of the workings of the nature. And yet, they constitute basic physical knowledge, simply because they work (in the spirit of Dewey's "what works is true" [Dewey, 1910]). Thus design research does not seem to have the exclusive rights on the utility.

But what about the realist perspectives? Can it be argued that design research could be viewed at some macro level as quest for the truth? To tackle this issue let's borrow a puzzle-solving metaphor used by Kuhn in his work on paradigms (Kuhn, 1962). According to Kuhn in the normal mode of science researchers act as efficient puzzle-solvers filling in the gaps dictated by an adopted paradigm. Now, if we accept that the mechanisms that the science is trying to uncover lie deeper beyond the experienced world of sense-perception (the observation made by ancient philosophers, notably Plato and Aristotle), we would soon realize that this is not a kind of regular puzzle that we are accustomed to.

Let us call the level at which the presumed hidden structures and workings of various domains of scientific interest (e.g. nature, society, etc.) take place the noumenal, or N-layer. These manifest themselves through observable events and structures at the phenomenal, or P-layer. Science attempts to grasp the N-layer by constructing scientific theory artifacts (the S-layer) using hints provided by the P-layer (Figure 1). Thus, there is an N-layer puzzle that is being reconstructed as the S-layer puzzle using signals from the P-layer (at least, according to the realist views). A better S- puzzle (than a rival one) illuminates more phenomena at the P-layer and thus is assumed to have a closer correspondence with the N-puzzle. It sort of has a higher truth value than a rival S-puzzle. When a science cannot explain some set of phenomena in its reflective domain, the S-puzzle may be said to be incomplete, although N puzzle is complete. Now let's entertain the possibility that in some domains the N-puzzle itself could be incomplete. It, as it were, has not yet evolved to the point of completion. In such cases the S-puzzle-solving may be regarded as a sort of prediction concerning the future evolution of the N-puzzle. The incomplete N-puzzle is the characteristic of design-type research disciplines. A design researcher by advancing an artifact concept makes a prediction that could be regarded as having a truth value. How a truth value is established then? Since the truth of theoretical concepts is ultimately judged against the set of illuminated phenomena at the P-layer, then the same could be said of newly created generic artifacts. Suppose a design researcher produces a novel conceptual artifact. If this is followed after some time by report of observations that manifest the presence of this artifact in one form or another in the targeted domain of the artifact's usage, then one could (arguably) say that the artifact as a theory is a *true* one. The N-puzzle has evolved in the expected direction. Regardless of whether the (true) N-puzzle is or is not complete at the time of the activity, both traditional, as well as design researchers are engaged in solving the same-layer puzzle (in this respect it is worthwhile to recall the discussion on the ontological status of artifacts introduced earlier in the chapter).

Figure 1. Science as puzzle-solving

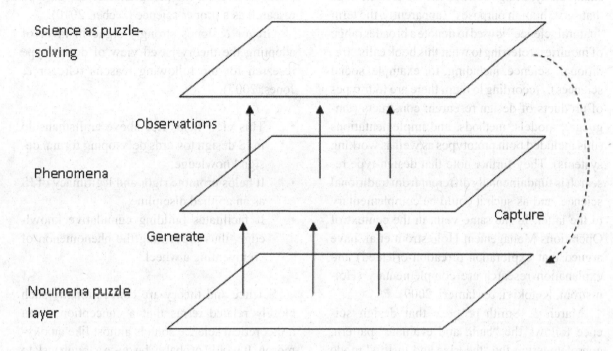

Consider an example of a relational data model as an abstract artifact (also referred to in Gregor & Jones, 2007, in the context of design theories). Its wide adoption as almost a universal means of organizing data storage attests to its truth value. A relational model is in some respect beyond useful; it is a true one (at least within present time context). Thus, in design research respect the wide adoption and usage of an artifact form (within the scope of its targeted applicability) amounts to it being true. Furthermore, because of the scope and range of observations where the designed form is manifest, it could be said that the proposal of the relational model was a true discovery, rather than invention. Thus, the lines between discovery and invention are blurred. Inventions of higher impact (such as the desktop metaphor in human-computer interactions) would be more appropriately called the discoveries, as they reveal ("unconceal") the major ways in which the technology will evolve. Design research is inherently future-oriented predictive enterprise. It aims at designing (predicting) the general forms

including their structure and behavior. In this regard Galle notes: "design predictions can be meaningful and true, because, like mathematical discourse they acquire their meaning from the structures they describe, (artefact structures, rather than mathematical structures), regardless of whatever makes up those structures" (Galle, 2008).

THEORY, PRESCRIPTION, PREDICTION, AND CAUSALITY

In an influential paper on comparison between natural science research and IT-related research March & Smith wrote: "It could be argued that research aimed at developing IT systems, at improving IT practice, has been more successful and important than traditional scientific attempts to understand it." (March & Smith, 1995). They deny the role of theory and theorizing in design-type research, focusing instead on the produced outcomes: "whereas natural science tries to understand reality, design science tries to create things that serve human purposes" (apparently, the term "natural science" is used to denote a broader range of inquiries, referring to what this book calls "traditional" science, including, for example, social sciences). According to them there are four types of products of design research: constructs (language), models, methods, and implementations (this included both prototypes as well as working systems). They further note that design-type research is fundamentally different from traditional science, and as such it could be complementary to the latter. In the same vein, in the context of Operations Management Holmström et al. have argued that exploration (creation-oriented) and explanation research are complementary (Holmström, Ketokivi, & Hameri, 2009).

March & Smith propose that design science follows the "build and evaluate" pattern, complementing the "theorize and justify" mode of the conventional science. They also stressed the paramount importance of the utility over the truth in design science, but unlike (Venable, 2006) who attempted to synthesize this utility orientation with the notion of a scientific theory (utility theories), March & Smith placed the theory firmly outside the domain of design science. Thus, they argued that the very notion of science needs to be broadened to include a-theoretical disciplines.

In an introduction to the special issue of the Information Systems and E-Business Management journal on design science Gregor and Hevner point at the emergence of two schools of thought among the design science researchers: one that advocates a design theory view, and the other one that puts the notion of a theory beyond the scope of design-type research (Gregor & Hevner, 2011). The work by March & Smith cited above exemplifies the latter view. The perspectives of Venable and Walls et al. (Walls, et al., 1992) are clearly on the design theory side. The apparent lack of theoretical contributions is one of the primary factors hindering the acceptance of design-type research as a proper science (Weber, 2010).

Gregor & Jones strongly argue in favor of adopting the theory-based view of design-type research for the following reasons (Gregor & Jones, 2007):

- This view helps rise above craftsmanship in IS design towards developing formal design knowledge;
- It helps promote rigor and legitimacy of IS as an applied discipline;
- It facilitates building cumulative knowledge, thus preventing the phenomenon of "reinventing a wheel."

Science and theory are conventionally such closely related terms that a conception of an a-theoretical science sounds almost like an oxymoron. It would probably be quite a tough task to promote the adoption of a-theoretical discipline as a legitimate science among the philosophers of science and scientific communities. Dropping the theory requirement from the characterization of a science would open up numerous possibilities for all kind of activities to be counted as science, and would remove an important demarcation principle between science and practice. It is, one could argue, a truly dangerous position, as the emerging design research community in IS could shoot itself in a foot by engaging in non-theoretical, thus, arguably, less rigorous design activities.

Scientific theories look to uncover the hidden principles, forms and workings of the given domain of interest with the purpose of illuminating the multitude of the observable phenomena. Thus, theories are inherently generality-oriented in that they seek manifestation of more fundamental elements in the events and objects of the experienced world. Design research should aim at generality, so that the result of designing is not a particular artifact. Design theories, if feasible, thus would be able to account for the multitude of observations (i.e. systems) that exhibit characteristics of common structures and behaviors expressed in form of theories. Thus, design theories would promote generality.

Therefore, many researchers believe that theories should be an integral part of design-type sciences (e.g. (Gregor & Jones, 2007; Kuechler & Vaishnavi, 2008; Purao, 2002)). Purao stresses the importance of theory building and theory testing in design research in technology of IS, noting that one of the challenges include demonstrating that "designing an artifact does not involve atheoretical tinkering" (Purao, 2002). But what is a design theory? What are its essential components? How does it relate to the observations in the domain?

The improvement-orientation of any design naturally leads to the prescriptive (Iivari, 2007) or utility-centric (Venable, 2006) characterization of the theories in design research, and as such they are assumed to have no truth value. Despite this, the previous section tried to show deeper links with the science in general both on the accounts of truth, as well as utility. As we shall argue, the proposals for the structure of design theories, at least to some extent blur the lines between pre-scriptive and descriptive orientation. A seminal work by Walls et al. had proposed the notion of a "design theory" for information systems, in part as an attempt to build theories endogenous to the area of information systems (Walls, et al., 1992). They envisaged the use of "kernel theories" in the design of a class of artifacts. According to them design theories include as their components:

1. Type of requirements (R) that an artifact is theorized to address (meta-requirements);
2. Type of system solution (S) or class of arti-facts that addresses the meta-requirements (meta-system);
3. Type of methodology (M) used to develop concrete artifacts which correspond to (1) and (2);
4. Kernel theories from the related disciplines that inform the design principles;

5. Testable design hypotheses that question whether S addresses R;
6. Kernel theories from the related disciplines that inform the design process and
7. Testable design process hypotheses ensuring that the method M leads to an artifact of type S.

Kernel theories are theories that guide the conceptual development of a meta-artifact. For example, the models related to human informa-tion processing helped definition of a decision support system as a meta-artifact. Consumer buying behavior guided the definition of meta-requirements and meta-design for agent systems that support online shopping processes. If we consider the structural core of design theories, then we could limit it to <R, S, M> tuple, as kernel theories belong to the related disciplines, while various hypotheses provide the means of testing the theoretical core. The authors had used their experience with the design of "vigilant executive information systems" to present an example of a design theory. More recently, Markus et al. em-ployed this concept of a design theory to devise the characteristics of a broad class of systems that the authors called "systems that support emergent knowledge processes" (Markus, Majchrzak, & Gasser, 2002).

Figure 2 graphically shows the components of a design theory according to Walls et al. Here *r* and *s* refer to particular observations, i.e. to the actual context-dependent requirements and specific system artifacts. Kernel theories inform various components of the theoretical core. The arrow leading from R to S implies a hypothetical relationship expressing the expectation that a given class of requirements demands a particular kind of meta-artifact. This hypothetical relationship is not directly testable, though. What could be tested empirically is that particular instantiated systems of type S fit the specific observed requirements of type R. The M component is also hypothesized to include the type of the method best suitable to produce specific systems.

Let us take a closer look at the components of the design theory and their relationships. It is curious to note that both prescriptive/utility as well as descriptive/explanatory theoretical schemas could be applied here. From a micro perspective, it is easy to see the prescriptive nature of the design theory. Though design theories do not have to be (and are actually required not to be according to Iivari, 2008) reducible to the corresponding kernel theories, nevertheless they are constructed based on the knowledge expressed in the latter. Basically an outcome of a design research project could be summarized as: "this is the type of a system to meet this type of requirements, and use this methodology to build actual systems whenever such requirements are manifest in specific problem contexts."

However, let us reflect about the contents of a theory taking a macro-perspective. The R component is essentially either an existential or predictive statement. It states that the particular type of requirements exist, or is about to come into existence in the near future, otherwise there is no need for design. It could potentially be tested by managing questionnaires or building mock-up prototypes (without having to conceptualize the full S) that are targeted to detect the evidence for R in experimental settings. It could be argued that detecting R is not a subject of design research, but more, probably of behavioral studies. However, R *is* the component of design theory, and as such can be viewed as either descriptive or a predictive statement.

Furthermore, let us try to reformulate the prescriptive interpretation of the relationship between R and S. R is usually linked to the goal, or effect, while S as an artifact is viewed to be the means,

Figure 2. Design theory

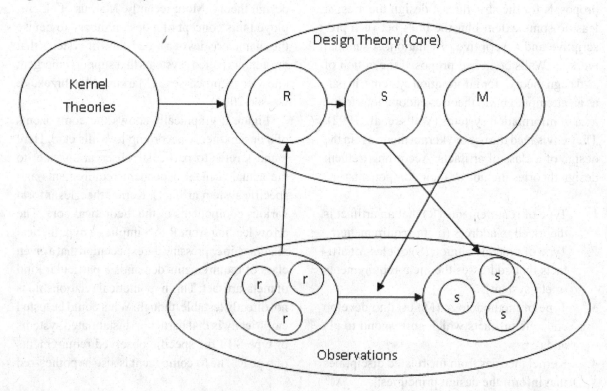

or the cause. In Chapter 1 we've seen that some researchers in design studies provocatively suggest that design reverses the relationships between the goal and the effect. That is first goal as a desired effect is realized and the cause is "designed" to bring about that effect. Again looked at micro-level this seems to make sense to some extent, especially since the design studies focus on particular design projects and their improvement. But in design-type research in IS the target is on theoretical knowledge. In science, it is myopic, and indeed meaningless to say that the effect precedes the cause (although some peculiarities of quantum physics probably challenge this long-held view). Thus we cannot say that the requirements precede the solution, we cannot regard the latter as cause and the former as an effect.

Let us now assume that a statement is made that a particular type of requirements, R *causes* a specific type of a solution, S. Could this be applied to design theories. One way to take an alternative look at the theory is to abstract away from the process of generating designs and development and think about what such a theory expresses. From this vantage point one could say that a design theory makes an existential (or predictive) statement that there is (or will be soon) a substantial set of situations, which could be described as R in the abstract way. Then, the presence of the type of requirements of the type R would cause the appearance of particular artifact-solutions, which are of the form S. R would also cause the specific kind of processes of the type M to produce particular systems. Looking from this perspective we arrive at the interpretation of design theories quite indistinguishable from those used in conventional sciences.

The perspective also provides insights into the value of design and design research. By theorizing about R, S, and M, and developing these constructs the design researcher facilitates a quicker, systematic, and more efficient and effective change in practice in the desired direction (that is, of

course if research is carried out rigorously, and the results properly disseminated to the respective practitioner groups). Now, the above account is admittedly speculative, but it demonstrates, at least how fuzzy the lines are between design-type science and the traditional one.

The version of a design theory structure by Walls et al. is the most commonly cited model. Other views on design theories have also been suggested, and we will mention them briefly here. Basing on the work by Walls et al. Gregor & Jones have proposed eight components for a design theory (Gregor & Jones, 2007), including:

1. Purpose and scope (met-requirements);
2. Constructs (representation of the entities of interest in the theory);
3. Principle of form and function (blueprint of an artifact: meta-system);
4. Artifact mutability (potential for evolution);
5. Testable propositions (hypotheses);
6. Justificatory knowledge (kernel theories);
7. Principles of implementation (method); and
8. Expository instantiation.

Kuechler & Vaishanavi examined the relationships between a kernel theory and a design theory. The former includes causal relationships between the entities in the domain of interest. The latter describe relationships between the prescribed actions and goals. The correspondence between the two types of theories is provided by so-called "mid-range" theories. Building on work by Bunge and Van Aken (Bunge, 1967; Van Aken, 2004), Carlsson had recommended the adoption of technological rules as the way to express design knowledge (Carlsson, 2005). The suggested form of such a rule could be expressed as: "If you want to achieve A (outcome) in Situation B (problem) and C (context) then something like action/intervention D can help because E (reason)" (Carlsson, 2005).

One important point to be emphasized in relation with design theories is that they often (if not always) involve meta- entities (e.g. types or classes of systems, requirements, etc.). Thus one could conclude that the primary interest of a design researcher (as opposed to a designer) is conception of abstract artifacts. As Galle notes the subject area of design contains abstract entities (Galle, 2008). Thus, strictly speaking, a design researcher should not aim above all at producing an actual working instantiated system, just like a researcher in conventional science is not primarily interested in producing observations as the major outcome of his/her work. As in traditional science, in design science observations matter only inasmuch as they serve the purpose of testing theories or triggering new research initiatives. This does not mean that implementing working artifacts is unimportant to a design researcher. Instantiating systems facilitate progress in a given direction and help bringing out artifact forms in concrete artifacts. Yet the key outcome should be of theoretical nature.

METHOD

The philosophy of science has generated a substantial volume of work related to the method the scientists are advised to employ to conduct their inquiries. The path that modern science tends to follow (more or less) fits under the hypothetico-deductive schema. According to this widely adopted scientific method, theories are devised first, followed by the deduction of hypotheses, which are then tested based on the observations, and subsequently analyzed. The analysis may lead to corroboration of the theories, their revision, or rejection (the discussion in Chapter 3 of various viewpoints on the philosophy of science revealed that there could be disagreements among the philosophers on some of the aspects of this simplified pattern, but they need not to concern

us in the context of this chapter where a macro-comparison is made between science and design science). The question related to design-type science is whether some methodology analogous to the scientific method can be proposed for doing design-type research.

Unlike natural and social sciences, which had sufficient time for their respective methodologies to evolve, the methodology in design-type research is still immature (Winter, 2008). Cole et al. suggested that in idealized settings the design method would imply two subprocesses running continuously on two semiotic levels with respect to potentiality and feasibility. Potentiality implies surveying the outer (organizational, economic, etc.) environment with the purpose of identifying the possibilities for a type of intervention by design to improve the current state of affairs in the problem domain. Examining the feasibility of a type of intervention implies surveying the inner (technological) environment in order to identify the possibility of realizing the potentiality (Sandeep Purao, 2002).

Pfeffers et al. proposeed a method for conducting design research projects that includes the following steps (Peffers, Tuunanen, Rothenberger, & Chatterjee, 2008):

- Identification of problem and motivation;
- Definitions of the objectives of a solution;
- Design and development;
- Evaluation; and
- Communication (scholarly and professional).

They illustrated application of various phases using four cases, including the development of a data warehouse to keep track of community health in U.S.; development of a SIP-based Voice and VOIP software, and others. The proposed method appears to have much more affinity with the methods for the design of particular artifacts (discussed in Chapter 2), rather than a scientific method. The cases mentioned also seem to target specific requirements. In the pursuit of achieving scientific rigor, the authors of the "memorandum" have suggested similar phases in design-type research, including analysis, design, evaluation, and diffusion (Österle, et al., 2011).

Gregg et al. have proposed a framework for doing design in software engineering (an allied discipline) (Gregg, et al., 2001). They had identified three basic types of design research projects, including conceptual, formal, and development. These types together with the possible overlaps among them define more specific types of design research. All kinds of design projects are seen as progressing through the steps of generation (conceptualization), creation, and confirmation.

Wieringa had introduced a distinction between what he called knowledge problems vs. practical problems (Wieringa, 2009). In knowledge problems the key question is understanding phenomena of interest. In practical problems call for actions to change the state of affairs to better suit the objectives of the problem solver. Traditional science deals with the knowledge problems. Note that in this respect scientific research is viewed as problem solving, i.e. as a kind of design, the point that had been stressed earlier in this book. In design science research the solver deals with both knowledge as well as practical problems. He or she tries to understand the problem context, while also attempting to generate a suitable solution. Thus, Wieringa proposes that design science is a sort of nested problem solving activity.

Design science project, according to Wieringa represents a set of nested problems, where the top level problem is always the one of a practical kind. He then proposes that the method for design research is circular: the process structure that he calls "regulative cycle." The regulative cycle includes the following phases: problem investigation; solution design; design validation; solution implementation; and cycling back to implementation evaluation/problem investigation.

Problem investigation is a knowledge kind of problem which could be of different kinds, depending on the emphasis, including problem-driven; goal-driven; solution-driven; and impact-driven. Very briefly, in problem driven investigation there is a concrete problem that needs to be resolved; in goal-driven type there may be no problem, but the change is required to achieve some given goals; in solution-driven investigation a known solution is applied to new problems; and in impact-driven case evaluation of past solution implementations is done.

Solution design phase is largely a practical problem. Design validation on the other hand is a knowledge task. Here different kinds of validities are addressed. Internal validity involves answering a question of whether a given design, if implemented would indeed lead to a desired outcome. This issue is further broken down into to subcomponents one termed causal validation (would solution have expected effects) and value question (would these effects satisfy stakeholders criteria). Two other types of validities aim at investigating the effects of slight changes in the problem context and the solution. Trade-offs has to do with evaluating the impacts of slight changes to a design on the set criteria. External validity looks to examine if the design would still be valid if contextual factors are slightly changed.

In a recently published book Vaishnavi & Kuechler have introduced a pattern-based approach (based on Alexander's work) to inform design research projects (Vaishnavi & Kuechler, Jr., 2008). They started with the general design cycle that includes awareness of problem; suggestion (conceptual); development; evaluation; and conclusion. They went on to present a large number of patterns related to idea generation, literature search, and others. They then matched these against different phases of the design cycle.

According to Vaishnavi & Kuechler's suggestion one could iterate through various phases of the cycle and employ the suitable patterns depending on the particular design research project's nature and context. Some of the patterns related to the phases are presented below.

- Awareness
  - ○ Problem selection and development patterns
    - Examples: Research conversation; Experimentation and exploration
  - ○ Literature search (e.g.)
    - Familiarization with new area
- Suggestion and development
  - ○ Suggestion & development patterns
    - Examples: Easy solution first; Elegant design
  - ○ Creativity patterns
    - Examples: Wild combinations; Brainstorming
  - ○ Literature search
    - Example: Industry and practice awareness
- Evaluation
  - ○ Evaluation patterns
    - Examples: Demonstration; Experimentation; Simulation
- Conclusion
  - ○ Publishing patterns
    - Writing conference papers
    - Writing journal papers

Each pattern is presented in terms of intent, context and applicability, description, consequences and examples of published work.

Carlsson proposed a design science research cycle that has explicit analogies with the scientific method (Carlsson, 2005). The starting point is the conception of a theory, which he views as referring to the type of IS intervention involving IS or IT artifact. Based on the theory hypotheses are developed. Carlsson maintains that technological rules mentioned earlier can be treated as the equivalents of the hypotheses of the traditional science, as they express expectations, which could be tested. The next step is actual testing, which implies use of a constructed system or a prototype. The outcomes of testing are then analyzed in regards with the expectations expressed in the hypothesis. Thus, the question asked in the beginning of the section can be answered affirmatively: there is a proposed method for design that follows the principles and the vocabulary of the scientific method.

In addition to the method, a number of guidelines have been described by Hevner et al. to ensure the rigor in the design process (Hevner, et al., 2004). These include:

- Design as an innovative artifact;
- Problem relevance;
- Design Evaluation;
- Contribution to research;
- Research rigor;
- Design as a search process; and
- Communication of research.

In (Kuechler, Park, & Vaishnavi, 2009) the authors have noted the similarities between design science research and qualitative research. They noted that such characteristics as situated understanding, ongoing data analysis, and employment of inductive iterative processes make the two modes of inquiry similar. Like in qualitative research, in design-type research there maybe pre-existing (kernel) theories to guide the process, or the researchers may have to start with a clean slate. Thus, they argue, qualitative research methods can be adopted by design-type research. In particular, they propose the use of such techniques as triangulation, comparative analysis, analytic induction, and developmental process for building design theories.

The question of the methodology for conducting design-oriented research is crucially important for establishing scientific rigor. Hopefully, future contributions in this direction will help solidifying the patterns for acceptable research practices.

DESIGN-TYPE RESEARCH VS. PLAIN DESIGN

The somewhat nagging question that arises when considering design practices is how to distinguish design-type research from plain design. Carlsson points that there has been little discussion about what design science is, what should be included and excluded (Carlsson, 2005). The question is of central importance to the design research community as there is a need for identifying true research projects, which could be disseminated as academic work through scholarly and professional outlets. Failure to identify such a demarcation criterion may lead to the proliferation of non-scientific work in the field, and ultimately loss of a reputable position as an academic discipline (yet to be fully gained).

Many researchers in the community recognize this potential danger as they attempted to provide some guidelines for the discriminatory principle between research and practice. Iivari suggests that there are two demarcation options that could be used to distinguish design research from practitioner inventions. The first one would limit research activities to scientific evaluation of new artifacts. However, this, he points leads to a reactive mode of research, which provides little guidance in the creation of new types of artifacts. A second, more preferable option would be to stress rigor in the process of designing an innovative type of a solution (Iivari, 2007).

Vaishanavi & Kuechler write in this respect: "We propose that design science research is distinguishable from design by the *production of interesting (to a community) new knowledge*" (Vaishnavi & Kuechler, Jr., 2008, p. 26). Therefore, the emphasis is explicitly made on knowledge, presumably in the form of design theories. Morrison emphasized the necessity for rigor in software engineering type of research (Morrison & George, 1995). Novelty, value and generalizability are mentioned as key factors contributing

towards "legitimacy" of design research. Burstein and Gregor listed the following criteria for the acceptability of design research: significance, internal validity, external validity (generality), objectivity/confirmability, reliability, dependability, and auditability (Burstein & Gregor, 1999).

Gregg et al. mention that some software development is clearly not research (Gregg, et al., 2001). However, they point that it is difficult to distinguish between research and non-research. Application of existing kinds of solutions to varied contexts may not constitute research. However, a fundamental innovation, such as the advent of databases would clearly qualify as research. "If a researcher proposes an entirely new way of looking at a problem and wonders if a system can be developed that addresses the problem, then the engineering of such software would constitute research" (Gregg, et al., 2001).

Österle et al. have stressed that design-type research should abide by the following set of principles (Österle, et al., 2011):

- Abstraction, i.e. applicability to classes of problems;
- Originality, i.e. advancement of knowledge;
- Justification; and
- Benefit (to stakeholders).

As mentioned earlier some researchers suggested adopting an action research perspective in design research. Järvinen had picked the principles of action research and gradually refined them to produce a set that has much similarity with the characteristics of design research (Järvinen, 2005). He notes that action research:

- Emphasizes utility;
- Produces knowledge;
- Implies both action taking and evaluation
- Is carried out in collaboration between action researcher and client, etc.

Since action research is an established method of inquiry, adoption of these principles in design research could also help to legitimize the latter. However, as we mentioned earlier, action research perspective has been criticized by Iivari on the grounds that much innovative design takes place away from practice (Iivari, 2007).

The discussion of different viewpoints expressed in regards with the desired demarcation principle suggests that for design to be considered research:

- A newly created artifact should be innovative in an important way; and
- It should be elevated to the status of knowledge, i.e. theory.

The second point implies that the artifact must be generic in its applicability to a variety of contexts. In other words it should refer to a class of concrete artifacts, be a meta-artifact. Unfortunately, there is no clear cut-off line, as various artifacts could have various degrees of generality. For some the scope could be limited to particular types of organizations or user groups, for others it might include various types of organizations. This difficulty suggests the continuity in the progression from plain design to design research. In many cases the distinction would probably be easy to make. But in general, the only way to address the issue is for the journal editors and reviewers to exercise their judgment in deciding whether a particular design represents the case of research.

REFERENCES

Baskerville, R., & Myers, M. D. (2004). Special issue on action research in information systems: Making IS research relevant to practice - Foreword. *Management Information Systems Quarterly*, *28*(3).

Becker, J., Niehaves, B., & Pfeiffer, D. (2008). *Case study perspectives on design science research*. Paper presented at the Third International Conference on Design Science Research in Information Systems and Technology. Atlanta, GA.

Bunge, M. (1967). *Scientific research II: The search for truth*. Berlin: Springer Verlag.

Burstein, F., & Gregor, S. (1999). *The systems development or engineering approach to research in information systems: An action research perspective*. Paper presented at the 10th Australasian Conference on Information Systems. Wellington, New Zealand.

Carlsson, S. (2005). Developing information systems design knowledge: A critical realist perspective. *The Electronic Journal of Business Research Methodology*, *3*(2), 93–102.

Carlsson, S., Henningsson, S., Hrastinski, S., & Keller, C. (2011). Socio-technical IS design science research: Developing design theory for IS integration management. *Information Systems and E-Business Management*, *9*(1), 109–131. doi:10.1007/s10257-010-0140-6

Chen, H. (2011). Editorial: Design science, grand challenges, and societal impacts. *ACM Transactions on Management Information Systems*, *2*(1), 1–10. doi:10.1145/2037661.2037663

Cole, R., Purao, S., Rossi, M., & Sein, M. (2005). *Being proactive: Where action research meets design research*. Paper presented at the International Conference on Information Systems, ICIS 2005. Las Vegas, NV.

Davison, R. M., Martinsons, M. G., & Kock, N. (2004). Principles of canonical action research. *Information Systems Journal*, *14*(1), 65–86. doi:10.1111/j.1365-2575.2004.00162.x

Dewey, J. (1910). A short catechism concerning truth. In *The Influence of Darwin on Philosophy and Other Essays* (pp. 154–168). New York, NY: Henry Holt and Company.

Galle, P. (2008). Candidate worldviews for design theory. *Design Studies, 29*, 267–303. doi:10.1016/j.destud.2008.02.001

Gregg, D. G., Kulkarni, U. R., & Vinze', A. S. (2001). Understanding the philosophical underpinnings of software engineering research in information systems. *Information Systems Frontiers, 3*(2), 169–183. doi:10.1023/A:1011491322406

Gregor, S., & Hevner, A. (2011). Introduction to the special issue on design science. *Information Systems and E-Business Management, 9*(1), 1–9. doi:10.1007/s10257-010-0159-8

Gregor, S., & Jones, D. (2007). The anatomy of a design theory. *Journal of the Association for Information Systems, 8*(5), 312–335.

Hevner, A., & Chatterjee, S. (2010). Design science research in information systems. In *Design Research in Information Systems* (*Vol. 22*). New York: Springer. doi:10.1007/978-1-4419-5653-8_2

Hevner, A., March, S. T., Park, J., & Ram, S. (2004). Design science in information systems research. *Management Information Systems Quarterly, 28*(1), 75–105.

Holmström, J., Ketokivi, M., & Hameri, A.-P. (2009). Bridging practice and theory: A design science approach. *Decision Sciences, 40*(1), 65–87. doi:10.1111/j.1540-5915.2008.00221.x

Iivari, J. (2007). A paradigmatic analysis of information systems as a design science. *Scandinavian Journal of Information Systems, 19*(2), 39–64.

Iivari, J. (2008). *Twelve theses on information systems as a design science.* Paper presented at the Third International Conference on Design Science Research in Information Systems and Technology. Atlanta, GA.

Järvinen, P. (2005). *Action research as an approach in design science.* Retrieved from http://www.cs.uta.fi/reports/dsarja/D-2005-2.pdf.

Kasanen, E., Lukha, K., & Siitonen, A. (1993). The constructive approach in management accounting research. *Journal of Management Accounting Research, 5*, 243–264.

Kuechler, B., Park, E. H., & Vaishnavi, V. (2009). *Formalizing theory development in IS design science research: Learning from qualitative research.* Paper presented at the AMCIS 2009. New York, NY.

Kuechler, B., & Vaishnavi, V. (2008). *Theory development in design science research: Anatomy of a research project.* Paper presented at the Third International Conference on Design Science Research in Information Systems and Technology. Atlanta, GA.

Kuhn, T. S. (1962). *The structure of scientific revolutions.* Chicago, IL: University of Chicago Press.

Lewin, K. (1946). Action research and minority problems. *The Journal of Social Issues, 2*, 34–46. doi:10.1111/j.1540-4560.1946.tb02295.x

March, S. T., & Smith, G. F. (1995). Design and natural science research on information technology. *Decision Support Systems, 15*, 251–266. doi:10.1016/0167-9236(94)00041-2

Markus, M. L., Majchrzak, A., & Gasser, L. (2002). A design theory for systems that support emergent knowledge processes. *Management Information Systems Quarterly, 26*(3), 179–212.

Morrison, J., & George, J. F. (1995). Exploring the software engineering component in MIS research. *Communications of the ACM, 38*(7), 80–91. doi:10.1145/213859.214802

Österle, H., Becker, J., Frank, U., Hess, T., Karagiannis, D., & Krcmar, H. (2011). Memorandum on design-oriented information systems research. *European Journal of Information Systems, 20*, 7–10. doi:10.1057/ejis.2010.55

Owen, C. (1997). Design research: Building the knowledge base. *Journal of the Japanese Society for the Science of Design*, 5(2), 36–45.

Peffers, K., Tuunanen, T., Rothenberger, M., & Chatterjee, S. (2008). A design science research methodology for information systems research. *Journal of Management Information Systems*, 24(3), 45–77. doi:10.2753/MIS0742-1222240302

Piirainen, K., Gonzalez, R., & Kolfschoten, G. (2010). Quo vadis, design science? – A survey of literature. In Winter, R., Zhao, J., & Aier, S. (Eds.), *Global perspectives on design science research* (*Vol. 6105*, pp. 93–108). Berlin: Springer. doi:10.1007/978-3-642-13335-0_7

Poser, H. (1998). On structural differences between science and engineering. *Philosophy and Technology*, 4(2), 81–93.

Purao, S. (2002). *Design research in the technology of information systems: Truth or dare*. Unpublished Working Paper. Retrieved from http://purao.ist.psu.edu/working-papers/.

Purao, S., Baldwin, C. Y., Hevner, A., Storey, V. C., Pries-Heje, J., Smith, B., et al. (2008). The sciences of design: Observations on an emerging field. *Communications of the AIS, 23*(29).

Rohde, M., Stevens, G., Brödner, P., & Wulf, V. (2009). *Towards a paradigmatic shift in IS: designing for social practice*. Paper presented at the 4th International Conference on Design Science Research in Information Systems and Technology. Malvern, PA.

Simon, H. A. (1996). *The sciences of the artificial* (3rd ed.). Cambridge, MA: MIT Press.

Stahl, B. C. (2008). *Design as reification, commodification and ideology: A critical view of IS design science*. Paper presented at the 16th European Conference on Information Systems in an Innovative Knowledge-Based Society. Galway, Ireland.

Vaishnavi, V. K., & Kuechler, W. Jr. (2008). *Design science research methods: Innovating information and communication technology*. Boca Raton, FL: Auerbach Publications.

Van Aken, J. E. (2004). Management research based on the paradigm of design sciences: The quest for field-tested and grounded technological rules. *Journal of Management Studies, 41*(2), 219–246. doi:10.1111/j.1467-6486.2004.00430.x

Venable, J. R. (2006). *The role of theory and theorising in design science research*. Paper presented at the First International Conference on Design Science Research in Information Systems and Technology. Claremont, CA.

Walls, J. G., Widmeyer, G. R., & El Sawy, O. A. (1992). Building an information system design theory for vigilant EIS. *Information Systems Research, 3*(1), 36–59. doi:10.1287/isre.3.1.36

Weber, S. (2010). *Design science research: Paradigm or approach?* Paper presented at the Americas Conference on Information Systems, AMCIS 2010. New York, NY.

Wieringa, R. (2009). *Design science as nested problem solving*. Paper presented at the 4th International Conference on Design Science Research in Information Systems and Technology. Malvern, PA.

Winter, R. (2008). Design science research in Europe. *European Journal of Information Systems, 17*, 470–475. doi:10.1057/ejis.2008.44

Chapter 6
Representing Meta–Artifacts

ABSTRACT

The concept of a design theory includes, among others, the components of meta-requirements and meta-systems. As an artifact, according to Simon, it is characterized in terms of its outer and inner environments, and the interface, design-type research projects may focus on one or another aspects of meta-artifacts. The purpose of this chapter is to describe a representational framework incorporating different views of meta-artifacts. The chapter introduces such a framework based on Zachman's model for information architecture. The two dimensional model includes perspectives and categories dimensions. The former is defined in terms of four layers, including analytical, synthetic, technological, and implementation layers. The latter includes the categories of motivation, structure, behavior, and instantiation. At each layer alternative meta-artifact conceptualizations may be proposed by different researchers, implying a third dimension in the framework. A complete design research work on any given layer would correspond to a research project. A work targeting the entire matrix would constitute a design-type research program. Efforts by different design researchers on alternative conceptualizations could be regarded as research stream.

META-ARTIFACTS: THE RIGHT FOR EXISTENCE

The previous chapter has introduced the concepts of observation and theory (by Walls, et al.) in design-type research in information systems. We have seen that a design theory contains at its core

a meta-system artifact. In other words, the product of the design researcher's work is not a concrete system, but the abstract one. One could say that design researchers propose systems, which cannot be implemented. This statement, of course cannot be interpreted literally, to mean that the workings of the proposed solution type are not demonstrable. It rather means that whatever instantiation comes

DOI: 10.4018/978-1-4666-0131-4.ch006

out of the meta-artifact's conception, it will necessarily have a mixture of the generic as well as specific instantiating elements. It is impossible to implement the meta-artifact form in its purity.

The design researcher, thus, unlike a designer, is not so much interested in the marketability of a particular software, since his or her interest lies beyond a specific package. What would really attest to the legitimacy of the design research question he or she had set out to tackle, and the appropriateness of the proposed artifact-theory is the adoption of systems, through which the proposed artifact form manifests itself. Adoption, thus, serves as an indicator of the prevalence of the meta-need that the meta-artifact seeks to address. In other words, it positively signals the existence of the context in the shape hypothesized by a design researcher as well as the hypothesized form devised to fit the context. Admittedly, adoption is not the definitive criterion, just like a few observations confirming a given scientific theory cannot serve as decisive evidence. Nevertheless, these adoption-observations are the only tangible means of assessing meta-artifact's viability. In this sense, one might suggest that adoption serves to provide evidence to attest to the *truth* or *falsity* of a given meta-artifact.

Adoption though is heavily influenced by the very factors that design-type research would rather ignore, according to our position, in particular by market forces. Thus, design researchers appear to face a curious dilemma: while they tend to ignore the interplay of particular market forces in their projects aiming at producing meta-artifacts for potentially wide adoption, these forces are the ones that crucially contribute to the very adoption. The escape from this dilemma lies in the belief that truly good meta-artifact forms will manifest themselves in one particular way or the other, no matter what paths markets evolve in. While this belief may not have always been supported by the history of technology, it is hard to accept that a discovered artifact form, which suggests a sufficiently significant improvement over its

rivals, would not turn up in particular designs sooner or later.

For example, a desktop metaphor and Graphical User Interface (GUI) is a human-computer interaction form, which tremendously advanced the wide adoption of micro-computers by non-technical users. Initially developed at Xerox, GUI way of interacting with machines had reached the markets via Macintosh and Windows for IBM PC. Regardless of the prevalence of a particular commercial product, the GUI as a form proved to be far superior to the text command-oriented rival form. Another example of a successful meta-artifact is a computerized spreadsheet form. Although it appeared in concrete product manifestations throughout its short history as VisiCalc, Lotus 123, or MS Excel, it's the general structural and behavioral aspects of the (tremendously successful) spreadsheet form that truly matter from a meta-artifact design perspective.

In design-type research a scientist tries to discover such potentially successful forms. Elements of these forms may already exist in some instantiated system cases, but the task of the designer-scientist is to explicitly define the structural and dynamic aspects of a purely abstract meta-artifact. The criterion of truth here is elusive, and before the artifact has been built and used, there's little to empirically attest to its viability. When a novel system concept is conceived and introduced a design researcher anticipates that it will be useful to the target user group within a given class of business contexts. Utility thus, is a practical criterion to assess the potential value of the artifact. When an artifact type actually finds its place in the technological arsenal of organizations, markets, and individuals, it becomes a part of the infrastructure. It fills an intended gap, and in this sense, becomes *true*. Utility, thus, provides a temporary judging principle for the artifacts that will eventually turn out to be true, or false. It serves a role of a probe in approaching the issue of the artifact's right for existence.

In conceiving novel IS meta-artifacts, the design researcher inevitably is faced with the necessity of considering their right for existence. For instance, suppose a researcher envisages a solution for automating negotiations in a supply chain (such approaches have actually been proposed). Does this concept have a right to exist? Is the nature of negotiations sufficiently structured (however complex) to enable automation? Would businesses ever subscribe to this model? What would be the scope of the applicability of this new form? Where would it fit, if it actually would? How about conceiving a software agent solution to negotiate prenuptial agreements or divorce settlements? Would anybody need such an autonomous tool?

In approaching the issue of the right for existence, a design researcher acts in some sense as a matchmaker between the common business needs/opportunities and the technological possibilities. Metaphorically speaking, the researcher should be akin to the double-faced Roman deity Janus, with one face turned towards business environments, and the other one facing technological environment and design-related disciplines. An emerging IS concept is, thus a complex artifact, that can be characterized from different perspectives. Thus, a question of what is a meta-artifact and how should it enter the relevant design theories must be addressed. This chapter describes a framework for representation of IS meta-artifacts first proposed in Vahidov (2006).

DESIDERATA FOR META-ARTIFACT CONCEPTUALIZATION

Researchers in DTR in IS have been using the terms like meta-system, meta-requirements, and meta-artifacts. But what do these terms refer to? Is meta-system a code written in some computer language, or in form of a pseudocode? Is it an architectural representation of major system com-

ponents? Is it a collection of user interfaces? A list of (meta-) functions supported? Perhaps, in different contexts all of these representational means could be valuable. But is it possible to propose a generic framework that would cover the essential aspects of system meta-artifacts (including requirements and systems) in a meaningful way? Is it feasible to have a unified model that could serve as a reference for both design researchers, as well as those engaged in behavioral studies? What would be the desired characteristics for such a meta-system framework?

Naturally, since we are speaking about research, and not system construction, a representational model should be focusing on generality. Since researchers are primarily interested in studying general or generalizable phenomena, the aim of design researchers is not to produce a concrete system, but an *abstract* meta-system. Thus, as pointed earlier, design researchers can be distinguished from the designers of the systems that the former are not interested in producing concrete systems, other than as means of exemplifying abstract systems. Rapid pace of technological change sometimes makes IS research obsolete and thus, less relevant, since a time is needed to carry out rigorous research projects and disseminate the results (Kock, et al., 2002; Robey & Markus, 1998). However, with an appropriate abstraction level it should be possible to conceptualize meta-systems in a way that enables isolating these concepts from the influences of technological fluctuations. For example, whether a meta-system is implemented as a component-based or service-oriented architecture may not make any difference in the representation of its key constituents and their interactions. Thus, the first desideratum states:

D1: The representational framework for meta-IS should adopt the abstract view of information systems.

Interestingly, different researchers seem to disagree on what should constitute the core of the IS discipline. Various attempts to define the "core" of the IS research field had been proposed in the past. Early work by Wand & Weber had attempted to formalize the ontological representation of information systems by advocating the adoption a "white-box" view of IT that largely ignored organizational contexts (Wand & Weber, 1988; Wand & Weber, 1990. Benbasat & Zmud had placed IT artifact and related phenomena at the heart of IS research. They defined the IT artifact "… as the application of IT to enable or support some task(s) embedded within a structure(s) that itself is embedded within a context(s). Here, the hardware/software design of the IT artifact encapsulates the structures, routines, norms, and values implicit in the rich *contexts* within which the artifact is embedded" (Kim & Benbasat, 2003). Weber had pointed that information systems, not IT-related phenomena should be the focus within the discipline (Weber, 2003). Alter had repeatedly criticized adoption of the IT-centric view (Alter, 2003) and promoted instead what he called "IT-reliant work systems," which he defined as "work systems whose efficient and/or effective operation depends on the use of IT" (Alter, 2003). El-Sawy pointed that there is nothing inherently wrong with either of these views as they represent alternative models of reality (Walls, Widmeyer, & El Sawy, 1992). He further proposed the "fusion" view of IT where the technology is "fused into" business environment to such an extent that both become inseparable and indistinguishable in a very strong sense.

It thus becomes evident that proper representational framework for meta-IS should attempt incorporating these various views. While it would be understandable to regard them as "alternative models," the various vantage points could be manifesting the critical disconnect between IT-centric vs. work-centric models. Hence, the framework should desirably represent the unified model, where various seemingly opposing views can organically co-exist and contribute towards a truly comprehensive ontological meta-model for meta-IS. Thus, the second proposed desideratum states that:

D2: *The representational framework for meta-IS must be unified in a sense that it must incorporate various pertinent perspectives on IS.*

Earlier in the book a very brief overview of the state of research in information systems has been provided. In particular, it had been noted that much of research have ignored the actual salient characteristics of systems being studied. For example, the technology acceptance model focuses on the relationships between system design features (as one of the "external variables") and a host of perceptive measures including ease of use, usefulness, intention to use, and usage (Davis, 1993; Davis, Bagozzi, & Warshaw, 1989; Davis & Venkatesh, 2004; Sultan, Urban, Shankar, & Bart, 2002). However, the system design features have effectively been reduced to dummy representation, which is essentially even beyond the black-box treatment. The task-technology fit model that focuses on explaining system utilization and performance impacts based on the adequate fit between task, technology, and individual characteristics, also reduces representation of "technology characteristic" to a dummy (Goodhue & Thompson, 1995).

While these models by now represent the classical part of IS literature (and can be easily "applied" to any kind of a tool, indeed), an informative inquiry into the questions of fit and usefulness should be based on an adequate representation of information systems. There must be a way to represent the *essence* of a given type of information system using an appropriate framework. Theorizing about IS should involve positioning of IS in the picture. A solid representa-

Figure 1. Integrating design theory with task-technology fit model

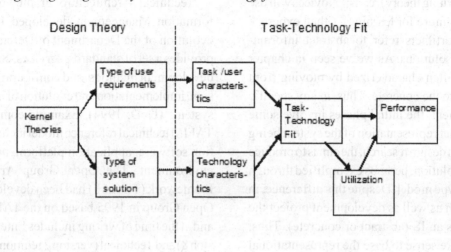

tional model for IS can be helpful for both design as well as behavioural studies, and what's more important, it could facilitate organic linking of the theoretical models originating from both (behavioral and design) sides. Consider, for example a possibility of integrating the task-technology fit model (Goodhue & Thompson, 1995) with the concept of a design theory for information systems (Walls, Widmeyer, & El Sawy, 1992). The former looks to explain system utilization and performance impacts based on task, technology, and individual characteristics and their fit. The latter employs what is called "kernel theories" in order to investigate and propose type of user requirements, type of system solution, and the method for system development.

One way to conceptually integrate these two (slightly modified) models is shown on Figure 1. Essentially, kernel theories are used to derive the meta-requirements that map onto task and individual characteristics, and type of system solution that would correspond to technology characteristics. These, in turn, would be the basis for conceptualizing fit, as well as the utilization and performance implications. The natural question would then be what kind of representation to employ at the dashed line, the outcome of one,

and the input of the other sides? The following desideratum states:

D3: *A meta-IS representational model should ideally incorporate relevant categories, or aspects that serve as a basis for describing the essence of information systems, which could be viewed from design as well as behavioral perspectives.*

Examples of such aspects include salient features and processes of a given IS type. One example of investigating the applicability of one technology-supported capability that spans both design and behavioural parts of information systems and their contexts is work by Gregor and Benbasat that concentrates on explanations generated by intelligent systems (Gregor & Benbasat, 1999). Aiming to propose a conceptual link between types of explanations generated by some advanced types of systems (e.g. knowledge-based systems, intelligent agents, etc.), the authors had grounded their model on cognitive theories and Toulmin's model of argumentation (kernel theories). They had devised a number of propositions that link types of explanations and types of task and user characteristics and behavioural impacts. An example of such a proposition (derived from cognitive learning theory) reads: "Novices will use explanations more for learning ... than experts."

IS meta-artifacts refer to abstract information system solutions. As we've seen in chapter 1 design is often characterized by moving from the abstract to the concrete. Thus, in any specific IS development, the initial phases involve some sort of abstract representation of the system being developed. In design research, the aim is to produce an abstract solution, perhaps exemplified through some prototype model. Despite this difference, in both research as well as development project the key output is an IS (abstract or concrete). Thus, it would make sense to base the representational framework for design researchers on the adaptation of some architectural model for specific IS. This practice-driven approach to developing a representational schema for meta-IS has a benefit of maintaining the links with the industry practices, and thus promote the relevance and communicability of design researchers' outputs:

D4: A meta-IS representational framework must be traceable to some established model for representing information systems in the industry.

ZACHMAN'S FRAMEWORK FOR INFORMATION SYSTEMS ARCHITECTURE

In light of the above desiderata we could start with some established architectural framework for representing concrete information systems in organizations, and further modify it accordingly to suit the requirements of meta-IS representation. Architectural models for IS have been advanced in the past, in particular for communicating the vision and enabling the evolution of enterprise systems (Armour, 2007; Sowa & Zachman, 1992; Zachman, 1987). Although a thorough review of these frameworks is beyond the scope of this work, we will briefly mention a few of them here.

Technical Architecture Framework for Information Management developed for guiding evolution of the Department of Defence systems provides a set of standards, services, components, development methods, and configurations for design, implementation and evolution of information systems (DoD, 1994). Example components of TAFIM technical reference model include application software, application platform, and external environment. The Open Group Architectural Framework (TOGAF) had been developed by the Open Group in 1995 based on the TAFIM model and at the time of writing includes Enterprise (version 8) and Technical (version 7) editions (TOGAF, 2001a, 2001b). In the Enterprise architecture TOGAF includes Business, Data, Application, and Technical architectures as its components. The Enterprise Architecture Planning model provides guidance for business model – driven system development while paying less attention to the design and implementation issues. The major principles include providing accessibility to enterprise data, adaptability of information systems to changing business requirements, high integrity and standards, integration, and cost-effectiveness of solutions (Spewak, 1992).

A particularly interesting framework had been proposed by Zachman, and subsequently extended by Sowa and Zachman (Sowa & Zachman, 1992; Zachman, 1987). Zachman had recognized the level of complexity of enterprise information systems and devised an elegant framework which could serve as a basis for representing systems in an organized fashion. The framework can serve as a prism through which various stakeholders can gain a relatively complete picture of a particular IS according to their level of description. The two-dimensional matrix organization of this model is the major motivation for us to adopt it as a starting point, as it neatly addresses the desiderata outlined earlier.

One dimension of the Zachman's framework (rows) captures perspectives of various stakeholders, including Planner (scope), Owner (enterprise model), Designer (system model), Builder (technology model), Subcontractor (out-of-context model), and, finally, functioning system. Zachman's insight was that any given IS can be *completely described* from each of the above perspectives. The second dimension (columns) then, introduces the pertinent categories that can be used for such descriptions. These are conceptualized as "different abstractions from or different ways to describe the real world" to contain the complexity of information systems (Sowa & Zachman, 1992).

The categories introduced in (Zachman, 1987) and further formalized and extended in (Sowa & Zachman, 1992) include Data (what), Process (how), Network (where), people (how), Time (when), and Motivation (why). The Data category describes the system as entities along with their structural relationships (things, tables, files, etc.) for a given level of representation. The Process category models the dynamic properties of the system (processes, functions, data flows, etc.). The Network column captures the fashion in which system architecture is distributed (locations, logistics, network architecture, etc.). The People column describes the human and organizational contexts of an IS (organization chart, human interface, security, etc.). The Time column focuses on pertinent events and synchronization of operations (list of events, master schedule, timing definitions, etc.). Finally, the Motivation category shows the rationale for the IS solution, and viewed vertically can be regarded as having ends-means-ends structure.

In addition to the matrix, the authors have devised a set of rules of the framework, e.g. "The columns have no order." An attractive feature of this model is that it helps identifying the non-overlapping gaps that must be addressed for the complete description of the system from any chosen vantage point. Thus, instead of prescribing that a particular conceptual tool (e.g. entity-relationship diagram) must be used to cover s given

cell in the matrix, the framework recognizes the cells that ought to be addressed.

In assessing the potential applicability of the Zachman's framework to conceptualize IS for research in light of the mentioned requirements, one is led to conclude that (in addition to D4) it is capable of addressing the requirements D2 and D3. First, it offers a truly unified view of IS, where various columns and rows are legitimate chunks of description of one and the same complex system. Second, it combines various relevant perspectives on an IS, which could be used as pertinent reference lenses through which an IS could be chosen to be viewed. Third, while the lower levels of the framework approach representations that are increasingly technical, the overall architecture cannot be regarded as a way to "white-box" the system. At the same time, since the upper levels also describes important aspects of the system, the framework provides a basis for informative characterization of IS without necessarily having to describe its internal organization and workings. Last, the model provides an invariant set of pertinent categories descriptive of an IS at each representation level.

The above analysis provides justification for the employment of Zachman's model as a starting point for developing a design researcher's representational framework for IS. One important requirement not addressed by the model is the generality of the represented IS. In other words, we are interested in modeling the ways in which entire classes of IS could be represented. The subsequent sections will thus re-examine the two dimensions of Zachman's framework with the aim of modifying them to suit the needs of IS researchers.

THE PERSPECTIVES FOR META-IS REPRESENTATIONAL FRAMEWORK

When it comes to conducting research in information systems, one could outline several salient perspectives on IS. Behaviorists tend to focus on questions concerning how information systems are used in organizations, markets, and by individuals and groups. Much of the past behavioral research in IS tended to ignore the features of the systems under consideration. In fact, IS has been viewed as a sort of homogeneous commodity. Theoretical models were devised with the assumption that they are applicable to any sort of systems. This approach cannot really lead to an informative theorizing about IS/IT. "One-fits-all" philosophy had displaced information systems completely out of the focus. With such a great variety of different IS types, one would wonder how anything useful and informative could be said about IS artifacts without incorporating their salient properties and processes explicitly in the models. Conceptualization of meta-systems in terms of key capabilities and processes they support may improve the relevance of behavioral studies in IS.

Design researchers should be interested in discovering the pertinent meta-requirements for a given problem context, and thus consider the questions of which functions should a system concept incorporate. The meta-requirements, however, are a starting point for the design-type research programs. Next, the structure and behavior of the abstract IS artifact needs to be outlined. This demands a separate view of meta-system at a different representation level. This additional level would focus on the overall logical organization of a given type of solution. The composition of a meta-system in terms of the key components, and the working principles defined in generic terms would constitute the design concept proposed to meet the meta-requirements. Technical aspects are of secondary importance at this layer.

Furthermore, the meta-system could be refined as a sound technological solution, which could be adapted to particular contexts to facilitate instantiation of specific IS artifacts. The purpose at this level is to propose a sound technological meta-artifact. The issues related to produce the sound technical design are addressed. Yet it does not mean that the system at this stage turns into a specific, rather than general solution. It means that technical generality that would enable realization of a synthetic solution is pursued. These three perspectives relate to the conceptualization of meta-systems in terms of organizational and technological connects, and the IS as an interface described in chapter 4.

The issue of identifying pertinent perspectives is not only important for providing adequate reference models for behavioral and design studies, but also for *distinguishing different types of design research projects*. For example, in a given design research projects, would it be appropriate to ask what is the logical architecture and dynamic properties of a given class of IS? What are the technological platform choices? What is the computational complexity of the algorithms employed? Is the design of the system efficient? Clearly, these questions belong to different levels of IS representation, and can, therefore, be separated to better manage the scope of research projects.

The need to explicitly incorporate IT (IS) artifact conceptualizations in theories about IS has been voiced in the past (Orlikowski & Iacono, 2001). Poser, referring to technology in general has separated three levels of technological hermeneutics: the level of real action (implementation); the level of engineering, i.e. the actual design; and the level of local conditions, referring to the conditions under which a given design applies. Within IS Iivari has identified three levels of abstraction for IS (Iivari, 2003), including organizational (representing users and their activities); conceptual; and technical layers. In our view the layering of representations could be organized to reflect the different espoused views of IS, e.g. IT-reliant work systems (Alter, 2003), IS artifacts, and IT artifacts (Kim & Benbasat, 2003; Orlikowski & Iacono, 2001).

Having identified the need for different research perspectives on IS we could now attempt to associate them with the corresponding entries in Zachman's framework to adapt it for the needs of design-type research. Re-examining Zachman's framework we could relate the planner and owner perspectives to compose what would be most descriptive as IT-Reliant Work System (ITWS) layer (the terms perspectives, levels, or layers will be used interchangeably). We will refer to this layer as the *"analytical"* perspective on IS. The major purpose here is to represent the IS a set of relevant work-system characteristics and processes supported. The essence of the layer is to model an IS as truly indistinguishable from the work system it supports, to a large extent similar to El Sawy's conception of the "fusion" view (Walls, Widmeyer, & El Sawy, 1992). As Alter aptly put it "information systems and the work systems they support are increasingly like Siamese twins that are inextricably connected" (Alter, 2003). Since the traditional conception of systems as being strictly internal to organizations need to be extended in light of ubiquitous networks to include the external users (businesses and consumers), the term analytical is proposed instead of "organizational." Broadening the context allows studying new forms of systems, for example the ones that provide guided on-line shopping support.

The analytical layer is of prime importance as it may serve as a point of convergence of behavioral and design studies. Behavioral studies about information systems usage could incorporate the characteristics pertinent to the layer to theorize about potential impacts on organizational/individual performance. Design researchers could conceptualize novel features and functions within the context of ITWS. In some respect the analytical layer erases sharp boundaries between description/explanation and design. For example, theorizing about active features of decision support would lead to the description of active decision support, and at the same time prompt design-type research initiatives for conceptualizing such systems.

Keeping in mind the IS meta-artifact as an interface and its inner environment (the techno-

logical connect) we could split the "design" of meta-IS that supports the analytical representation into two layers. The first of these focuses on the overall structure of the artifact to support the requirements of the work system. In other words, the basic issues addressed here is how to synthesize an information system class from its components in order to achieve the "specifications" of the upper layer. The overall architecture and working principles of the system can be pictured here. We call this layer a *"synthetic"* perspective.

The synthetic layer shows a way to employ the "knowledge base" from respective reference disciplines (March, Hevner, & Ram, 2000), utilizing applicable concepts, methods, and system frameworks to compose an abstract system ("meta-system") in order to support the desired mode of fusion of IT in target problem contexts. It corresponds to the Designer (system model) view of Zachman's framework. It does not necessarily focus on the questions of the *optimality and efficiency* of the design of the proposed type of solution per se. In other words it should propose a way to build an artifact, but not necessarily the *optimal* way. Investigation of the optimality and efficiency of the solution is a question of the *technological* layer, or IT artifact layer for the IS representation. This layer corresponds to what is usually referred to in specific IS development as "detailed design." However, the layer does not contain a description of concrete artifacts, but rather a more technical representation of generic IS solutions. For example, if at the synthetic layer the system employs a search method, at the technological layer the question would be to investigate which search method promises the best performance in the context of the task that needs to be accomplished. In terms of Zachman's framework this layer would correspond to the builder's, and to some extent, subcontractor's view. It is important to stress that the solutions devised at this layer should aim at providing informative guidance, a sort of generally defined specifications in order to implement concrete systems.

Finally, the last level of representation captures concrete system implementations. While research is primarily interested about general phenomena, the *implementation* layer serves as the ultimate connection with the real business environments. Design researchers in particular would like to see the results of their higher level artifacts to be implemented in practice. Metaphorically speaking the representations at this layer serve as *observations* to the generic constructs of the higher layers.

Table 1 summarizes the proposed layers that belong to the "perspectives" dimension. An interesting question for design researchers would be the nature of relationships between different layers of representation. Suppose a design researcher conceptualizes a new type of a meta-system, say at the analytical layer. Then should he or she ignore completely the underlying layers. In other words, if a description for a new type of a system is given, how do we know that it is feasible to build such a system if lower-layer views are ignored? For example, stating that a system "actively adapts to the user profile" would not be sufficient; there has to be at least some tentative way to show how this capability could be achievable to distinguish grounded design from something akin to science fiction. Thus, some "gray box" view of the lower level representations is necessary to be included in the design researchers' constructs of the higher levels. They have to show that their solutions,

at least in principle, are feasible in a technical sense. In this connection, it might be worthwhile employing the "skyhooks and cranes" metaphor introduced by Dennet (1987). The point is that for design research projects "skyhooks" will not be sufficient to represent a system at a higher level without some reference to the possible lower level "cranes" (how the capabilities are supported).

The organization of perspectives follows the "organizational connect – IS – technological connect" pattern. The meta-requirements defined at the analytical layer describe a meta-system from the outside. In other words, they describe the outer context in which a given synthetic solution would operate. The solution itself would presuppose the possibility of being refined as a technological meta-artifact. The technological layer, thus, serves as a context in which the artifact could be defined in terms of more technical arrangement of its components and their interactions, i.e. it would constitute a meta-artifact's inner environment. Therefore, the dimension of perspectives in the framework parallels Simon's conception of an artifact being an interface between the inner and outer environments. It, hence would be appropriate to refer to the perspectives dimension using the term *"Simonian."*

To briefly illustrate how a design of particular type of a system type can be pictured along the perspectives dimension, we will refer to the

Table 1. Summary of perspectives of the representational framework

Perspective	Description	Related terms	Relationship to Zachman's framework
Analytical	Models salient system features and processes supported as characteristics of work/tasks performed within organizational/ human contexts	IT-reliant work system	Planner, Owner (user)
Synthetic	Focuses on the organization of the system in terms of key capabilities of components to support the analytical representation	Information system	Designer
Technological	Focuses on the questions of the optimality and efficiency of the artifact's design	IT Artifact	Builder, Subcontractor
Implementation	An instantiation of a system for a given concrete problem/ organization.	Concrete IS	Functioning System

design theory for systems supporting emergent knowledge processes (Markus, Majchrzak, & Gasser, 2002). In this work authors have investigated the characteristics of Emergent Knowledge Processes (EKP) as having "challenging" information requirements. Kernel theories helped the authors to describe the meta-requirements for such systems. The nature of meta-requirements led them to propose the features of the systems that support EKP in terms of key characteristics and processes supported. Examples of such characterization include: "system must translate expert knowledge into actionable knowledge for non-experts…," and "system must implicitly, not explicitly, guide users' deliberations in desirable directions, without restricting them to a prescribed process…." These descriptions clearly refer to the analytical perspective as no internal design decisions are elaborated at this level.

The set of meta-requirements lead to the development of the blueprint for the type of systems that support emergent knowledge processes. From the synthetic perspective, the overall composition of the (meta-) system consists of the knowledge base, inference engine, and the interface parts. The authors have provided a set of design principles to guide the development of systems supporting EKP. One such principle reads "componentize everything"—a recommendation that would be most applicable to the technological perspective of the proposed framework. Finally, the concrete system (called Top Modeler) architecture was described detailing technical choices made, e.g. object-oriented query generator, and relational databases, that would most properly be regarded from the implementation perspective.

THE CATEGORIES FOR META-IS REPRESENTATIONAL FRAMEWORK

Previous chapters had outlined some views on the nature of artifacts, noting in particular the importance of their abstract representation. In this regard the essence of the artifact could be expressed at a high level of abstraction as structure and behavior. It was also noted that in design context the Aristotelian final cause could be invoked as a matter of convenience for the completeness of an artifact's description. In this section an attempt will be made to reconcile these views with the second dimension of Zachman's framework.

The second dimension deals with different categories or aspects that can be used to represent the type of IS being studied. In line with the generality requirement, we will be interested in capturing those categories that are appropriate for conceptualizing classes of IS, i.e. those conveying the essence of a given type of systems. Thus, in Wand & Weber (1990) an emphasis has been made on eliciting "deep structure" of IS that reflects "the *meaning* of the real world system that the information system is intended to model." The two obvious categories include the ones that capture static and dynamic properties of the system being studied. Thus an ontological model proposed included both static (e.g. things, properties, system structure), as well as dynamic (e.g. events, transitions) elements. Modeling of static and dynamic aspects has long been used in software engineering, where the focus is on providing tools and methods to produce concrete systems in an effective and efficient manner. Examples include entity-relationship and class diagrams (static), and flowcharts, state, and sequence diagrams (dynamic).

The static part of representation corresponds to the "Data" view of Zachman's framework, while the dynamic description would primarily relate to the "Process" or "Function" as well as "Time" columns. These views allow the description of systems as structures and behaviors from each relevant perspective. For example, analytical layer could serve as a segment where the salient features as well as processes that describe business information systems are conceptualized.

Another important category derived from Zachman's framework is "Motivation." This view represents the system as the purpose (the "final cause") that it aims to fulfill at the given level of representation. As the development of specific systems is driven by specific business needs, the motivation behind classes of systems must be guided by the common needs and opportunities of the respective problem domain. Thus, for instance, the raison d'être for Decision Support Systems has traditionally been informing decision makers in ill-structured tasks. Inclusion of this motivational category allows describing systems as purposes they fulfill. Thus, at any given level of representation one could obtain a full picture of how the static and dynamic properties of the systems relate to the major motivations behind them. In this sense, the *structural* (static), *behavioral* (dynamic), and *motivational* (teleological) aspects of IS contribute towards the *completeness* of IS representation.

Revisiting some of the discussion provided in earlier chapters, it could be noted that there is a stronger twist to the motivational view of complex systems, which could potentially lead to their useful treatment as "intentional" systems. As already mentioned earlier, Searle had argued that intentionality is a legitimate part of basic ontology of the world (Searle, 1980, 1995). Dennet suggested that adopting the "intentional stance" can lead to a more convenient way of reasoning about complex artifacts than adopting the "design stance" (Dennet, 1987). Johnston and Milton have suggested the view of information systems as intentional systems as a way to provide "parsimonious, high-level description of the behavior of these entities," thus promoting the "agency" view (Johnston & Milton, 2001). In fact, intentional notions have been employed by researchers in the area of intelligent agents (sometimes explicitly in the design), to the point that Wooldridge and Jennings in their often-cited paper have related the "strong notion" of agenthood to the appropriateness of employing intentional characteristics (e.g. "beliefs," "desires," "intentions") in their description (Wooldridge & Jennings, 1995). As

exotic as these ideas may appear, it seems that the motivational lens provides a substantative and distinct way to conceptualize systems.

In view of the abstract nature of meta-systems, it could be suggested that the "network" component of Zachman's array not to be included in the framework for researchers as it is more adequate for the description of concrete system instantiations. Furthermore, we will also omit the "People" column to emphasize the inseparability of human users and their tasks from the IS representation at the analytical layer. However, we feel that there is one more important category missing. While Zachman's framework shows various views of one concrete system instantiation, in our opinion each layer of our framework representing abstract artifacts can be complemented by specific instantiations, or prototypes. March and Smith have included instantiations as one of the key outcomes of design research, mentioning that these could include both prototypes as well as implemented systems (March & Smith, 1995). In our view it would be useful to provide instantiations at each layer of the representational framework that serves the purposes of illustrating, exemplifying, or implementing the contents of other cells of that layer. Table 2 summarizes the four categories that can be employed to describe types of IS at any perspective layer.

The framework categories could be related to some extent to the products of design research as proposed by March & Smith, including constructs, models, and implementations, but not the methods, as the framework is concerned with the meta-IS ontology, and not the methodology of development. Furthermore, in regards with categories, there is an obviously strong analogy with Aristotle's four causes: formal, efficient, final, and material. The structure category of the framework can be tied to the formal cause; the dynamic category relates to the efficient cause; the motivational aspect aligns itself with the final cause; and instantiations view corresponds to the material cause (as it is the one that defines the indi-

Table 2. Summary of framework categories

Perspective	Description	Related terms	Relationship to Zachman's framework
Structure	Defines meta-IS using structural and static descriptions, e.g. properties, subsystems, and relationships.	Static	Data
Behavior	Shows dynamic aspects of meta-IS, e.g. supported processes, working principles, and methods employed.	Dynamic	Function, Time
Motivation	Provides the description of meta-IS from a given perspective as a set of primary motivations.	Teleological	Motivation
Instantiation	Shows example instantiations for various perspectives, e.g. prototypes.	Prototype	N/A

viduations of the entities). This parallel allows linking the framework to its earliest logical predecessor. Thus, the "categories" dimension of the framework can also be termed *"Aristotelian."*

Note, that while we disregarded the final cause in a macro-perspective on technological developments in earlier discussions, we have still included it in the framework as means of convenience for explaining directing design initiatives.

THE MATRIX FOR IS REPRESENTATIONAL FRAMEWORK

Similar to Zachman's model we can structure the researcher's representation for information system meta-artifacts using a two-dimensional matrix. Table 3 summarizes the framework in terms of dimensions introduced above.

The analytical layer represents the view of meta-IS that not only informs the subsequent design decisions, but can also be used in behavioral studies to conceptualize the type of systems being investigated. The structure category allows the description of IT-reliant systems in terms of their salient features. The behavior category permits incorporating processes that are supported/exhibited by meta-IS. The motivation category clarifies the description of the common business need addressed by the meta-system. The Instantiation category allows the inclusion of an example representation of the system. In this aspect

Table 3. Summary of the framework

Category Perspective	Structure	Behavior	Motivation	Instantiation
Analytical	Salient properties and features of IT-reliant systems	Processes supported by IT-reliant systems	Major generic business/organizational motivations	Mock-up prototypes
Synthetic	Overall logical organization (architecture) of IS	The dynamic behavior of IS; its working principles	Motivation for the type of IS solution as related to requirements	Working prototype that illustrates the concept
Technological	Refined structural design for the type of IS	Refined methods, algorithms, interactions employed by IS	Objectives for the design	Generic packages, frameworks, shells.
Implementation	Architecture, design of implemented systems	Dynamic aspects of implemented systems	Specific business motivations	Implemented functioning systems

a mock-up prototype or verbal description would be equivalent to a high-level instantiation. In this connection it is worthwhile mentioning work by Davis and Venkatesh, who have recently proposed that pre-prototype testing can help predicting the perceived usefulness of implemented systems (Davis & Venkatesh, 2004). Such a "pre-proto-type" representation can be instantiated using descriptions and screenshots that accompany the questionnaire. An entry in the analytical/instantiation cell could then be exemplified by employing such a "pre-prototype."

At the synthetic layer the design researcher would aim at synthesizing a type of the system solution that would conform to the requirements defined at the analytical layer. The major motivation here is to propose a solution that would accomplish this goal, while postponing the refinement of the detailed design per se. The structural aspect would show an overall organization of the system in terms of its key components. The dynamic category would detail the behavior of the components, and interactions that take place among them, as well as with the user. Instantiation would contain a working prototype that exhibits the major essential features and processes supported. Such a prototype can demonstrate the feasibility of the solution, and also can be used in experimental assessments of the value of the concept.

The major motivations in the technological layer would most typically address the efficiency of solution, its technical generality, ease of development, optimality of technical choices, and the like. In a word the layer addresses the question what is the best technical design of the given system type. Thus, the architectural and behavioral aspects would be refined here, and the instantiations would ideally include frameworks, shells, patterns, components that could be used to efficiently build concrete systems. If we adopt the guideline suggested in (Hevner, March, Park, & Ram, 2004) to treat design as a search process, we could see that often the search for adequate conceptualization at the analytical layer could be complemented by the search for the synthetic model that supports the former. Essentially this corresponds to a search for a problem that itself is vaguely defined. Thus, until the value and validity of representations at the higher levels is supported by empirical evidence, it would be best to postpone the search for the adequate refined technological model.

Recent work on the design of customer-centric web sites can illustrate how some of the cells in the framework could be covered (Angehrn & Jelassi, 1994). The authors presented the major analytical motivation of the work as the necessity to connect the intentions of the users and the delivered experience in quest for attracting and retaining the visitors. The objective was not to produce a single system, but rather to provide description and guidance for designing a class of systems, namely, the customer-centric websites. The authors chose an adapted version of so-called "microsegmentation framework" as a kind of kernel theory that drove the analytical conceptualization. In the analytical/structure cell the basic concept introduced was that of "nanosegment." In other words, nanosegments were used to derive analytical representation of these systems. These segments were used to represent individual characteristics of the visitors. The analytical/behavioral representation was built upon the notion of the "nanoflows," that is the interactive aspects of customer experiences of the websites, which had been operationalized further as navigation sequence (in terms of content and interactivity). The authors have also offered a method for providing adaptability by monitoring and handling the gaps or mismatches between nanosegments and nanoflows.

The authors have further introduced an information architecture in form of a "stylized" entity relationship diagram that most closely relates to the structural representation at the synthetic layer. They discussed pertinent aspects of dynamics and methods employed by the system, including data analysis and data mining methods. In addition, the authors have provided a case study detailing how a system was implemented in a concrete environment, mentioning concrete technical choices (e.g. using "BroadVision" platform for web presence).

Apparently producing a technological solution, i.e. frameworks, components, patterns, libraries, etc. was not the primary purpose of the work, and it would have been well out of the scope of the project. In fact, the conceptualization at each layer of the framework could constitute a project, while addressing various perspectives would be akin to research program. One possible issue here is whether technological layer truly belongs to the realm of IS, and not other computing disciplines. Our motivation for its inclusion is that the work conducted by a design researcher in this layer does not attempt to make contributions to other related disciplines (in terms of methods, structures, etc.) per se (although such contributions may incidentally occur), but it aims at producing a technical meta-solution to a given business meta-problem.

It is interesting to re-visit the notions of deduction vs. induction mentioned in the previous chapter in connection with the framework. It might appear that the natural progression through the layers for design researchers would be top-down, i.e. triggered by kernel theories, which may be described as *deductive* process. However, as the vast majority of innovative solutions are grounded in practical problems, and thus arise from the industry, the design research programs could be actually progressing from the bottom up. For example, proactive autonomous components had been in use before autonomous agents emerged as a research field. The issues facing the researchers then would be to investigate the applicability, generalizability, extensions and value of innovations in broader contexts. Such a process could be described as being essentially *inductive*.

Let us know re-consider the components of the design theory by Walls et al. that refer to the meta-artifact. The type of the requirements (meta-requirements, R) are represented by the analytical layer. The representation of a type of system solution is split between the synthetic layer (S) and the technological layer (T). Thus, the meta-artifact as part of the design theory can be represented as $<R, S, T>$. The essential structure of the theory can be expressed as

$$\exists R$$
$$R \rightarrow S$$
$$S \rightarrow T$$

In other words, the theory expresses that a given type of requirements (as expressed by the analytical layer) exist; this type of requirements implies a particular synthetic meta-IS concept; and this concept leads to a certain technological conceptualization of meta-IS. The implementation layer provides observations that could ideally be related to assess the validity of the above statements.

PLURALISM: THE THIRD DIMENSION FOR IS REPRESENTATIONAL FRAMEWORK

The aforementioned "search" nature of the design research implies that multiple promising conceptualizations and generic solutions may be proposed in the search process. The point is that the framework should explicitly allow for such pluralism to prevent "this gap has been covered" type of responses from the referees of design research projects.

Pluralism has had a long tradition in the philosophy of science. As one may recall from qn an earlier chapter, Popper has stressed the conjectural nature of the scientific theories, thus implying theoretical pluralism as a key factor in the growth of scientific knowledge (Popper, 1962). Lakatos has further argued in favor of diversity in scientific communities by introducing the notion of the "protective belt" of auxiliary hypotheses around the "hard core" of research programs (Lakatos, 1980). He pointed that the theoretical

Figure 2. The three-dimensional space for researcher's representation of meta-IS

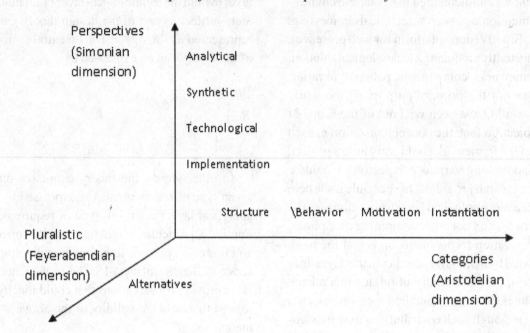

pluralism was superior to monism. Feyerabend characterized science as an essentially anarchistic enterprise, where "anything goes" (Feyerabend, 1975). Feyerabend repeatedly used the phrase "inventing hypotheses," which gives a strong design flavor to this pluralistic approach to conducting research. These different views emanating from the philosophy of science will be elaborated in more detail in later chapters.

A case for a methodological pluralism in IS research has also been presented (Mingers, 2001). In our opinion, there is an even stronger need to tolerate multiple alternative views for the design researchers in IS. Since design researchers are concerned with providing generic solutions, there may be alternative conceptualizations for the problems, alternative ways to synthesize types of systems to address those problems, and multiple ways to offer technological solutions. Thus, we propose to explicitly incorporate the third, pluralistic dimension in the framework, which could be called "Feyerabendian" dimension, after one of the most ardent advocates of pluralism.

Figure 2 shows schematically a three-dimensional space for a researchers' IS representations. Roughly speaking, a research initiative that addresses one or perhaps two perspectives aiming to propose solutions for different categories would correspond to a research project. A larger goal of generating representations for all perspectives would be akin to a research program. An expansion in the dimension of pluralistic treatment of a given business problem could be reflecting a research stream.

An interesting question regarding expansion in the pluralistic dimension of higher layers is whether at any given period there is a predominant accepted conceptualization (alternative). Such an "accepted" alternative would correspond to Kuhnian "paradigm" as applied to design-type research. Like in ordinary science the Kuhnian model suggests that for any type of a problem context a certain way of conceptualizing it would be prevalent. For example, in the decision support domain, for decades the prevalent view has been that human decision makers need to be in control of the process when interacting with a given decision support tool. The stream of research known as "active DSS" had challenged this position to advocate some level of proactiveness on the system's part. When a given "theory" does not yield expected observations, there is room for the alternatives. From the design-type research point of view, this implies that a given meta-system form does not seem to make appearance in the reality. Emergence of other alternatives and growing role of some of them could lead to a "paradigm shift."

Naturally, alternative conceptualizations of problem contexts, which would subsequently lead to a diversity of meta-requirements, are always a possibility for researchers to explore. For example, much of the past research in decision support systems had targeted ill-structured problems. This focus had led to a set of meta-requirements for guiding design research efforts in the area. A more recent characterization of some decision support contexts proposes an alternative view: that of "wicked" problems, i.e. the ones, which are particularly difficult to tackle (Courtney, 2001).

Each particular (meta-requirements) context conceptualization may lead to a variety of competing synthetic meta-system forms. Each synthetic meta-system may itself be supported by a diversity of technological meta-artifacts. For example, a particular synthetic form of a business intelligence solution maybe refined into a component-based, or, alternatively, a service-based technological meta-system. It could appear that such a view of alternative forms generation suggests a tree-like hierarchical structure of relationships between different layers. However, a given type of a solution at one layer may actually link with several alternatives at the higher layer. For example, assume that in a given domain alternative conceptualizations of decision support have been proposed: one relying on a passive model, and the other one featuring proactive elements. Then a corresponding technological artifact may incorporate the features of both conventional decision support, as well as decision automation.

Apart from purely scientific value of pluralism in search for an adequate theory, alternative conceptualizations may be valuable in designing specific solutions. The recently advanced concept of "design theory nexus" relies on the existence of alternative design theories (Pries-Heje & Baskerville, 2008). The authors propose to harness the diversity of the existing design approaches in searching a sound design for an artifact. In their vision, existing alternative design theories help drive the solution search, influenced by particular design goals and the organizational factors. They define nexus as a set of constructs that "enables the construction of models that connect numerous design theories with alternative solutions." Through establishing such a connection the nexus helps define a particular design solution.

In introducing the design theory nexus, the authors emphasize that alternative design theories should differ in terms of the respective targeted sets of criteria. This brings up an interesting question as per the nature of diversity among the alternative models. Although Kuhn is commonly regarded as espousing a monistic view of normal science, his concept of disciplinary matrix helps identifying the possibilities for the emergence of pluralism in scientific communities. The four components of the matrix include symbolic generalizations; metaphysical presumptions; values; and exemplars. The metaphysical component has to do with the beliefs (and commitments) held within a given scientific community. Values relate to the criteria adopted for judging theoretical models, e.g. prediction accuracy. Abstracting away from the monistic nature of paradigms per se, these two components may suggest the two kinds of sources for pluralism. In the context of theory nexus the authors had clearly referred to the value component as a source of pluralism.

The idea of harnessing the power of pluralism for computational problem solving had been proposed about three decades ago (Kornfeld & Hewitt, 1981). In their work the authors have relied on the works of Popper and Lakatos to propose a computational model, based on the simulation of pluralism in scientific communities. A more recent publication devised a model for pluralistic decision support directly based on the components of Kuhn's matrix, namely views (which corresponded to the metaphysical part of the matrix) and values (Vahidov & Fazlollahi, 2004). Portfolio selection was chosen as an example application. Here the diversity in regards with the values derived from the two alternative schools of thought in security analysis, namely technical and fundamental analyses. Diversity with respect to values came from two profiles: low-risk, and high-risk investment objectives. These two dimensions in combination produced four types of "artificial" financial advisors. The four advising "agents" then analyzed historical data on different securities to propose four alternative portfolios for the investor's consideration. Coming back to design-type research, then one could say that alternative conceptualizations for the meta-requirements and meta-systems may arise from the difference in views (beliefs), or values (criteria) targeted.

REFERENCES

Alter, S. (2003). 18 reasons why IT-reliant work systems should replace "the IT artifact" as the core subject matter of the IS fiel. *Communications of the Association for Information Systems*, *12*(23), 366–395.

Angehrn, A. A., & Jelassi, M. T. (1994). DSS research and practice in perspective. *Decision Support Systems*, *12*, 267–275. doi:10.1016/0167-9236(94)90045-0

Armour, P. G. (2007). Twenty percent: Planning to fail on software projects. *Communications of the ACM*, *50*(6), 21–23. doi:10.1145/1247001.1247020

Courtney, J. F. (2001). Decision making and knowledge management in inquiring organizations: Toward a new decision-making paradigm for DSS. *Decision Support Systems*, *31*, 17–38. doi:10.1016/S0167-9236(00)00117-2

Davis, F. D. (1993). User acceptance of information technology: System characteristics, user perceptions and behavioral impacts. *International Journal of Man-Machine Studies*, *38*(3), 475–487. doi:10.1006/imms.1993.1022

Davis, F. D., Bagozzi, R. P., & Warshaw, P. R. (1989). User acceptance of information technology: A comparison of two theoretical models. *Management Science*, *35*(8), 982–1003. doi:10.1287/mnsc.35.8.982

Davis, F. D., & Venkatesh, V. (2004). Toward preprototype user acceptance testing of new information systems: Implications for software project management. *IEEE Transactions on Engineering Management*, *51*(1), 31–46. doi:10.1109/TEM.2003.822468

Dennet, D. (1987). *The intentional stance*. Cambridge, MA: Bradford Books/MIT Press.

DoD. (1994). *Technical architecture framework for information management (TAFIM)*. Reston, VA: DISA Center for Architecture.

Feyerabend, P. K. (1975). *Against method: Outline of an anarchistic theory of knowledge*. London, UK: NLB.

Goodhue, D. L., & Thompson, R. L. (1995). Task-technology fit and individual performance. *Management Information Systems Quarterly*, *19*(2), 213–236. doi:10.2307/249689

Gregor, S., & Benbasat, I. (1999). Explanations from intelligent systems: Theoretical foundations and implications for practice. *Management Information Systems Quarterly*, *23*(4), 497–530. doi:10.2307/249487

Hevner, A. R., March, S. T., Park, J., & Ram, S. (2004). Design science in information systems research. *Management Information Systems Quarterly, 28*(1), 75–105.

Iivari, J. (2003). The IS core – VII: Towards information systems as a science of meta-artifacts. *Communications of the Association for Information Systems, 12*(37), 568–581.

Johnston, R. B., & Milton, S. (2001). *The significance of intentionality for the ontological evaluation of information systems.* Paper presented at the Seventh Americas Conference on Information Systems. Boston, MA.

Kim, D., & Benbasat, I. (2003). Trust-related arguments in internet stores: A framework for evaluation. *Journal of Electronic Commerce Research, 4*(2), 49–64.

Kock, N., Gray, P., Hoving, R., Klein, H., Myers, M., & Rockart, J. (2002). IS research relevance revisited: Subtle accomplishment, unfulfilled promise, or serial hypocrisy? *Communications of the Association for Information Systems, 8,* 330–346.

Kornfeld, W. A., & Hewitt, C. (1981). The scientific community metaphor. *IEEE Transactions on Systems, Man, and Cybernetics, 11*(1), 24–33. doi:10.1109/TSMC.1981.4308575

Lakatos, I. (1980). Falsification and the methodology of scientific research programmes. In Worrall, J., & Currie, G. (Eds.), *The Methodology of Scientific Research Programmes* (*Vol. 1,* pp. 8–101). Cambridge, UK: Cambridge University Press. doi:10.1007/978-94-010-1863-0_14

March, S., Hevner, A., & Ram, S. (2000). Research commentary: An agenda for information technology research in heterogeneous and distributed environments. *Information Systems Research, 11*(4), 327–341. doi:10.1287/isre.11.4.327.11873

March, S. T., & Smith, G. F. (1995). Design and natural science research on information technology. *Decision Support Systems, 15,* 251–266. doi:10.1016/0167-9236(94)00041-2

Markus, M. L., Majchrzak, A., & Gasser, L. (2002). A design theory for systems that support emergent knowledge processes. *Management Information Systems Quarterly, 26*(3), 179–212.

Mingers, J. (2001). Combining IS research methods: Towards a pluralist methodology. *Information Systems Research, 12*(3), 240–259. doi:10.1287/isre.12.3.240.9709

Orlikowski, W., & Iacono, C. (2001). Desperately seeking the "IT" in IT research - A call to theorizing the IT artifact. *Information Systems Research, 12*(2), 121–134. doi:10.1287/isre.12.2.121.9700

Popper, K. R. (1962). *Conjectures and refutations: The growth of scientific knowledge.* New York, NY: Basic Books.

Pries-Heje, J., & Baskerville, R. (2008). The design theory nexus. *Management Information Systems Quarterly, 32*(4), 731–735.

Robey, D., & Markus, M. L. (1998). Beyond rigor and relevance: Producing consumable research about information systems. *Information Resources Management Journal, 11*(1), 7–15.

Searle, J. R. (1980). Intrinsic intentionality. *The Behavioral and Brain Sciences, 3,* 450–456. doi:10.1017/S0140525X00006038

Searle, J. R. (1995). *The construction of social reality.* London: Penguin Books.

Sowa, J. F., & Zachman, J. A. (1992). Extending and formalizing the framework for information systems architecture. *IBM Systems Journal, 31*(3), 590–616. doi:10.1147/sj.313.0590

Spewak, S. H. (1992). *Enterprise architecture planning.* New York: John Wiley & Sons.

Sultan, F., Urban, G. L., Shankar, V., & Bart, I. Y. (2002). *Determinants and role of trust in e-business: A large scale empirical study*. MIT Sloan School of Management Working Paper 4282-02. Cambridge, MA: MIT Press.

TOGAF. (2001a). *The open group architectural framework, version 7, December, 2001*. New York: The Open Group.

TOGAF. (2001b). *The open group architectural framework, version 8, December, 2002*. New York: The Open Group.

Vahidov, R. (2006). *Design researcher's IS artifact: A representational framework*. Paper presented at the 1st International Conference on Design Science Research in Information Systems and Technology, DESRIST 2006. Claremont, CA.

Vahidov, R., & Fazlollahi, B. (2004). Pluralistic multi-agent decision support system: A framework and an empirical test. *Information & Management, 41*(7), 883–398. doi:10.1016/j.im.2003.08.017

Walls, J. G., Widmeyer, G. R., & El Sawy, O. A. (1992). Building an information system design theory for vigilant EIS. *Information Systems Research, 3*(1), 36–59. doi:10.1287/isre.3.1.36

Wand, Y., & Weber, R. (1988). *An ontological analysis of some fundamental information systems concepts*. Paper presented at the International Conference on Information Systems. Minneapolis, MN.

Wand, Y., & Weber, R. (1990). An ontological model of an information system. *IEEE Transactions on Software Engineering, 16*(22), 1282–1292. doi:10.1109/32.60316

Wand, Y., & Weber, R. (1990). *Towards a theory of deep structure of information systems*. Paper presented at the International Conference on Information Systems. Copenhagen, Denmark.

Weber, R. (2003). Editor's comments: Still desperately seeking the IT artifact. *Management Information Systems Quarterly, 27*(2), iii–xi.

Wooldridge, M., & Jennings, N. (1995). Intelligent agents: Theory and practice. *The Knowledge Engineering Review, 10*(2), 115–152. doi:10.1017/S0269888900008122

Zachman, J. A. (1987). A framework for information systems architecture. *IBM Systems Journal, 26*(3), 276–292. doi:10.1147/sj.263.0276

Chapter 7
Application of the Representational Framework:
The Case of e-Negotiation Systems

ABSTRACT

The representational framework introduced in the previous chapter could help design researchers organize their work by choosing to focus on analytical, synthetic, or technological kinds of projects. This chapter presents the case of electronic negotiation systems as an example of the application of the framework. Theoretical background of negotiations allows deriving the analytical picture of systems designed to support them. The chapter discusses two system concepts: one providing an example of a synthetic meta-artifact for conducting electronic negotiations; and the other one representing the case of design-type research with the emphasis on obtaining a sound technical meta-system. Alternative meta-requirement or meta-system concepts could be devised at each layer of the framework.

NEGOTIATIONS

Negotiations are an integral part of normal business and personal activities. People rarely realize how often they engage in negotiations in their daily lives (Raiffa, 1982). Engaging in a negotiation the parties attempt to find an agreement that

DOI: 10.4018/978-1-4666-0131-4.ch007

would be suitable for them. In retailing the most common sort of exchange mechanism between a company and its customers is a catalog model, where a price for a given product or service is fixed and non-negotiable. Companies attempt to find such price levels, which would maximize their profits, subject to a number of other factors, such as mission, profile, reputation and the like. This is "take it or leave it" philosophy. However, even in the mass-volume catalog-oriented retailing there are elements of negotiations. Economically speaking, negotiation is a too attractive and flexible mechanism to avoid completely. Businesses realize the value of this flexibility for maximizing their profits and market share.

During the course of negotiations one party makes an offer, and the other one either accepts, or rejects it. The other party may also make a counter-offer. Thus, negotiation is about exchange of offers which leads to an agreement or termination without an agreement. In a sense, many businesses do engage in negotiations with their customers, but in an implicit way. This is done through realizing that customers may not react to basic offers and anticipating the offers to which customers may react. For example, while shopping at amazon.com a shopper may be considering buying a given item. The site then offers this item in combination with some other, similar item at a reduced total price. The site sort of "negotiates" with the customer, while the latter does not necessarily realize it. It is not a true exchange of offers, but it is a hidden one. First, customer sees the item of interest. The site at this point has no clue as for whether the customer intends or does not intend to purchase the item. A customer may or may not be interested in the item. In any case, if the customer does not proceed directly to check out, he or she notices the new offer, which might be of interest. A customer may so easily leave the site. This is why the latter makes a number of offers in *parallel*, rather than interactively. Many businesses, ranging from established online stores to fast-food restaurants make such offers including "value packs" and limited-time discounts.

In any exchange the issue is in determining the value of goods or services being exchanged. In retailing, the value is easier to estimate as many exchange instances occur on a daily basis. In some other contexts, e.g. in real estate the value of a given property is influenced by many factors. A given property is not traded multiple times in a short time interval, which makes its value less ob-

vious. As a rough approximation, one could check the prices of properties in a given neighborhood. However, there is typically a multitude of other details. For example, selling it quickly could be one of the motivational factors of the owner. The value of an *exchange* has to be *discovered* through the negotiation process.

Somewhat arbitrarily in the above discussion a business context of exchange has been adopted. While negotiations between business partners and those involving decisions of a strategic kind, e.g. mergers between companies present interesting cases for analysis, the objective was to argue, that even in routine exchanges the elements of negotiations are present. Negotiations are omnipresent. Surely, negotiations in general are not limited to purely economic transactions. They are an important mechanism in social, legal, and political domains as well. Formally, negotiation can be defined as "a process of social interaction and communication about distribution and redistribution of power, resources, and commitments" (Kersten, 2003). Usually, when speaking about negotiations, one thinks of the two parties involved in the offer – counter-offer sequences. However, in general negotiations may involve several parties. For example, negotiations over the legal status of the Caspian Sea involved representatives of five countries (four of which used to be parts of Soviet Union): Azerbaijan, Iran, Kazakhstan, Russia, and Turkmenistan. Two-party negotiations are referred to as "bilateral." Those involving multiple parties are called "multi-lateral." It is also common to have a scenario, where one party negotiates with multiple other parties, but these negotiations are independent from each other. In this case we have multi-bilateral negotiations.

The simplest type of negotiations involves two parties entering into interaction with the purpose of reaching an agreement on some subject. For example, a person could be negotiating with another person about a sale of a vehicle. In this case offers and counter-offers may concern a single dimension: the price. Dimensions over which negotiations take place in negotiation theory terminology are called the "issues." Issues contain a set of possible values included in the offers. These values are called "options," and they could be continuous or discrete. In single-issue negotiations the gain of one party necessarily entails the loss of the other. Suppose, each party has its own reservations as per the minimum desired level of an issue he or she would still be willing to accept. For example, say, a seller would not accept any price below some level (reservation level). Likewise, a buyer would not accept an agreement that implies the price higher than his/her reserved level. If there is a non-zero length intersect between the buyer's and seller's acceptable prices, the interval between the two is called the zone of possible agreement, as it contains the set of values, which might be acceptable for both parties (Raiffa, 1982). In the case where the zone contains an empty space of such points, no agreement is possible. Knowing the zone of agreement by some mediating body could simplify the solution sought by the parties. However, in negotiations the reservation levels are typically kept private.

In single issue negotiations different points of agreement may have different levels of attractiveness to the parties. For example, difference between two price levels close to the reservation point may be of much higher importance, than the difference of the same magnitude further away from the reservation point. This is a well-established subject of utilities, first systematically studied by von Neumann and Morgenstern (1944). Therefore, in single issue negotiations the "optimal" point of agreement from the aggregate perspectives of the two parties is not necessarily the center of the zone of possible agreement. Nevertheless, if a single issue is involved with opposite directions of in the objectives of the parties, the gain on one side would necessarily imply the loss of the other party. This is akin to dividing a given pie. Such negotiation cases are generally referred to as "distributive," as the shares of a given "pie" need to be distributed between the parties.

If more issues are involved, there are more possibilities for the parties to "maneuver." These different issues may be of different importance to the negotiators. For example, if a seller of a property is in a situation demanding that he or she has to sell it as quickly as possible, the time issue acquires a heightened level of importance. Multi-issue negotiations allow for a wider set of possibilities for the negotiators to explore. Adding an issue often is desirable in exploring the avenues of possibilities of mutually acceptable agreements. More degrees of freedom are available in negotiations. A person selling a car may offer winter tires as an additional issue to the price. Repairing a roof of a house or including appliances as part of an offer may help the proprietor to successfully complete the transaction. The pie could be made bigger, after all. Negotiations could be moved from a distributive mode to an "integrative" one, whereby joint gains could be achieved by the parties.

However, the addition of more issues leads to higher cognitive demand on the part of negotiators. It is much easier to react to an offer including a couple of issues, than to the one that features a half-dozen of them. It is very easy for someone's rationality to stumble in multiple dimensions. Could there be ways of supporting decision making in such circumstances? Traditionally, negotiators could go back to evaluate the offers received using some sort of calculators, to see if an offer is acceptable. In other words, they would be relying on some means of decision support. They would have to take the situation at hand from the world of the Real, to the world of the Digital. What if the Digital was organically embedded in the modes of interaction between the parties? What if the Digital became, indeed, the part of the "Real," the "Virtual Real"? Then it could be integrated into analysis of offers and construction of counter-offers organically. Enter the electronic negotiation systems.

E-NEGOTIATION SYSTEMS: ANALYTICAL LAYER

Theoretical body of knowledge on negotiations is extensive and its coverage is well beyond the scope of this book. Here, the purpose is to show how negotiations could be supported by electronic systems, or rather how these systems could be visualized at the analytical, synthetic, and technological levels. Sure enough, at each layer the focus is on classes of requirements or systems. Concrete instantiations serve as specific examples within those classes. The above discussion helps clarify the basic terminology, typology and structure of negotiation processes to be supported by electronic negotiation systems. It is important to bear in mind, that unlike in specific system development, where the analytical, design, and implementation perspectives refer to the process of refining one particular solution, in design-type research, these perspectives refer to different kinds of design research projects. They are not focusing on a stage-wise development of a particular system.

Motivation

Traditional way of conducting negotiations commonly involves parties meeting face-to-face to explore the possibilities of arriving at some joint solution. The parties have to be at the same time and same place to engage in an interaction. Normally, each party would have done their homework in terms of setting the objectives, deciding on the minimum levels of acceptability of agreements, choosing the tactics to follow, investigating other alternatives in regards with the issues to be negotiated, assessing the importance of the issues, and making other preparatory decisions. Each party would not know what private negotiation-related objectives, preferences, and tactics the other party has. During the course of negotiations the parties exchange their offers while trying to assess the

chances of reaching a desirable outcome. They may have to adjust their preferences and tactics in response to the moves by the other parties, in particular if new issues are added in the process.

What would be the motivation behind developing a system solution for supporting negotiations? In what sense it would be beneficial to the negotiators in this process? One important motivational dimension is in enabling negotiations when the parties cannot be at the same place and same time. Globalization trends are fostering the types of economic relationships that span across the countries and continents. The rising importance of such critical activities as effective supply chain management, outsourcing and outtasking requires extensive coordination and search for joint solutions by the parties located in different parts of the world. The bulk of these activities, in particular in relational exchanges (Blois, 2007; Larson, 2005) can be viewed as negotiation processes where agreement is sought in accordance with the objectives and preferences of the interacting parties. Ways of managing offer exchanges between geographically separated parties would allow for much broader scope of interactions. System solutions that specifically target effective facilitation of such interactions may play a major role in improvement of both the processes and outcomes of business negotiations.

Apart from pure communication issues, the dynamics of the global business and technological environment imposes significant stress on the decision makers in their search for adequate responses to arising challenges and opportunities. Modern businesses often have to adopt agile strategies in choosing the partners to interact with. This means that they often have to act in the face of uncertainty with little time left to adapt to the specifics of transacting with dynamically changing set of partners. Moreover, the rapid technological advancements bring about new types of products and services further complicating the options and issues to be agreed upon regarding production, distribution, and retail of these products and services

An important motivational component is that a system could help the parties get organized by means of tracking the history of interactions and help them understand their preferences more clearly. In the absence of some sort of decision support parties would find it somewhat difficult to clearly assess offer packages that include various combinations of options on multiple issues. In multi-issue negotiations, it is also quite possible that the parties may eventually converge to an inferior agreement. In other words, their agreement may not be Pareto-optimal, from the point of view of their preferences. This is known as "leaving money on the table" as an agreement made may indeed be substituted by another potential agreement, which suggests an improvement to at least one of the parties.

Electronic negotiations (e-negotiations) are those conducted using electronic media. The major technological factor behind the interest in E-Negotiation Systems (ENS) has been the emergence and quick development of the web that has allowed geographically and temporally separated parties to engage in interactions involving exchange of offers, as well as advances in the development of models and software components that could be useful for the parties in planning, conducting, and analyzing their negotiation processes (Kersten & Noronha, 1999).

In light of the above discussion there is a potential need for appropriate analytical tools and software solutions, which would empower the negotiating decision-makers with the capabilities facilitating clarification of own, and understanding other parties objectives and preferences, adequately assessing offers, counter-offers and potential agreement points, and acting in the "sense-respond" mode to quickly react to any market challenges and opportunities. In summary, ENS seek to address the following important needs among the others:

- Providing means for informational and analytical support for improving negotiation processes and outcomes;
- Facilitating effective communication between the parties; and
- Provisioning flexibility for dynamically changing the range of issues to negotiate over.

Structure

ENS as a concept had originally emerged through the attempts to apply the prior work on Negotiation Support Systems (NSS) to web technologies (Kersten & Noronha, 1999). NSS had originally been conceived as possessing communication and decision support capabilities. Thus, the key salient features of ENS are support of communications between the negotiating parties, as well as analytical support.

The communication component of ENS can vary in its ability to represent items of interactions. Simple forms would enable free text messaging, similar to e-mail communications, but with better facilities to keep track of the history of such interactions. In more structured exchanges, the offers are specified using some predefined format and following a given negotiation protocol. In structured exchanges the issues and options are specified explicitly during the course of negotiations. Protocols define what kinds of state transitions are allowable in the process. This mode of interaction tends to be more formal, and it helps better organize issues and options, and facilitate quick and impartial interpretation of offers. Strictly following a structured approach may translate into somewhat lowered level of propensity to form stable relationships between the parties. A combination of structured exchanges as well as limited-length freestyle messages could contribute towards getting the benefits of both approaches. This may result in learning more about the opponent's profile and use argumentation and substantiation techniques during the course of negotiations.

One of the essential communicational aspects of characterizing negotiations is the participants involved in the process (Kersten, 2003). As pointed earlier in a simple case only two parties would be involved in a bilateral negotiation. A system targeting bilateral negotiations would only need to track exchanges of offers by two sides. Support of multilateral exchanges would require more complex protocols, and means of communicating offers to multiple recipients. In multi-bilateral setting a certain negotiating party will be interacting with a number of other parties in parallel with the objective of finding the most suitable agreement. This could involve cases where only one agreement with a single party is sought (Nguyen & Jennings, 2004) or multiple agreements could be made with a subset of other negotiating entities (Vahidov, 2007). In general, the set of issues within each of the one-to-many negotiation instances could vary. The capabilities of displaying multiple offers received in a fashion that facilitates their effective and efficient evaluation would be of critical value to the negotiator.

The purpose of endowing ENS with analytical capabilities is to enhance users' powers for the assessment of a given interaction context and improvement of decision making. Use of information search and retrieval facilities could inform users about market situation, possible options and issues (Liang & Huang, 2000). Various analytical tools and techniques could help the negotiators to better understand their own preferences, as well as the preferences of the other parties. For example, Coehoorn and Jennings (2004) propose a method for evaluating opponent preferences using kernel density estimation. While the above approaches focus on supporting individual negotiators, ENSs could also help both parties achieve mutually beneficial agreements. This could involve cases where private preferences of the parties could be revealed to the system (Thiessen, Loucks, &

Stedinger, 1998), or if they have to be inferred (Dzeng & Lin, 2005).

Another important characterization of ENS is the mode of support, which could be passive or active. In a "toolbox" mode and the system would provide the informational and analytical resources to the user, and the latter has to use them properly in preparing and conducting negotiations. On the other hand, the user could specify the aspiration and reservation levels, preferences, and strategies for negotiation, but the actual negotiation could be carried out by autonomous software agents. While research into completely automated negotiations has been extensive (e.g. see Beam & Segev, 1996; Chavez & Maes, 1996; Faratin, Sierra, & Jennings, 2002) such delegation can only take place when the problem is well-structured, which may apply to a fairly restricted set of business contexts. In cases where multiple operational-level negotiations can be conducted in parallel, users could be involved in managing a fleet of autonomous negotiating agents (Vahidov & Neumann, 2008). An intermediate level of ENS proactiveness is when both the system and the user are actively involved in the process. In such cases an embedded agent could act as an assistant to provide the user with advice. For example, an agent could provide recommendations as to whether to accept or reject an offer, and propose alternative counter-offers (Chen, Vahidov, & Kersten, 2005), or be endowed with the capability of predicting opponent's moves in order to calculate the counter-offer that it deems to be the best (Carbonneau, Kersten, & Vahidov, 2008).

Summarizing the above, some of the important salient features of ENSs include the following:

- Communicational
  - Support for structured vs. unstructured exchanges
  - Support for bilateral, multi-bilateral, or multilateral negotiations
- Analytical
  - Information search and retrieval

- Modeling negotiator's preferences
- Modeling opponent's preferences
- Search for mutually beneficial agreements
- Mode of support
  - "Toolbox" (passive)
  - Automated and semi-automated
  - Assistance and guidance

Behavior

The dynamic aspects of negotiation processes prepared and conducted with the use of ENSs *depend not only on the particular context (e.g. domain, number and type of participants) but also* on the capabilities provided by the systems. In general, negotiation processes progress in a number of identifiable stages or phases. Gulliver has identified eight phases that commonly apply to a wide class of negotiation tasks (Gulliver, 1979). These phases include:

1. Searching for an arena;
2. Formulating an agenda and working definitions of the issues to be negotiated;
3. Making preliminary statements of demands and offers, exploring issues and differences between the parties;
4. Narrowing the differences and reaching agreement on some issues;
5. Preliminaries to final bargaining;
6. Final bargaining;
7. Ritual confirmation of the final outcome; and
8. Implementation of the outcome.

These phases can be further aggregated into three major steps: pre-negotiation, negotiation, and post-negotiation (De Moor & Weigand, 2004; Kersten & Noronha, 1999). The pre-negotiation phase involves activities related to preparation for the negotiation. These typically involve exploring current situation in the problem domain, defining the key issues for the possible inclusion

in the agreement, setting objectives for the task, exploring alternative possibilities for reaching the objectives (e.g. alternative methods of obtaining products or services to be negotiated over), defining aspiration and reservation levels for the issues, clarifying the relative importance of the issues, and deciding on negotiation strategies/tactics. In the pre-negotiation phase the system could help users in retrieving information about problem domain and potential negotiators, help eliciting and modeling the preferences of the negotiator, and conducting what-if analysis in assessing the implications of possible agreement points.

During the negotiation stage actual interaction between the parties in form of offers and counter-offers takes place. In structured negotiation an explicit set of rules is defined that stipulates such aspects as: how offers are made and counter-offers produced; whether and how new issues could be added during the negotiation process; and when and how the agreement could be reached. For well-structured negotiation problems software agent tools could be adopted, which would completely automate the execution of this phase (note that a well-structured problem has a different meaning from structured negotiations. In a well-structured the tactics of the negotiation task could be formulated as an algorithm). ENS could help users by providing analytical tools to help them assessing of offers and counter-offers in light of the specified preferences.

The post-negotiation (post-settlement) phase can involve formalizing the agreements (e.g. through contracts), their execution and follow-up. Additionally, a system could propose the ways of improving the achieved agreement. To this end the system could evaluate the agreement to see if it is Pareto-optimal. This is possible to do if the system knows the private preferences of the parties. Note, that the system should not reveal the preferences of any one party to the other one. The negotiators' preferences could be captured by the system in form of utility modeling. Then, knowing the agreement achieved the system could evaluate the agreement in terms of its utilities to both parties. Employing a search method within the vicinity of an agreement, the system could then try to improvement. An improvement would imply that the new solution would be beneficial to one or both of the parties. In doing so the system would ensure that the new potential agreement point would not translate into utility deterioration for any negotiator. If such solution is found, it could then be proposed to both parties as an alternative. If the parties agree to renegotiate with this new suggestion, this may lead to better joint outcomes than the previously agreed-upon solution. Certainly, the system might not capture the preferences of the negotiators correctly. In this case the new agreement may not be truly an improved one. However, this would be up to the negotiators to judge.

Instantiation

Instantiation at the analytical level serves as a way of exemplifying the meta-requirements to promote their clarification and communication. It does not imply that a full system solution, representing an instance of a meta-system should be developed. At this point, example scenarios or mock-up prototypes could be used to better convey the idea, to add some "meat" to the description of a given class of requirements.

To illustrate how human negotiators could negotiate in business settings through the use of hypothetical ENS capabilities we will use a case described on the Interneg website (http://invite. concordia.ca/inspire/demo.html). Interneg is one of the leading research centers in electronic negotiations focusing on the issues related to study of electronic negotiations and design of e-negotiation system concepts. The case features a bilateral negotiation example, which involves the representatives of two companies, nicknamed "Misty" and "Smiley." These representatives negotiate the sale of an aircraft by one party to the other.

The case is relatively simple (from the point of view of the negotiation task) as it involves just two issues: price and warranty. Despite the simplicity of this particular scenario, the ENS must support multi-issue negotiations. During the preparation stage each negotiator might be able to specify their preferences by assigning relative weights to the issues. For example, one party could come up with 70% importance assigned to the price issue, and 30% to the warranty. The other party one could have a different allocation of importance, for example 50-50 scheme. The aspirations of the parties regarding the issues are in the opposite directions, i.e. the buyer wants a lower price and better warranty, while the sellers preferences are the reverse. If the weights for the issues were the same for both parties, the negotiations would be distributive and essentially equivalent to one issue case. The difference in the importance of issues allows the parties to explore the solutions which would entail higher satisfaction levels compared to the distributive situation. This difference, therefore, in general would lead to a higher likelihood of reaching an agreement.

Furthermore, apart from identifying the issues, the options for the issues need also to be specified. Issue values could be continuous or discrete. To limit the size of the search space, a continuous issue could be transformed into a discrete one. For example, in the case described, it may be decided that price is negotiated at three levels. To be able to specify the utility values for the issue values an ENS could use formulas and/ or look-up tables. For example the utility values for the price (for the selling side) could be 0 for $300,000, 45 for $310,000, and 70 for 320,000, since the price is allocated 70% of importance (alternatively, the values for the set of the options for an issue could be expressed on a scale from 0 to 100, and then multiplied by a weight to obtain its contribution to the total utility score). System could also use preference elicitation techniques (e.g. AHP) to derive/clarify negotiators' preferences. Communicating relative weights, as well as the desirability levels of various options to the system would allow quantitative analysis of different offers. Moreover, the preferences could change in the process of negotiation due to dynamic contextual factors, and the system should be able to accommodate for these changes.

After the preparation phase is complete one of the parties could make an initial offer. Typically one would start with the most attractive offer in terms of the issue values and enter these into the system using web form-like interface. The submitted offer would remain in the system until the other party checks for new offers received. The other negotiator may evaluate the offer in light of his/her utility schema and decide whether to accept it, make a counter-offer, or terminate the negotiations. He or she can evaluate possible counter-offers against their utility structure and choose what kind of counter-offer to make. This offer would then be evaluated by the first party, and a possible concession could be made in the next offer, if any. In addition to structured offers the system could also support messaging facilities. The process would continue until an agreement is made, or one of the negotiators decides to terminate the process.

A difference in issue ratings between the two parties is a double-edged sword. On one hand, as mentioned earlier, due to this difference the parties could make mutually attractive agreements. Yet on the other, they could in general reach a non-Pareto-optimal solution. In the post-settlement phase the system could use preference information to decide if the agreement made is dominated by some other possible solutions. In the latter case the system may offer possible improvements to the negotiated agreement to the parties which they may decide to accept. This would avoid "leaving money on the table" especially in cases where number of issues is large and there are significant differences between preference vectors of the negotiators.

SYNTHETIC LAYER

In the remaining sections, two types of ENS concepts will be discussed. One project aimed at producing a meta-artifact with the emphasis on synthetic side, while the other primarily addressed technological view of the ENS artifact. Thus, the first case emphasized logical organization, while the second one the technological architecture. First we will look into the synthetic meta-solution.

Motivation

The "Inspire" e-negotiation system (Kersten & Noronha, 1999) has probably been the first working web-based negotiation support solution. The purpose of the Inspire project was to demonstrate the feasibility of implementing ENS, propose the architecture and working principles for ENS, and investigate its use by offering its facilities to the volunteer users over the Internet located in different regions of the world. As the project was undertaken at the time the web technologies were maturing and the community of web users was on the sharp rise, the key question to address was whether it was possible to provide negotiators on the web with effective means for preparing and conducting negotiation activities using only web browser interface. Little attention had been paid to the questions of technical generality.

The system concept had envisaged use of its facilities in bi-lateral settings, where communication capability would allow easy construction, submission and retrieval of offers through the web. The exchange of offers followed a structured format that could also be accompanied by sending short free-style messages if the user chose to do so. The negotiation process itself was based on a protocol with well-defined procedures for starting, conducting, and terminating negotiation sessions.

The analytical capabilities included in the concept were incorporated in form of decision-theoretic models, which enabled the users to model their preferences and analyze offers and counter-offers. Additionally it was deemed promising to include visual aids as part of the analysis toolbox. Each user could view the history of his or her offers in terms of their utilities graphically. Additionally, the user could also see the opponent's offers graphically in terms of the given user's utilities (and not those of an opponent, since the preference information was private). Thus both users could watch the dynamics of interactions graphically with the two graphs being, in general different from each other, due to the difference of preferences. Graphical representation of the ongoing exchanges in terms of their utility to the user was thought to facilitate intuitive insight into the process, assess the progress and get a feeling for the convergent tendencies and estimate possible agreement point between the negotiating parties.

As the ENS concept targeted three-phase model outlined earlier, the possibility of addressing the post-settlement phase was also considered. Thus, the Inspire concept included the possibility of acting in the mediating mode, whereby after the agreement has been made between the negotiating parties it could decide to "softly" intervene if it determined that the agreement made was not Pareto-optimal. This could involve re-negotiation of the issues if both parties agreed to do so.

In summary the major objective for the project was to synthesize a solution concept and develop a working prototype of an ENS that would accomplish the following features related to the analytical-layer representation:

- Support of structured bi-lateral negotiations;
- Offer formulation and messaging facilities;
- Analytical tools for preference elicitation;
- Means for analysis of offers and counter-offers in terms of their utilities;
- Visual aids for graphically viewing the progress of negotiations;
- Mediation facilities for proposing possible improvements to the agreements.

Structure

The architecture of the Inspire system concept in the contexts of supporting individual negotiators vs. mediation mode is shown on Figures 1 and 2, respectively. The central part of the ENS is the Inspire engine that implements much of the communication, storage, and analytical support. Users interact with the front-end in order to indicate their preferences and submit offers and messages. The engine contains negotiation database server that allows storing user profiles and information on on-going negotiations (e.g. issues, options, offers, etc.). The message engine allows free-style messaging by the use of the system front-end or the regular e-mail clients.

Preference specification module allows the users to provide ratings for the offers and issues in the fashion exemplified by the case briefly described in the previous section. User-specified preferences may be somewhat "rough" as people find it difficult to assign numbers to desirability and importance levels, especially in the case of many issues and options. Therefore, additionally, in order to refine the preferences a conjoint analysis approach has been incorporated in the solution and it allows human negotiators to indicate their preferences in a more natural way by assessing hypothetical fully or partially complete offers. The extracted information is stored in the database and used by the utility construction module to calculate the utility (attractiveness) of any given offers and counter-offers. The history module allows retrieving past interactions for a given negotiation. The graphical facility uses historical information as well as the elicited preference to graphically display the history of negotiations in light of the negotiator's utility. Lastly, the module termed "Methodologies and control" is the main controlling unit of the engine that orchestrates the process of negotiations in interaction with other modules and the user. It implements the protocol of interaction and decides in which context which modules/tools should be invoked.

Figure 1. Inspire architecture: individual mode (Kersten & Noronha, 1999)

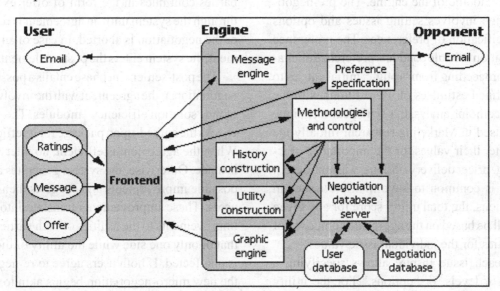

Figure 2. Inspire architecture: mediation mode (Kersten & Noronha, 1999)

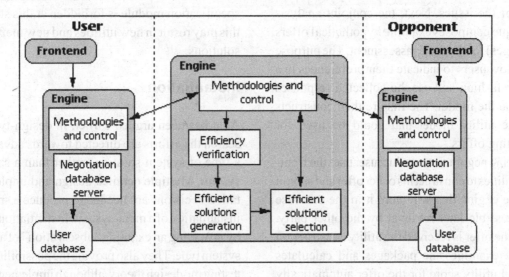

In the mediation mode the system architecture could be viewed as consisting of two negotiation engines for individual support as described above and an additional one for the mediation. This engine has a module for the analysis of the agreement in the context of given negotiation and latest preference structures provided by the users. Based on these the modules perform verification of the efficiency of reached agreements, and if the latter are found to be inefficient, generation of efficient potential agreements and their selection for the presentation to the parties.

Behavior

The three negotiation phases mentioned earlier lie at the basis of the Inspire process model. They are largely controlled by the "Methodologies and

Control" module of the engine. The pre-negotiation stage involves setting issues and options and specification of preferences. The preference specification module conducts preference elicitation by proceeding from "rough" initial entries to more refined estimates of user utilities with the help of conjoint analysis: a statistical technique widely used in Marketing research. Initially the users enter their values for the importance of issues (e.g. price, delivery options, warranty, etc.). Since it is common to have multiple issues in negotiations, the total utility score for any given offer will be based on the aggregate composed of the utilities for the individual issue values.

For each issue Inspire allows specifying a number of levels, or "options." For the utility construction, the user is asked to rate each option for each value on the scale defined by the importance of the issues. Next, the conjoint analysis technique composes example hypothetical offers (packages) for the user's assessment. The purpose is to allow users to indicate their preferences in a holistic fashion and use the collected responses to refine the model. The Inspire then constructs additive utility model that could be used for evaluating offers.

During negotiation conduct user uses the front-end facilities to construct his or her offer and submit it to the engine that will store it in the database for a possible later retrieval by the other party. When the offer is received the utility construction module examines the packages and calculates the total utility score for the offer automatically to complement the visual analysis. Additionally, history of exchanges can be provided to the user, as well as graphical representation of the history depicting the user's and the opponent's offers up to the point. Since the other party's preferences are not revealed to the user, both set of offers are shown in terms of their scores of the given user's utility function. User can also decide to invoke preference specification module to modify his or her preferences. Interaction between the two

parties continues in the form of offer exchange through the system until an agreement is reached, or the negotiation is aborted. In case of an agreement, the system enters the post-settlement phase.

The post-settlement phase entails a possible re-negotiation of the agreement with the involvement of the "solution efficiency" modules. The system checks the agreed-upon package for its efficiency. When the agreement is efficient, no intervention is made. Otherwise, the system generates a set of possible improvements and suggests them to the users. These improvements translate into either improvements to the utilities of both parties, or to that of only one side while the utility of the other is unaffected. If both users agree to re-negotiate, the new micro-negotiation begins akin to that of the main negotiation phase. To make this process stable and convergent, the use of the preference specification module is forbidden at this stage as this may result in new utilities and new inefficient solutions.

Instantiation

As it has been argued earlier, in design-type research the efforts are directed towards advancing a type of system solution, rather than a specific system. Multiple detailed design and implementation decisions are needed to produce a specific instantiation of a meta-system. Instantiations help by providing an example "observation" of a given system type. They also provide the possibilities for testing the design theory, although implementation details may interfere as confounding influences.

The Inspire system had been implemented using HTML, JavaScript and Applets for the front-end, and largely C++ code for the engine (Kersten & Noronha, 1999). As mentioned in the "behavior" section, in the pre-negotiation stage negotiators prepare for the negotiation, in particular they clarify their preferences and objectives. Figure 3 shows the example screen that a negotiator uses to indicate their ratings for the options for each of

Figure 3. User ratings of options

Price	Rating (Max = 70)	Warranty	Rating (Max = 30)
300 000 $	0	No warranty	30
310 000 $	45	6 months	30
320 000 $	70	One year	10
		Two years	0

the issues. As one can see, there are two issues to be included: price and warranty. There are three levels (options) of price to be considered in an offer exchange: $300,000, $310,000, and $320,000. The most preferable price is $320,000, and the least preferable is $300,000 (one could guess that the ratings are for the seller). Maximum rating is 70, and the minimum is 0. For the warranty, there are four options: no warranty (most desirable), 6 months, one year, and two years (least preferable).

As it can be easily seen, the total number of possible offers (if no new issues are added during the course of negotiation) equals twelve. This is quite a small set of possible offers, but with more issues and options, the search space could be significantly larger. Thus, the worst possible agreement (from the seller's perspective would be {Price = $300,000; Warranty = 2 years}, and the best one is {Price = $320,000; No warranty}).

Note, that the ratings have been specified for each issue separately. In the case of small number of issues, the ratings might, more or less, correspond to the true preferences of the negotiator. However, with a larger set of issues, the ratings could be too rough to provide a useful way of modeling the intrinsic preferences. In order to attune the modeled preferences, conjoint analysis is employed. Figure 4 displays complete packages with the purpose of soliciting user preferences to be used by the conjoint analysis.

The user is asked to provide ratings on a scale from 0 to 100 for the examples of option/issue combinations. Instead of asking for the rating of a specific option, the user is given a set of potential offers to evaluate, e.g. {Price = $320,000; Warranty = 1 year}. This information is used by conjoint analysis to adjust the model.

After the preparation stage the negotiator could start the session by making an initial offer to a counterpart. Typically, the first offer made would be the one that is most desirable to a given negotiator. A counter-part can accept an offer or propose a counter-offer. This process goes on until an agreement is made, or one of the parties decides to terminate the negotiation. Figure 5 shows an example where a negotiator proposes a counter-offer to the other party along with the accompanying message.

When analyzing a given offer, the negotiator can assess its utility in terms of his or her preferences. History graph shows the progression of offers and counter-offers in terms of a given negotiator's utility. The graph could help estimate the potential for an agreement, and its possible value to the negotiator. Figure 6 shows a history graph displaying the dynamics of exchanges up to a certain point from the perspectives of two negotiators' utilities.

Figure 4. User ratings of packages

Price	Warranty	Rating
320 000 $	No warranty	100
320 000 $	One year	80
310 000 $	6 months	75
320 000 $	Two years	70

TECHNOLOGICAL LAYER

Motivation

The major motivation behind the synthetic concept, exemplified by the development of the Inspire system was to demonstrate the feasibility of providing negotiation support facilities on the web and proposing an overall design for such systems. Thousands of negotiation sessions have been held through Inspire and they provided a rich set of data for research in e-negotiations. The purpose of the Invite project (invite.concordia.ca) was to propose an ENS solution type with the emphasis made on the technical side of design. In other words, the objectives were set to produce a technological solution that would be flexible enough to accommodate a variety of business negotiation contexts, and would allow easily modifying or enhancing its capabilities through adding new components if necessary. Development of new web technologies allowed for pursuing the principles of good design, in particular those of cohesion and loose coupling.

Inspire, both as a concept, and as an instantiated system followed a pre-defined process, or protocol to manage negotiations between the parties involved. In Invite the vision was to propose such an architecture that would allow for flexible specification of the process the system should follow, as well as the features included for a given set of negotiation situations. In fact, Invite had been conceptualized as a negotiation platform, rather than a particular system, in that it allows to produce (or emulate) other example ENSs. As such, the Inspire model could be produced through Invite by entering specifications for the protocol and support. In this respect Invite could be viewed as an "ENS generator."

Structure

The architecture of the Invite platform (Kersten, Law, & Strecker, 2004) is shown on Figure 7. The overall organization follows a three-tiered approach with persistency, application logic, and

Figure 5. An example offer

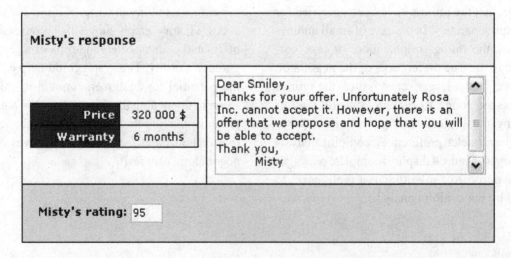

Figure 6. History graphs

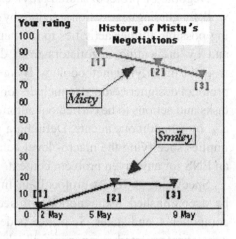 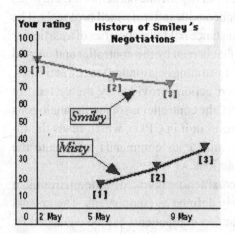

presentation tiers. The design of the platform follows component-oriented philosophy, whereby new components can be developed and added to the system flexibly. These components could be used in specifying new processes and capabilities supported by the system.

Presentation layer contains web pages generated dynamically depending on the particular ENSs user interface. Page composer component of the business logic layer generates pages that follow some layout according to given specifications. For example, page composer could emulate the layout and elements of the Inspire system.

Page contents depend on the particular settings specified for the given emulated ENS type. For example, if an ENS supports only freestyle messaging, then only the part where such messages could be viewed and composed would be included on the page. If it targets structured negotiations, then each of the issues would be shown separately along with the particular options per an issue, making up an offer would be displayed.

The "brain" of the application logic layer is the negotiation controller that is sufficiently generic to be free of peculiarities of any particular protocol. The controller implements actions and instructs

Figure 7. "Invite" architecture

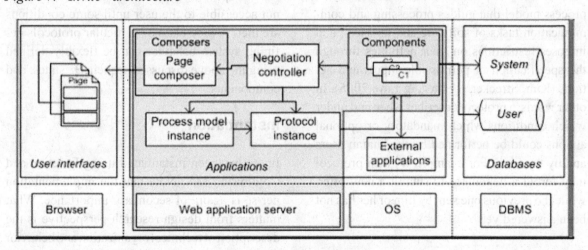

page composer to generate particular page layouts in accordance with softly defined protocols. The protocol instance holds the specifics of a particular protocol that is read by the controller and carried out for orchestrating negotiation stages, activities, and support actions provided by the system. In this respect, the controller is somewhat analogous to the control unit in CPUs, which reads the instructions and sends commands to execute the required actions.

The actual actions invoked by the environment are flexibly defined as components. The arsenal of these action components can be enhanced by developers in order to adapt the system to particular problem contexts, or enhance its capabilities. Thus, the system architecture as defined allows for its evolvability. For example, preference construction methods, optimization or other decision support methods could be included as components and invoked when necessary. New components could also include the capabilities of providing advice and guidance to a negotiator in the course of negotiations. Furthermore, as some of the generic functions could already be pre-existing as external applications or services, Invite makes a provision of utilizing such external tools in its actions.

Behavior

The behavior of an ENS is largely described by the protocol it implements, which is defined as a process model that guides processing and communication tasks of software and its users, and imposes restrictions on their activities through the specification of permissible inputs and actions (Kim, Strecker, Kersten, & Law, 2005). In other words, a protocol describes when and under which conditions which mandatory or optional actions could be performed by the human users and by the ENS. For example, a given protocol may forbid a negotiator to submit a new offer, while the previous one sent by him or her has not been answered yet.

Negotiation protocol should provide a framework for guiding negotiation activities by suggesting possible further activities to the negotiators and by preventing negotiators from deviating from the underlying methodology. By means of a protocol designer could also include some of the tasks and actions to be carried out automatically, e.g. by autonomous agents. Defining a protocol implies specifying the macro- level behavior of an ENS for any given problem context.

Specifying different protocols in Invite can be accomplished using notions of sequences, components, and states. Sequence is defined as a set of interrelated components which together determine all possible activities that can be undertaken in a given negotiation situation (Kim, Kersten, Strecker, & Law, 2005). Component is defined as a software module associated with composing a page that supports activity of the user on a page. A sequence must have at least one component. Components in a sequence are classified into initial, mandatory, optional, and hidden optional states depending on their roles.

Initial state denotes a component, which a user is forwarded to when entering a sequence is the initial state of the sequence. Mandatory state refers to a component which the user has to enter in order to exit to another sequence is the mandatory state of the sequence. Optional states include set of components accessible to the user. Hidden optional states relate to set of components not accessible to the user until some conditions are met. A wide class of particular protocols defining system behavior can be flexibly defined using the above discussed sequences, states, and components.

Instantiation

Invite has been instantiated using Fusebox and ColdFusion MX. Note that the implementation per se is again, of secondary importance. What matters from design research perspective is the description of technical organization and behavior of the system, regardless of particular technologies chosen. As Invite is a platform rather than a specific ENS, instantiation involves implementing particular ENS features and processes using Invite protocol specification and component models. For example, Inspire as a synthetic concept has been instantiated on Invite: a technological concept. The instantiation of Inspire on the Invite platform emulates the functionality of the original system. An example screenshot from Inspire implementation is shown on Figure 8.

ALTERNATIVES

Design research projects may vary in their primary objectives not only by their target artifact classes, but also by the type of questions they are seeking to answer. Some projects may be directed towards better understanding the design problem and type of meta-requirements, while others may propose a conceptual type of solution for a given class of problems, and still others may aim at producing more technological solution. A representational

framework introduced earlier seeks to distinguish between these types of research objectives and indicates aspects that need to be addressed regardless of the questions posed.

Analysis of meta-requirements for ENS briefly discussed in this chapter derives from kernel descriptive and normative theories related to the study of negotiations, as well as the fields of negotiation and decision analysis and negotiation support systems. Based on the kernel theories, the analytical layer allows specifying what kind of capabilities and features and processes must be supported by the electronic negotiation system solutions. The salient system features and processes identified in this layer could be tied to other human factors related to the adoption and use of such systems in light of behavioral studies. For example, experimental assessment of the impact of providing agent assistance in negotiations has been carried out in (Vahidov, Chen, & Feng, 2005). Other work investigated the value of including visual analytical aids in the process of negotiations (Weber, Kersten, & Hine, 2006).

Figure 8. "Invite" implementation of "Inspire"

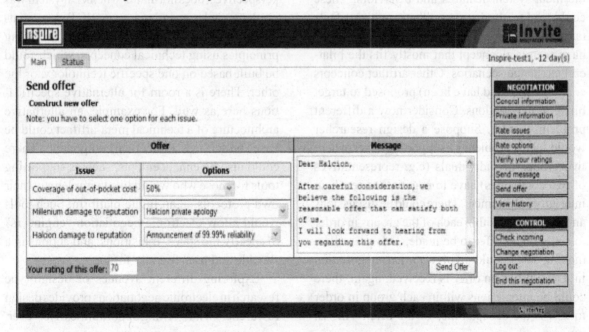

The Inspire project provided a synthetic concept that showed how different communicational and analytical components could be combined in an architecture that would provide a basis for negotiation support on the web with enhancing and complementing negotiators' natural intellectual capacities. Goodness of design has been the driving motivation behind the Invite project that resulted in a platform flexible enough to enable designers to spell out specific protocols and "look and feel" for the user interface. The flexibility of the platform is highly beneficial to the researchers, e.g. it allows comparing different negotiation mechanisms while maintaining the same user interface, or varying user interfaces while preserving the same mechanism to effectively study the impacts of the both.

The analytical study of ENS and Inspire/Invite systems can be viewed as different design research projects. These projects essentially constitute a design research program in electronic negotiation systems. Alternative approaches to ENS are possible at each layer of the framework, and in totality could be viewed as design-type research stream.

Different types of problem contexts could lead to different meta-requirements in terms of the meta-system features and behaviors. These could lead to alternative synthetic meta-artifacts targeting those meta-requirements. Inspire, as we have seen is a concept that mostly fits the bilateral exchange scenarios. Other artifact concepts could also be (and have been) proposed to target bilateral negotiations. Consider now a different problem context. Suppose a design researcher would face a problem of supporting cases where two groups of individuals (e.g. representatives of two companies) have to negotiate to reach an inter-group agreement. There could be discussions and exchanges within each of the groups in order to settle on an offer to be made. This pre- offer-making stage could involve a micro-negotiation in itself. When an offer is received, again, there could be interactions within each group in order to assess the acceptability of the offer. This is, metaphorically speaking a case of a "wheel within a wheel."

What kind of system solution could effectively address supporting the participants in the case like above? Certainly, there would be separation of modules managing interactions within and between the groups. There would be group-level "private" sections for interactions within the group, and perhaps also individual-level "private" sections to model an individual's preferences. Perhaps, the architecture could be more adapted to serve group decision making, rather than negotiation within the group. In this case, tools like Analytical Hierarchy Processing could be used to aggregate preferences within the group and weight alternative offers to submit. The possibilities of design meta-solutions for such cases are numerous and fascinating.

What about the alternatives for the technological layer? Since Invite can accommodate a variety of bilateral negotiations, could it be said that it is the only viable technical meta-solution? It does provide an elegant framework for specifying a wide variety of ENS, regardless of the choice of particular technologies used in its instantiation. At the technological layer, from the design research perspective it does not matter whether a system was implemented, say, in Java, or in .NET. What matters is that it shows the architecture and working principles using technical concepts, which could be built based on one specific technology, or the other. There is a room for alternative specifications here as well. For example, an alternative architecture of a technical meta-artifact could be based on services, rather than components. There could also be enhancements, such as supporting tools for those who would like to implement their own protocols on an Invite platform. Such tools would allow electronic negotiation "engineers" to specify the states, transitions, and actions in a flexible and user-friendly format.

Exploring different avenues of design-type research in electronic negotiations provides design researchers with exciting opportunities. However, rather than embarking on such problems in a haphazard manner, it would be useful to provide researchers with an informative guiding framework could help them better organize and scope their research projects. In this respect, at least from the analytical point of view some typology of possible negotiation problems would be helpful.

In Ströbel (2003) a taxonomy for electronic negotiations, called "The Montreal taxonomy" is described. The authors present the taxonomy "as a contribution to a more structured and methodological electronic negotiation engineering approach." One of the key goals of the taxonomy is "assist the conceptual design of electronic negotiations and support the abstraction necessary for the development of the generic electronic negotiation engines."

The taxonomy focuses only on the types of negotiations where certain rules apply. It does not consider completely unstructured cases, where any participant could make any proposition without restrictions. The taxonomy adopts the phase model of negotiations, and targets what is referred to as "intention" and "agreement" phases. The intention phase includes the following tasks: offer specification; offer submission; and offer analysis. The agreement phase involves offer matching; offer allocation; and offer acceptance. Furthermore, the taxonomy distinguishes between exogenous vs. endogenous, and explicit vs. implicit classification criteria. These, in combination result in four criteria categories.

Exogenous criteria are defined by the problem context, and thus are not under the control of a designer. Explicit exogenous criteria serve as the basis for formal description of the business context. Within this quadrant two categories of criteria are suggested: business domain and business model. The business domain criteria can be formulated to describe the essence of the business context, e.g. market structure, nature of negotiation object, relation of the negotiating agents (e.g. buyers vs. sellers). Business model specifies the role of the business within the domain, e.g. consulting com-

pany. As a result of defining the explicit criteria a set of implicit criteria may be derived. These are less formal, "soft" sort of criteria; however, they can have a significant impact on the course of negotiations. Examples include culture, ethical standards, reputation, and the like.

The endogenous criteria describe "the choices made, the parameters determined within the design of electronic negotiation instance." The explicit endogenous criteria represent the most well-defined and comprehensive part of the taxonomy. We will briefly discuss some of the categories. First, the taxonomy proposes criteria based on the roles of participants. Within this category the subcategories of participation, agents, admission, identity, and collusion are defined. With respect to participation, there are cases of bilateral, multilateral, and mediated settings. With respect to agents, there could be a single or multiple agents per each side involved in negotiations. Admission refers to whether there are restrictions on admission of agents. Identity relates to whether the negotiations are conducted in an anonymous or exposed mode. Collusion refers to whether collusions among the agents are allowed.

The next major category concerns the overall rules governing the negotiation process. The following subcategories are included: variation, specifying whether the rules are fixed or could be modified during negotiation; rounds, i.e. single- vs. multi- round process; stages, which provide the possibility of changing rules at each stage; and concurrency, dictating whether a given agent could be involved in only one negotiation at a time, or could interact with multiple counterparts.

The third category relates to the issues related to offer specification. The subcategories include: attributes (issues), which could be single, multiple, or undetermined; values, specifying whether in an offer a given attribute may have single or multiple values; relaxation, relating to whether values could be specified as flexible vs. fixed; structure, implying whether the number and types of the attributes may or may not change during negotiations; relation, defining whether offers could be made in an independent, parallel, or sequential fashion; and object, mostly dealing with whether offers could be made regarding a single object, or object bundles.

The offer submission category includes the subcategories of sides, referring to whether only one or multiple sides could make offers; position, meaning if an agent could assume only a single role (e.g. a seller) or multiple roles; activity, including unrestricted mode, when an agent can submit as many offers as he or she desires vs. restricted mode, where certain rules apply; and direction, which includes reverse mode, when, say a buyer makes an offer to the seller vs. forward mode, when a seller advertises a deal first, vs. haphazard mode. Other major categories include offer matching, offer allocation, offer acceptance, information, and strategy. The list of possible implicit criteria includes: Pareto-efficiency, social welfare, fairness, convergence, stability, truth revelation, and nature of gains.

The taxonomy gives an idea of how many possibilities of designing e-negotiation system concepts are there for the interested design researchers. Past work on such systems could be viewed in light of the multi-dimensional taxonomy in order to identify major gaps to be addressed by design researchers. It would be highly beneficial for design-type research to develop similar taxonomies or typologies for other types of meta-artifacts.

REFERENCES

Beam, C., & Segev, A. (1996). *Automated negotiation: A survey and the state of art*. Berkeley, CA: Hass School of Business.

Carbonneau, R. A., Kersten, G. E., & Vahidov, R. (2008). Predicting opponent's moves in electronic negotiations using neural networks. *Expert Systems with Applications, 34*, 1266–1273. doi:10.1016/j.eswa.2006.12.027

Chavez, A., & Maes, P. (1996). *Kasbah: An agent marketplace for buying and selling goods*. Paper presented at the First International Conference on the Practical Application of Intelligent Agents and Multi-Agent Technology. London, UK.

Chen, E., Vahidov, R., & Kersten, G. E. (2005). Agent-supported negotiations in the e-marketplace. *International Journal of Electronic Business, 3*(1), 28–49. doi:10.1504/IJEB.2005.006387

Coehoorn, R. M., & Jennings, N. R. (2004). *Learning on opponent's preferences to make effective multi-issue negotiation trade-offs*. Paper presented at the 6th International Conference on Electronic Commerce. Delft, The Netherlands.

De Moor, A., & Weigand, H. (2004). Business negotiation support: Theory and practice. *International Negotiation, 9*, 31–57. doi:10.1163/1571806041262106

Dzeng, R.-J., & Lin, Y.-C. (2005). Searching for better negotiation agreement based on genetic algorithm. *Computer-Aided Civil and Infrastructure Engineering, 20*, 280–293. doi:10.1111/j.1467-8667.2005.00393

Faratin, P., Sierra, C., & Jennings, N. R. (2002). Using similarity criteria to make issue trade-offs in automated negotiations. *Artificial Intelligence, 142*(2), 205–237. doi:10.1016/S0004-3702(02)00290-4

Gulliver, P. H. (1979). *Disputes and negotiations: A cross-cultural perspective*. Orlando, FL: Academic Press.

Kersten, G., Law, K. P., & Strecker, S. (2004). *A software platform for multi-protocol e-negotiations: An InterNeg research report 04/04*. Montreal, Canada: InterNeg Research Center.

Kersten, G., & Noronha, S. J. (1999). WWW-based negotiation support: Design, implementation, and use. *Decision Support Systems, 25*, 135–154. doi:10.1016/S0167-9236(99)00012-3

Kim, J. B., Kersten, G. E., Strecker, S., & Law, K. P. (2005). *Component-based software protocol approach: InterNeg research papers INR 01/05.* Montreal, Canada: InterNeg Research Center.

Kim, J. B., Strecker, S., Kersten, G. E., & Law, K. P. (2005). *Towards a theory of e-negotiation protocols.* Paper presented at the Group Decision and Negotiation (GDN). Vienna, Austria.

Liang, T.-P., & Huang, J.-S. (2000). A framework for applying intelligent agents to support electronic trading. *Decision Support Systems, 28*(4), 305–317. doi:10.1016/S0167-9236(99)00098-6

Neumann, J. V., & Morgenstern, O. (1944). *Theory of games and economic behavior.* Princeton, NJ: Princeton University Press.

Nguyen, T. D., & Jennings, N. R. (2004). *Coordinating multiple concurrent negotiations.* Paper presented at the 3rd International Conference on Autonomous Agents and Multi-Agent Systems. New York, NY.

Raiffa, H. (1982). *The art and science of negotiation.* Cambridge, MA: Belknap Press of Harvard University Press.

Thiessen, E. M., Loucks, D. P., & Stedinger, J. R. (1998). Computer-assisted negotiations of water resources conflicts. *Group Decision and Negotiation, 7*(2), 109–129. doi:10.1023/A:1008654625690

Vahidov, R. (2007). Situated decision support approach for managing multiple negotiations. In Gimpel, H., Jennings, N. R., Kersten, G., Ockenfels, A., & Weinhardt, C. (Eds.), *Negotiation and Market Engineering* (Vol. 2, pp. 179–189). Berlin, Germany: Springer-Verlag. doi:10.1007/978-3-540-77554-6_13

Vahidov, R., Chen, E., & Feng, Z. (2005). *Experimental evaluation of agent-supported e-negotiations.* Paper presented at the Group Decision and Negotiation 2005. Vienna, Austria.

Vahidov, R., & Neumann, D. (2008). *Situated decision support for service level agreement negotiations.* Paper presented at the 41st Hawaii International Conference on System Sciences (HICSS). Waikoloa, HI.

Weber, M., Kersten, G., & Hine, M. (2006). Visualization in e-negotiations: An inspire ENS graph is worth 334 words, on average. *Electronic Markets, 16*(3), 186–200. doi:10.1080/10196780600841571

Chapter 8
Scientific Principles Applied to Design–Type Research

ABSTRACT

If design-type research shares deep roots with the traditional scientific research, then the principles advanced by the philosophers of science should be applicable to it as well. The purpose of this chapter is to show how these principles could be interpreted through the lens of design-type research. Induction in DTR implies extracting features of the implemented particular solutions with subsequent generalization. Deduction means inferring meta-requirements and, subsequently, features of meta-systems based on kernel theories. Ockham's razor as a criterion favors simpler designs. Popper's falsifiability criterion means that design of meta-artifacts should be informative. Lacatos's protective belt translates into separating the immutable core of a design theory from the part that is potentially modifiable. Kuhn's paradigms in design establish a given core design statement for a particular kind of meta-artifact, which drives focused research in that area. Feyerabend's anarchy encourages alternative design visions. The aesthetics criterion plays an important part in recognizing forms in meta-artifacts.

LEARNING FROM TRADITIONAL SCIENCE

The previous chapters advanced various arguments in support of the claim that there is no essential difference between traditional scientific research and that of the design-type. Science aims at discov-ering hidden mechanisms behind the multitude of world phenomena to simplify our understanding of the reality and enable prediction of unfolding events. We have argued that design can also be seen as a kind of discovery, whereby predictive statements are made about future evolution of the needs of humankind and the emergence of the corresponding forms in response to this evolution.

DOI: 10.4018/978-1-4666-0131-4.ch008

Professional designers engage in the procreative type of work devising new types of products, processes, tools, techniques, and the like in their attempts to tackle new specific requirements in their respective fields. The new artifacts exhibiting elements of various pertinent forms appear in the course of technological evolution, and some of them prove to be valuable for the given problem contexts. Many fail to fulfill the requirements, either because of the inappropriateness of the solution, or the failure to correctly describe the requirements (including the case of their sheer non-existence). Yet some others appear to serve the purpose for a limited time until a better solution is prompted, most likely by the advances in the technological (inner) environment.

In the course of design it is only natural to rely on the elements of the existing familiar objects and incorporate them as part of the new designed environments to promote ease of learning and use by the target artifact users. The use of metaphors, therefore, has been one of the crucial techniques in the designer's arsenal. The desktop metaphor, for example had proven to be tremendously successful in promoting computer usage by non-technical professionals. So was the employment of shopping cart by the online retailers as it eased the transition to the electronic ways of shopping. On the other hand, not all metaphors are necessarily useful. Virtual beings that create the illusion of a personality and battle the machine nature of computers agreeably catch one's imagination. However, use of the synthetic characters in various application contexts is not readily justified. A meta-study of the value of providing synthetic animated characters did not reveal any evidence of their usefulness other than in gaming applications (Dehn & Mulken, 2000). The clip character introduced in Microsoft Office was of the dubious value to the users. Perhaps, in this case there was no need for an "artificial" metaphor.

There are also examples of requirements that are valid, but the solutions offered are relatively short-lived and are soon superseded by the newer solutions, typically incorporating the elements of newer technological advances. The floppy disks have enjoyed the popularity for about two decades or so as they have been an adequate solution for the truly existing requirement. Zip disks, introduced in 1994 were seen as a new promising technology, but had a much shorter life as an innovation. CD and DVD technologies proved to be superior in providing much larger storage capacities. In the domain of databases the early suggestions of data organization included hierarchical and network models. These, again had a valid requirement to address: the need to properly store large amounts of data and facilitate their effective and efficient access and manipulation. However, the emergence of the relational model had proved to address this requirement much better, and thus is the most popular format employed in modern systems. Even the more "advanced" object-oriented database model does not seem to be replacing the relational schema, while the vendors of the latter incorporate some object-oriented features in their products without having to make significant changes to the relational core.

In the search process, thus, the artifacts appear as the representatives of the new species in the course of technological struggle for survival, and many of them perish because of sheer inadequacy, or because they are replaced by better fit rivals. Then, why not let this evolution flow in its natural turbulent course? Why bother about design-type research and predictions about "meta-requirements" and "meta-artifacts"? What is the value of the design-type science?

The ultimate response to this nagging question is to consider the value of science to the practice. Why do science at all? Why not let in any individual case the observer to make his or her conclusions about the observations and make the corresponding specific interpretations and predictions without the employment of scientific knowledge? While any observation is particular in some sense, science allows employing the knowledge of inherent commonalities to minimize the errors and the associated waste of resources in practice. Similarly, design-type research also aims at capturing the commonalities in an attempt to make the practical designer's work more structured. Evolution is a powerful process, but it is tremendously wasteful. Failed products, temporary solutions, wastage of resources and turbulent economies with all the negative impacts on humankind are the by-products of technological evolution.

Employing design as a kind of science can help minimize wastage and help steer technological progress in promising directions. Scientifically capturing the present or imminent type of needs and suggesting general types of solutions could help the practitioners make more informed and substantiated decisions. Abstract artifacts as ultimate products of design-type research could help in more definitive description of the present and imminent future needs in multiple domains of human practice. Thus, design-type research, properly conducted and communicated could play a significant positive role in the course of progress.

Yet, what does it mean for design-type research to be properly conducted? What are the principles, or guidelines the designer-researcher should follow to ensure that a particular project would result in a solid generic solution/finding? Is there a need for establishing a completely novel tradition for such research? As cited earlier, an influential work on design-type research proposed a number of guidelines to be followed for design researchers (Hevner, March, Park, & Ram, 2004). With all due respect to this awareness-rising publication, one would wonder whether reliance on the existing millennia-long tradition of conducting scientific inquiries could be of any use in directing design-type projects.

If we are convinced that design type research is akin to the traditional scientific research, then the teachings of the philosophy of science should be applicable to directing design-type inquiries, albeit with some adaptations and interpretations. Perhaps, there is no need to re-invent the wheel in building up the methodological body of knowledge

for design-type research. While this is, agreeably, a speculation, why not direct our attention to the modus operandi of traditional scientific research as the first attempt to define structural elements for less traditional "design as a science" activity.

This chapter looks into the application and interpretation of some of the well-established principles of science as they apply to design-type science. By no means is the coverage of the principles claimed to be comprehensive and complete in some sense. Rather, it illustrates (hopefully) the possibility of putting the teachings of the philosophy of science into the design-type research perspective.

INDUCTION AND DEDUCTION

Major components of design theory, as mentioned in the previous chapters has been conceptualized as a tuple $< R, S, M >$, including meta-requirements, meta-system, and method for developing systems of type S to satisfy requirements of type R (Walls, Widmeyer, & El Sawy, 1992). The two essential approaches in the history of science to arriving at theoretical knowledge are induction and deduction. How can these be applied in the context of design-type research?

Induction is the method of arriving at the knowledge of the general from the observations of the particular cases. Thus, a zoologist studying particular instances of different plants may find commonalities among them and suggest a new category of plant species. Though, as we've seen induction as an approach of generating new scientific knowledge has been criticized by some philosophers of science (in particular, by Popper) it could help a scientist in formulating theories, whose implicit hypotheses could in turn be further tested. In short, induction represents an attempt at a progression from observations to concepts, typologies, laws, and other components of scientific knowledge.

In design studies the term "constructive induction" has come to signify the approach by which design concept and problem representation co-evolve in the absence of a theoretical framework for a given type of artifact (Arciszewski, Michalski, & Wnek, 1995). It involves borrowing design elements from other related domains in an attempt to address the design problem at hand. For example, in Haverty (2002) the constructive induction has been advocated as a viable method for defining information architecture. This is somewhat different from the use of term "induction" implied in the context of the present book. Here, induction is understood as a process of moving from observations to generalizations, as it is traditionally understood in the context of scientific research.

In design-type science perspective, as we have noted earlier, an observation relates to a particular case of requirements in a given organizational/functional context, or a particular instantiation of a system, or a specific method employed. Thus, given a set of instances of similar particular requirements in a given general problem context one could view them as a set $\{r_1, r_2,...,r_n\}$, where n denotes the number of observations (i.e. the number of instances in which a particular type of requirements is being examined). These requirements could be broken into their key elements as describing a given desired function or feature the required system needs to support. Thus, r_1, for example can be further broken down into $\{r_{11}, r_{12}, ..., r_{1m_1}\}$. One could aggregate all of the requirement elements to create a "requirements space," and represent the presence of a particular element in for a given observation as 1 (exists) or 0 (does not exist) in a matrix form. Some of these elements may appear similar, and, thus could be combined into a single, more general (and abstract) requirement element. This is similar to "attribute construction" in the context of "constructive induction" method in engineering proposed in

(Arciszewski, Michalski, & Wnek, 1995). Then one could, in principle examine clusters of requirement elements and identify common types of requirements pertinent to a subset of instances. One could even attempt to identify typologies of such common meta-requirements. In other words, for a subset of similar requirement instances one could decompose these as follows:

$$\{r_1, r_2,...,r_n\} = \{R \cup sr_1, \{R \cup sr_2, ...\{R \cup sr_n\}$$

Here R represents the common part of requirements (meta-requirements), while sr refers to the part specific to that instance. In case several such sets could be extracted, a number of meta-requirements can be identified. The R, is thus factored out of the specific instances. This is similar to Aristotle's enumeration approach to induction. In practice, extracting requirements is not an easy task, as they do not exist as tangible objects, but are inherent in the needs and desires of system users. One possible method of collecting such requirements could be through a questionnaire. In creative problem solving Ackoff had described a method of eliciting the "wishlist" of telephone users (Ackoff, 1978). Something similar could be employed in research projects directed towards meta-requirements elicitation.

While the requirement collection for the subsequent induction may be a challenging task, treating existing systems as manifestation of requirements is more straightforward. Here, the analytical-level representation of existing systems, including their features and functions could serve as a surrogate for representing the requirements. The synthetic-layer description would help outline the characteristics of meta-systems (S). Again, the relevant features and functions of specific systems can be represented in a form

$$\{s_{i1}, s_{i2},...,s_{im_i}\}, i = \overline{1, n}$$

for *n* different system instances. Similar to the above, a meta-system concept(s) can be extracted as

$$\{ s_1, s_2,...,s_n \} = \{ S \bigcup ss_1, \{ S \bigcup ss_2, ..., \{ S \bigcup ss_n \},$$

where *S* refers to a meta-system, and *ss* relates to the specific part of the system. A method could also be constructed in a similar fashion by observing particular methods involved.

An early work by Alter on Decision Support Systems (DSS) can serve as an example of inductive generalization for clarifying the DSS concept and providing a taxonomy for such systems (Alter, 1977). This exploratory research has examined eight instantiated examples of DSS, outlining, in particular, their characteristics and further deriving different classes of DSS which fit a taxonomical dimension according to the degree in which system determined the decision output. The derived classes included file drawer systems, in which access to individual data items was provided; data analysis systems, which allow for means of data manipulation for ad-hoc retrieval; analysis information systems, which provide means of combining data from different sources; accounting models, which allow for accounting and financial type of calculations to assess the impact of decisions; representational models, which simulate the reality for assessing decisions; optimization models, which, provided with problem description allow for optimization of the solution; and suggestion models, which generate a proposed decision. The first three types were further categorized as data-based DSS, while the rest were fit under model-based DSS. Thus, an inductive process, in this classical case moved from the observation of real-life systems to the definition of various meta-DSS.

The scope of the inductive study may be more general, or it may instead focus on a specific type of a meta-system. For example, with regards to DSS research in (Zopounidis, Doumpos, & Matsatstinis, 1997) a survey of knowledge-based decision support systems for financial applications was performed (although not all of them were applied in real-life settings). The study had underlined some important implications of utilizing the DSS with the knowledge base component (meta-system) in the financial management contexts (meta-requirements).

Just to give another example of exploratory work that could be related to the inductive mode, in (Miles & Howes, 2000) a survey of various e-commerce sites have been presented that outlines some of the features of such sites. This potentially could also help at arriving at different meta-concepts of online commercial websites. The sites surveyed varied in their complexity, including, among others, the means for providing search, browsing, auctions, and 3D environments.

The inductive method ideally would start with the real-life applications, and thus has an advantage of being grounded in practical observations. But induction has its own drawbacks, in particular as applied to design-type research. First, as noted earlier, observing the present or imminent latent requirements is far from being an easy process. Requirements elicitation is by itself a non-trivial task for analysts studying particular requirements. Making claims on the nature of generic (meta-) requirements is, thus based on a shaky ground. Second, though an argument could be made that existing (relatively novel) systems may serve as "negative prints" manifesting the hidden requirements; they may not be adequately fitting the latter. Furthermore, these "novel" systems may be short-lived. Third, the focus on the existing systems and their features per se says little about the imminent new developments in the given type of meta-requirements. Fourth, even if all the previous points are answered satisfactorily, such an induction, although valuable, does not foster a true innovation on the part of a design science researcher (which, as argued previously does not invalidate the effort as a research and design, yet exclude the important innovation aspect of work).

Deduction implies progression from more generic to specific, i.e. from theoretical core to particular statements inferred from the theory. Deduction implies some creative non-observational component in advancing the theories. Thus, deduction is inherently more "design-oriented." In chapter 1 the conflicting views on the design process have been pointed, one that espouses systematicity in designing, and the other, which maintains that design is an inherently creative, sort of artistic activity that defies systematization. For the most part the implication of the former view is that a certain theoretical knowledge about a given problem domain and the related artifact types could be applied to guide the design process. This is, basically deduction. A theoretical core (generic design principles and knowledge of a given domain) is used to make inferences from (i.e. to design) in regards with specific conditions (requirements) to produce predictions about expected observations (actual artifacts).

In (Zeng & Cheng, 1991) a proposed definition of an artificial system is given in terms of a syllogism "...as a logical system of deduction, where the major premise is the behavior principle of the system subjected to the natural law, the minor premise is the form of the system and the natural actions alike exerted on the system, and the conclusion is the function of the system in the environment. As deduction involves making inferences based on the rules of logic, the formal approaches to design fit well under this category of design efforts. For example, in (Brazier, Van Langen, Ruttkay, & Treur, 1994) formalization of design tasks and concepts has been proposed in terms of first-order predicate logic.

To mention a couple of examples of deduction-oriented views in a particular area, in (Carroll & Kellogg, 1989) the importance of theoretical knowledge (specifically related to the area of psychology) in design of Human-Computer Interaction (HCI) artifacts has been upheld. The authors argued that while hermeneutics plays a valuable role in this respect, the scientific body of knowledge about the problem domain, properly applied could be critical in informing the HCI design. In regards with HCI a process model incorporating deductive process into the iterative design of HCI artifacts has been introduced in (Mackay & Fayard, 1997). The authors showed how theories borrowed from psychology, sociology, anthropology and areas of engineering and arts could be employed and complemented by field studies and evaluation in the process of design.

Deductive approach in design-type research implies that a researcher claims the existence of a certain type of meta-requirements not simply based on generalization from the observations. These requirements are, so to speak, "invented" to some extent. The existing solution to the given type of problem must be shown to have some inadequacy. A new meta-solution is then advanced, largely based on logical reasoning.

To understand the similarities between deductive reasoning in traditional vs. design-type sciences consider an example of Einstein's special theory of relativity in physics. Einstein (through pure mental modeling) was concerned with the behavior of light in relation to a traveling observer. Having a solution that would adequately describe such behavior in accordance with Maxwell's description of electromagnetic waves was the requirement in this case. The then existing Newtonian solution failed to serve as a valid explanation. Thus, he invented a new solution by making a central claim of the constancy of the speed of light in relation to an observer. The special theory of relativity then was developed in a deductive fashion as a new solution.

Now let's take an example from the decision support (design) area. By the late Sixties computer technology had advanced to the point where its potential for improving managerial decision making was becoming clear. The nature of managerial decision making was being described as ill-structured, in particular through the works of Simon. This signaled the type of meta-requirements needed for supporting decision makers. The existing type of solution at the time featured management information systems, which were largely standard-report generating tools. The inadequacy of these in fulfilling the information needs of decision makers was pointed, in particular by Ackoff (1978). The newly posited requirements included delivering decision-centric information, ad-hoc querying, and "what-if" analysis among others. The kind of a solution that was being advanced in the 70s, termed decision support systems included capabilities and components that were thought of being better fit to the existing type of a problem. These were assumed to have a database, a model base, and user interface at the very generic levels. They proposed flexibility, interactivity, ease of use, possibility of "what-if" analysis, data querying, and other features, which were deemed to be adequate for managerial decision support.

Thus, the emergence of DSS was largely a deductive process, in the course of which theoretical claims were advanced concerning the requirements, which guided the development (invention) of a theory/meta-artifact. One could clearly see the parallels between these two examples as being different versions of the same general deductive process. Once the theoretical core is in place theory can expand and apply to more specific domains, perhaps in conjunction with theories from other disciplines. For example, financial applications of DSS would be considered as a subtype of generic model enhanced by the theoretical apparatus from the area of Finance. Just like a traditionally scientific theory can be tested through predictions and observations, the particular instantiations of meta-artifacts serve as a way to produce concrete system-observations, thus concluding the deductive chain. Although observations (concrete systems) per se are not the aim of a researcher, they serve as a way to assess the theoretical core, and thus the validity of the deductive process. Some journals (e.g. "Interfaces") require the system concept to be implemented within a specific context for a given research work to be publishable.

Can the emergence of the DSS concept be elevated to the status of a scientific finding? Was the DSS-form an invention or a discovery? As we have argued earlier, the criterion of truth espoused by the traditional science can be expanded to DTR as well, meaning in this respect the adoption and usage of the given artifact-form. In other words to ask whether the DSS meta-artifact is true is the question of assessing its wide usage across multiple application areas, both for private or organizational decision support. But it could only be done with the hindsight. DSS as a form has found a multitude of applications and its essential features are behind many different decision support tools in usage. Modern spreadsheets with their impressive arsenal of tools are so widely adopted that knowing how to use them has become the matter of basic computer literacy. Their capabilities allow quick creation of model-based DSS instantiations. The rise of data warehouses, on-line analytical processing, business analytics and other related terms all point in the direction of data-based decision support. Thus, at least in its most generic form the DSS is a *true* meta-artifact, and its appearance was a result of scientific *discovery*.

Like induction, deduction has its own potential pitfalls. With deductive process, there is always an element of invention in the core theory. The central claims and the components of the theory are not simply results of mere generalization. In the chapter on science we have seen that alongside with the legal scientific disciplines, the pseudosciences had developed with their own set of (unsupported) premises, claims, and predictions. An overly inventiveness at the core of the deductive process may lead to models far distanced from their respective aspects of reality. This is not to imply that branches of pseudo-design-type sciences can be seriously expected to develop. However, the claims of a given design theory must be carefully investigated and checked with the intended real-life application domain. Often, design publications start out with the claim stating that there is a need for a certain type of artifacts. The typical cliché opening sentence in many publications proposing a new type of a solution reads something like "modern business environment is characterized by globalization trends, growing importance of technology, intensified competitive pressures…" etc., and thus there is a need for artifact X that would somehow improve our abilities to cope with all those challenges. In the best case a couple of common references would be added to add the flavor of legitimacy of these claims.

However, is there really a need for the artifact X? While it is true that its impact (and thus, its truth) may only be assessed with the hindsight, there must be some way to at least initially verify the validity of the claims. Before committing to the particular direction of meta-artifact development that could lead, in some cases with high-impact papers, to a new stream of research, some effort is needed to legitimize the central claims, and, perhaps stop the deduction from going in the wrong direction. For example, is there need for automating business negotiations? Is it feasible at all? Would business subscribe to conduct, let's say supplier contract negotiations in an automated fashion? Automated negotiations perhaps are beneficial in some well-structured domains, but their wide-spread adoption as a model of managing relationships with different groups of stakeholders seems highly doubtful. As one of my colleagues puts it "automation is fine when the printers negotiate between themselves." This is not in any respect to deny any value in research on software negotiation agents for business applications, but simply to point that critical questions need to be answered to avoid a potentially wasteful effort.

Both deductive as well as inductive processes in design-type research have their value, place, advantages, and shortcomings. They have been the basic workhorses of the traditional scientific. Their adequate application can help improve the efforts in producing successful meta-artifacts.

OCKHAM'S RAZOR

"Entia non sunt multiplicanda praeter necessitatem": this Latin phrase by William Ockham is what has become known as the Ockham's (or Occam's) razor. It translates as "things should not be multiplied beyond necessity." It has been accepted as one of the prime guiding principles of advancing scientific theories and explanations. It can be interpreted as follows: of the two alternative theories, which equally well predict a given set of phenomena, the simpler one should be preferred. The principle does not necessarily express an absolute truth, in other words, there is no guarantee of any sort that the simpler models will always be the true ones, the ones corresponding to the actual mechanisms behind the real-life phenomena. It is only based on the belief that the reality works in the simplest possible way. This is echoed by a famous quote from Einstein: "everything should be made as simple as possible, but not simpler." Indeed, a handful of basic formulas and specific values for physical constants define fundamental relationships based on which all of the complexity of the world builds. Simplicity or parsimony of hidden mechanisms and essential relationships is a fundamental belief shared by the scientists and the philosophers of science, and thus in evaluating newly advanced theoretical models it serves a critical role, indeed very much like the razor to deny overly complex constructions.

Parsimony does not imply that a simpler model should be chosen even if it comes at a cost of the accuracy of predictions. It becomes a guiding criterion if there is no other reason to judge one model more accurate than the other. Newtonian mechanics describes the behavior of moving objects with sufficient accuracy at speeds much lower than that of the light. If we were unable to gather observations at much higher speeds and have necessary equipment of sufficient precision, we might have been unable to decide between the

Newtonian and Einsteinian mechanics. Indeed, since the latter features more complexity to it, by employing Ockham's razor we would have to discard it (at least for a time). However, numerous observations (e.g. related to the decay of pions traveling at the near-light speed) have shown the predictions of the special theory of relativity to be precise. And precision is what the science values more than simplicity.

A classic example of the application of Ockham's razor in Astronomy is the advance of heliocentric model by Copernicus over the older Ptolemaic system. Ptolemy had earth at the center of the solar system, but had to introduce additional complexity (epicycles) to account for an apparent backward movement of the planets. Copernican model was more elegant, providing similar predictions, and thus, in the absence of other evidence it is preferred for its parsimony.

Can Ockham's razor be used in design of artifacts? In a short paper on commonality of quality criteria for design and science Bartneck lists several scientific principles, including Ockham's razor (Bartneck, 2009). Simplicity in design, implying the preference for the least complex solution to achieve objectives, is the analog of parsimony espoused by the science. Indeed, the value of simplicity has been stressed extensively in the design of systems and processes. Many authors advocate simplicity in design of artifacts. In a concise book on the topic Maeda had proposed ten laws of simplicity for design applicable, in particular to business processes and practices (Maeda, 2006). These included:

- **Reduce:** the simplest way to achieve simplicity;
- **Organize:** makes the system of many appear fewer;
- **Time:** savings in time feel like simplicity;
- **Learn:** knowledge makes everything simpler;
- **Differences:** simplicity and complexity need each other;

- **Context:** what lies in the periphery of simplicity is not peripheral;
- **Emotions:** more emotions are better than less;
- **Trust:** in simplicity we trust;
- **Failure:** some things can never be made simple;
- **The one:** simplicity is about subtracting the obvious and adding the meaningful.

It is easy to draw some parallels between these laws and guidelines in designing software artifacts and human-machine interfaces. For example, it has been pointed that simple designs promote trust – an important success factor for commercial websites (Karvonen, 2000).

Simplicity has been long recognized as one of the key principles in building usable systems. Since usability promotes system adoption, it is easy to see that among the alternative design concepts for a given problem context the simpler solution forms are likelier to appear in implemented artifacts. Therefore, simpler meta-artifacts have higher probability of being the "true" ones. In this sense, simplicity in design and Ockham's razor in science clearly have a common ground. Simplicity intuitively points in the direction of truth.

Since here we are mostly concerned design of software-based meta-artifacts, it is worthwhile to briefly mention the issues of complexity as they are treated in software engineering. The evolution of software construction processes had emphasized the importance of modularity, well reflected in the general system principles. The two crucial principles include those of cohesion and loose coupling. Cohesion relates to the degree to which parts of software module is focused on performing related tasks. Coupling refers to the degree of reliance of one software module on the other. These metrics relate to the simplicity of software design. Increasing cohesion and weakening the couplings lead to simpler software organization.

Apart from the above, other metrics of software metrics have been developed. In this respect, three types of complexities are distinguished: problem complexity, structural complexity, and procedural complexity (Tegarden, Sheetz, & Monarchi, 1995). Problem complexity deals with the inherent complexity of requirements. The so-called function point metric, which attempts to reflect the inherent complexity of the required solution could be regarded as an example (Albrecht, 1979). This type of complexity is generally assumed to be outside the designer's control.

Structural complexity relates to the organization of the software system in terms of its constituent modules and their interrelationships. Cohesion and coupling mentioned above fall in this category. Other well-known metric includes fan-in and fan-out with the former related to the number of other modules making calls to the given module; and the latter one to the number of other modules being called from the given one (Lucas, 1999). Procedural complexity reflects the complexity of the flow in implementing the logic of different parts of application. One well-known metric in this respect is cyclomatic complexity, which is based on the number of various paths through which the module logic could flow (McCabe, 1976). It has been recommended to control the complexity of the modules by monitoring their cyclomatic complexity metric. With the advance of the object-oriented paradigm in software development, new specific metrics have been proposed, including the categories of system-, object-, variable-, and method- level metrics (Tegarden, Sheetz, & Monarchi, 1995). For example, system level metrics included number of classes and maximum depth of class hierarchy, among others.

The above simplicity-oriented metrics and guidelines were proposed to improve design of concrete instantiated systems. Here we are concerned with the design of meta-artifacts, i.e. design as a scientific research process. The key ideas in software design improvement can be expanded to the domain of design-type research as well, albeit with significant changes. The three types of software complexity can be mapped to various aspects of design theories. The problem complexity, for example has much in common with the meta-requirements part of such a theory. Structural and procedural complexities correspond to the structure and behavior components of meta-system representations. However, the sets of actual metrics are hardly applicable directly to the artifacts-as-knowledge in a straightforward fashion.

Consider the meta-requirements, for example. In software engineering, the requirements are assumed to be given, thus being outside of the designer's control, as it has been mentioned above. The issue is to capture them correctly, and their implicit complexity can be estimated for the purposes of scoping the development project and assessing the required effort and time. For meta-requirements the picture is different. These relate to classes of requirements, and thus are much harder to capture. Their higher abstraction level makes it difficult to measure them using some sort of requirements-gathering process. Following the hypothetico-deductive process, the meta-requirements are often inferred from the respective kernel theories. The meta-requirements are essentially predictions, whose validity may only be reliably assessed with the passage of time and observation of multiple implemented solutions.

Thus, the meta-requirements are just predictions and alternative models for them may be proposed and they could co-exist simultaneously. Consider an example of on-line shopping support. Based on the kernel theories from cognitive psychology one could advance an argument (and it had been advanced many times) that in the presence of volumes of information and a large number of purchase decision alternatives shoppers are susceptible to information overload. Thus, there could be a (meta-) requirement to provide guidance to the shoppers by employing methods to rank product choices available through a particular retailer's website, in addition to conventional browsing and searching. The alternative meta-requirement is to provide the shopper with simple traditional searching and browsing tools. The latter is clearly a simpler model of meta-requirements. If an experiment involving the two versions of website prototypes does not reveal significant differences in relevant variables (e.g. satisfaction, usefulness, correctness of choice, etc.) then Ockham's razor may be invoked. This is, admittedly, somewhat simplified example, as a lot depends on which ranking method was employed. A more comprehensive approach would compare multiple ranking methods, or conduct a survey of such studies before arriving at a conclusion. But, suppose a survey of the assessments of various ranking mechanisms had lead to inconclusive results. Then, by Ockham's razor, the search & browse meta-requirement should survive and the ranking-based one should be abandoned.

Assuming that meta-requirements are well-justified, the next step is to advance a type of solution, which would satisfy them. Here, the meta-system is essentially a prediction about the form and behavior, which will be present in the instantiated systems addressing the targeted type of requirements. Ockham's razor dictates that among several meta-system proposals, which perform (more or less) equally well the simplest one should be preferred over the more sophisticated alternatives. The design implications of simpler solutions are evident: they would most likely require less time to be implemented in concrete systems; the latter would be better testable, maintainable, and evolvable. For these reasons the practitioners would most probably opt for these simpler forms, and this justifies application of Ockham's razor for the prediction of future meta-artifact structures.

In terms of complexity of meta-systems one could distinguish (following the different kinds of complexity measures in software engineering) structural and behavioral complexities. We have mentioned fan-in and fan-out as being classical metrics in software design. This essentially relates to the number of components of the system and the intensity of links among them. As meta-systems consist of a number of components, which in turn may be broken down into their constituent components, the structural complexity of a meta-system depends on the number of its constituent parts, and the complexity of the parts themselves.

To give an example, consider a kind of software entity, which is referred to as "agent." We will say more about the agents later in the book, but essentially they can be viewed as active software units, something akin to the metaphor of "software robots." Among different types of agents the category called "deliberative" or "planning" agents features the most sophisticated designs as they are designed with the purpose of mimicking explicitly the different kinds of mental states of human beings (Wooldridge & Jennings, 1995). These are fairly complex systems both in their architecture and behavior. Many forms have been proposed, one example being the Procedural Reasoning System (PRS), which had components for representing Goals, Beliefs and Intention Structure, Knowledge Area Library, Reasoner, Sensors, Monitor, Command Generator, and Actuator (Ingrand, Georgeff, & Rao, 1992). There may be problem domains where the structural and behavioral complexity of this level can be justified by the performance gains. However, a critical question is whether a much simpler solution type would suffice without having to recourse to more complicated designs.

Consider the domain of automated negotiations (assuming this is a justified meta-requirement of a sufficiently relevant scope). There have been proposals of "Belief-Desire-Intention" (BDI) agent solutions to promote improved negotiation process and outcome measures, in particular emphasizing the use of argumentation among the agents (Rueda, Garcia, & Simari, 2002; Sierra, Jennings, Noriega, & Parsons, 1998). As opposed to using BDI agents, consider a simple algorithm proposed in (Faratin, Sierra, & Jennings, 2000), which follows the heuristic: in determining the next offer in negotiations, calculate the one which minimizes the distance between the current offer and the opponent's latest offer without dropping the utility level; if such an offer cannot be found make a small concession and find the offer that minimizes this distance. Such a heuristic is easy to implement, both structurally and procedurally. If a study that compares the performance of the latter with the BDI agent solution does not reveal a significant superiority of the latter in terms of relevant criteria (e.g. joint gains), then the Ockham's razor would advocate abandoning of the idea of BDI agent use in negotiations.

Concerning the constituent components of a meta-artifact, their complexity should also be taken into account. This refers to both structural and procedural/time aspects. For example, consider an example where a module is used in some application context (e.g. supply chain management) for predictive purposes. One could think about using linear regression or neural network model for predicting the values of the variables of interest. Neural network models feature non-linearity, and thus are more complex than linear models. If performance-wise there is no significant difference, then one should opt for the simpler, linear model.

Nature appears to work on the basis of simplest possible mechanisms discovered by science. As humans are also part of the nature, then it is only natural to suppose that the evolution of human creation will favor simpler forms of artifacts. Design-type researcher would then be encouraged to be inclined more towards meta-artifact predictions that are simpler both in structure, as well as behavior.

POPPER'S FALSIFICATIONISM

Rigor and criticality are the key distinguishing characteristics of scientific endeavors. Empirical sciences, in particular are concerned about uncovering truths about the nature of their respective domains in order to provide descriptions, explanations, and predictions. Popper, as it has been discussed earlier provided a demarcation principle to distinguish between what constitutes a legitimate theory in empirical sciences from pseudoscientific and metaphysical inventions and speculations (Popper, 1969).

Popper maintained that a legitimate scientific theory should allow deduction of definitive hypotheses, which could be tested by experimentation and observation. These hypotheses should allow for possible observational outcomes, which would overthrow, or falsify them. In other words the hypotheses should be falsifiable, which means that the theories themselves should be falsifiable as well. Moreover, the more room for potential falsification a theory allows (the more "risky" it is) the more preferable it should be.

Figure 1 compares schematically the case of three theories. The blank portion of the circle refers to all possible observational outcomes. The blackened portion covers those predicted/allowed by a theory. In this example theory I is superior to theory II in it empirical content. Theory three is not a scientific theory according to Popper, as it "explains" every possible outcome.

It is interesting to note the similarity between Popper's falsifiability principle and Shannon's notion of information content. Information content of a message, according to Shannon is inversely related to the probability of that message. The lower is the likelihood of receiving a particular message, the richer information it carries. Now, according to Popper, the higher room the theory allows for its falsification, the more empirically rich it is. Or to continue along the same lines, a good theory is the one that has *a priori* lower chances of surviving the falsifiability test, i.e. lower probability for a prolonged existence. If one can think of a theory as a sort of sophisticated message, then one would be able to say that the less probable this theory-message is (as it is allows for more restrictive hypotheses) the higher information content it has. In this sense, Shannon's information content and Popper's falsification principle are closely related.

But is there any guidance regarding the nature of a theory that would allow making judgments

Figure 1. Comparison of three theories

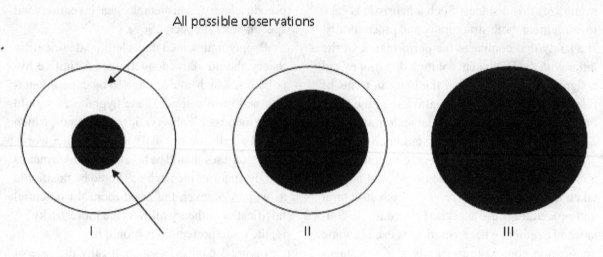

about its potential falsfiability? Popper proposed that simpler theoretical models are, in general, more susceptible to falsification. Thus, simplicity again was advanced as a key criterion, albeit from a different angle: as the means of assessing the empirical strength of a theory. In this regard, Popper proposed that models proposing linear relationships are more easily falsified than those advocating non-linear ones. Thus, a linear relationship between some variables of theoretical interest would constitute a stronger, bolder claim than non-linear one, which could be adjusted in case if its particular form is proves not to be in accordance with observation.

How would these insights help adapt the falsification principle to a design-type theory. It is not sufficient to say that simpler meta-artifacts should have a higher preference (as it has already been implied by Ockham's razor). After all, simplicity was proposed as a *consequence* of advising the falsificationist view. Bartneck very briefly mentions the role of falsifiability in design (Bartneck, 2009). He gives an example of inventing a certain device that increases somebody's karma. The effectiveness of such device, he notes is not possible

to falsify, and thus a design does not survive the Popper's criterion. He notes, however that "falsifiability plays a less important role in design in comparison to science, since it often deals with concrete and well-defined problems. The effects of a solution are usually easy to observe." Design-type research deals with meta-artifacts, which are not so much concrete, and the problems are not so well-defined. It will be argued in the remainder of the section that the falsifiability criterion plays the key role in design-type research and its value is in no way less important than in traditional science.

To understand the role of falsifiability, let's revisit the very essence of the principle. In a nutshell it states that a legitimate theory should be capable of exposing itself to observations, which would be contradicting its implications. A major part of "design" theory is a meta-artifact, which is abstract in nature, and thus unobservable in principle. The observations relate to concrete instantiated systems. If the description of a meta-artifact is vague by nature, it could potentially fit a multitude of observed systems, and thus wouldn't be falsifiable.

Let us consider a meta-artifact as an interface as suggested by Simon. Vagueness of description (and thus that of design) could relate to its outer or inner environments or the interface itself. Let's assume a particular design-type work targets the design of a shopping assistance tool to help customers of online retailers. Suppose a claim is made that online shoppers need an adequate level of automation in locating and purchasing the products they are looking for. Would this count as a definitive claim as part of meta-requirements? As long as electronic retailing survives, its customers will have some sort of support, which is "automated" to some extent. Whatever part of searching, browsing, ranking, filtering, auctioning and the like is automated in real websites, the above claim cannot be defeated. It is impossible to falsify it as any level of automation could be considered as "adequate."

Now, moving on to the "artifact-as-interface" perspective, suppose the designer presents an architecture of the system for shopper support as the one shown on Figure 2. Is there anything wrong with the proposed "meta-system"? It has the three major components denoted as user interface, program, and database. If the claim is that in response to the (meta-) needs for "adequate" shopping support the meta-systems of this structure should appear, then what are the chances of disproving this claim? Any information system can be considered as having three major parts. The claim, i.e. the design is not falsifiable. And it is utterly uninformative. The author has actually witnessed a presentation where exactly the same, admittedly very general "architecture" for a particular type of systems has been shown by the presenter.

What about the inner environment? Assume further, that a more detailed breakdown of the system into its key components is presented. For facilitating effective shopping support the designer introduces the module that would adjust to the shopper's profile as it dynamically changes throughout the shopping process. To this end

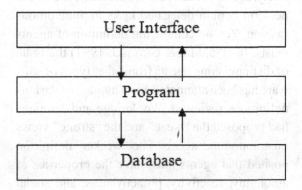

Figure 2. Uninformative design

the designer introduces the "adjustment" module in his/her system architecture, but fails to describe by what means the adjustment is actually implemented. In other words, while the adjustment itself as a function is part of the system, and yet any reference to the way it might be performed is omitted. It is a "miracle" component. In a more descriptive architecture, at least some kind of reference to the underlying model (e.g., a neural network, a decision tree, etc.), probably borrowed from other related disciplines would have to be provided. Otherwise, any means of implementing the adjustment would fit the proposed "design."

Thus, one way to translate Popper's falsifiability principle to design-type research context is through the demand for the definitiveness of the requirements, of the solution structure and behavior, and of the nature of the components from which a solution is synthesized. In particular, in terms of the structural representation of a meta-artifact it should differ in some respect from a more generic type (similar to object-oriented design where a subclass should differ in at least one feature from a superclass). As we've discussed the link between falsifiability and the concept of information content, the former implies that the design of the meta-artifacts should be *informative*.

To conclude the topic of falsifiability, it is well worthwhile to consider an example of "software agents," a research stream that became popular in computing disciplines in the nineties. Intuitively, agents are active software units, which can perform certain delegated tasks in autonomous fashion. Yet, no convincing definition of agents exists. In (Franklin & Graesser, 1997) the issue of distinguishing agents from other types of software has been attempted and a number of various definitions reviewed. Wooldridge and Jennings had proposed the "weak" and the "strong" views on autonomous agents. The "weaker" definition posited that agents must have the properties of autonomy, reactivity, proactiveness, and social ability (capability to communicate with user and/ or other agents). Now consider a word processing application, such as MS Word. It counts word may save a copy of a document in an autonomous fashion. It reacts as the user misspells words. It corrects minor misspellings autonomously. It proactively suggests the ways to re-word sentences as the user moves cursor over the dubious sentence. It has social ability as it clearly understands user commands and has the capability of conveying important messages to the user. Is it an agent? The "stronger" notion relates the possibility of ascribing mental categories, such as beliefs and desires to the artifacts. Then an elevator may be ascribed the desire to move people between the floors. A pressed button would make an elevator believe that someone needs its services. It then forms an intention to cater the service whenever it finishes its current task in progress.

Another popular definition of agents envisages a system that can sense its environment through sensors and affect it through effectors (Russell & Norvig, 2003). Then would read/write queries sent to a database count as sensing and affecting? The difficulties in defining the properties of agents make their outer environments ill-defined. Since much of ordinary software could more or less fit the definition of software agents, the claim that there is a need for agent solutions is virtually non-falsifiable. Moreover, apart from few types of BDI agents there is also no definitive accepted structure of agent software. The structural aspects

of agent designs range from means of modeling beliefs and intentions to simple computational models. Thus, in terms of being a meta-system the concept of a software agent is ill-defined. Software agent as a meta-artifact seems to be non-falsifiable. This is not to criticize attempts to build "truly" autonomous proactive solutions, yet the concept is in a definite need for clarification.

LACATOS'S PROTECTIVE BELT

The falsifiability criterion taken in its pure form is fairly (if not overly) critical to the process of advancing and testing theories. It dictates that, no matter how sell theory was constructed a single counter-example would suffice to discard it. Imre Lakatos has proposed the idea of protecting theoretical constructions from hasty blind falsification (Lakatos, 1980). He contended that a theory could be divided into its major component—the theoretical core, and the secondary one. The latter contains hypotheses, which he called "auxiliary" and they help make predictions based on the knowledge expressed in the core. Observations contradicting predictions would not necessarily lead to the dismissal of the whole theoretical build-up. What could be dismissed includes the auxiliary hypotheses, while the core could still be compatible with alternative hypotheses. Thus, this layer of hypotheses was termed a protective belt.

What would be the pattern of progress of a research programme (to use Lacatos's term) that reflects the presence of a protective belt? Let's start with the assumption that a theoretical core has been advanced by researchers. The core may be surrounded by the additional hypotheses, which help in advancing falsifiable statements concerning future observations. In case these predictions are indeed falsified, it deals a blow to the underlying theory, and results in a setback. However, as some insightful dedicated researchers recognize the weakness of the secondary, auxiliary hypotheses, they may attempt proposing alternative ones, which could lead to new predictions that are consistent with observations. Therefore, the presence of the protective belt may manifest itself through the theory advance, testing – setback – and further possible revival. This is, undoubtedly a speculative conclusion, but it appears to fit the "adjustment" philosophy behind the protective belt.

Could there be an analog of protective belt applied to design-type of research work? By drawing parallels with the above pattern of possible theory progression, it is easy to note that such a trial – modification – re-trial is quite characteristic of any design. In terms of design research, the streams that grew popular at some point and then subsided only to re-emerge in a stronger form are good candidates for signaling the presence of auxiliary hypotheses. The subsiding of a stream with further resurgence may not be the only indicator, and much research into various design-type research streams would be valuable in this respect.

There are some examples when a given type of an artifact, with its essential features and behavior had been abandoned by a majority of researchers, only to re-emerge strongly in a somewhat renewed form after its "recession." As an example, consider the evolution of neural networks. Initially conceived in the early forties, neural network models appeared to hold a strong promise to mimic cognitive tasks, such as perception. However, by the late Sixties, it became apparent that simple two-layer networks could not handle classification tasks in which the classes were not linearly separable (e.g. the famous "exclusive OR" problem). This deficiency has been pointed in a celebrated book by Minsky & Papert (1969).

Consider the example of neural network research in the context of the discussion of this section. The core belief was that neural networks, which combined units, which performed simple arithmetical transformations in a homogeneous fashion are capable of handling pattern recognition-related tasks. The "auxiliary" hypothesis (implicitly) was that they needed to be presented

with input and output signals for all neurons in order to learn the patterns. However, the cases were presented in which such networks would fail to perform. To make neural networks more powerful, introduction of other "hidden" layer units between the input and output one was necessary. But then, what should serve as an example output for such hidden neurons was not intuitive at all. This almost led to the abandonment of the entire core. After Minsky & Papert's publication only few believed in the future of neural nets. However, the discovery of the error back-propagation algorithm in the Eighties had resulted in an impressive renaissance in neural network area (Rumelhart, Hinton, & Williams, 1986). The auxiliary hypothesis that all neurons must have "natural" example output signals was abandoned and replaced by the new one. The latter resided on the insights that errors of neural network output (as compared to the desired output) could be propagated back through the layers, thus providing the way for all neurons to participate in the learning process. The success and further development of the area has been substantial.

KUHN'S PARADIGMS

Thomas Kuhn had introduced the concept of paradigms in the course of the evolution of sciences (Kuhn, 1962). He had distinguished between the "normal" periods of scientific development vs. the episodes of scientific revolutions leading to paradigm shifts. A paradigm can be described as an accepted framework, within the boundaries of which scientists operate during the normal period as "efficient puzzle solvers." Thus, Newtonian mechanics had defined a paradigm which lasted for over two centuries until Einstein's theory of relativity had entered the stage, thereby dethroning the by-then established system of views on the motion of bodies.

Following the hypothetico-deductive model of scientific progress, one could note that established paradigms help provide the momentum and direction of scientific research. They, as it were, assist the members of scientific communities to focus on research problems to tackle and help defining the gaps that need to be filled. This is truly the way of turning scientific progress into efficient puzzle-solving. Paradigms, once established, not only point the direction for the researchers to explore (possibly wrongly), but also resist attempts to accept changes. Thus, paradigms, unfortunately, make scientific progress somewhat susceptible to stagnation and help reviving the ghosts of Bacon's idols. In this respect, as mentioned previously, scientific progress viewed as a succession of different paradigms replacing one another is akin to the "punctuated equilibrium" model of biological evolution, cherished by Gould.

In this respect, it is interesting to draw an analogy between scientific research process and general search methods from Artificial Intelligence. One basic uninformed search method is the "depth-first" search. Consider a network of interconnected nodes with one node being designated as the starting one, and some other as the target one. The depth-first method would choose one of the nodes neighboring the initial one, and then progress by exploring the subsequent one, and so on moving on deeper and deeper until it finds the target one. The nodes could be considered as logical deductions from the theoretical core within the accepted paradigm. This is a somewhat stretching example, as there is no ultimate "target" hypothesis or observation in the course of scientific progress. Rather, as these "nodes" are explored additional evidence, or counterevidence in respect to the accepted paradigm accumulates. In fact, scientific progress is a kind of informed search. Yet, the paradigms provide the momentum to move in established directions while withstanding the attempts to explore other, alternative sets of views.

Depth-first search could be indeed effective if the paradigm indeed happens to lead in the right direction. Yet, certainly, it could lead to the dead end. As an example, the nineteenth-century thermodynamics could not cope with the problem of black body radiation. This dead end was resolved by the scientific revolution kindled by the invention of quantum physics. Nonetheless, the depth-first search is known to be efficient for its low memory requirements. Thus, by analogy, paradigms help dealing with the potential overload on the researchers that could be introduced if multiple alternative viewpoints on the basic theoretical assumptions were allowed. The analogy between the memory efficiency of the depth-first strategy and the efficient puzzle-solving view of the researchers in normal periods of science are hardly coincidental.

Is there evidence of the existence of paradigms in design-oriented research disciplines? Within the domain of computing sciences, perhaps the best example of paradigms and paradigm shifts comes from the area of software engineering. The latter does not so much target introduction of new meta-systems, but rather generic tools, techniques, principles, and processes to produce software-based systems. In other words, software engineering research produces (meta-) artifacts that help build well-designed concrete systems. From the ages of chaotic software development, when little structure was in place in developing software, the field had been moving in the direction of proper organization of software systems. Perhaps the biggest jump (paradigm shift) in this respect has been the advance of object-oriented development. One of the key insights has been the introduction of the information hiding principle. It had been a common assumption in the pre-object-oriented era that all the information within a particular application should be available to all modules within that application, it was hardly realized that this principle had led to the increased dependencies between different parts of the system, and thus it impeded the testability and maintainability of the systems. Information hiding, along with other principles of object-oriented design (e.g. moving away from hierarchical decomposition models) can truly be considered as a major paradigm shift—a very successful one, considering a wide adoption of object-oriented development tools nowadays.

Another example more closely related to the information system field is the emergence of data warehouses. Data-based decision support tools had been in existence before, and these largely relied on the possibility of forming ad-hoc queries to the existing operational database. However, it had been realized by the nineties, that informational needs for managerial analysis differ somewhat from what the operational databases have to offer. In particular, in terms of business analysis, managers needed access to information that displayed the development of key variables of interest through time. Furthermore, the capabilities of providing summary information, as well as "drill-down" facilities became deemed as important. This had led to the advanced of data warehouses, which were not intended for supporting date-to-date operations, but purely for managerial analysis and decision making purposes. One of the key characteristics of the data warehouses is that data entered there would remain unchanged for prolonged periods of time. Now, one of the key design activities of designing a good operational database is a proper level of normalization. The latter is done to avoid various anomalies related to the adding, deleting, or editing data (e.g. inconsistent records, loss of information). However, since data in data warehouses is not modified and is durable, the need for normalization is no longer there. This "dethroning" of the normalization principle in designing data-based decision support can be viewed as (however minor) an example of paradigmic shift.

FEYERABEND'S ANARCHY

The presence of paradigms and the hypothetico-deductive method employed by the scientists enables a logical, structured, in a certain sense even algorithmic progress of science towards new discoveries. The role of the major part of scientific communities as puzzle-solvers endows a scientist with the job of finding gaps in an incomplete puzzle and filling those gaps using efficient established procedures.

Feyerabend spoke against the somewhat bureaucratic organization of scientific communities. Indeed, he raised the issues to counter the established scientific method (Feyerabend, 1975). He noted, that any newly introduced theories and hypotheses, which are radically different from the established older theoretical frameworks would immediately find themselves at a disadvantage. Suppose there are two competing theoretical models, one that comes from the established theory, and the other one that is invented anew (perhaps by negating some parts of the existing theory). Then, according to the scientific method, the former one would be favored, and the latter one would be rejected as an unsubstantiated speculation, even if it happens to be closer to truth. The former model is, sort of a child of a well-respected theoretical parent, while the latter one is a poor unknown orphan, who has to make extraordinary efforts to succeed.

Feyerabend discussed a historical example concerning Galileo' findings in mechanics. He pointed that Galileo had to give up some of the old-standing assumptions to make his discoveries. Feyerabend proposed an anarchistic view on scientific progress, arguing that all invented hypotheses have a right for existence. "Anything goes" is his motto. Indeed, breadth of scientific explorations is what could characterize the anarchistic attitude. Here, an analogy with breadth-first search that looks to explore all available nodes from the given one can be made. More than that, the search in all direction would be massively parallel under the anarchy model.

Traditional science does not espouse the anarchistic approach. Rigor largely dictates a disciplined approach to advancing science in various domains. Yet, it is important to keep in mind that scientific theories are, in fact artifacts, and as such they can be said to be invented. Alternative conjectures and their theoretical offshoots are helpful in avoiding possible "dead ends" in scientific explorations.

In design-type research alternative problem and solution formulations could only be considered even more valuable, as researchers are attempting to "invent" the right meta-requirements and meta-systems while employing different candidate tools from the related disciplines. The author once submitted a paper on agent-based decision support and had one of the referees recommend rejection on the basis that some other agent-based solution had already appeared in the literature. "This gap has been covered" was the referee's comment without further detailed assessment of the work. The gaps are not covered that easily, especially in design-type research. For a gap to be covered there should be sufficient observational evidence (e.g. instantiated, adopted solutions), that speaks for the superiority of one solution over the other.

As another example of "anarchism," consider the case of dealing with uncertainties in decision making. Traditionally, uncertainties are tackled by the probability theory and statistics. However, the area of fuzzy sets and related possibility theory appeared as alternative ways of describing uncertainties. In fuzzy sets a given element may belong to a given set to some extent. For example, in traditional set theory a person who is 38 years old is classified either as young or not. In fuzzy sets, that person may belong to the set of young people to some degree. It would be awkward to speak about a probability of the person being young. In possibility theory the likelihood of an event is described in terms of possibilities, and these do not have to add up to unity, as it is the case with probabilities. The probability theorists are rather non-receptive of the developments in the fuzzy sets community. For the details the reader is referred to an excellent discussion of the topic in (Kosko, 1993). Despite the stronger, more rigorous mathematical foundations of the probability theory, systems based on fuzzy sets and fuzzy logic have found impressive range of applications from technological process control to consumer electronics.

ON BEAUTY

In his famous book, *An Essay on the Psychology of Invention in the Mathematical Field*, Jacques Hadamard set out to explore how mathematicians succeed in making crucial mathematical discoveries (Hadamard, 1954). He maintained that a solution to a given problem the mathematician has been working on often appears suddenly in a flash in its wholeness. Referring, among others to the experiences of Henri Poincaré he notes that these "eureka" moments can strike when a scientist is not even thinking about the problem he/she is trying to tackle. There are many other similar examples, e.g. Mendeleev allegedly invented the periodic table while he was dreaming (although some doubts in this case have been voiced [Baylor, 2001]).

Hadamard proposed that the scientist's brain is actively seeking the solution, even though the person may not be conscious of it. During this "incubation" period various combinations are tried out, and the brain performs a selective function, by which it chooses which solution to present to the consciousness. The criterion for the selection used, according to Hadamard, is the aesthetic beauty of the solution.

The aesthetic beauty, supposedly being in the realm of arts, appears to play an important role in guiding scientific explorations as well. Often findings are described as being "elegant" in some respect, although it is hard to define what exactly it means. Simplicity is often linked to beauty, and it appears to be the latter's important correlate. However, arguably, not everything simple is necessarily beautiful. Early human stone tools are quite simple, but they can hardly be called beautiful. The comprehensive discussion of the

Figure 3. Divergence – convergence

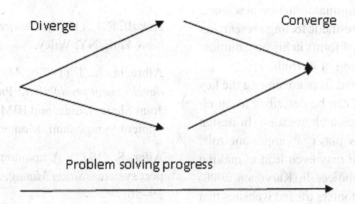

role of beauty in science is outside the scope of the present book, but few insights are worthwhile mentioning.

In a book called "The equation that couldn't be solved" the author entertains the idea that symmetry and proportion are the essential components of aesthetics (Livio, 2005). In particular, he discusses the highly abstract mathematical artifact advanced by French mathematician Galois, known as Group Theory as being highly aesthetic with inherent symmetry at its heart. He also draws a parallel showing how symmetry is present in beautiful musical pieces by Bach. The beauty and symmetry are also discussed at length in a book by Hofstadter that links patterns in mathematics, music, and fine arts (Hofstadter, 1979).

In February 2000 issue of Discover magazine an article titled provocatively "Do you love this face" was published along with the picture of a female face (Lemley, 2000). The face was actually created by aggregating the photographs of sixteen real females, and the author contended that the "average" was even more beautiful than any of the actual participants. While the topic is controversial, and the article is by no means "academic," however if the claim has some validity to it, how could this be explained? Why "averaging" would yield an aesthetic appearance?

It is interesting in this respect to re-visit Plato's doctrine of forms. Plato believed in the actual existence of pure forms in some domain, different from that of real objects. He found these forms to be beautiful in themselves, while earthly objects shaped after these forms had imperfections, i.e. additional details that made them somewhat less aesthetic. For example, while there is a form of a perfect circle (at least in somebody's mind) one cannot find one in the reality. Perhaps, averaging different people's faces does reveal a picture of the "form." If that's the case then Plato's forms indeed have aesthetic side to them. And since it is through forms (whether they do have their own domain of existence or are simply mental constructions) the scientists are attempting to

Figure 4. Divergence – convergence through phases of problem solving as a form

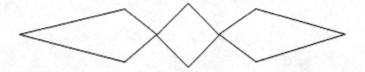

provide explanation of phenomena, then beauty does appear to be a legitimate criterion in science. It is then through the aesthetic feeling a researcher recognizes presence of forms in his/her solution, and the intuitive feeling of its truth.

Thus, symmetry and form are among the key components of what can be described as an elegant solution to a research question. In design in general aesthetics plays an important role. In user experiences it may even lead to making somewhat irrational choices. In (Karvonen, 2000) it was found that customers trusted websites that appeared aesthetic: "If it looks pleasant, I just trust it." But how does the beauty come into play in design-type research? Perhaps solutions that feature presence of forms and symmetries of some sort appear more aesthetic and will be preferred at some rather not obviously rational level.

Consider an example from the area of general problem solving that focuses on devising methods, techniques, and tools to help handle ill-structured problems. One well-known principle is known as divergence-convergence, implying that in the initial stages of problem solving the divergent processes should be stressed, followed at later stages with the convergent ones. Schematically, this principle can be shown as in Figure 3. The shape shown exhibits form and symmetry, and thus it adds an aesthetic flavor to the principle.

In Basadur (1994) the principle of convergence-divergence has been linked with the intelligence-design-choice model by Simon. The author has argued further that divergent processes should be stressed more during the intelligence phase, while convergent ones should be emphasized in the choice phase. The design phase should have a balanced mix of divergence and convergence. Graphically this model is expressed through a beautiful shape shown in Figure 4.

REFERENCES

Ackoff, R. L. (1978). *The art of problem solving*. New York, NY: Wiley.

Albrecht, A. J. (1979). *Measuring application development productivity*. Paper presented at the Joint Share, Guide, and IBM Application Development Symposium. Monterey, CA.

Alter, S. (1977). A taxonomy of decision support systems. *Sloan Management Review*, *19*(1), 39–56.

Arciszewski, T., Michalski, R. S., & Wnek, J. (1995). *Constructive induction: The key to design creativity*. Paper presented at the Third International Round-Table Conference on Computational Models of Creative Design. Heron Island, Australia.

Bartneck, C. (2009). *Using the metaphysics of quality to define design science*. Paper presented at the Fourth International Conference on Design Science Research in Information Systems and Technology. Malvern, PA.

Basadur, M. (1994). Managing the creative process in organizations. In Runco, M. A., & Chand, I. (Eds.), *Problem Finding, Problem Solving, and Creativity* (pp. 237–268). Norwood, NJ: Ablex.

Baylor, G. W. (2001). What do we really know about Mendeleev's dream of the periodic table? A note on dreams of scientific problem solving. *Dreaming*, *11*(2), 89–92. doi:10.1023/A:1009484504919

Brazier, F. M. T., Van Langen, P. H. G., Ruttkay, Z., & Treur, J. (1994). On formal specification of design tasks. In Gero, J. S., & Sudweeks, F. (Eds.), *Artificial Intelligence in Design* (pp. 535–552). Berlin, Germany: Kluwer Academic Publishers. doi:10.1007/978-94-011-0928-4_31

Carroll, J. M., & Kellogg, W. A. (1989). *Artifact as theory-nexus: Hermeneutics meets theory-based design*. Paper presented at the SIGCHI Conference on Human Factors in Computing Systems: Wings for the Mind. Austin, TX.

Dehn, D. M., & Mulken, S. V. (2000). The impact of animated interface agents: A review of empirical research. *International Journal of Human-Computer Studies, 52*, 1–22. doi:10.1006/ijhc.1999.0325

Faratin, P., Sierra, C., & Jennings, N. R. (2000). *Using similarity criteria to make negotiation trade-offs*. Paper presented at the 4th International Conference on Multi-Agent Systems. Boston, MA.

Feyerabend, P. K. (1975). *Against method: Outline of an anarchistic theory of knowledge*. London, UK: NLB.

Franklin, S., & Graesser, A. (1997). Is it an agent, or just a program? A taxonomy for autonomous agents. In Muller, J. P., Wooldridge, M. J., & Jennings, N. R. (Eds.), *Intelligent Agents III: Agent Theories, Architectures, and Languages* (pp. 21–36). Berlin: Springer Verlag. doi:10.1007/BFb0013570

Hadamard, J. (1954). *An essay on the psychology of invention in the mathematical field*. New York: Dover Publications.

Haverty, M. (2002). Information architecture without internal theory: An inductive design process. *Journal of the American Society for Information Science and Technology, 53*(10), 839–845. doi:10.1002/asi.10096

Hevner, A. R., March, S. T., Park, J., & Ram, S. (2004). Design science in information systems research. *Management Information Systems Quarterly, 28*(1), 75–105.

Hofstadter, D. R. (1979). *Gödel, Escher, Bach: An eternal golden braid*. New York: Basic Books.

Ingrand, F., Georgeff, M., & Rao, A. (1992). An architecture for real-time reasoning and system control. *IEEE Expert: Intelligent Systems and Their Applications, 7*(6), 34–44.

Karvonen, K. (2000). *The beauty of simplicity*. Paper presented at the ACM Conference on Universal Usability. Arlington, VA.

Kosko, B. (1993). *Fuzzy thinking: The new science of fuzzy logic*. New York, NY: Hyperion.

Kuhn, T. S. (1962). *The structure of scientific revolutions*. Chicago, IL: University of Chicago Press.

Lakatos, I. (1980). Falsification and the methodology of scientific research programmes. In Worrall, J., & Currie, G. (Eds.), *The Methodology of Scientific Research Programmes* (*Vol. 1*, pp. 8–101). Cambridge, UK: Cambridge University Press. doi:10.1007/978-94-010-1863-0_14

Lemley, B. (2000, February). Do you love this face?. *Discover*.

Livio, M. (2005). *The equation that couldn't be solved: How mathematical genius discovered the language of symmetry*. New York, NY: Simon & Schuster.

Lucas, H. C. (1999). The state of the information systems field. *Communications of the AIS, 1*, 1–5.

Mackay, W. E., & Fayard, A.-L. (1997). *HCI, natural science and design: A framework for triangulation across disciplines*. Paper presented at the 2nd conference on Designing Interactive Systems: Processes, Practices, Methods, and Techniques. New York, NY.

Maeda, J. (2006). *The laws of simplicity*. Cambridge, MA: MIT Press.

McCabe, T. J. (1976). A complexity measure. *IEEE Transactions on Software Engineering, 2*(4), 308–320. doi:10.1109/TSE.1976.233837

Miles, G. E., & Howes, A. (2000). A framework for understanding human factors in Web-based electronic commerce. *International Journal of Human-Computer Studies, 52*(1), 131–163. doi:10.1006/ijhc.1999.0324

Minsky, M., & Papert, S. (1969). *Perceptrons: An introduction to computational geometry.* Cambridge, MA: MIT Press.

Popper, K. R. (1969). *Conjectures and refutations: The growth of scientific knowledge.* London: Routledge & K. Paul.

Rueda, S. V., Garcia, A. J., & Simari, G. R. (2002). Argument-based negotiation among BDI agents. *Journal of Computer Science & Technology, 2*(7), 1–8.

Rumelhart, D. E., Hinton, G. E., & Williams, R. J. (1986). Learning representations by back-propagating errors. *Nature, 323*, 533–536. doi:10.1038/323533a0

Russell, S. J., & Norvig, P. (2003). *Artificial intelligence: A modern approach* (2nd ed.). Upper Saddle River, NJ: Prentice Hall.

Sierra, C., Jennings, N., Noriega, P., & Parsons. (1998). A framework for argumentation-based negotiation. In M. P. Singh, A. Rao, & M. J. Wooldridge (Eds.), *Intelligent Agents IV: Agent Theories, Architectures, and Languages: 4th International Workshop,* (pp. 193-208). Berlin: Springer-Verlag.

Tegarden, D. P., Sheetz, S. D., & Monarchi, D. E. (1995). A software complexity model of object-oriented systems. *Decision Support Systems, 13*(3-4), 241–262. doi:10.1016/0167-9236(93)E0045-F

Walls, J. G., Widmeyer, G. R., & El Sawy, O. A. (1992). Building an information system design theory for vigilant EIS. *Information Systems Research, 3*(1), 36–59. doi:10.1287/isre.3.1.36

Wooldridge, M., & Jennings, N. (1995). Intelligent agents: Theory and practice. *The Knowledge Engineering Review, 10*(2), 115–152. doi:10.1017/S0269888900008122

Zeng, Y., & Cheng, G. D. (1991). On the logic of design. *Design Studies, 12*(3), 137–141. doi:10.1016/0142-694X(91)90022-O

Zopounidis, C., Doumpos, M., & Matsatstinis, N. F. (1997). On the use of knowledge-based decision support systems in financial management: A survey. *Decision Support Systems, 20*, 259–277. doi:10.1016/S0167-9236(97)00002-X

Chapter 9
An Example of Application of Scientific Principles to Design–Type Research:
The Case of Online Shopping Support

ABSTRACT

This chapter aims at illustrating the application of important scientific principles using a sample design-type research project, which featured the development of a method for online shopping support. Existing schools of thought are described as potentially competing paradigms. A deductive approach is utilized to derive the required features of the artifact based on kernel theories. Falsifiability criterion is met by the development of the concrete form (in terms of structure and behavior) and the proposal of specific testable hypotheses. An example of auxiliary protective hypothesis is given. Ockham's razor is used in order to refute a more complex version of the method.

THE PROBLEM

This section aims to demonstrate the application of the scientific principles outlined in the previous chapter to a particular design-type research initiative. Needless to say, it is difficult to show in a comprehensive fashion how these different principles come to guide research process within the boundaries of a single project. A thorough approach would demand a meta-analysis of a particular design-type research stream targeting a given class of problems. Such a project, however is well beyond the scope of the book. Rather, here

DOI: 10.4018/978-1-4666-0131-4.ch009

the purpose is to illustrate the potential applicability of the guidelines advanced by the philosophers of science using the concrete case of design-type research work. The initial stages of the project have been published earlier in (Vahidov & Ji, 2005).

The case of a design project for online shopping support has been chosen in this chapter to serve as an illustration. This particular choice is an interesting one, as it represents a relatively recent type of problems for design-type research. Thus, in this respect it is somewhat premature to speak about an established (design research) paradigm, and a diversity (anarchy) of various approaches may be proposed by the researchers. On the other hand, the approaches may be based on the application of the previously developed generic methods, or adopted from other problem similar problem contexts. In such a case if an online shopping problem can be shown to be belonging to some known class of problems (problem solving, ranking, etc.), then there would be something akin to a pre-existing paradigm expanded to this particular one.

The problem is also interesting from the point of view of "design-as-a-prediction." Currently, it is not obvious, whether basic online shopping tools would be complimented in some substantial manner by more advanced capabilities. There are many exciting questions related to such a "predictive" perspective. Would the shoppers be willing to use advanced support tools? Would such a usage help companies in increasing their sales and customer satisfaction levels? Would the benefits of provisioning support tools offset the costs associated with their development and maintenance? Are their specific problem contexts or customer classes to which the tools would be beneficial? In short, do these tools have the right for existence? Are they the true IS meta-artifact forms? Only time could help answering these questions, yet design-type research attempts to illuminate the way the future may progress on one hand, and speed up this progress on the other.

The rapid rise of electronic commerce had opened new opportunities for design researchers as it allowed considering innovative ways in which the computational and communication capabilities of computer networks could be employed to improve performance of individuals, groups, and organizations. The degree of automation entertained by different researchers ranged from the effective and efficient delivery of information, to suggestion generation, and to automated decision making, including bidding and negotiation. For example, various software agent concepts were proposed to tackle different phases of buying, in particular those that could automated negotiations on behalf of buyers and sellers (Guttman, Moukas, & Maes, 1998). Some researchers have even speculated that customers in the digital economy would be equipped with powerful computational tools, which could seriously jeopardize businesses, since the assumption of bounded rationality may no longer be valid (Conway & Koehler, 2000).

The basic mechanisms employed by the majority of online retailers are browsing and searching capabilities bundled with the product catalogs (Detlor, Sproule, & Gupta, 2003). These represent fairly marginal improvements over the traditional paper-based catalogs, including: maintaining up-to-date product information; convenience of using drill-down capabilities via links; and quick access to information about product(s) of interest using provided search criteria. Could there be other ways to enhance the shopping experience, while harnessing the computational and communication powers of computer networks?

The potential possibility of improving online shopping process represents an opportunity offered by technology. The ease with which product information can be delivered to the shoppers though, is a double-edged sword. On one hand customers can have access to much richer information environments, on the other, the phenomenon of information overload may seriously hinder their decision quality (Lurie, 2004), and this is a threat to effective decision making, which could be battled by providing adequate support solutions. The past studies have shown that increases in the number of alternatives and attributes have a detrimental effect on the quality of consumer decisions (Chernev, 2003; Keller & Staelin, 1987). By itself, this is hardly a surprise, as the increase of the decision space could translate into higher probability of making less-than-adequate choices. Perhaps, a somewhat less intuitive finding is that consumers are *less* likely to make a purchase decision when a store has an extensive selection of a given product (Iyengar & Lepper, 2000). Hence, a design research project may offer a type of solution, which would mitigate threats and exploit the opportunities of online shopping.

Thus, the motivational aspect work of on online shopping support is in addressing the question of providing adequate assistance for decision making. In particular, a design researcher would envisage an e-commerce outlet that helps customers in make their choices in an effective and efficient manner. This is especially important in cases of ill-defined criteria and preferences the shoppers have in regards to the products sought. Studies have revealed that consumers often lack a well-defined a priori preference structure; rather they *construct* preferences during the shopping process (Bettman, 1979; Haubl & Trifts, 2000).

PARADIGM COMPETITION

It might be premature to speak about an established paradigm in the area of online shopping support. Perhaps it would be more appropriate to speak about classes of approaches, or "schools" of thought. One could expect that one of these schools will become dominant enough to constitute a paradigm. This section focuses on the development of research in the area of online shopping support, emphasizing the role of the two paradigms looking to establish themselves as predominant frameworks for addressing the problem outlined above. One of these schools has a longer history as it derives from general multi-criteria decision making context, while the other is relatively new and is mainly supported by the advance of the Web.

In the context of online shopping support the term "recommender (or recommendation) systems" has emerged to signify solutions that are capable of proposing "best" candidate products based on some prior historical or otherwise elicited knowledge about the users (Stohr & Viswanathan, 1999). A variety of approaches have been employed to this end including: data mining; content-based filtering; and collaborative filtering (Karacapilidis & Moraitis, 2001; Kim, Cho, Kim, Kim, & Suh, 2002; Kim, Lee, Shaw, Chang, & Nelson, 2001; Kim, Kerschberg, & Scime, 2002; Liu & Shih, 2005; Maes, Guttman, & Moukas, 1999; Prasad, 2003; Sarwar, Karypis, Konstan, & Riedl, 2000; Schafer, Konstan, & Riedl, 2001; Seo & Zhang, 2000; Srikumar & Bhasker, 2004; Stohr & Viswanathan, 1999; Wang, Chuang, Hsu, & Keh, 2004).

Content-based filtering involves relating the contents of a product description with the user needs and desires. In this respect the problem could be regarded as a particular subclass of a broader class of problems, where eliciting decision maker preferences and ranking decision alternatives is considered. Preference and utility modeling in general has been researched extensively, and work in this area dates back at least to the classical work by von Neumann and Morgenstern (Neumann & Morgenstern, 1953). While comprehensive coverage of past research is well beyond the scope of this book, few key points summarizing the accumulated work can be emphasized here. First, there could be several attributes upon which different possible choices can be mapped. Second, decision maker's preferences in regards to different attribute values and the trade-offs among the attributes are not well-defined. Third, the decision maker cannot directly articulate these preferences in terms of specific numbers: this would be too rough of an approach. Therefore, some method of preference elicitation should be used to collect these. Fourth, a mathematical model (e.g. additive, multiplicative, etc.) that intrinsically incorporates user preferences can be used to evaluate the attractiveness of a particular decision alternative to the decision maker. Fifth, the decision alternatives could be ranked and presented to the decision maker in the order of decreasing attractiveness. In other words, the alternatives can be ordered (albeit with some of them being equivalent) from the best choice to the worst one.

When weighing of attributes is used to model consumer preferences, the accuracy of the recommendations is highly dependent on the accuracy of weights. One possibility to obtain the weights for the product attributes is to employ Analytic Hierarchy Process (AHP) (Saaty, 1980). In a nutshell, AHP simplifies the task of assigning weights to different criteria by reducing it to a series of pairwise comparisons. The weights could be then calculated based on the matrix of preferences. For example, in (Schmitt, Dengler, & Bauer, 2002) an application of AHP to generating product recommendations was proposed with an illustration of automobile purchasing. Another family of methods for eliciting shopper's preferences, long used in marketing research is conjoint analysis (Green, Krieger, & Wind, 2001). In conjoint analysis the user is asked to indicate his or her preferences while making trade-offs between different alternative "packages," which are built by including subsets of attributes. The method then determines the weights, which are implicit in user's choices. For example, mySimon site used to offer in the past the "active buyer's guide," which employed conjoint analysis to elicit user preferences, and then presented him or her with an ordered list of products available from the retailers.

Along with the traditional modeling techniques, more novel approaches mainly based on artificial intelligence have also been proposed. Mooney & Roy have employed content-based filtering for recommending books (Mooney & Roy, 2000). In their approach machine learning was employed to learn customer preferences through example ratings by the user. Lee et al. used the content-filtering-based approach (i.e. using a vector of weights, each of which represents the relative importance of a given attribute to the customer) in their agent-based recommender system for DVD selection (Lee, Liu, & Lu, 2002). They used Genetic Algorithm to learn about customer's preferences through minimizing the error of prediction. For infrequently purchased products they have let the users specify the weights for the product attributes and then provide ordered set of recommended products based on those weights. Similarly, Pazzani and Billsus used the vector of weights to model preferences for the source of document recommendation in their adaptive website agents. In their approach the agent system increases/decreases the weight by a constant factor so as to adapt the user's preferences when the recommendation is/is not accepted (Billsus & Pazzani, 1999).

Modeling user preferences adequately requires that the method somehow should extract this information from the user. Multi-criteria decision making methods, for example, need to acquire this information by "interviewing" the user. Typically, the number of questions (judgments) the user needs to answer grows quickly with the number of product attributes considered. This places a significant cognitive effort on the shopper, which considerably hinders the adoption and usage of such support tools in practice. Furthermore, purely content-based systems have been criticized for "over-specialization" problem, i.e. for being overly restrictive (Balabanovic & Shoham, 1997).

An alternative school of thought had appeared from the belief that shoppers will be receptive to the equivalent of "word-of-mouth" recommendations. People tend to rely on the reaction of others to purchased products or services. However, while in the past shoppers were restricted in this respect to the opinions of their personal acquaintances; the communicational powers of the Internet had provided the possibilities of sharing information within large communities of shoppers. The collaborative filtering family of approaches looks to exploit this potential to offer a less obtrusive way of offering product or service choices (Balabanovic & Shoham, 1997; Fisk, 1997; Guttman, Moukas, & Maes, 1998; Prasad, 2003; Sarwar, Karypis, Konstan, & Riedl, 2000). These techniques rely on the basic premise that like-minded people will tend to prefer similar products. An example approach would employ a distance metric to find nearest neighbors for a given customer. This distance could be based on the previously elicited ratings of products by customers, or the past purchases. Then the highly-rated items that are not yet purchased by a given customer can be recommended to him or her. Firefly was an early example of such systems that generated music and book recommendations (Maes, Guttman, & Moukas, 1999). In another, more elaborate example, collaborative filtering approach has been used to generate movie recommendations (Fisk, 1997). The elegance and generality of collaborative filtering derives from the fact that it requires little concentration on the detailed analysis of product attributes. In fact, it seems that collaborative filtering has becoming the dominant paradigm as it is being used by some of the well-established businesses (e.g. Amazon). One significant drawback of such an approach to recommendation generation is that it requires the availability of past data, which makes its application to new or highly customizable products somewhat problematic.

Another family of approaches to product recommendation relies on the employment of data-mining techniques. These methods aim at discovering patterns in buying decisions based on available historical data. Decision tree induction aims at deriving decision trees that categorize set of cases into a set of distinct classes (Kim, Cho, Kim, Kim, & Suh, 2002). For example, Kim et al. had employed decision trees to propose product categories to online customers based on demographic data (Kim, Lee, Shaw, Chang, & Nelson, 2001). Association rule mining is a technique based on correlations between items, which aims at deriving probabilistic rules relating them (Aggrawal, Imielinski, & Swami, 1993; Changchien, Lee, & Hsu, 2004; Wang, Chuang, Hsu, & Keh, 2004). Thus, the technique is best applicable for detecting complementarities among the products. The measures of confidence and support are employed to indicate the strength of such rules. Wang et al. had used association rules as part of their method for generating recommendations for the cosmetic business (Wang, Chuang, Hsu, & Keh, 2004). In general data mining techniques assume availability of historical data for generating recommendations.

In order to improve the quality of recommendations and overcome the shortcomings of individual technique classes, hybrid approaches had also been proposed. For example, in (Balabanovic & Shoham, 1997) content-based and collaborative filtering had been combined into one method in the "Fab" system. In (Liu & Shih, 2005) the authors integrated AHP, clustering, and association rule mining for generating recommendations. In (Wang, Chuang, Hsu, & Keh, 2004) content-based, collaborative filtering, and data mining techniques had been combined. The project presented here diverges somewhat form the above schools. Next section shows how deductive method is used to this end.

INDUCTION AND DEDUCTION

The project described here had followed a deductive pattern. Induction as a method is valuable in cases where observations are readily available. It does not, in general, as we had discussed earlier, culminate in the arrival at reliable knowledge in a straightforward and mechanistic fashion. It could be rather employed to set the stage for theorizing, to inform the process of theory formation. In case of design-type research induction is more difficult to apply as there is a good chance that particular observations (instantiated systems and the methods embedded in them) already exist. If they do, the job of a researcher would be in advancing a generic model based on these specific observations. Yet, typically, in the IT-related area the pace of progress is too quick to accumulate sufficient number of observations for the inductive purposes. This is not to deny the role of induction, but rather to point at its limitedness as applied to design.

One way to foster inductive processes is to attempt extracting the desired features and processes to be supported by the meta-system through questionnaires, perhaps supplemented by mock-up prototypes of system variants. In the context of online shopping support, one could decide which features and processes should be included in the questionnaire. These would be presented through few design alternatives to the user. For example, the user would be asked to evaluate the attractiveness of such features as providing (vs. not providing): guidance and product recommendations; ranking of products; product critique, etc. The questionnaire could be asked within different shopping contexts, such as shopping for computers, books, music, etc. This would represent, essentially, an attempt to elicit meta-requirements. The analysis of this data could then help inducing the desired characteristics of the new type of a meta-artifact. There is little methodological guidance in conducting such type of design-type research work, though, and the typical research project follows the deductive path.

Deduction starts with a pre-existing theoretical model (models) and it tries to apply it in a given problem context to arrive at a design theory (including type of user requirements and type of system solution). Since shopping-related theories are in the area of Marketing, the relevant theoretical insights from this area could illuminate the deductive process. Among these, the Consumer Buying Behavior (CBB) model has been employed extensively by the researchers working on improving buyer support (Guttman, Moukas, & Maes, 1998; Karacapilidis & Moraitis, 2001; Maes, Guttman, & Moukas, 1999; O'Keefe & McEachern, 1998). In this respect, while discussing the applicability of software agents in supporting buying process by individuals Guttman et al. (Guttman, Moukas, & Maes, 1998) adopted the version of the model comprised of six stages of consumer behavior, including: 1) need identification (the consumer identifies the need for a product); 2) product brokering (the consumer identifies products that can satisfy the need); 3) merchant brokering (the consumer decides the seller of the product); 4) negotiation (the customer and the seller negotiate over the terms of the transaction); 5) purchase and delivery; and 6) after purchase evaluation.

Decision making by an online shopper is involved throughout these stages. Thus, adopting the decision support perspective, Miles, Howes, and Davis focused on the early stages of decision-making processes in e-commerce shopping that have more psychological demands on consumers: 1) search for products, 2) management of search criteria, and 3) comparison of found products (Miles & Howes, 2000). They have further drew a parallel between these stages and Simon's classical three-phase decision-making process (Simon, 1960), i.e. design, intelligence and choice, wherein *intelligence* refers to defining the problem and collecting relevant information, *design* largely focuses on discovery of viable alternatives, and *choice* include systematic examination of the alternatives and making the final decision. They have surveyed thirteen alternative types of websites that have searching, browsing, and/or product comparison capabilities to propose a framework for guiding interface design for supporting buyer decisions.

Simon's model had also been employed to analyze consumer satisfaction with a channel in an empirical study using structural equations modeling (Kohli, Devaraj, & Mahmood, 2004). In particular, stronger evidence was found in favor of the support of design and choice phases. Furthermore, the influence of support of the decision process on satisfaction was strongly mediated by the cost and time savings (thus, the efficiency consideration) by the online consumers. It seems, thus, that there is empirical evidence in favor of providing effective and efficient decision support tools for online consumers.

As it has been mentioned earlier, there are two basic common traditional modes of informing consumer decisions: *browsing* and *searching* (Detlor, Sproule, & Gupta, 2003; Nah & Davis, 2002; Rowley, 2000). *Browsing* (or navigation, surfing, information discovery, information exploration) is "an activity in which one gathers information while scanning an information space without an explicit objective" (Toms, 2000, p. 424). As applied to e-commerce shopping, it takes place when the consumer does not have a well-defined goal towards what exactly he or she is looking for. Therefore the browsing process may be described as largely experimental, and less predictable. *Searching* (or directed search), on the other hand, requires explicit objectives and is a goal-directed behavior (Detlor, Sproule, & Gupta, 2003; Nah & Davis, 2002). Building on Miles et al.'s work, Nah and Davis (Nah & Davis, 2002) suggested that e-commerce sites' searching capability is more suitable for the customers who have a clear idea of what they are looking for, while browsing capability seems to fit those who do not have well-defined product preferences (Detlor, Sproule, & Gupta, 2003).

To propose a blueprint for a method of buyer support, an informative description of different buyer types would be useful. Based on buyer's prior product knowledge, buyers can be categorized into low-knowledge, moderate-knowledge, and high-knowledge buyers (Alba & Hutchinson, 1987; Rao & Monroe, 1988; Smith & Wortzel, 1997). The low-knowledge buyers depend on holistic information processing rather than analytic processing, and they tend to make similarity-based inferences. Moderate-knowledge buyers, on the other hand, have a fair level of familiarity with product attributes and are able to examine detailed functional attribute data. Their capability to assess and analyze complex attribute data approaches to that of high-knowledge buyers. Finally, high-

knowledge buyers possess highly comprehensive knowledge of the product category, brands, and attributes, and they are able to process attribute information analytically and brand information spontaneously. High-knowledge buyers may only need search capability employed by the websites, and thus are less likely to need more advanced support tools. Moderate knowledge buyers may use browsing and/or search to combine direction with exploration. Low-knowledge buyers appear to be in higher need for shopping assistance than the basic mechanisms can provide. Therefore, the decision support perspective is more applicable to this buyer group. Moreover, with frequent shopping it is likely that buyers will gain more knowledge of the given product category. Therefore, the decision support perspective is applicable to cases and items for which a typical buyer goes shopping infrequently. This is a deductive conclusion that helps outlining the birds' eye view of the problem/solution pair: infrequent shopping / decision support.

Further deduction will help refine better the context (problem) as well as the form (solution). Prior knowledge about the product significantly affects the way customers process product information and make choices. Experts are more likely to deduct when it comes to information gathering and problems solving, while novices (or non-experts) tend to induct. To be more specific, experts tend to spend more effort on identifying and defining the problem as if "formulating hypotheses and then test these by acquiring relevant information"; the non-experts, on the contrary, would "… explore information to look for differences and generate propositions. Thus they initially appear to have only vague ideas about what they want." (Selnes & Troye, 1989, p. 425) Therefore, to effectively support novice customers, the system has to take into account their inductive behavior in framing the problem. To this end, the system should be able to handle vaguely expressed preferences, and help maximizing the experiential and learning components of the shopping processes.

Do the approaches to shopping support discussed earlier fit the outlined problem context? Since recommender systems essentially aim at providing decisional guidance for the potential buyers, the relevant theoretical contributions in the analysis of DSS may be important in guiding the design of an effective consumer decision support. We will include in our discussion the two concepts from the DSS literature, namely system restrictiveness and intelligence density to aid our analysis.

Silver had introduced the concept of system restrictiveness as a way to analyze various modes of decision support (Silver, 1991). System restrictiveness is defined as "the degree to which, and the manner in which, a Decision Support System limits its users' decision-making process to a subset of all possible processes" (p. 115). In introducing system restrictiveness, Silver primarily referred to the capabilities that a system would provide to a user. For example in approaching multi-attribute decision problems (making a major purchase referred to as an example), the system will effectively restrict the users to the subset of techniques it has to offer. Silver distinguished between "absolute" (i.e. objective) vs. "perceived" (i.e. subjective) restrictiveness. Interestingly, the latter may be high even if the absolute restrictiveness of the system is low. This is due to the fact that system users may be overwhelmed by the range of system capabilities, and thus use only limited subset of interaction processes.

In our analysis we will use the restrictiveness of any given method, rather than a system. Our meaning of restrictiveness is somewhat different from Silver's, namely, we will use restrictiveness to signify the degree to which the method restricts the choices offered to the shoppers to a small set of "similar" in a certain sense, products. It is interesting to note certain analogies between Silver's original notion and restrictiveness of product recommending techniques. For example, as previously mentioned, content-based filtering approaches have been criticized for being overly

restrictive and limiting the choices to a set of similar products (Balabanovic & Shoham, 1997). On the other hand, as pointed earlier, marketing literature suggests that given the exposure to a large variety of product choices consumers will tend to make inferior decisions, presumably, because of being overwhelmed, or "restricted" in a sense. Thus, as in the case with system restrictiveness, the perceived restrictiveness of the product retrieval mechanism will tend to grow with the low absolute restrictiveness.

Another informative dimension (mentioned earlier) offered by in the context of decision support is known as intelligence density (Dhar & Stein, 1997). Intelligence density refers to how quickly a decision maker can get the essence of the underlying data from the output, or how much of the provided information will need to be examined in order to make a decision of a specified quality (p. 9). Thus, this metric is rather applicable to a particular decision tool, rather than a system. Increasing intelligence density of a method is viewed as a series of steps that move from simple access, to data integration and transformation, discovery, and, finally learning. A variety of DSS tool categories (including OLAP, Neural Nets, Genetic Algorithms, Inductive techniques and others) had been discussed in the context of intelligence density.

In supporting online buying decisions by consumers two considerations are important: 1) the available pool of products and their attributes and prices and 2) the consumer's preferences, needs and constraints. As discussed earlier, many consumers will tend to construct their processes in the process of shopping. Thus, in some respect the processes of product exploration and preference construction are often intertwined in the shopping process. A method with high intelligence density would facilitate efficient and effective exploration and learning of both structures.

The representational framework introduced in earlier chapters contained a number of layers for describing IS meta-artifacts from different perspectives. Restrictiveness and intelligence density are the examples of dimensions for meta-artifact characterizations at the analytical layer. In other words, they represent the part of description of meta-requirements for a given type of artifacts. There could be other dimensions to add to the description. System proactiveness and adaptability can be mentioned as examples. The design researcher should choose those analytical dimensions, which help yielding an informative guidance in arriving at a solution type, and, in particular clarify the differences between a new approach and the existing ones.

Table 1 roughly categorizes the existing product retrieval mechanisms according to the two dimensions of method restrictiveness and its intelligence density. Basic search and browse mechanisms are essentially data access type of approaches with little transformation or processing involved. Thus, they are viewed as possessing lower level of intelligence density. They differ on the (absolute) restrictiveness dimension, though. While search could be regarded as being more restrictive, since it only retrieves products in accordance with the exactly specified criteria, browse is essentially unrestrictive, since the consumer may be exposed to the unlimited number of choices (which may lead to higher perceived restrictiveness). Most basic retrieval mechanisms combining search and browse will tend to lie between the two extremes, yet still remaining within the category of simple data access.

The majority of recommender systems will have higher level of intelligence density since they employ methods to retrieve the products that supposedly match consumer preferences. However, it can be argued that they are essentially restrictive. Thus, content-based filtering will restrict the choices offered to the ones that match the user profile best, essentially restricting the consumer to a set of similar products, perhaps even ordered or ranked. Collaborative filtering restricts the choices to those that other "similar" consumers make. Inductive methods will rely on past purchase data to restrict the set of alternatives based on the historical patterns. Incidentally, all of these methods explore the various forms of *similarity*-based approaches for product recommendation.

Decision-making and problem solving are closely related (perhaps, indistinguishable) terms. Research in problem solving/decision making focuses on the advance of principles, techniques, and guidelines for tackling ill-structured (nonstandard) problem situations. Since infrequent shopping is more likely to be considered a subset of ill-structured problems (due to unclear preferences, low knowledge of product categories, etc.) the findings from these areas should be of importance for the design of shopping support.

Classical problem solving principles, advocate the use of divergence as a key ingredient in effective problem solving/decision making (see e.g. Ackoff, 1978; Basadur, 1994). Similarity in generated alternatives thus, seems to be in discordance with problem solving guidelines. Therefore, it follows that a less restrictive method would try to avoid making similar (in some sense) recommendations, and should; on the contrary, look to possibly explore *dissimilarity* to make the process

Table 1. Analysis of product retrieval mechanisms

Restrictiveness / Intelligence Density	Higher	Lower
Higher	Content based filtering, collaborative filtering, data mining	Divergent product recommendation
Lower	Basic Search	Basic Browse

more in line with "creative" problem solving. The lower restrictiveness/higher intelligence density quadrant offers an opportunity for the potential solutions that would facilitate efficient process of exploring and learning the product landscape, as well as constructing preferences. This paper proposes and evaluates a diversity-based approach that, in our view fits well in the above quadrant.

It is worthwhile to summarize the above analysis in order to highlight its deductive nature. The theoretical process description (kernel theory) for online shopping support is provided by consumer buying behavior model. This has been shown to be similar to general problem solving/decision making. The area of problem solving/decision making mostly addresses ill-structured problems. In online shopping, search for infrequently purchased products is a case of an ill-structured problem. In ill-structured problem solving divergent processes are emphasized, in particular it concerns generating differing alternatives. In online shopping the available support tools, other than basic browsing are similarity-oriented. Thus, they are less applicable to the task of supporting infrequent shopping. Furthermore, intelligence density and system restrictiveness help identifying the characteristics of solution. In particular, for infrequent shopping the desired system characteristics would include low restrictiveness and high intelligence density. The available support mechanisms do not satisfy this condition. Therefore, the analytical description of problem/solution includes: support for infrequent shopping (motivation)/divergent approach (behavior), high intelligence density, low restrictiveness (structure).

AGAINST THE PARADIGM

Having identified the features of the meta-artifact we can proceed to the synthesis phase, i.e. elaborating on its generic design that would fit the meta-requirements deduced above. Let us review the major principles of the multi-attribute problem solving paradigm mentioned earlier.

1. There could be several attributes upon which different possible choices can be mapped.
2. Decision maker preferences in regards to different attribute values and the trade-offs among the attributes are not well-defined.
3. Decision maker cannot directly articulate these preferences in terms of specific numbers. A preference elicitation method should be used to quantify these.
4. A mathematical model (e.g. additive, multiplicative, etc.) that intrinsically incorporates user preferences can be used to evaluate the attractiveness of a particular decision alternative to the decision maker.
5. Decision alternatives could be ranked and presented to the decision maker in the order of decreasing attractiveness.

Now, while the statements 1 and 2 well fit the requirements of the infrequent shopping support, the adequateness of the claims 3 to 5 can be questioned. If a decision maker cannot directly articulate preferences, it may not be simply due to the fact that many attributes/criteria are present, and human brains have limited capacities. In infrequent shopping the decision maker may truly have vague preferences. It would be inadequate to employ whatever method to come up with a precise numeric value expressing a specific preference (denial of [3]). It would be an inappropriate model. Furthermore, a mathematical model cannot generate the precise assessment of the attractiveness of product alternatives, while the preferences are intrinsically imprecise (denial of [4]). Therefore, there could be no adequate way to rank order the alternatives in a strict sense (denial of [5]).

How would then the above set of statements change as a result of the denial of statements 3 to 5? Let's propose the following set of statements replacing the original claims 3 to 5, and in addition to (1) and (2).

3. Decision maker *can* directly articulate their preferences, albeit *vaguely*. Preference elicitation is *not* needed.
4. A mathematical model that incorporates user preferences can be used to evaluate the *approximate* attractiveness of a particular decision alternative to the decision maker.
5. Decision alternatives *cannot* be ranked strictly. ·

Note, that these changes partially deny the existing paradigm in multi-criteria decision making. In particular, the new number 3 has a specific flavor of Feyerabend's anarchy: "anything goes."

We will show next, how the proposed approach to online shopping support fits the new set of statements. As we've mentioned the approach is essentially diversity-oriented. Actually, we had developed two variants of the approach, but first, we will present the first one that had been also described (in a more comprehensive fashion) in Vahidov & Ji (2005).

As shown earlier, basic search and browse mechanisms have high and low restrictiveness respectively. It has also been pointed out that a combination of the two could effectively be used to manipulate the level of restrictiveness. In any case one could expect that basic browse and search generate information of a low intelligence density for an average consumer. Thus one way to look at the problem is how to increase the intelligence density of browse and search while maintaining the relatively low level of restrictiveness.

The approach presented here looks to facilitate preference-driven search for interesting product candidates in the presence of ill-defined consumer preferences is to allow the users to express these in inexact (soft) form. Thus, the importance of a CPU frequency, for example for a non-technically oriented shopper could be expressed in essentially vague terms. The subsequent retrieval of the set of products would then include products, among which there is no essential ordering in terms of preferences. Potentially, a method could be pro-

posed, where products are divided into several "classes," or "grades," each of them representing a certain level of desirability of the products contained within them, but without explicit ranking inside each class.

The approach is based on facilitating effective browsing of a set of candidate products through emphasizing the interplay of divergent and convergent processes, in line with the problem solving principles (Basadur, 1994). This would result in an essentially dissimilarity-driven alternative generation. Among the set of possible candidates a small number of most diverse products is presented to the user. As the user chooses to explore one of the possibilities, the most diverse products within the vicinity of the choice will be generated. Thus, while the process can be viewed as a sequence of divergent and convergent phases, the overall pattern will be stressing more divergence in the early phases, and convergence in the later ones.

In order to capture and model "vague" information (shopper preferences) fuzzy sets and fuzzy arithmetic has been selected as proper modeling tools (Kaufmann & Gupta, 1985; Klir & Yuan, 1995). Interestingly, the area of fuzzy sets had emerged as an alternative to the traditional probabilistic paradigm. As such, despite the multitude of successful practical applications, it is subject to criticism on part of the proponents of the more conventional schools (Kosko, 1993). Instead of relying on "crisp" values, the method employs fuzzy numbers to represent the importance placed by the customer on different product attributes (e.g. price, memory, etc.). Fuzzy sets are sets where a membership value is associated with elements indicating the degree of belonging of that element to a fuzzy set. Fuzzy numbers are fuzzy sets defined over real numbers that have bounded support and a single maximum value of unity for the membership function. In this particular work the triangular shape for fuzzy numbers has been adopted for the sake of conceptual and computational simplicity. The importance of the attributes can be elicited using leftmost, peak, and rightmost values of the fuzzy weights. For example, the user might indicate that the brand name is at least moderately important, most likely very important, and at most extremely important. These terms will have associated numbers similar to Likert scale. Since we are not dealing with precise crisp numbers we can ask the user to specify imprecise weights directly. This information will be treated in a very liberal fashion to form a set of "promising" products for the customer without strict ranking or ordering.

The modeling approach is related to the "fuzzy weighted averages" method that incorporates vagueness in the desirability of different attribute values of alternative solutions (Dong & Wong, 1987; Vanegas & Labib, 2001). In particular, the application of this approach to design process with gradually reducing vagueness has been elaborated in (Antonsson & Otto, 1997). In this work an additive aggregation model with fuzzy weights and crisp or fuzzy utilities of individual attributes has been adopted. Most of the product attributes could be mapped into crisp utilities (e.g. memory, screen size, etc.). However, there may be some qualitative aspects of the products that could be represented by fuzzy utilities (e.g. reputation of the manufacturer). In such cases expert or user judgment could be used to specify imprecise utilities.

The purpose of using the fuzzy-linear model is to partition the set of all alternatives into few "classes" or "grades" representing different "desirabilities" for the customer. For example, first-grade products would constitute the set of all interesting products (an "A" class), second-grade products would be less desirable ("B" choices), and so on ("C," "D," etc.). This partition is achieved this by specifying a parameter ranging from 0 to 1 used to derive the "cuts" through the fuzzy utilities. The higher the value the fewer alternatives will be assigned per grade. When it is set to 1 the procedure will simply return ordered list of products with one assigned per grade. Since the purpose here is not ordering, but rather determining the set of

"good" alternatives, lower cut level should be used. In a nutshell, the procedure determines the sets of products that are utility-wise indistinguishable at a given level and assigns them to the grades. For a more detailed description the reader is referred to (Vahidov & Ji, 2005).

THE BEAUTY

In the previous chapter we have seen that aesthetic aspects play an important role in the course of scientific research. Symmetry and proportion inherently drive researchers in their search for the forms. The word elegance is often used to mean the intrinsic attractiveness of a theoretical structure or method. One example that was sited revealed the aesthetic pictorial representation of the role of divergence/convergence principle throughout the phases of problem solving. Somehow, as an unwritten law, in the lack of actual observations the more aesthetic models receive higher priority in researcher's work and its acceptability, than the alternative ones. Could there be an aesthetic aspect in the project being described?

Once the set of promising candidates has been identified, the next task is to present shopper with choices that would convey the most information about the product space. As we have seen, one of the fundamental principles of solving ill-structured problems is promoting divergent (idea generation) and convergent (systematic evaluation) activities during different phases of problem solving. In an early work Evans argued that a computer algorithm for supporting problem solving would generate diverse alternatives in preferably a single run (Evans, 1990). While divergent and convergent activities should be used in all phases of problem solving, the divergence is stressed more during the earlier phases, while the convergence is emphasized more in later phases (Basadur, 1994).

In the present approach we follow the logic that is consistent with the above discussion: we look to provide more diverse (dissimilar) product

Figure 1. Divergence and convergence in online shopping

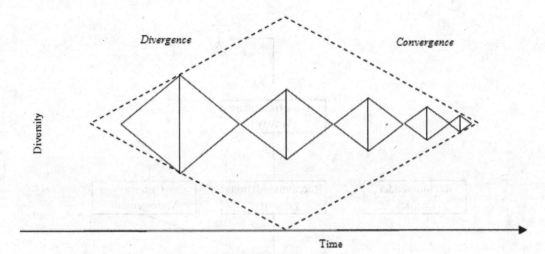

alternatives in the beginning and more convergent (similar) ones towards the end of the shopping process. While browsing the class "A" product set, the shopper is presented with the most diverse product offerings. When he or she chooses to explore more the neighborhood of one of these products, the system generates a new set of diverse alternatives, but at this step the level of diversity is lower than at the previous one. The shopper, as it were, "zooms into" the selected neighborhood of products. Within this neighborhood then, the new most divergent recommendations are generated.

We have chosen a technique that is widely used by recommender systems. While cluster analysis is usually employed to find similarities, here we utilized it in order to provide the most dissimilar choices. This maybe one way to convey the essential difference between recommendation generation for frequent vs. infrequent shoppers. Our clustering algorithm uses Euclidian distance metric for measuring distance between products. Specifically, hierarchical clustering method was chosen for its relatively high speed. The method tracks at what point in the decision process the user is and produces a small number of alternatives close to the centroids of clusters. When the user chooses to explore similar products in some

cluster (in the vicinity of one of the alternatives) the new (sub-) cluster centroids within that cluster will serve as the basis for generating new alternatives. This process will continue until the user makes a final choice. The user may move back ("zoom out") to explore a different cluster of products at any time. Our expectation is that the users will be able to quickly learn the structure of the product space in light of their preferences and will have better chances of finding the right product. Overall one could say that in the early stages the divergence is predominant, while at the later phases the convergence is more stressed.

The process is graphically depicted on Figure 1. While, understandably the aesthetic aspects are hardly quantifiable, it is hard not to notice the glimpse of beauty present in the picture. In particular, different types of symmetry and proportion are noticeable.

FALSIFIABILITY

Falsifiability, as we have seen, means that for a theory to be considered scientific there must be claims inferred from that theory, which could be, in principle tested by observations. We have

Figure 2. Structure of shopping support system

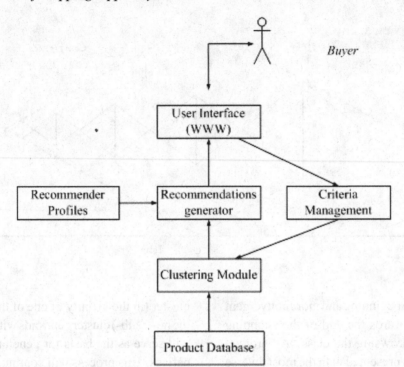

argued that in design-type research this translates into advancing meta-artifacts, which have a level of specificity that allows distinguishing them from other, wider classes of artifacts. Let's say, for example that the system presented here was described in terms of three major components: database, application logic, and user interface. The expectation would be that such forms will appear in the future. But specified in this way, the model would be indistinguishable from nearly any other type of a system. It would be, therefore non-falsifiable.

The behavior of the model has been described in the previous section, and it is specific enough to separate it from other classes of methods. The logical structure of the system is shown on Figure 2. The criteria management module allows the user to specify preferences in a vague fashion. Recommender profiles (not discussed above) contain terms that help user identify different product choices. Three profiles have been

included: inexpensive, value, and luxury. When a user sees different product selections, these terms are attached to them to help user identify the type of a product. Recommendation generator interacts with the clustering module to generate diverse recommendations.

The form presented here has a sufficient level of specificity to be subject to falsifiability. The claim is then, that such design forms will appear in particular implemented systems (observations). In other words, the claim is that this is the true form for the given problem context. From the macro perspective of design as a science the behavior and the structure presented here constitute, in essence a prediction, an expectation that they will appear in reality as means of supporting infrequent shopping. The real future mechanisms provided to this end may deviated from those presented here in few respects, yet the core idea of imprecise preference modeling coupled with divergent browsing constitute the essence of the form. This is a falsifiable claim.

Design-type researcher would not typically wait, though for the form to make its presence in reality. For "preliminary" evaluation of its viability, the form will be instantiated in a concrete prototype and used for the experimentation purposes to assess its right for existence. The truth criterion implies that the form (as a theoretical model) fits better the problem context than the rival models. Therefore, standard (testable) hypotheses in design-type research always imply that the proposed solution is better on a selected set of criteria than the alternative candidates. Thus, within the context of this particular project, it is expected that the proposed method that combines fuzzy filtering with subsequent divergent/convergent product suggestions will lead to an improvement in relevant dependent variables as compared to other methods.

To start making claims about the fitness of the form, one must compare its performance on key criteria against an alternative form. The alternative that has been adopted for comparison is the basic browsing mechanism as it is present in nearly all commercial websites. It would appear that choosing other recommendation approaches would be a better approach in this case. However, many recommendation systems, such as collaborative filtering assume some data on past purchases (or ratings) and a sizeable database of other customers' behaviors to provide effective guidance. However, this would imply that subjects have had some considerable experience shopping for this type of items, which is not typically the case with "infrequent" shopping. On the other hand, employing basic search, content-based filtering, or some sort of preference elicitation method would translate into narrowly defined set of alternative products, and also imply one's well-defined preference structure as well as familiarity with product attributes and specifications. Browsing is an unrestrictive mechanism by means of which the subjects would have access to the whole set

of offerings and could construct their preferences as they shop. Thus, to make a fair comparison browsing was adopted as a baseline mechanism.

The degree to which solution fits the problem context is reflected by a set of criteria. Since it has been suggested above to treat the shopping problem as a particular case of general decision support, the corresponding literature can provide us with the choice of such criteria. The DSS literature suggests that evaluation of these systems must be performed using a variety of criteria, that could be divided into decision outcomes, perceived measures, and process measures (Aldag & Power, 1986; Barr & Sharda, 1997; Keen & Morton, 1978; O'Keefe, 1989; Sharda, Barr, & McDonnell, 1988). The decision outcome in our case is not objectively measurable easily, thus we will rely more on the subjective measures. The important perception-based measures derive from the IS theories, partly discussed in an earlier chapter. Thus, perceived usefulness of the system, satisfaction with the outcome, and satisfaction with the process have been adopted as criteria. Note that these now appear on the dependent side of the study as we look to measure the impact of alternative design solutions on them. Furthermore, since the support is provided within the context of e-commerce, we have also incorporated intention to return to the website as a significant variable (Palmer, 2002).

The form's (falsifiable) claim for existence now can be assessed (preliminarily) by a set of concrete hypotheses. The hypotheses express statements, comparing the presented divergent method against the basic browsing mechanism in light of the criteria mentioned above.

Hypothesis 1. *Use of the system incorporating the divergent method will lead to higher perceived usefulness of the system than that of system with the browsing mechanism.*

Hypothesis 2. *Use of the system incorporating the divergent method will lead to higher* satisfaction with the outcome than that of system with the browsing mechanism.

Hypothesis 3. *Use of the system incorporating the divergent method will lead to higher satisfaction with the process than that of system with the browsing mechanism.*

Hypothesis 4. *Use of the system incorporating the divergent method will lead to higher level of intention to return than that of system with the browsing mechanism.*

To test the above claims two website prototypes have been developed: one featuring the product catalog that could be browsed in a familiar fashion, and the other, incorporating the divergent method. An experimental task included shopping for note book computers and indicating the final choice. The divergent method first asked the user to indicate their preferences in terms of importance of such product attributes as CPU speed, memory size, brand name, and others. Figure

3 shows the example screenshot for this stage. Then the products were categorized into classes and the subject was presented the most diverse alternatives from the "top" class. To this end, once the product classes had been identified, the hierarchical clustering method was used once per each class to make dissimilar suggestions. The subject could move into the neighborhood of one of the recommendations to obtain further three diverse choices within that neighborhood. The process finished once the subject had indicated the final choice.

The subjects for the experiment were recruited among the graduate and upper-level undergraduate students of a major North American university. Of these, ninety had duly completed the tasks and the questionnaires. The participants were asked to assume the role of an online notebook computer shopper and explore the products using one of the prototypical sites with the aim of finding a notebook that they may wish to buy.

Figure 3. Capturing imprecise preferences

The subjects were randomly assigned to one of the two systems in the experiment all of which had access to a database with fifty different notebook choices

The participants then browsed through the notebooks, navigated to various clusters of products, and requested detailed information for informing their shopping process. When an adequate notebook was found, the subjects had indicated their intention to purchase by clicking on the "Buy Now" button on the product page. A questionnaire was then presented to the participants to measure their satisfaction with the system process, satisfaction with the system outcome, the intention to return, and the perceived usefulness of the system adopted from the literature discussed earlier. The Likert scale ranging from 1 (strongly disagree) to 7 (strongly agree) was used to collect the responses.

Factor analysis was performed to measure the impact of the two alternative designs on the four criteria shown above (the details are not discussed here, but they indicated the adequateness of the questionnaire items). The average factor score of perceived usefulness for the users of the divergent method was higher than that for the users of basic browsing mechanism by 2.8 with the standard error being 0.4. This confirmed the hypothesis 1. The average factor score of perceived usefulness for the users of the divergent method was higher than that for the users of basic browsing mechanism by 2.80 with the standard error being 0.4 (p = 0.00). This confirmed the hypothesis 1. The average factor score of the satisfaction with outcome for the users of the divergent method was higher than that for the users of basic browsing mechanism by 2.5 with the standard error being 0.38. Thus, hypothesis 2 was also confirmed. The average factor score of satisfaction with the process for the users of the divergent method was higher than that for the users of basic browsing mechanism by 2.63 while the standard error was 0.33. This confirmed the hypothesis 3. Finally, the average factor score of the intention to return for the users

of the divergent method was higher than that for the users of basic browsing mechanism by 2.7 with the standard error being 0.34. Thus, all of the hypotheses have been confirmed.

The results are, thus encouraging in that the proposed method had outperformed the existing prevalent browsing mechanism in the context of infrequent shopping. However, from Popper's point of view, the presented artifact merely survived the first test. According to Popper, by no means can the result be considered as having established truth. Perhaps, in shopping for other types of products, with other kinds of subjects, or employing other mechanisms as alternatives we could see different results.

THE RAZOR

Ockham's razor, as applied to design-type research implies the preference for simpler models, if these perform equally well as the more complicated artifacts. The project described in this chapter provides a good example for the application of the razor. Although it hasn't been mentioned in the sections above, the project actually included two versions of the approach. In the basic method, the clustering structure does not change as the shopper explores the subset of the product space. In order to make the divergent and convergent components of the process more dynamic the more adaptive approach has also been developed. The idea is that the method would allow for flexible adaptation to shopper's profile in the process of shopping.

In this adaptive divergent approach the pre-filtering of the product catalog is performed similar to the way it is done in the basic divergent method. However, in the adaptive version the system tracks the user's exploratory trajectory and changes the way clustering is carried out. We pointed that the initial system version had a number of "recommender profiles," which essentially reflected different categories of products. The profiles were intended to mimic fixed preference

Figure 4. The adaptive divergent method

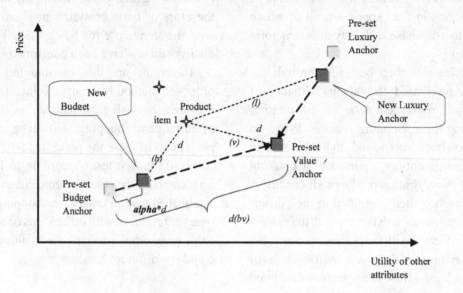

"packages" that represented customer classes, and these included the categories of budget, luxury, and value products. These three points in product space were defined a priori as initial "anchors" that reflect different "values" customers may be driven by. These anchors were then treated as cluster centroids for the clustering algorithm. In an adaptive method a nearest-neighbor clustering is performed to assign products to clusters. Thereafter, the anchors dynamically adapted their positions according to the customer's interactions with the system.

Figure 4 depicts such movements of the anchors. Assume, for example, that the customer has chosen to explore the Value cluster (i.e. the customer retrieves detailed information on products in that category). All the anchors will then move towards the pre-set Value anchor by a specified factor of *alpha* (alpha is used in the case of anchors of different clusters, e.g. Budget anchor to Value anchor and Luxury anchor to Value anchor). The higher the factor, the faster the anchors will move. The value anchor will then move to its originally pre-set position by a factor of *beta*. In essence, the shopper's interest in a particular cluster will tend to pull other anchors towards that cluster. By doing this, the system adjusts

and focuses itself to the customer's interests. In this particular study, both alpha and beta were set to 0.1. It was expected that this adaptive nature of divergence and convergence in the shopping process will yield an improvement over the basic method. But first, we expected that, at the least the adaptive divergent approach outperforms the basic browsing mechanism:

Hypothesis 5. *Use of the system incorporating the adaptive divergent method will lead to higher perceived usefulness of the system than that of system with the browsing mechanism.*

Hypothesis 6. *Use of the system incorporating the adaptive divergent method will lead to higher satisfaction with the outcome than that of system with the browsing mechanism.*

Hypothesis 7. *Use of the system incorporating the adaptive divergent method will lead to higher satisfaction with the process than that of system with the browsing mechanism.*

Hypothesis 8. *Use of the system incorporating the adaptive divergent method will lead to higher level of intention to return than that of system with the browsing mechanism.*

The next set of hypotheses compares the adaptive divergent method with the basic one. It was expected that the use of the adaptive method will yield an improvement on the dependent variables as it intends to adjust the recommendations based on the users' browsing patterns.

Hypothesis 9. *Use of system incorporating adaptive divergent method will lead to higher perceived usefulness of the systems than that of system with the divergent method.*

Hypothesis 10. *Use of system incorporating adaptive divergent method will lead to higher satisfaction with the outcome than that of system with the divergent method.*

Hypothesis 11. *Use of system incorporating adaptive divergent method will lead to higher satisfaction with the process than that of system with the divergent method.*

Hypothesis 12. *Use of system incorporating adaptive divergent method will lead to higher level of intention to return than that of system with the divergent method.*

In fact, all three types of approaches (browsing, divergent, and adaptive divergent) have been tested in one experiment. However, the discussion of the adaptive method has been postponed until this section to demonstrate the application of Ockham's razor. Ninety subjects had participated in this experiment and they were assigned randomly to one of the three prototypes. As a result of this assignment, 27 subjects interacted with the prototype that featured basic browsing, 36 were assigned to the site featuring divergent method, and 27 used the site that incorporated adaptive divergent method.

Of the hypotheses 5 to 8 all have been confirmed at a significant level. Indeed, in this respect the results were quite similar to those obtained from comparing the performance of the divergent method with basic browsing. Thus, one could claim

that the adaptive divergent method significantly outperforms the traditional browsing mechanism.

What is more interesting, though, is comparison between the two divergent methods. The average factor score of perceived usefulness for the users of the adaptive divergent method was lower than that for the users of divergent method by 0.13 with the standard error being 0.34. Thus hypothesis 9 was not confirmed. The average factor score of satisfaction with outcome for the users of the adaptive divergent method was lower than that for the users of divergent method by 0.05 with the standard error being 0.4 ($p = 0.38$). Thus, the hypothesis 10 was not confirmed either. The average factor score of the satisfaction with the process for the users of the adaptive divergent method was higher than that for the users of divergent method by 0.06 with the standard error being 0.38. Thus, hypothesis 11 was also not confirmed. Finally, the average factor score of the intention to return for the users of the adaptive divergent method was lower than that for the users of adaptive method by 0.26 with the standard error being 0.34. Thus, none of the hypotheses have been confirmed.

The results showed that the divergent and the adaptive divergent methods were virtually indistinguishable. The latter is a more complex method than the former, and yet it did not yield improved results. This could be due to a number of reasons: the choice of the particular parameter values, for example. And yet, following the Ockham's razor, one would have to give up on the adaptive divergent approach in favor of the simpler method.

THE BELT

The falsifiability criterion looks to expose theoretical models to the possibility of refutation by means of rigorous and critical testing of the hypotheses derived from them. Theories, which pass such a test are only provisionally kept, while their failure to do so would imply their immediate refutation. To soften such harsh survival conditions Lacatos had proposed the use of auxiliary hypotheses, which could be refuted, without having to abandon the theoretical core.

As we have seen in the example research project the proposed artifact had successfully survived the first test. In other words, the defined method and form appeared to fit the problem context. Assume, however that the model did not yield any substantial improvement over the widely utilized rival. Would this mean that the method should be abandoned and forgotten? Aside from re-examining the peculiarities of prototype implementation and the adequateness of experimental setup, would there be any hope for salvaging the situation?

It seems that it would have been possible to defend the approach by keeping its core idea, and focusing, instead on any implicit assumptions that could be considered to be a part of the "protective belt." If we try to preserve the form from being rejected, perhaps we could focus on the nature of the assumed form/problem context linkages. One such assumption would be that the proposed approach would be helpful to all the shoppers regardless of their problem solving/information processing styles. This protective auxiliary hypothesis, then could be sacrificed in order to preserve the core form (theory).

Instead, a new auxiliary hypothesis could be proposed that the method would fit a subgroup of potential shoppers sharing specific decision-making style(s). In this regard, a deeper insight into the types of online shoppers might be worthwhile. Or, perhaps, the researcher might be interested in linking psychological styles with the characteristics of a shopping task and the support provided by the method. One such possibility would be looking into informational requirements of different psychological styles as they relate to decision making process. A researcher may propose a new

auxiliary hypothesis, for example, claiming that the method would better suit intuitive rather than sensing shoppers (as defined by Myers-Briggs Type Indicator). This might be due to the fact that intuitive people tend to make decisions based on lesser amount of information than the sensing people. Thus, the method that helps to complete the browsing job in a more efficient and informative manner would be more attractive to them, as they will be able to quickly learn about the product space without having to go through the extensive browsing process.

Such a hypothesis, though would require additional experimentation. In the new setup three types of supporting prototype would be needed: one with the basic browse, one with the divergent approach, and one where people could make a choice over which mechanism to use. Then it would be expected that the latter prototype should outperform both other choices as it would allow the subjects to make the choice of a mechanism that fits their needs best. If that would turn out to be the case the form of the support could be said to have survived the test.

REFERENCES

Ackoff, R. L. (1978). *The art of problem solving: Accompanied by Ackoff's fables*. New York: John Wiley and Sons.

Aggrawal, R., Imielinski, T., & Swami, A. (1993). *Mining association rules between sets of items in large databases*. Paper presented at the ACM SIGMOD Conference on Management of Data (SIGMOD 1993). San-Diego, CA.

Alba, J. W., & Hutchinson, J. W. (1987). Dimensions of consumer expertise. *The Journal of Consumer Research*, *13*(4), 411–454. doi:10.1086/209080

Aldag, R. J., & Power, D. J. (1986). An empirical assessment of computer-assisted decision analysis. *Decision Sciences, 17*(4), 572–588. doi:10.1111/j.1540-5915.1986.tb00243.x

Antonsson, E. K., & Otto, K. N. (1997). Improving engineering design with fuzzy sets. In Dubois, D., Prade, H., & Yager, R. R. (Eds.), *Fuzzy Information Engineering: A Guided Tour of Applications* (pp. 633–654). New York: John Wiley & Sons.

Balabanovic, M., & Shoham, Y. (1997). Fab: Content-based collaborative recommendation. *Communications of the ACM, 40*(3), 66–72. doi:10.1145/245108.245124

Barr, S. H., & Sharda, R. (1997). Effectiveness of decision support systems: Development or reliance effect? *Decision Support Systems, 21*, 133–146. doi:10.1016/S0167-9236(97)00021-3

Basadur, M. (1994). Managing the creative process in organizations. In Runco, M. A., & Chand, I. (Eds.), *Problem Finding, Problem Solving, and Creativity* (pp. 237–268). Norwood, NJ: Ablex.

Bettman, J. R. (1979). *An information processing theory of consumer choice*. Reading, MA: Addison-Wesley.

Billsus, D., & Pazzani, M. J. (1999). *A personal news agent that talks, learns and explains*. Paper presented at the Third International Conference on Autonomous Agents. Seattle, WA.

Changchien, S. W., Lee, C. F., & Hsu, Y.-J. (2004). On-line personilized sales promotion in electronic commerce. *Expert Systems with Applications, 27*, 35–52. doi:10.1016/j.eswa.2003.12.017

Chernev, A. (2003). When more is less and less is more: The role of ideal point availabilty and assortment in consumer choice. *The Journal of Consumer Research, 30*(2), 170–183. doi:10.1086/376808

Conway, D. G., & Koehler, G. J. (2000). Interface agents: Caveat mercator in electronic commerce. *Decision Support Systems, 27*(4), 355–366. doi:10.1016/S0167-9236(99)00046-9

Detlor, B., Sproule, S., & Gupta, C. (2003). Pre-purchase online information seeking: Search versus browse. *Journal of Electronic Commerce Research, 4*(2), 72–84.

Dhar, V., & Stein, R. (1997). *Intelligent decision support methods: The science of knowledge work*. Upper Saddle River, NJ: Prentice-Hall.

Dong, W. M., & Wong, F. S. (1987). Fuzzy weighted averages and implementation of the extension principle. *Fuzzy Sets and Systems, 21*(2), 183–199. doi:10.1016/0165-0114(87)90163-1

Evans, J. R. (1990). *Creative thinking in the decision and management sciences*. New York: South Western Publishing Co.

Fisk, D. (1997). An application of social filtering to movie recommendation. In Nwana, H. S., & Azarmi, N. (Eds.), *Software Agents and Soft Computing* (pp. 117–131). Berlin: Springer-Verlag.

Green, P. E., Krieger, A. M., & Wind, Y. (2001). Thirty years of conjoint analysis: Reflections and prospects. *Interfaces, 31*(3), S56–S73. doi:10.1287/inte.31.3s.56.9676

Guttman, R., Moukas, A., & Maes, P. (1998). Agent-mediated electronic commerce: A survey. *The Knowledge Engineering Review, 13*(3).

Haubl, G., & Trifts, V. (2000). Consumer decision making in online shopping environments: The effects of interactive decision aids. *Marketing Science, 19*(1), 4–21. doi:10.1287/mksc.19.1.4.15178

Iyengar, S. S., & Lepper, M. R. (2000). When choice is demotivating: Can one desire too much of a good thing? *Journal of Personality and Social Psychology, 79*(6), 995–1006. doi:10.1037/0022-3514.79.6.995

Karacapilidis, N., & Moraitis, P. (2001). Building an agent-mediated electronic commerce system with decision analysis features. *Decision Support Systems, 32*(1), 53–69. doi:10.1016/S0167-9236(01)00100-2

Kaufmann, A., & Gupta, M. M. (1985). *Introduction to fuzzy arithmetic: Theory and applications*. New York, NY: Van Nostrand Reinhold.

Keen, P. G. W., & Morton, M. S. S. (1978). *DSS: An organizational perspective*. Reading, MA: Addison-Wesley.

Keller, K. L., & Staelin, R. (1987). Effects of quality and quantity of information on decision efectiveness. *The Journal of Consumer Research, 14*(2), 200–213. doi:10.1086/209106

Kim, J. K., Cho, Y. H., Kim, W. J., Kim, J. R., & Suh, J. H. (2002). A personalized recommendation procedure for internet shopping support. *Electronic Commerce Research and Applications, 1*, 301–313. doi:10.1016/S1567-4223(02)00022-4

Kim, J. W., Lee, B. H., Shaw, M. J., Chang, H.-L., & Nelson, M. (2001). Application of decision-tree induction techniques to personalized advertisements on internet storefronts. *International Journal of Electronic Commerce, 5*(3), 45–62.

Kim, W., Kerschberg, L., & Scime, A. (2002). Learning for automatic personalization in a semantic taxonomy-based meta-search agent. *Electronic Commerce Research and Applications, 1*(2), 150–173. doi:10.1016/S1567-4223(02)00011-X

Klir, G. J., & Yuan, B. (1995). *Fuzzy sets and fuzzy logic: Theory and applications*. Upper Saddle River, NJ: Prentice Hall.

Kohli, R., Devaraj, S., & Mahmood, M. A. (2004). Understanding determinants of online consumer satisfaction: a decision process perspective. *Journal of Management Information Systems, 21*(1), 115–136.

Kosko, B. (1993). *Fuzzy thinking: The new science of fuzzy logic*. New York, NY: Hyperion.

Lee, W., Liu, C., & Lu, C. (2002). Intelligent agent-based systems for personalized recommendations in e-commerce. *Expert Systems with Applications, 22*, 275–284. doi:10.1016/S0957-4174(02)00015-5

Liu, D.-R., & Shih, Y.-Y. (2005). Integrating AHP and data mining for product recommendation based on customer lifetime value. *Information & Management, 42*, 387–400. doi:10.1016/j.im.2004.01.008

Lurie, N. (2004). Decision-making in information-rich environments: The role of information structure. *The Journal of Consumer Research, 30*(4), 473–486. doi:10.1086/380283

Maes, P., Guttman, R. H., & Moukas, A. G. (1999). Agents that buy and sell. *Communications of the ACM, 42*(3), 81–87. doi:10.1145/295685.295716

Miles, G. E., & Howes, A. (2000). A framework for understanding human factors in Web-based electronic commerce. *International Journal of Human-Computer Studies, 52*(1), 131–163. doi:10.1006/ijhc.1999.0324

Mooney, R. J., & Roy, L. (2000). *Content-based book recommending using learning for text catecorization*. Paper presented at the 5th ACM Conference on Digital Libraries. San Antonio, TX.

Nah, F. F.-H., & Davis, S. (2002). HCI research issues in e-commerce. *Journal of Electronic Commerce Research, 3*(3), 98–113.

Neumann, J. V., & Morgenstern, O. (1953). *Theory of games and economic behavior* (3rd ed.). Princeton, NJ: Princeton University Press.

O'Keefe, R. M. (1989). The evaluation of decision-aiding systems: Guidelines and methods. *Information & Management, 17*, 217–226. doi:10.1016/0378-7206(89)90045-1

O'Keefe, R. M., & McEachern, T. (1998). Web-based customer decision support systems. *Communications of the ACM, 41*(3), 71–78. doi:10.1145/272287.272300

Palmer, W. J. (2002). Web site usability, design, and performance metrics. *Information Systems Research, 13*(2), 151–167. doi:10.1287/isre.13.2.151.88

Prasad, B. (2003). Intelligent techniques for e-commerce. *Journal of Electronic Commerce Research, 4*(2), 65–71.

Rao, A. R., & Monroe, K. B. (1988). The moderating effect of prior knowledge on cue utilization in product evaluations. *The Journal of Consumer Research, 15*(2), 253–264. doi:10.1086/209162

Rowley, J. (2000). Product search in e-shopping: A review and research propositions. *Journal of Consumer Marketing, 17*(1), 20–35. doi:10.1108/07363760010309528

Saaty, T. L. (1980). *The analytic hierarchy process*. New York, NY: McGraw Hill.

Sarwar, B. M., Karypis, G., Konstan, J. A., & Riedl, J. (2000). *Analysis of recommendation algorithms for e-commerce*. Paper presented at the ACM Conference on Electronic Commerce. New York, NY.

Schafer, J. B., Konstan, J. A., & Riedl, J. (2001). E-commerce recommendation applications. *Data Mining and Knowledge Discovery, 5*(1/2), 115–153. doi:10.1023/A:1009804230409

Schmitt, C., Dengler, D., & Bauer, M. (2002). *The MAUT machine: An adaptive recommender system*. Paper presented at the ABIS Workshop 2002: Personalization for the Mobile World. Hannover, Germany.

Selnes, F., & Troye, S. V. (1989). Buying expertise, information search, and problem solving. *Journal of Economic Psychology, 10*(3), 411–428. doi:10.1016/0167-4870(89)90032-9

Seo, Y.-W., & Zhang, B.-T. (2000). *Learning user's preferences by analyzing Web-browsing behaviors*. Paper presented at the Fourth International Conference on Autonomous Agents. Barcelona, Spain.

Sharda, R., Barr, S. H., & McDonnell, J. C. (1988). Decision support system effectiveness: A review and an empirical test. *Management Science, 34*(2), 139–159. doi:10.1287/mnsc.34.2.139

Silver, M. (1991). *Systems that support decision makers: Description and analysis*. New York: Wiley.

Simon, H. A. (1960). *The new science of management decision*. New York: Harper.

Smith, G. E., & Wortzel, L. L. H. (1997). Prior knowledge and the effect of suggested frames of reference in advertising. *Psychology and Marketing, 14*(2), 121–143. doi:10.1002/(SICI)1520-6793(199703)14:2<121::AID-MAR2>3.0.CO;2-F

Srikumar, K., & Bhasker, B. (2004). *Personalized recommendations in e-commerce*. Paper presented at the Management of Electronic Business: 25th McMaster World Congress. Hamilton, Canada.

Stohr, E. A., & Viswanathan, S. (1999). Recommendation systems: Decision support for the information economy. In Kendall, K. E. (Ed.), *Emerging Information Technologies* (pp. 21–44). New York: SAGE Publications.

Toms, E. G. (2000). Understanding and facilitating the browsing of electronic text. *International Journal of Human-Computer Studies, 52*(3), 423–452. doi:10.1006/ijhc.1999.0345

Vahidov, R., & Ji, F. (2005). A method for infrequent purchase decision support in e-commerce. *Electronic Commerce Research and Applications, 4*(2), 143–158. doi:10.1016/j.elerap.2004.09.001

Vanegas, L. V., & Labib, A. W. (2001). Application of new fuzzy-weighted average (NFWA) method to engineering design evaluation. *International Journal of Production Research, 39*(6), 1147–1162. doi:10.1080/00207540010023592

Wang, Y.-F., Chuang, Y.-L., Hsu, M.-H., & Keh, H.-C. (2004). A personalized recommender system for the cosmetic business. *Expert Systems with Applications, 26*(3), 427–434. doi:10.1016/j.eswa.2003.10.001

Chapter 10
Family of Information System Meta–Artifacts

ABSTRACT

Development of the informative classification scheme for information system artifacts would be highly useful for design researchers in focusing and organizing their research projects and identifying gaps. There have been few dated attempts at IS classification mostly focusing on intra-organizational systems. This chapter stresses the need for newer frameworks, which would accommodate for recent developments in IS from the design-type research perspective. The chapter outlines one possible approach, which incorporates individuals, groups, organizations and markets as possible components. Classification could span through the layers of the representational framework presented earlier to produce the families of meta-requirements and synthetic and technological meta-systems. Design research frontier helps in identifying possible developments from the existing meta-systems towards true future system forms. Along this path design researchers are expected to encounter phantom forms.

DISCOVERING THE TYPES OF INFORMATION SYSTEMS

Design-type research in IS aims at discovering generic forms for such systems or their constituent components, which would be beneficial for improving performance of individuals, groups,

organizations, and markets. These forms, as pointed earlier, are essentially abstract entities, which could be instantiated in particular environmental contexts. While design-type science is, essentially, a C-type of science, design activities begin by producing the proper description of the (generic) problem context and examination of the existing solution forms. In order to provide guidance for researchers and help them organize their

DOI: 10.4018/978-1-4666-0131-4.ch010

projects, a descriptive typology of the existing problem contexts and solutions would be highly valuable. In other words, a general typology of existing information system solutions, including those widely used in practice, as well as the ones proposed by researchers and not-yet adopted by the practitioners, would be very much desirable.

An ideal model for classification of the IS would have a form of a hierarchy. Hierarchical typologies are well-organized and have a relatively low level of complexity. It would have been easier for researchers to position their work somewhere along the branches of such a hierarchy, perhaps by adding an additional "leaf" to the terminal branches. This would have been very much akin to the way different living forms are classified in the biological domain. Each type of organism is classified as particular species. At a higher level the similar forms are aggregated into genera, and so on. Thus, as one progresses towards higher levels in the hierarchy, the forms become more and more abstract. Applied to the IS domain, this would translate into the hierarchies of system forms of varying levels of abstractness. For example, one could position an active decision support system form as a subclass (species) of the DSS genus, which, in turn would be a subtype of a superclass of Information Systems, which, in turn is a sub-class of computing artifacts. Then, just like in the biological domain, the system types could be informatively described in terms of their features, structure, and behavior. The design researcher, could then be viewed as a discoverer of new "species" of IS, rather than an inventor of an artifact.

Unfortunately, an adequate way to arrive at such a clean classification hierarchy seems to be much more difficult compared to the biological model. The way biological evolution is working is not quite similar to the technological progress. Every species has one and only one parent genus. Interchange of form and behavior aspects between the individuals of different species is impossible, as these do not interbreed or their offspring is fertile. The biological taxonomy is well-aligned with the chronological order of the succession of living forms. The difficulty with developing a hierarchical classification schema for IS lies, partially in the fact that classes of systems may actually be regarded as subclasses of several more generic types. There is no particular rule in technological evolution that prohibits the mixing of various higher abstraction level form elements to produce a more specific subform. For example, a knowledge-based decision support system form may be regarded as an offspring of general DSS and general expert system forms, and thus, it would be inheriting some features and behaviors from both parents. This type of permitted relationships between classes is known as multiple inheritance, and it could lead to quite complex structures. In this regard, in object-oriented development the designers and programmers are well-advised to refrain from using multiple inheritance; in fact it is forbidden in later languages, including Java and C#, as opposed to earlier ones (e.g. C++). Chronological approach would not work either, as the evolution of technology is not quite as or-derly as the natural evolution. It would be highly doubtful to have the applications that had histori-cally appeared first at the root of the classification hierarchy. Indeed, it would be inadequate to put early payroll applications as the most generic type of information systems.

In view of the difficulty of developing a hi-erarchical classification model, one could try to adopt a tabular classification format, similar to the way it is done in Chemistry. The periodic table of elements nicely organizes them according to their atomic numbers. The latter here serves as a natural dimension that alleviates the classification task. The difficulty of applying such format to derive IS typology lies in the fact that systems could be classified according to several dimensions. For example, in textbooks it is common to list classes of IS, which include Transaction Processing Systems (TPS), DSS, Expert Systems, office productivity tools, and so on. On the other hand, one could also consider classification along functional areas, e.g.

marketing systems, operations support systems, etc. There doesn't seem to be a natural numeric scale by which system artifacts could be ordered.

Yet another hindrance to this descriptive task is that the characteristics of IS forms and behavior are not always accessible easily. While a natural scientist might be able to find a new organism type in the wild, or discover a new type of an element (lately by means of synthesis in the labs) the features and design aspects of instantiated systems are often protected by organizations, which makes the feature elicitation and classification task more difficult.

It is not surprising, thus that there is no solid accepted classification structure that nicely binds together all types of IS artifacts. The classification task seems to become easier, though when one considers a specific type of IS, e.g. decision support systems. While developing a complete classification model for information systems would be a very considerable effort, this section looks at earlier attempts and proposes a tentative schema for such a structure.

PAST WORK

There was some work in the past aiming to produce a solid classification framework for organizing various types of information systems. One early attempt in this regard dates back to 1980. The authors defined MIS as "a computer-based organizational information system which provides information support for management activities and functions" (Ives, Hamilton, & Davis, 1980). They noted, however that researchers also focus on transaction processing systems as well. In general the term MIS refers to a narrow class of systems mainly restricted to information reporting functions. Thus, generally the term "information systems" is preferred. Note also that this early definition refers to the systems, which are contained strictly within organizational boundaries. With the technological advances of the past two

decades, however, classes of systems have grown beyond the limits of a single organization.

The authors reviewed even earlier approaches to identify variables describing the essence of information systems to be used in IS research models. In this respect, it is interesting to mention the work by Chervany et al. (1971). In that work (truly limited to MIS) the authors had proposed a framework, according to which the dependent variable of decision effectiveness is influenced by the characteristics of decision maker and those of the decision environment, as well as the features of information systems. The decision environment was described in such terms as function (finance, marketing, etc.) and level (strategic, tactical). Information systems were characterized, in particular by format, including content, form, presentation, and media; and decision aids. It looks like this early characterization contained items, which could be mostly related to the analytical layer of the descriptive framework described earlier in the book. Such characteristics of information systems could, in principle, serve as the basis for their classification. Indeed they could help define the classes of meta-requirements.

The authors proposed the model for IS research, which includes the environmental variables, specifically: external environment, the organizational environment, the user environment, the IS development environment, and the IS operations environment (Ives, Hamilton, & Davis, 1980). The other two factors include the information subsystem and process variables. The information subsystem contains three classes of variables, including content (data and decision models), presentation form (the way information is provide to the user), and time dimension. Here, the presentation form seems to better fit the analytical layer description, while content most likely refers to the synthetic layer. The process variables include development process, operations process, and use process. The authors proceeded to recommend the categories of research derived from their model, which will not be discussed here, as the focus of this chapter is on the categories of IS.

Another widely cited early work for viewing managerial information systems (predominantly from the decision support view) looked to categorize them by the level of management control and the level of structuredness of the decision making task (Gorry & Scott-Morton, 1971). In this two-dimensional framework the kind of managerial activity relates to the scope of the decision at hand and includes operational, management (tactical), and strategic levels. The second dimension distinguishes between structured and unstructured decision situation. The structured decisions relate to cases where standard procedures for executing decisions are in place. In such case decision systems are the appropriate form of information system solutions. In the unstructured case decision support tools are more adequate. By now the framework has become a standard part of major textbooks on decision support systems.

Based on the framework discussed above (Ives, Hamilton, & Davis, 1980), in (Barki, Rivard, & Talbot, 1988) a keyword classification scheme for IS research has been proposed, which was subsequently updated in (Barki, Rivard, & Talbot, 1993). The authors noted that classification scheme for the keywords was important as it helps researchers organize and scope their work. The following top-level categories for keyword classification were proposed: reference disciplines; external environment; technological environment; organizational environment; IS management; IS development and operations; IS usage; information systems; and IS education and research. The list of keywords had been compiled from top IS outlets, as well as the textbooks. The authors produced a list of keywords that contained about 2000 of them. These were then classified according to the categories identified.

Each of the top-level categories was further subdivided into subcategories. For the present discussion some of these subcategories are more relevant than the others. Reference disciplines included, among others behavior science; computer science; decision sciences; information theory; systems theory; management science; artificial intelligence; and others. The technological environment included computer systems and software. IS usage included organizational use of IT; types of IS support, access, and processing. Most importantly, information systems contained the subcategories of types of information systems; IS application areas; components of IS; and IS characteristics (features).

Within the "types of information systems" category the following keywords had been compiled: transaction processing systems; management information systems; decision support systems (including group DSS and distributed decision-making systems); expert systems; executive support systems; inter-organizational systems (including electronic markets); computer-based communication systems; information storage and retrieval systems; document management systems; electronic meeting systems; collaborative work systems; model management systems; image systems; and authoring systems. The IS application areas subcategory included various functions (e.g. financial, marketing) or types of organizations (e.g. banking, government) as application domains. The components of IS included user interface; database; programs; input; output; information resource; knowledge base; and modules. IS characteristics included interface characteristics; database characteristics; and IS structure.

Clearly, since it has been a fairly long period since the last update of the classification, it would require a major expansion nowadays and, most likely deletion of obsolete keywords. The scheme, though does not classify IS per se, but only the keywords found in research publications about IS.

Another paper (again, somewhat dated) focused directly on IS classification rather than on identifying types of research in IS (Ein-Dor & Segev, 1993). The work is quite comprehensive and interesting and, thus, it is worthwhile to take an in-depth look into the findings and insights by the authors. The paper looks to explore the deep patterns behind diversity of IS artifacts to promote better understanding of their range. The definition of IS by the authors is much broader than the one cited earlier as it includes "any computerized system with a user or operator interface ... provided the computer is not physically embedded." Thus, it spans systems beyond what one typically considers to be a business application, such as transaction processing or management information systems. The authors exclude from the consideration embedded systems, such as self-guiding missiles, while manufacturing robots are judged to be a borderline case.

In order to identify the major types of IS the authors had conducted an extensive review of the publications in the area. They had identified seventeen major types of systems, while acknowledging some degree of arbitrariness in their analysis and the possibility of omitting some major classes, which they argue are subtypes of the wider classes. For example, marketing information systems constitute a subcategory of MIS. The types of IS identified in the work included: Early Computation; Early Data Processing; MIS; DSS; Office Information Systems/Office Automation (OIS/OA); Executive Information Systems (EIS); Group Decision Support Systems (GDSS); Expert Systems (ES); Mature Data Processing; Scientific Computation; Material Requirements Planning; Manufacturing Resource Planning; Computer-Aided Design (CAD); Computer-Aided Manufacturing (CAM); CAD/CAM; Manufacturing Robots; and Command, Control, Communications, and Intelligence.

Admittedly, the boundaries of the information systems domain are not clear-cut, and this raises a question of whether some of the categories listed by the authors truly constitute IS. Also, due to the rapid and significant changes in the technological environment new important types of systems had appeared since the paper had been published. Nonetheless, what is more important is the method used by the authors in conducting their analysis to arrive at a taxonomic characterization of IS meta-artifacts. To proceed with such an analysis there must be a way to characterize existing types of systems in a meaningful descriptive fashion. Important aspects of such characterization can serve as means of defining a given type of IS.

The authors noted that there are two sorts of definitions given in the literature. Firstly, the system could be defined in terms of its functionality; secondly, it could be described in terms of its attributes. Two examples of EIS definitions have been mentioned in this respect. For the sake of the discussion here, it is useful to cite the definitions the authors had referred to. The first one reads: "...EIS should use the following techniques: a non-keyboard interface...; the ability to combine text and graphics on the same screen; relational, time-series information storage; electronic communication facilities integrated with office automation" (Kogan, 1986). The second one states that EIS "support the information monitoring needs of executives and managers by providing flexible, user controllable displays of operational results and external information (DSS-89, 1989). (Both definitions have been cited in (Ein-Dor & Segev, 1993)).

Despite the fact that both definitions are over twenty years old, and the term EIS itself has been largely abandoned (in favor of "business intelligence" and "business analytics"), it is worthwhile to take a closer look at the components of definitions, as the insights may help future classification attempts, in particular in the context of design-type research. If one tries to relate the elements of the above definitions to a layered model of IS artifacts presented in this book, one could notice that some of these (within the same definition) elements relate to different layers. For example, in the first definition, the terms "non-keyboard interface" and "ability to combine text and graphics" would fit under the analytical level of representation. The terms "time series information storage" and "communication facilities with office automation" would probably be linked with the synthetic level of description. The term "relational" relate to the concrete type of technology, and would fit in the technological layer. The second definition completely lies within the analytical layer, as it does not refer to the structural or behavioral aspects of the system from the architect's point of view. Thus, it would be a desirable characteristic of a system definition to include only components from one layer. Then related definitions could be given of a meta-artifact as meta-requirements and meta-solution (synthetic or technological).

It appears from the authors' discussion that functions relate more to the analytical description, while attributes describe the structural aspects of the given type of system-as-design. This relation though is not completely definitive, as both requirements and solutions could be described in terms of structural, as well as behavioral aspects. The authors noted that for the completeness of description and classification, both functions and attributes of the systems must be included in the study. Thus, in the authors' vision, these constituted the vectors describing major types of information systems.

The authors had scanned a large number of system definitions to derive 31 attributes and 27 functions. Some examples of the attributes included: graphics; real time; interactive; user control. Examples of functions included: data collection; arithmetic computation; symbol processing; learning. Some of these clearly belonged to different levels of description. Compare, for example "supporting structured decisions" with "inference" and with "distributed processing" (physical). The first function definitely describes a meta-requirement, the second one relates to a capability of the system delivered by some type of an inferencing module, and the third characterizes physical implementation aspects.

The attribute and function vectors were then used to calculate the differences between the systems by comparing binary vectors. A multidimensional scaling technique was then used to arrive at dimensions along which different types of systems were positioned. On the graphs featuring these systems (as dots) curves were drawn separating clusters of systems. For example, the separating curves on the attribute scaling graph distinguished between non-interactive (e.g. early data processing, MIS, MRP) and interactive systems (e.g. DSS, CAM). Other curves on this graph included non-batch mode; natural language text; and user control. The separating lines on the function scaling graph included making structured decisions; controlling processes; communicating; and supporting unstructured decisions.

Interestingly, the authors also discussed the possibility of interpreting the results from the point of view of technological evolution. To this end they considered the evolutionary framework that distinguishes technological evolution from the natural one and proposes four basic concepts in approaching the study of the former: diversity, continuity, novelty, and selection (Basalla, 1988). Based on this framework the authors had attempted to position the development of different types of systems in chronological order. Their partial map of system difference by attributes aligned along the chronological dimension shows possible paths of evolution. Overall, the authors pointed two major paths of development, which they called "applied artificial intelligence path" and "human interface path." One example path of evolution, according to the authors proceeds from early computation to early data processing, to MIS, to DSS and to GDSS. While the evolutionary view of technological progress may certainly be interesting in many respects, as discussed earlier, it does not naturally lead to the type of classification schema as it would in biology. For example, CAD/CAM systems seem to evolve both from CAM and CAM, which represents the case of multiple inheritance, mentioned earlier. Some types of system do not seem to fit the succession of artifacts naturally and were left out of the map, e.g. expert systems. Another difficulty with putting a chronological perspective in regards with technology evolution is the possibility of evolving terminology. When new terms replace the old ones (e.g. application vs. program) it creates an additional noise in judging the distances between systems that appeared at different times. Thus, systems that co-existed in the same epoch may be judged to be closer, just because of the similarity of terminology.

INFORMATION SYSTEM TYPES AND REPRESENTATIONAL FRAMEWORK

As it has been pointed in the above section some classification attempts in the past distinguished between system functions and their attributes (features). It appeared, though that the distinction did not explicitly separate between the analytical vs. design views of the system. From the analytical point of view, a (meta-) system is described by means of (meta-) requirements. Thus, to say that a given class of systems features high degree of autonomy would be essentially a reflection of a requirement, which implies that a task the system performs is highly structured. The analytical view treats a system as a black box. On the other hand to say that a system incorporates a module, which performs optimization implies a synthetic (design) perspective. To describe an artifact in terms of the design of an application framework or a package means to provide technological description.

In their seminal work, Hevner et al. have provided a framework for IS research, in which this research is influenced by an influences the environment (including people, organization and technology) and the "knowledge base" (including foundations, e.g. theories, frameworks, instruments, methods, etc. and methodologies, e.g. data analysis techniques, formalisms, etc.) (Hevner, March, Park, & Ram, 2004). From the point of view of the structure of a design theory (Markus, Majchrzak, & Gasser, 2002; Walls, Widmeyer, & El Sawy, 1992) it is easy to see similarities between the knowledge base of the framework

and the kernel theories. In an earlier discussion, it might have appeared that kernel theories help define the meta-requirements, which then translate into meta-system design. In light of the work on IS classification, the kernel theories actually help define not only requirements, but also inform the design of the artifact. Here, we will not make distinction between the terms "kernel theories," "knowledge base," or "reference disciplines." The relationship between a meta-artifact and kernel theories is shown schematically on Figure 1.

Theories from the problem description-related category help describe the meta-requirements for an artifact. For example, the consumer buying behavior model helps define the phases to be supported by an online store. Theories related to solution description provide means of outlining the design of an artifact type. For example, available optimization techniques may guide the design of an electronic market system. Technology related theories may guide the choice of technologies used in producing generic artifact packages. For example, expert system shells may be used as part of a knowledge-based system composition.

Table 1 shows examples of the theory and artifact descriptions (in no particular order) mostly using classifications provided in (Barki, Rivard, & Talbot, 1988, 1993; Ein-Dor & Segev, 1993). On the left hand the knowledge base (kernel theories) provides knowledge that helps shaping the meta-requirements, meta-synthetic solution, and meta-technological solution. Admittedly, it is hard to see how technological terms could be regarded as theoretical components. Yet, from the perspective of an artifact as knowledge, these technological types of solutions help the design-type researcher in constructing a generic type of a solution. Potentially, using descriptive subset of terms from the right side, three different types of classifications are possible: families of meta-artifacts as meta-requirements, as meta-systems, and as meta-technological solutions.

Figure 1. Kernel theories and meta-artifact

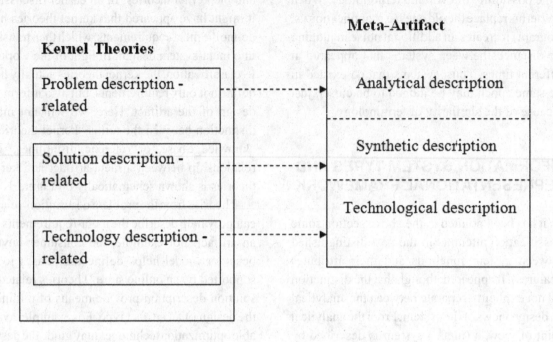

Table 1. Examples of keywords related to kernel theory and meta-artifact descriptions

Kernel theories	Meta-artifact
Problem description-related Behavioral science Human information processing Individual differences Decision making styles Management style Management techniques Agency theory Social science Problem solving	**Analytical** Supporting operations Supporting structured decisions Making structured decisions Supporting unstructured decisions Learning Text processing
Solution description-related Decision theory Information presentation Management science Optimization Simulation Heuristics Artificial Intelligence Neural networks Deduction and Reasoning	**Synthetic** Transaction processing systems MIS DSS Group DSS Expert systems Inference engine Real-time Model base Database
Technology description-related Computer architecture Distributed systems Web-based systems Client-server Database management systems Software packages Object-oriented systems Software architecture Algorithms	**Technological** Application package Application framework Software component Expert system shell Object Service Grid

FAMILY OF META-REQUIREMENTS

Undoubtedly, the classification schemes presented in this chapter are somewhat outdated. Significant technological developments of the past two decades have brought about novel system forms. In the past information systems were considered to be lying entirely within organizational boundaries of the firm. With the proliferation of networks this assumption is no longer valid. Newer approaches to categorizing the types of systems are much needed. This chapter does not attempt to develop a complete classification of IS types. This is a sizable work that lies beyond the scope of the present manuscript. Nonetheless, such an effort should be valuable, especially when undertaken from a design-type research perspective. Here, one potential framework for identifying the major types of systems will be advanced, with few examples given.

Since systems are no longer confined to particular organizational contexts, it is important to recognize various context categories, where IS could be used. One possibility is to follow up on the work mentioned earlier in the book that looked to uncover major topics in IS research (Sidorova, Evangelopoulos, & Valacich, 2008). To recall, in this work five research areas have been identified, including IT and organizations, IS development, IT and individuals, IT and markets, and IT and groups. Thus, it seems appropriate that the components for the classification framework could include the following contexts: individuals, groups, organizations, and markets (perhaps, with minor deviation from what these were referring to

in the above paper). Moreover, it could be useful to consider relationships between the components as IS application contexts as well. For example, there could be systems supporting business processes within organizations, as well as those involved in organization-to-organization interactions. One possibility to outline context categories is shown in Table 2.

To avoid confusion, here individuals include those persons who are not part of organizations. The individuals working within organizations are considered as integral parts of these organizations. Thus, individuals here mostly relate to consumers. Groups, on the other hand may be parts of organizations or include members from two or more organizations. Thus, since the composition of the groups may lie within or cross organizational boundaries, we do not consider their interaction with organizations. Markets are separate from organizations as they provide mechanisms for finding products, services, vendors and customers, and facilitating the exchange processes. Markets may provide these exchanges for use between businesses, individuals and businesses, and between individuals.

Another dimension for classification can be adopted from the earlier mentioned work on categorizing DSS (Gorry & Scott-Morton, 1971). The level of structure in performing a task has significant implications for the degree of potential automation and emphasis on the type of support. For each requirement category the nature of requirements may differ by the degree of structuredness. For simplicity, we could focus here on structured vs. unstructured task dichotomy. In the

Table 2. IS application context types

	Self	Individual	Organization	Market
Individual	V		V	V
Group	V			
Organization	V	V	V	V
Market	V	V	V	

remainder of the section we will briefly discuss the nature of requirements for each of the checked cells in Table 2. Ideally, one would come up with the complete description of behavioral and structural (feature) aspects of these categories of requirements, but this, as mentioned, would constitute a separate substantial effort, and it is not the central objective of the present monograph.

Systems supporting individuals. Structured tasks here would require systems with capabilities of typing, performing simple calculations, personal data entry, etc. For unstructured tasks, applications, which allow analysis and personal decision support, including what-if analysis and optimization are appropriate. For example, to enable analysis of personal spending an application could have the facilities of tracking and reporting an individual's spending, perhaps enhanced with summary and exception reporting. Another example in decision making context would be a personal decision support tool that allows an individual to perform a what-if analysis in choosing a type of mortgage. Optimization tools may also be used as part of decision support. For example a system supporting tax preparation may have optimization capabilities to recommend tax filing strategies if the respective laws allow for some degree of flexibility.

Systems supporting groups. For structured tasks the systems supporting the work of multiple individuals should focus on communication and coordination of work. Depending on the context of group work, the need for the capability to jointly author the documents, including document retrieval policies, revisions, commenting, and imposing the overall policies and procedures may be needed. For the work in project-centric groups the systems having capabilities for project management and organizing the coordination of activities and organizing workflow would be useful. For unstructured tasks the focus would move from coordination (which still may be required) to group decision support facilities. As such, such system could include the capabilities of gathering the input of individuals and communicating it to others, preference elicitation methods, capabilities for clarifying criteria, evaluating and ranking alternatives and estimating their impact on the criteria. In inter-organizational group settings in the potential presence of substantial difference between the objectives of different subgroups, the group decision support facilities may be complemented by negotiation support tools, which would enable for the privacy of the part of the subgroup information and discussion.

Organizational systems. This is the category, which includes oldest types of requirements addresses within organizations and it includes a wide range of applications. Up until recently (before the internet revolution) all information systems were considered as being internal organizational systems. For structured tasks the requirements of entering, editing, updating, and deleting business records (transactions) are most prominent. In maintaining the key processes within organizations the respective systems should follow the business logic as reflected in operational procedures. Routine information reporting capabilities for managers help them to have the control of the operations. Individuals within organizations also use document management and general office productivity tools. For unstructured tasks, such as analysis and decision making the systems may have the capabilities of on-demand information reporting, producing summary and detailed information, "what-if" scenario analysis, "What's-best" capability, knowledge management facilities, and others.

Market systems. These include requirements for various forms of markets, which could be implemented electronically. Markets could support exchanges between the organizations, organizations and individuals, and between individuals. The structured market forms could feature products listed in a catalogue-like fashion by different vendors, typically for the fixed price. A more advanced type of market includes various types of mechanisms allowing parties to make bids. For unstructured exchange tasks a market may offer different types of negotiation capabilities. A market may have additional features, which could help the participants to form an economic relationship, e.g. matchmaking and reputation tracking.

Individual-to-market and organization-to-market systems. These systems would fulfill the requirements of organizations or individuals in finding vendors/products, monitor market developments, and implement selling/purchasing tactics. For structured tasks automated tools could be used, for example, to implement pricing or bidding tasks. For unstructured tasks the decision support tools may be used to monitor market developments, make predictions, and implement decisions through bidding or negotiation. This category represents a good opportunity for design researchers to explore, as there seem to be few real-life widely used solution types.

Organization-to-organization systems. These systems aim to support direct relationships between partner organizations. Typically the tasks would fall under supply chain management category. For structured tasks the systems would allow efficient data interchange, such as sending orders between the parties. For unstructured tasks such as contract negotiation the systems may be equipped with communication, negotiation and joint document storage and authoring facilities.

Organization-to-individual systems. The systems in this category support customer needs for product search, product catalog browsing and ordering. They may also include the possibility of accepting customer offers, although this is far from being a common practice. They further include facilities for customer support to handle a variety of requests. The means to provide such support range from frequently asked questions pages to online tutorials and chats.

The above scheme for requirements classification may be suffering from a number of disadvantages. Firstly, some given category (e.g. organizational systems) may incorporate a much

richer and wider range of requirements than some others (imbalance). However, this seems to be inevitable in light of the desire to neatly categorize a rather large number of different requirements types within the framework provided by the four components. To deal with this imbalance each of the categories would need to have its own, more detailed sub-classification. Secondly, some of the described categories may not actually have a substantial presence in real-life (error of commission). For example, individual-to-market systems mostly appear in research projects, rather than real-life. This is, however not an issue, as the topic of the book is design-type research the aim here is not to classify existing systems, but the potential ones. After all, the design researcher's interest is in discovering the non-existent. Thirdly, some of the cells in Table 2 were left blank indicating no existence for a certain type of requirements (error of omission). For example, the need for market-to-market systems may be overlooked here. However, the fact that the cell was left blank does not imply that a given type of system is denied the right for existence. The filled cells indicate categories for which either existing and widely adopted systems are used in real-life, or (as shall be seen in the next section) they were conceptualized in one way or the other in design research projects. It is well-admissible that future developments will show the significance of the omitted categories as well.

FAMILY OF SYNTHETIC META-SYSTEMS

Family of meta-requirements describes various broad classes of problem contexts in terms of generic, somewhat abstractly defined expected features and behavior of systems. The latter are to a large extent treated in a blackbox fashion. Family of meta-systems would consist of types of solutions for the classes of meta-requirements. Ideally such a classification would be done in terms of all essential structural and process aspects. Here, a blackbox view would be replaced with the outline of internal organization of a given meta-system, albeit at a certain level of abstraction. Subclasses of systems could then be added with extra-features in addition to those inherited from the higher-level classes. In this section we will not be concerned with the thorough and rigorous classification, but, rather we will mention the major types of systems with few features outlined.

At the synthetic layer, it may be the case that a given system form, at some level of abstraction could serve several classes of requirements as outlined earlier. For example, a form for decision support may have similar major components, regardless of whether it is intended for supporting individuals within or outside an organization. Thus mapping of meta-requirements to meta-systems is not necessarily of one-to-one type. Below for each meta-requirement category mentioned above a type of meta-solution is presented. Admittedly, some of the meta-system descriptions may appear trivial. Nonetheless, for the completeness sake every category is briefly described.

Systems supporting individuals. Systems supporting structured tasks would place emphasis on ease of use, and ease of learning (intuitive interface). The category contains a range of systems commonly referred to as productivity tools. Such applications would have to have small data storage, which could be implemented as a database or a file. They may also have modules allowing for text creation and editing with a possible spell and grammar checking, a library of frequently used functions, modules for enabling customizability, and means of providing extendibility of functionality. For design researchers one interesting dimension to investigate is the degree of automation achievable in carrying out routine tasks. In this regard, the work on personal assistants looks to provide individuals with a kind of personal virtual secretaries. For example, artificial agent concepts have been proposed for calendar and time management tasks (Berry, et al., 2006; Modi,

Veloso, Smith, & Oh, 2005). For the unstructured tasks a classical solution is a personal decision support approach. Traditionally, these systems included data, models, and user interface. Various additions to these components could provide new types of decision support. For example, adding agents to basic DSS structure would most likely produce a system form that belongs to the subclass of "active" DSS. For design researchers personal decision support presents interesting opportunities with regards to separating automatable vs. non-automatable parts of human decision making under changing technological environment. For example, in (Fazlollahi, Parikh, & Verma, 1997) a personal DSS for asset allocation problem had been proposed. In addition to the basic DSS parts it also featured an "adaptation" component that, in particular, helped to adapt system recommendations to the decision maker profile. Another example design-type research in this category proposed a type of an active solution for personal finance management (Vahidov & He, 2010). In particular, it included such components as sensors, effectors, and an active "manager."

Systems supporting groups. The term "computer-supported collaborative work" historically referred to methods of facilitating work in groups. Other related terms also include groupware and collaboration support. The category contains a wide variety of systems, including such subclasses as collaborative document authoring and project management. The structural and process aspects vary, but at a broader level, such systems include components for facilitating communication, collaboration, and coordination (Wells & Kurien, 1996). This is an active area of research for design researchers looking to provide innovative solutions for improving group work. For the unstructured tasks, the analytical tools may also be included (e.g. the component for supporting analytical hierarchy process in ranking decision alternatives) in a type of systems known as group decision support systems (Watson, DeSanctis, & Poole, 1988). There are various opportunities for design researchers to investigate the ways of facilitating effective decision making in groups. For example, in (Briggs, Vreede, & Nunamaker, Jr, 2003) the modules called ThinkLets are used to improve the group work and decision making processes. ThinkLets incorporate various protocols to be used in group work, e.g. stressing convergence.

Organizational systems. Transaction processing systems represent a major class of applications in this domain. These are used to maintain operational records to run day-to-day business processes. Large data stores are used to maintain volumes of business records. Business logic layer software modules manage the execution of business processes. Management information systems have reporting modules, which pull the data from database to provide a variety of managerial reports. As these above types of systems are among the oldest business applications targeting well-structured processes, there seem to be little room for design researchers to try inventing radically new logical forms. For some other types of structured tasks though, there are opportunities for innovative design concepts to be applied. For example, there is a bulk of research looking to apply methods of artificial intelligence (e.g. expert systems, neural networks, fuzzy logic, etc.) to fraud detection problem. One example of such an approach is proposed in (Estévez, Held, & Perez, 2006). For unstructured problems various forms of decision support systems are used. These include, among others, data warehouse solutions, business intelligence/analytics software, data mining approaches, and others. Such systems include as major components data storage (separate from operational databases in case of data warehouse), models, modules to facilitate flexible data display (e.g. summary information and drill-down, slicing and dicing of data hypercubes, etc.), and toolboxes with different data mining means. There are various opportunities for design researchers to help expand the frontiers of such solutions. For example, there is a stream of research on providing

active data warehouse solutions (e.g. Thalhammer, Schrefl, & Mohani, 2001).

Market systems. Internet has enabled global electronic markets. Various forms of market systems facilitate exchanges between businesses and individuals. The simplest marketplace form may simply serve as a website where buyers and sellers could post their respective requests concerning products and services. In general form these marketplaces would need to have extensive storage with product and user information along with the appropriate access mechanisms, components for managing searching and browsing activities, and, possibly, reputation tracking components. They may also feature parts for alert generation and support for messaging and chatting (with a possibility for negotiation) between buyers and sellers. One such example is a business-to-business marketplace alibaba.com. Auctions, in their variety are well-structured markets in a sense that once bids are submitted the outcomes can be determined in an algorithmic way. They should include mechanisms for bid submission, components for deciding on winning bids, and those for calculating allocation of goods or services to ensure the proper clearance of the auction. These components may have to execute tasks of a varying degree of complexity depending on the type of an auction. Design researchers may be involved in discovering new types of market forms and various related methods. For example, in (Petric & Jezic, 2009) a reputation tracking mechanism had been proposed for reverse auctions; in (Sandholm, 2002) an algorithm for winner determination in combinatorial auctions had been described. Market engineering offers various other possibilities for creative meta-solutions (Gimpel, Jennings, Kersten, Ockenfels, & Weinhardt 2007).

Individual-to-market and organization-to-market systems. Electronic marketplaces typically have some support tools to match products/vendors with buyers and facilitate exchanges. Nonetheless, there are applications for providing means of individual's or organization's interaction with the markets, which are not necessarily an integral part of the latter. For example, there are sites, which enable customers to find deals while collecting information from other markets. One such site finds farming products listed on various auctions to present them to the user (http://www.farmauctionguide.com). Another site monitors auctions (e.g. eBay) to deliver information on a wide variety of products (www.auctionlotwatch.co.uk). It has a number of components to help the sellers properly prepare their postings, and the buyers find what they are looking for and pursue auction winning tactics. These components include auction speller, auction sniper, reminders and other tools. Another category of tools include software agents, which could automate much of human user-market interaction to fulfill the objectives of an exchange. Past research in this direction looked to provide means of automating the bidding process (e.g. Wurman, Wellman, & Walsh, 1998). Design researchers have exciting opportunities in proposing innovative methods to help organizations and individuals better achieve their objectives in interaction with different types of market mechanisms. In particular, one intriguing possibility is to explore the ways of combining decision support tools with automated components in managing buying or selling tasks in the presence of uncertainty and dynamics in markets and business environments.

Organization-to-organization systems. The major class of systems in this category includes those supporting automation of interactions between organizations in a supply chain context. A well-established type of a solution is electronic data interchange. It contains components ensuring information communication between the partners, and means of translating electronic orders into business formats. Another type of application includes software for RFQ/RFP preparation. Some opportunities for design researchers interested in this category include exploring application of agents and innovative decision and negotiation support tools in sourcing decisions, contract negotiations, RFQ/RFP preparation, and other activities. Examples of agent-based approaches to supply chain management can be found in (Kim & Cho, 2010; Nissen, 2001).

Organization-to-individual systems. These systems provide means for businesses to interact with customers directly. This is a well-known category of applications providing front-end facilities for the customers. Design researchers may explore the ways of providing intelligent shopping and customer service support and investigate the non-conventional ways of selling. For example, an online car dealer site (http://www.tonkin.com/) allows customers to negotiate the deals. According to one source (http://www.automotivedigitalmarketing.com/profiles/blogs/online-negotiation-almost) this feature had led to a considerable business performance improvement.

FAMILY OF TECHNOLOGICAL META-SYSTEMS

Synthetic meta-system view emphasizes overall logical organization of a system concept in terms of major components. These components relate to the existing types of solutions contained in the "knowledge base." Technological-layer meta-artifacts describe more detailed artifact design with the emphasis placed on technical aspects. The objective at this layer is achieving technical generality. Technological meta-systems (e.g. packages, frameworks, shells, application generators, toolkits, etc.) are located closest to the instantiated systems, and, from the design research perspective facilitate the progress from synthetic artifacts-ideas to their practical implementation. Since innovative approaches to designing and building these meta-systems is rather a subject for the practitioners and researchers in computer science and software engineering, rather than information systems researchers, we will briefly discuss few examples of meta-systems here.

As mentioned earlier transaction processing systems have been in use for a long time and their basic logical organization has been well-understood. However, their technological organization varied considerably due to the particular approaches to their design and implementation within organizations and the specific functions they handled. Enterprise Resource Planning packages had appeared in the Nineties as an elegant technological framework to address various requirements for supporting business operations. The keyword to ERP philosophy is integration, as they looked to offer a suite of capabilities within a single package and a common database to eliminate data redundancy and inconsistency.

The categories of functions supported by the ERP systems include manufacturing, financial applications, human resources, supply chain management and others. Thus, as one can see the ERP systems actually cover a range of synthetic meta-systems as described above, including, for example, organizational and organization-to-organization categories. Moreover, the integrated nature of the package allows expanding their capabilities for decision support purposes as well. Thus, while early ERP implementations were for a major part pure transaction processing systems, later developments also contained DSS category. In (Holsapple & Sena, 2005) benefits of ERP systems on decision support objectives has been investigated. The following categories of decision support contexts have been identified: individual decisions; multiple people making joint decision; multiple people making inter-related decisions; and people from inside and outside of an organization making cooperative or negotiated decisions. Thus, ERP packages cross the structured vs. unstructured tasks boundary as well.

Though ERP solutions may not be suitable for all types of organizations, studies have been performed in order to assess the causes of success and failure of ERP implementation projects (Gargeya & Brady, 2005). The technical design of an ERP package features components encoding standard business processes, which could be customized to some extent. Thus, as such the ERP concept is an example of a technological meta-artifact. Per se it does not introduce a new synthetic concept, but rather can be considered as a combination of several synthetic meta-systems. In this respect some synthetic-layer design research could still be performed on ERPs as they are mapped onto the synthetic layer. For example, in (Lea, Guptab, & Yuc, 2005) use of agents, including coordinating agents, task agents, data collecting agents, and user interface agents within the ERP concept has been proposed. The work is purely synthetic as it does not aim at producing a technical meta-solution.

While ERP systems primarily targeted support of operations, a class of applications had emerged to specifically aim at informing analysis and decision making processes in organizations. We had seen that the basic components of DSS include models and data components. Alter's early typology included various types of data-based DSS ranging in their capacity from simple data retrieval functions to systems retrieving and integrating information from various data stores. The advance of data warehouse solutions presented a new technical concept to building effective data-centric analysis and decision support applications. Coupled with modeling components these applications would provide powerful business intelligence/analytics tools to promote "integrated" decision support (March & Hevner, 2005).

The key technical design decision in data warehouses as opposed to regular databases is separation of operational data from that dedicated to analysis and decision-making. This is due to realization that the informational needs for the latter are different from those required to run day-to-day business processes. In particular, various operational databases may have inconsistent data formats. Thus, for analytical support one would require some way to integrate data from various sources in a consistent fashion. Analysis may be directed towards key subjects, e.g. customers, sales, etc. Therefore data needs to be organized according to subjects. It would be useful to study trends and developments in key business indicators. Thus, data needs to be time-stamped and durable. Also, it would be useful for the managers to view data along several dimensions to efficiently assess a given situation and developments, rather than in a traditional report format. Therefore, a multi-dimensional organization of data storage is required.

From the layered perspective of meta-artifact representation framework, it may appear that the work in analytical perspective would precede the conception of a synthetic meta-system, followed by the more technical design. This could be the case if the underlying technical components for a given synthetic solution are known to exist. For example, if a given synthetic solution type includes a database and a regression analysis module, then since the models, approaches and packages are available in the technical "knowledge base" to implement them, such a synthetic design would be feasible and well-understood. In case of data warehouses, though, the existing technologies could not be employed, but the new technical design solutions had to be made. For example, the organization of data storage, the idea of non-normalized data, the need for data extraction and conversion tools, and the concept of meta-data were all innovative technical design solutions. These, in fact enabled the emergence of the common data warehouse architecture and the type of support of analysis described above.

Since data warehouses can be largely considered as technological meta-artifacts, design research in the area tends to be of a more technical nature. For example, there is research stream on active data warehouses. Conventional solutions tend to periodically upload data from the operational stores to the warehouse. Active data warehouses are the ones that try to obtain data in real-time. This poses problems related to effectively managing

and coordinating data streams (Dayal, Castellanos, Simitsis, & Wilkinson, 2009; Polyzotis, Skiadopoulos, Vassiliadis, Simitsis, & Frantzell, 2007). For overview of research directions in data warehouse design one could be referred to (Rizzi, Abelló, Lechtenbörger, & Trujillo, 2006).

While ERP systems and data warehouses represented significant breakthroughs in information systems practice, the next type of technological solution type considered here has a much narrower application domain, comparatively limited adoption levels by the industry and is more subject of research projects. The emergence of intelligent agents as a field posed a question of the adequate internal design for these active software components. In the absence of commonly accepted definition a wide range of agent designs have appeared, some explicitly incorporating such categories as beliefs and desires, while others having much simpler organizations. A number of agent building toolkits have been developed, for example Jade (Bellifemine, Poggi, & Rimassa, 2001) and Zeus (Nwana, Ndumu, Lee, & Collis, 1999) to facilitate construction of agent systems (Shakshuki & Jun, 2004). Here we will briefly discuss the organization of a commercial agent construction toolkit AgentBuilder (http://www.agentbuilder.com) from Acronymics Inc.

The java-based package features a run-time system, containing agent engine, and an agent building toolkit. The latter includes project control tools; ontology manager; agent manager; agency manager; and agent debugger. The ontology manager allows the developers to define the concepts of the problem domain. It includes concept mapping tools; concept graphing tools; and object modeling tools. Agent manager can be used to define the model and behavior of individual agents. It uses such mental categories as beliefs, intentions, and commitments. The agency manager allows combining individual agents into a multi-agent system. The emphasis here is on communication and cooperation. The knowledge query manipulation language standard is used for inter-agent communications. Practitioners and design researchers interested in agent-based applications may adopt such a package, if suitable to produce agent-based solutions and research prototypes.

DESIGN-TYPE RESEARCH FRONTIER AND PHANTOM META-ARTIFACTS

This chapter reviewed some past attempts at deriving useful classification approaches to identify a typology for information system artifacts. One possible approach has been outlined albeit in a tentative fashion. Design researchers would greatly benefit from a descriptive classification, since it would help the focus and organize their research initiatives and help uncover existing gaps. Figure 2 shows schematically IS artifacts organized according to some possible hierarchical

classification scheme (while the difficulty with hierarchical classification has been admitted earlier in the chapter, it would still be possible to derive it by choosing the most "relevant" parent class as a single superclass for a given subclass). On the left hand existing adopted types of IS solutions are shown as darkened circles. On the right hand the dashed lines show possible paths of future IS evolution. Some of these would lead to true future meta-artifacts shown as white circles. Others may lead into wrong future forms, i.e. the types of systems that will not be adopted by the respective application domain users to a substantial extent. These are called, here, "phantom meta-artifacts." The curved dashed line displays the design-type research frontier. This is where design researchers can contribute towards discovering the new types of IS forms.

Like in traditional science, the new forms are discovered by the researchers as they add new types of objects to the tree of the existing knowl-

Figure 2. Design-type research frontier

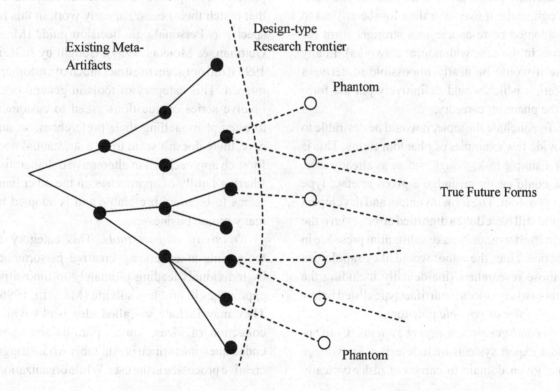

edge. Except, here the forms are discovered by designing. Their existent is latent, and the discovery process is not a linear and steady progression. As in other sciences many dead ends are taken and multiple phantoms are met (conceived) along the journey. Yet few of them, it is hoped, will lead to true future forms.

A classification scheme for design researchers should illuminate the existing work and make the design-type research frontier explicit. One way to derive it would be to study the recent design-type publications in established journals and conference proceedings. Such a study would involve documenting the features and functions of the invented IS forms, probably in a fashion consistent with the representational framework introduced in an earlier chapter. Then analysis of the data would help derive the common classes and subclasses of system types. It could also help identify the phantom forms. Let's say, if a research stream focusing on an artifact type X is clearly on the decline, while X does not seem to be adopted in practice, then that artifact type is a candidate phantom. This may not be the case, though, since it may take time for the artifact to be adopted or re-appear in a stronger form (as it was in the case with neural networks). In any case it would be nearly impossible to derive a criterion which would definitively put the form in the phantom category.

To conclude the topic, it would be desirable to provide few examples of phantom forms. This is not a simple task, though, since, as already said, one could easily misjudge a given artefact type as a phantom. The form inventors and developers would still have done a dignified effort, even if the form itself wouldn't make substantial presence in practice. Thus, the author would like to apologize to those researchers (incidentally including the author) who work on the artifact types listed below as examples of *possible* phantoms.

Second-generation expert systems. Conventional expert systems include expert knowledge on a given domain to carry out tasks typically performed by human experts, e.g. equipment malfunction diagnosis or credit request approval. The most common way of representing knowledge involves a number of "If – Then" rules. The so-called second-generation expert systems attempt at capturing deep knowledge behind the workings of the problem domain based on relevant theories and cause-and-effect chains (David, Krivine, & Simmons, 1993). The benefits of the approach include the apparent higher robustness as compared to the conventional systems and the reduced need for knowledge extraction from the experts. While this form may be applicable in some limited domains where theoretical workings are well-understood and easy to model, they don't seem to fit many business contexts, e.g. fraud detection. Even if a theoretical knowledge is obtainable to some extent, the conventional expert systems offer the simplicity which would discard more complex approaches by Ockham's razor.

Direct preference elicitation-based shopping tools. These often require a substantial effort on the consumer's side to help them make their preferences explicit and then search the products that match their needs. An early work in this respect was PersonaLogic decision guide (Maes, Guttman, & Moukas, 1999). Bought by AOL in 1998 it did not seem to attract much of customers' interest. This category of tools in general often involve series of questions asked to customers to attempt modelling their preferences. In any case, there doesn't seem to be a substantial need for such approaches. An alternative collaborative filtering family of approaches on the other hand seems to be more preferable and is adopted by many online businesses.

Creativity support tools. This category of tools aims at enhancing creative performance by individuals leading ultimately to innovative approaches in problem solving (Massetti, 1996). They may include so-called idea banks with a collection of ideas, topics, phrases and open-ended questions which presumably would trigger creative processes in the user. While organizations could benefit from such tools if they really had value, they don't seem to be a key component in common business application portfolios. An experimental study conducted with MBA students with the involvement of two creativity support packages did not reveal a significant improvement in individual creative performance (Massetti, 1996).

Electronic negotiation systems with analytical support. These systems allow users to exchange offers in a structured format through the web with the possible modelling of negotiator preferences (Kersten & Noronha, 1999). They have been described earlier in the book and further elaboration is unnecessary here. The use of electronic negotiation support systems is fairly limited to research and education, and they are yet to prove their value to organizations and individuals.

Admittedly there is a good deal of arbitrariness in listing the above system types as example phantom candidates. It would be appropriate to stress again that future developments may prove the author wrong and the above types of solutions will make their presence in the real practice.

REFERENCES

Barki, H., Rivard, S., & Talbot, J. (1988). An information systems keyword classification scheme. *Management Information Systems Quarterly*, *12*(2), 299–322. doi:10.2307/248855

Barki, H., Rivard, S., & Talbot, J. (1993). A keyword classification scheme for IS research literature: An update. *Management Information Systems Quarterly*, *17*(1), 209–226. doi:10.2307/249802

Basalla, G. (1988). *The evolution of technology*. Cambridge, MA: Cambridge University Press.

Bellifemine, F., Poggi, A., & Rimassa, G. (2001). *JADE: A FIPA2000 compliant agent development environment*. Paper presented at the Fifth International Conference on Autonomous Agents. Montreal, Canada.

Berry, P., Peintner, B., Conley, K., Gervasio, M., Uribe, T., & Yorke-Smith, N. (2006). *Deploying a personalized time management agent*. Paper presented at the Fifth International Joint Conference on Autonomous Agents and Multiagent Systems. Hakodate, Japan.

Briggs, R. O., Vreede, G.-J. D., & Nunamaker, J. F. Jr. (2003). Collaboration engineering with ThinkLets to pursue sustained success with group support systems. *Journal of Management Information Systems*, *19*(4), 31–64.

Chervany, N. L., Dickson, G. W., & Kozar, K. A. (1971). *An experimental gaming framework for investigating the influence of management information systems on decision effectiveness*. Unpublished manuscript.

David, J.-M., Krivine, J.-P., & Simmons, R. (1993). *Second generation expert systems*. Secaucus, NJ: Springer-Verlag New York, Inc.doi:10.1007/978-3-642-77927-5

Dawkins, R. (2004). *The ancestor's tale: A pilgrimage to the dawn of evolution*. Boston, MA: Houghton Mifflin.

Dayal, U., Castellanos, M., Simitsis, A., & Wilkinson, K. (2009). *Data integration flows for business intelligence*. Paper presented at the 12th International Conference on Extending Database Technology: Advances in Database Technology. Saint Petersburg, Russia. DSS-89. (1989, April). Ninth international conference on decision support systems: Call for papers. *OR/MS Today*, 50-51.

Ein-Dor, P., & Segev, E. (1993). A classification of information systems: Analysis and interpretation. *Information Systems Research*, *4*(2), 166–204. doi:10.1287/isre.4.2.166

Estévez, P. A., Held, C. M., & Perez, C. A. (2006). Subscription fraud prevention in telecommunications using fuzzy rules and neural networks. *Expert Systems with Applications*, *31*(2), 337–344. doi:10.1016/j.eswa.2005.09.028

Fazlollahi, B., Parikh, M. A., & Verma, S. (1997). Adaptive decision support systems. *Decision Support Systems, 20*(4), 297–315. doi:10.1016/S0167-9236(97)00014-6

Gargeya, V. B., & Brady, C. (2005). Success and failure factors of adopting SAP in ERP system implementation. *Business Process Management Journal, 11*(5), 501–516. doi:10.1108/14637150510619858

Gimpel, H., Jennings, N. R., Kersten, G., Ockenfels, A., & Weinhardt, C. (2007). *Negotiations, auctions and market engineering* (*Vol. 2*). Berlin, Germany: Springer-Verlag.

Gorry, A., & Scott-Morton, M. (1971). A framework for information systems. *Sloan Management Review, 13*, 56–79.

Hevner, A. R., March, S. T., Park, J., & Ram, S. (2004). Design science in information systems research. *Management Information Systems Quarterly, 28*(1), 75–105.

Holsapple, C. W., & Sena, M. P. (2005). ERP plans and decision-support benefits. *Decision Support Systems, 38*(4), 575–590. doi:10.1016/j.dss.2003.07.001

Ives, B., Hamilton, S., & Davis, G. B. (1980). A framework for research in computer-based management information systems. *Management Science, 26*(9). doi:10.1287/mnsc.26.9.910

Kersten, G., & Noronha, S. J. (1999). WWW-based negotiation support: Design, implementation, and use. *Decision Support Systems, 25*, 135–154. doi:10.1016/S0167-9236(99)00012-3

Kim, H. S., & Cho, J. H. (2010). Supply chain formation using agent negotiation. *Decision Support Systems, 49*(1), 77–90. doi:10.1016/j.dss.2010.01.004

Kogan, J. N. (1986). *Information for motivation: A key to executive information systems that translate strategy into results for management.* Paper presented at the Sixtrh International Conference on Decision Support Systems. Washington, DC.

Lea, B.-R., Guptab, M. C., & Yuc, W.-B. (2005). A prototype multi-agent ERP system: An integrated architecture and a conceptual framework. *Technovation, 25*(4), 433–441. doi:10.1016/S0166-4972(03)00153-6

Maes, P., Guttman, R. H., & Moukas, A. G. (1999). Agents that buy and sell. *Communications of the ACM, 42*(3), 81–87. doi:10.1145/295685.295716

March, S. T., & Hevner, A. R. (2005). Integrated decision support systems: A data warehousing perspective. *Decision Support Systems, 43*(3), 1031–1043. doi:10.1016/j.dss.2005.05.029

Markus, M. L., Majchrzak, A., & Gasser, L. (2002). A design theory for systems that support emergent knowledge processes. *Management Information Systems Quarterly, 26*(3), 179–212.

Massetti, B. (1996). An empirical examination of the value of creativity support systems on idea generation. *Management Information Systems Quarterly, 20*(1), 83–97. doi:10.2307/249543

Modi, P. J., Veloso, M., Smith, S. F., & Oh, J. (2005). CMRadar: A personal assistant agent for calendar management. In Bresciani, P., Giorgini, P., & Henderson-Sellers, B. (Eds.), *Agent-Oriented Information Systems II* (pp. 169–181). Berlin, Germany: Springer. doi:10.1007/11426714_12

Nissen, M. E. (2001). Agent-based supply chain integration. *Information Technology Management, 2*(3), 289–312. doi:10.1023/A:1011449109160

Nwana, H. S., Ndumu, D. T., Lee, L. C., & Collis, J. C. (1999). *ZEUS: A toolkit and approach for building distributed multi-agent systems.* Paper presented at the Third Annual Conference on Autonomous Agents. Seattle, WA.

Petric, A., & Jezic, G. (2009). Reputation tracking procurement auctions. In *Computational Collective Intelligence: Semantic Web, Social Networks and Multiagent Systems* (pp. 825–837). Berlin, Germany: Springer. doi:10.1007/978-3-642-04441-0_72

Polyzotis, N., Skiadopoulos, S., Vassiliadis, P., Simitsis, A., & Frantzell, N.-E. (2007). *Supporting streaming updates in an active data warehouse.* Paper presented at the 23rd International Conference on Data Engineering. Istanbul, Turkey.

Rizzi, S., Abelló, A., Lechtenbörger, J., & Trujillo, J. (2006). *Research in data warehouse modeling and design: dead or alive?* Paper presented at the 9th ACM International Workshop on Data Warehousing and OLAP. Arlington, VA.

Sandholm, T. (2002). Algorithm for optimal winner determination in combinatorial auctions. *Artificial Intelligence, 135*(1-2), 1–54. doi:10.1016/S0004-3702(01)00159-X

Shakshuki, E., & Jun, Y. (2004). Multi-agent development toolkits: An evaluation. In Orchard, B., Yang, C., & Moonis, A. (Eds.), *Innovations in Applied Artificial Intelligence* (pp. 209–218). Berlin, Germany: Springer. doi:10.1007/978-3-540-24677-0_23

Sidorova, A., Evangelopoulos, N., & Valacich, J. (2008). Uncovering the intellectual core of the information systems discipline. *Management Information Systems Quarterly, 32*(3), 467–482.

Thalhammer, T., Schrefl, M., & Mohani, M. (2001). Active data warehouses: Complementing OLAP with analysis rules. *Data & Knowledge Engineering, 39*(3), 241–269. doi:10.1016/S0169-023X(01)00042-8

Vahidov, R., & He, X. (2010). Situated DSS for personal finance management: Design and evaluation. *Information & Management, 47*(2), 78–86. doi:10.1016/j.im.2009.11.001

Walls, J. G., Widmeyer, G. R., & El Sawy, O. A. (1992). Building an information system design theory for vigilant EIS. *Information Systems Research, 3*(1), 36–59. doi:10.1287/isre.3.1.36

Watson, R. T., DeSanctis, G., & Poole, M. S. (1988). Using a GDSS to facilitate group consensus: Some intended and unintended consequences. *Management Information Systems Quarterly, 12*(3), 463–478. doi:10.2307/249214

Wells, D., & Kurien, A. (1996). *Groupware & collaboration support.* Washington, DC: Object Services and Consulting, Inc.

Wurman, P. R., Wellman, M. P., & Walsh, W. E. (1998). *The Michigan Internet auction bot: A configurable auction server for human and software agents.* Paper presented at the Second International Conference on Autonomous Agents. Minneapolis, MN.

Chapter 11
Science as Design

ABSTRACT

The purpose of this chapter is to demonstrate that traditional science is a kind of design. Scientific research can be viewed as a type of reverse engineering. Alternatively, one could entertain a highly hypothetical thought about how an engineer would have designed the world as we experience it. The artifact nature of scientific knowledge can be seen in different sciences through examples. Mathematics is the domain of the purely abstract, where the difference between the invented and discovered disappears. History of Astronomy provides examples of how the sense of beauty led the scientists to invent early models involving celestial bodies. Creativity and inventiveness are often needed in Physics to construct artifacts involving the unobservable. Purpose and corresponding design distinguishes Biology, which focuses on living forms displaying high levels of sophistication in their organization.

RE-INVENTING THE WORLD

Previous chapters have defended the view of design of meta-artifacts as being akin to traditional science. Thus, it was argued that the scientific principles and scientific method should be applicable to design-type research. As mentioned earlier, the opposite view suggested that science itself is a form of design (Glanville, 1999). These perspectives do not really contradict each other,
but imply a sort of equivalence between scientific and design-type research. The key point is that the focus is on discovering relevant common forms, either those manufactured by nature, or those yet-to-be-made by means of the human invention. The objective of this chapter is to treat some well-known examples of discovery in traditional sciences as acts of design. In this respect the chapter does not deals directly with information systems or their components. Nonetheless, demonstrating the artificial nature of scientific knowledge could

DOI: 10.4018/978-1-4666-0131-4.ch011

help conveying the parity between conventional notion of science and design-oriented science view.

Traditional explanation-oriented scientific research is essentially equivalent to the process of reverse engineering. By observing phenomena scientists are trying to get insight into the workings behind the observable. They invent models and put them to the test by comparing the outputs predicted by these models with the observations. Often these models are assumed to work under idealized conditions. The whole process has a strong design orientation. A scientist acts as a designer with the definite purpose in mind. The kind of phenomena studied represents a problem context. Finding a solution (form) to fit this context is the purpose of the scientist. Science, as design is thus a purpose-driven activity.

In fact it would be interesting to entertain an illusion of forward engineering in this respect. Suppose one would be given a problem of designing the world as ours with all of its key ingredients and physical laws. Notwithstanding pure philosophical implications of such an artificial scenario (the designer would have to exist in some world to do the designing), it would be curious to consider what kind of design choices would have been made. Or rather, assume that an engineer attempts to simulate some world with interesting dynamics of its own in a virtual environment. In fact, the well-known game of life is an example of constructing a simulated world which can exhibit a variety of dynamic stable patterns. Conceived by John Horton Conway (Gardner, 1970) the game runs on a grid of squares, which could be either turned on or off. If a given cell has any two of its neighbouring cells on, then that cell preserves its state. If three of the neighbouring cells are on, then this cell will be on in the next step. A Dennett puts it: *"The entire physics of the Life world is captured in that single unexceptional law"* (Dennett, 1995, p. 167).

The original motivation behind the design of the game was to enable artificial self-reproduction. A number of stable patterns have been discovered including, for example, gliders, eaters, pulsars, and others. Some of these stable patterns, in interaction could produce a form of a Turing machine. Dennett makes a beautiful insight into the implications of the game that to a large extent relates to the point of this book: "…notice how the distinction between Order and Design gets blurred here…Conway *designed* the whole Life world – that is he set out to articulate an Order that would *function* in a certain way. But do gliders, for instance, count as designed things, or as just natural objects? …the simplest glider would seem just fall out of the basic physics of the Life world "automatically" …it just was *discovered* to be implied by the physics of the Life world." (Dennett, 1995, p. 173).

Game of Life represented a remarkable attempt to define (design) the structure and physics of an artificial world in terms of very simple structure and law governing its dynamics. The area of artificial life looks to simulate a variety of different aspects of the living organisms and their populations (Adami, 1998). Here, again research can be considered as a form of forward engineering. Life is being re-invented in the digital medium. Human designers sort of "produce" the "natural."

The design attitude towards natural world taken literally inevitably leads to the theological stance. Religious views have long espoused the idea of a god-designed world. In theology there are two major categories of thought: deism and theism. The former tends to suggest that the deity had initially created the world along with its fundamental structures and laws and then let it unfold by itself. Theism holds the view that the deity can intervene through intentional actions in the flow of earthly events (e.g. by means of "miracles"). As an analogy, the deistic view is something similar to the game of Life, whereby the designer sets the laws and provides initial conditions to let the things evolve by themselves. Theistic view is, in a way, similar to systems development methods, where the maintenance phase is an on-going activity of changing the system functionality and features, by means of workarounds, and corrective and adaptive modification activities after it has been put into operation.

The designed world view dates back to ancient times, but, perhaps, the most famous way of putting it was by William Paley, an Eighteenth century British theologist (Paley, 2006). He had compared the world with the intricate and sophisticated clockwork. Now, if somebody finds a clock, say, on a desert island, it immediately suggests the necessity of existence (probably in the past) of a clockmaker, i.e. a designer. Since world undeniably shows the features of design, there must be a grand designer behind it. This piece of reasoning is known as teleological argument, or argument from design. It beats itself as the same reasoning could be applied to the grand designer, leading to an infinite regress (Dawkins, 2006b).

Presently, the role of a deity as a grand designer has been somewhat diminished in face of Darwinism's triumph. There are attempts to provide scientific basis for the belief in the existence of the world designer (Davis, 1992). There is a community the members of which believe in the necessity of design act, as they suggest that Science cannot explain everything. It is known under the name of "Intelligent Design" (Dembski, 1998). Their purpose is not to deny, say the role of biological evolution in face of a massive stock of evidence for the latter. Rather, they argue that evolution does not explain everything. They set out to search for the evidence of an intelligent design act behind the existing forms. In the above-cited volume, one of the contributors lists the fundamental physical formulas on one page as an evidence of a purposeful intelligent design act. The argument is based on the sheer simplicity of the fundamental principles, which, they claim is an evidence of the existence of the grand designer. An example par excellence of their critique of evolutionary theory includes the origin of life and the appearance of a DNA: a highly complicated macromolecule, and the accompanying machinery for reproduction. Another widely used example includes the design of an eye.

Since for the eye to function correctly one needs not only photo-sensitive cells, but also a lens to focus the images, how could have both evolved simultaneously, whereas each one of these parts is useless and costly to produce and maintain? In other words having either a retina or a lens (but not both) is costly, and should not be favored. This is an "Exclusive OR" (XOR) problem. Then how could an evolution make such a giant step to discover the eye form? Evolution cannot solve XOR problems. Dawkins had convincingly shown that a cluster of photosensitive cells is much more advantageous as compared to absolute blindness (Dawkins, 2006a). The sensing of light and darkness must have proved critical to the survival and reproduction of the organisms. Later, a membrane must have developed that were to assume a role of a primitive lens. Thus, in essence Dawkins has shown that the problem is not XOR after all.

It would have been an easy way out to adopt the intelligent design stance in order to promote the main argument of the book. In fact, if there is a designer behind natural objects and a multitude of somewhat less grand designers for the artificial objects, the line separating science from design would really appear to be thin. However, the author is very far from sharing intelligent design sentiments. Then what is the point of diverging into the grand designer-related issues? The very existence (and a substantial one) of the views expressing the presence of design behind the natural forms speaks in favor of the argument rejecting that there is a definitive line separating science from design. One could entertain an idea of a grand designer actually existing and ask oneself what design decisions would such an entity make. In short, one would be engage in reverse engineering. A scientist, then, could pretend being the deity and try to make (design) mechanisms which would lead to the desirable observable phenomena.

Let's pretend that a grand designer have created the world as we experience it. Sciences attempt to recreate (build) different aspects of this world (sometimes they actually do it by means of simula-

Table 1. A parallel between sciences and design

Science	Major Focus	Industrial Engineering	Software Engineering
Astronomy, Physics, Inorganic Chemistry	Objects, properties, relationships	Simple tools	Procedures, functions, variables
Organic Chemistry, Biochemistry	Complex compounds	Mechanisms	Common classes and components
Biology	Plants and animals	Machines and robots	Systems
Neuroscience, Cognitive science	Human brain and behavior	Intelligent robots	Intelligent agents and applications

tion models). Could a parallel be drawn between the creations of humans in producing new types of artifacts, and those who re-create world as a knowledge artifact? Table 1 shows one way to make such a comparison.

Physical sciences study classes of objects in order to understand their properties and relationships at macro- and micro-levels. Astronomy and Astrophysics aim at describing various types of celestial bodies and gaining insights into the processes involved. Particle Physics classifies elementary particles and examines their properties. Various types of nuclei and atomic combinations are the subject of Chemistry. A grand designer would have had to invent different object types and set the laws that govern their interaction. Human inventors make their own objects in order to cope with various needs. Simple tools are objects that human creators have been designing since the pre-historic times. In software engineering fragments of code, methods, procedures and modules and their relationships enable execution of simple information processing tasks.

The grand designer could then use the existing simple objects in order to build more complex mechanisms out of them. This is the domain of organic chemistry and biochemistry. The engineer at this point must have the basic objects with the desired properties in order to achieve such a purpose. Out of simple objects larger complex objects are constructed to enable building of various mechanisms to be used in a variety of contexts. DNA form and the accompanying cel-

lular machinery is designed to enable information copying and transportation. The hemoglobin object is invented to enable transportation of the oxygen objects. In human engineering there is a vast variety of mechanisms to accomplish tasks within a wide class of contexts. Wheels, belts, gears and bearings are example objects out of which mechanisms are built. These mechanisms help transforming one type of a motion (e.g. circular), into another (e.g. linear). In software engineering designers invent new types of classes and components, which provide some common type of functionality. Bundling of related methods and variables is the major means of achieving this end. These classes then could be used in a multitude of various application contexts wherever such a functionality is required.

With basic biochemical mechanisms in place, the grand designer could now move on to construct various living forms. In particular, three major types of living creatures are invented, which are termed plants, animals, and mushrooms. Some living machines are capable of moving around, while others are static. The key distinguishing features of these machines is their ability to reproduce, and their disposability. Human engineers have also designed a great diversity of machines to support technological processes in producing a desired good. The majority of these machines turn simpler inputs (e.g. raw materials) into more complex outputs (e.g. finished products). In software engineering such machines would be equivalent to different classes of applications. These help accomplishing various information processing types by turning inputs into outputs, and have to be designed accordingly.

Ultimately, the grand designer could entertain a thought of building a special type of a machine capable of planning, decision making, and action execution. The task would require conception of a mechanism which would enable such a high-level information processing. Cognitive scientists attempt to re-engineer the grand designer's invention. The mechanism would have to be supported by special type of technology. The designer would choose special types of objects, called neurons to facilitate higher-level cognitive processes. The need for automation would prompt human designers to build sophisticated machines, called industrial robots, some of them equipped with the capacity for planning and action execution. These robots would replace human beings in accomplishing tasks in manufacturing domains. In the domain of software the designers in the field of artificial intelligence investigate different ways to provide software components with intelligent capabilities. They would try to figure out how to achieve their objectives by imitating the way the grand designer had achieved it. They would reconstruct mechanisms for thinking and re-invent neural structures in their search. They would build software analogies of robots, and call them "intelligent agents." By doing this they would aim at freeing humans from a variety of ordinary tasks as far as artificial intelligence allows this. Yet, they wouldn't be quite as successful as the grand designer.

FRAUDULENT SCIENCE AND DESIGN

The artifact point of view on scientific knowledge can be well understood through citing cases of scientific fraud. Perhaps, the most common type of forgery in the academic world is fabrication of data. In this type of scientific misconduct data may be altered in a way that fits the hypotheses advanced by a researcher. Or, in extreme cases data may have never been collected, but simply made up to suit the purposes of the fabricator. In either case, the phenomena in their manifestation are simply invented, which might require a certain level of ingenuity. The insincere scientist may have a strong belief in his or her theoretical model ("don't confuse me with the facts") or, simply trying to publish the "results" to get a promotion or achieve a dubious fame. Notwithstanding the various motivations, the gap between the context (the target phenomena), and the theoretical solution outputs (predictions) is covered up by artificially moving the context in order for it to display a tighter fit with the solution.

What is more interesting to explore is the class of hoaxes, where scientific knowledge itself is designed artificially as a fraud, in many cases purposefully and intentionally. The position of this book is that all scientific knowledge is "invented" or "designed." Theories, models, hypotheses, typologies, and the like are all artifacts, although of a special kind. As any artifact they could be well-designed and properly functioning or not functioning as per designer's claims. Just like a claim for a certain design may be fraudulent, so could be scientific knowledge.

Perhaps, the most famous hoax in science is related to the "discovery" of Piltdown man (Adler, 1962). Ever since Darwin's development of evolutionary theory, and explanation of the descent of humans in particular, the scientists had been puzzled by the absence of evidence of the existence of intermediate forms between humans and apes. The theory implied the existence of a certain type of a form, for which no fossilized examples had been found. Then, in 1912 fragments of a skull were presented reported to be found in Piltdown, England that clearly showed structural features of both apes and humans. The evidence now had been discovered. The specimen had given rise to a form, a new hypothetical species, *eoanthropus dawsoni* in "honor" of Charles Dawson, a man who had first reported the finding. The missing piece in a chain of forms predicted by a theory had been filled. Only in 1953 a detailed examination of the "fossil" had revealed that it was made up of a skull of a modern human pieced together with the jaw of an orangutan.

This is an interesting case, as a certain degree of inventiveness was required to forge scientific knowledge. By manufacturing an example, implicitly, the forger (whose identity is still not known for certain) had "designed" a new form, new species. Unethical, as it was, the case showed the intervention of human invention in the course of science. Invention appeared not as means of conducting science, but as the ways of fabricating knowledge.

The other case relates to a story where a vague and untested theoretical idea had lead to the false applied practice. In the Eighteen's century many scientists had been attracted to the phenomenon of magnetism. It was known at the time that Earth was, in essence one huge magnet. An inventive mind could then conceive an idea that magnetic vibrations generated by the movement of the Earth could have an impact on the health of people, just like moon affected tides on Earth (Adler, 1962). Franz Anton Mesmer, a German physician hade conceptualized the idea of an animal magnetism, and he claimed it was essential for maintaining human health. Magnetism was thought to be manifesting the presence of a magnetic fluid, the lack of which in a person affected his or her health. Therefore, Mesmer proposed, the treatment of many diseases should come down to investigating ways of replenishing magnetic fluid. He had then proceeded to "design" artifacts for healing human illnesses. For example, he had a large water tank containing pieces of metal and glass with a cover through which metal pins were inserted. Patients would hold on to these pins as Mesmer approached them and touched them with a metal wand or his hand to transfer magnetism. A special committee formed later had performed rigorous tests and found the entire enterprise to be a fraud. Interestingly, some patients did report certain really felt effects, which had eventually led to the study of hypnotism.

Mesmer's case shows an example where a potentially interesting idea had to a hasty conclusion (whether intentionally fraudulent, or sincere) and application. The idea that magnetism could have effect on people's health, at a time, did not seem to be an outrageous one. But invention in this case had gone too far. The notion of animal magnetism was simply invented, without any attempt at testing. The tubs, pins, and all the accompanying "treatment" procedures were just built based on an imaginativeness of the mind. Design and invention went too far without testing.

The third example of fraudulent science has more design orientation than the ones mentioned above. It relates to the attempts at creation of perpetual motion machines (Collins, 2006). The perpetuum mobile had been something like a holy grail for the inventive engineering minds of the past, much like the philosophical stone was to alchemists. Not all of the designers were crooked as some of them sincerely believed in deriving the principles of such machines. The latter came in the variety of wheels with rolling balls, water buckets, and the like. With the advent of thermodynamics, and, especially its pessimistic second law, it became clear that such machines would be impossible to build. Yet, attempts had been made by many in pursuit of the source of perpetual self-sufficient motion. Among these, Johann Ernst Elias Bessler had claimed that he had succeeded in designing a machine that would do just that. His drawings did not reveal sufficient detail as per internal workings of a machine. Nonetheless, the machine kept running without interruptions indefinitely, as it appeared. Only later his maid had confessed that she was operating the machine from the adjacent room.

The example with perpetuum mobile refers primarily to the engineering fraud. Yet, this fraud has deep connections with the related scientific theories. This is the case, where, if the device really worked, it would have proven science to be wrong. Yet, the second law of thermodynamics cannot be wrong, as it can be derived almost entirely from mathematical reasoning alone (Lightman, 2000).

Fraud is not the most ethical type of activity in scientific communities. Yet, the examples of fraud cited here make the difference between science and design even vaguer. The idea that scientific knowledge is the result of invention implies the possibility of fake inventions, and fake science. The purpose of an ethical scientist, as well as an ethical design scientist, is to produce true artifacts, the ones, which they believe, have the right for existence.

MATHEMATICS: THE NON-EXISTENT

Mathematics is concerned with the study of the purely abstract. This is where the difference between design and science, invention and discovery disappears completely. Mathematics deals with classes of idealized objects and their properties. The actual existence of these objects has been a major question for the philosophers throughout millennia. The fact that mathematical notions could be applied to a variety of real-life objects and phenomena, including musical tonalities had fascinated the ancient Greek philosophers, the sheer ubiquity of mathematical structures in describing real world had led Pythagoras to an extreme claim that everything is a number. He is regarded as the father of numerology, who went on to form a religious sect of Pythagoreans who worshipped numbers (Dudley, 1997).

Plato, on the other hand had noticed the impossibility of having ideal mathematical structures in worldly objects. The existing objects always have irregularities, deviations from their ideal counterparts. Since the ideal is much more preferable intellectually and aesthetically, then could it be that they do not have existence? How is it that the beautiful and perfect does not exist, while the imperfect imitation does? Plato had concluded

that there is a godly domain, which contains all the perfect and abstract. In this domain there are pure ideas, or forms, how he called them, which Demiurge uses as templates to manufacture material objects (Copleston, 1993). However, matter inevitably corrupts the ideal forms by introducing irregularities. Thus, material objects have existence of a lower quality, something akin to the existence of shadows (the famous concept of Plato's cave).

How is it possible that humans can conceive ideal forms, such as a circle, whereas they never experience these through sense-perception. Our souls must have pre-existed among the perfect forms before being incarnated in the material world. Thus, Plato had invented the concept of a form along with the domain where those forms reside. According to him, though it follows that mathematical concepts are discovered, not invented. Plato's ideas have survived millennia and they re-appear in one form or another in modern mathematical thought. For example, Roger Penrose, an English mathematical physicist believes in an actual existence of the world of mathematical objects (Penrose, 1989). In his schema, mathematical forms are reflected in the worldly objects, of which humans are part, and the humans by studying mathematics re-discover the domain of ideas. The sheer beauty of mathematics is the foundation for belief of its actual existence.

The major schools of thought concerning the nature of mathematical objects include logicism, formalism, and intuitionism (Lindstrum, Palmgren, Segerberg, & Stoltenberg-Hansen, 2009). Logicism, introduced by Bertrand Russell and Gottlob Frege holds the view that all of the mathematics can be deduced from pure logic. Whitehead & Russel's monumental work *Principia Mathematica* represents such an attempt (Whitehead & Russell, 1927). Formalism, advanced by David Hilbert defends the view that mathematical findings can be derived by pure manipulation of formulas, according to a set of rules, without having to impose meanings to the symbols. Intuitionism, introduced by L.E.J. Brower contends that mathematical objects are mental constructions and any mathematical symbols or formulas that have no meaning attached are useless. Quine, referring to Fraenkel points that according to logicism classes of mathematical objects are *discovered*, while intuitionism implies that they are *invented* (Quine, 1999). As one can see from these views, both invention and discovery can be applied to mathematical research. Is there really need for distinguishing one from the other? Would it not be possible to claim that mathematics is both science and design? Is there need to classify it as one or another?

An interesting mathematical concept relevant to the design view is infinity. Before Cantor the infinity was treated more as a potentiality of continuing the process of finding larger numbers than any given one indefinitely. Cantor had considered infinity in itself and studied its properties. He found that some types of infinities are larger than others. The set of irrational numbers is larger than that of rational numbers. The latter set is equivalent to the set of integers. But could infinity exist in the reality? Is it a mathematical invention? Do irrational numbers exist anywhere in the actual world? Infinities give birth to paradoxes. One such paradox was advanced by a German astronomer Olbers, who had noted that if the universe is infinite and contains an infinite number of stars, then the night sky should be all glowing, instead of being dark (Maor, 1987). It is now known that the universe is not infinite, after all. It is, as if the reality defies the infinity. Other examples of paradoxes have been known since the times of Zeno of Elea. Hilbert's hotel is amongst the best known examples. A hotel that has infinite number of rooms, all of them occupied could still find free rooms for the new guests, in fact for an infinite number of them. Another paradox includes finding the result of the series $1 - 1 + 1 - 1 + \ldots$ Depending on grouping of the terms the sums would be completely different.

The fact that infinity produces paradoxes makes it difficult to imagine any kind of physical world where they would exhibit their presence in one way or another. Mathematically, at a purely abstract level they could be dealt with. Irrational numbers, which do incorporate infinity in their structures have been discovered by a Pythagorean. Well-known examples are the square root of 2 and the pi. These should be familiar to any high school student. It is even easy to show the square root of 2 by drawing a one-by-one right triangle and looking at the hypotenuse. Yet, there are no perfect lines or triangles in the real world. Infinity is, thus a pure mathematical invention. There is no physical equivalent to it, except in the approximation sense. The minimum meaningful distance according to Physics is Planck length. The minimum time interval is Planck time. The earliest time after the birth of the universe about which we can talk meaningfully about it is Planck epoch. Infinity, therefore, is an example mathematical concept, which suggests that mathematics is creation (design and invention) rather than science.

It is curious to note that as infinity leads to paradoxes, this suggests that the ideal world of mathematical concepts could never be translated perfectly into reality. Reality does not allow for paradoxes. Yet the sciences that study the real try to employ mathematical descriptions of the phenomena their studying. Here is the paradox: ideally, the physical sciences should succeed in arriving at mathematical descriptions, although mathematics a priori cannot serve perfectly for the description of reality.

The history of geometry provides other reasons for treating mathematics as design. Euclid in his *Elements* he had devised the axiomatic method of proof in geometry. Any proof is based on logical reasoning based on known truths. These truths could be, in turn proved based on more basic true statements. However, there has to be some point at which the statements cannot be proved any further. These have to be accepted as axioms. Note the parallel with the process of design. Any artifact is built using other objects. These objects, in turn could be components, i.e. types of artifacts invented earlier. Or else, they could be based on natural objects, like in the case of early human technologies. However, the designer must start with some objects in hand.

Euclid had proposed a set of five basic axioms (called postulates), from which much of the traditional geometry could be derived. It is, as if, by setting a few non-disputable design principles Euclid showed a way of how to engineer more complex geometrical statements by using the machinery of theorem proving. In essence, Euclidean axiomatic method is inherently constructive. Euclidean geometry still occupies a central place in general mathematical education. The five axioms constituted a simple set to which a large knowledge base of geometry statements could be reduced. The question for generations of mathematicians to follow was whether this set could be reduced even further. In particular, some mathematicians believed that the fifth postulate could be reduced to the four others, and, thus would prove to be unnecessary. They had spent considerable efforts in this respect, yet to no avail. The fifth postulate, in one version, states that through a given point lying outside a given line one and only one parallel line could be drawn.

One could look at Euclid's system of postulates from the design point of view. In design creativity plays a key role. One of the methods of inducing divergent creative thinking is to reject some of the accepted, almost dogmatic assumptions. What if the fifth postulate could be treated as an assumption, rather than indisputable truth? What if it really represented a decision of the designer of a given type of geometry artifact? Lobachevsky and Bolyai took this route by rejecting one of the Euclid's design principle. The abandonment of the fifth postulate gave birth to new fascinating types of geometry. Essentially, Euclidean geometry was designed for studying objects on a plain surface. Non-Euclidean geometries allow building self-consistent statements about the nature of objects

in curved spaces. The surface of the Earth itself is not plain, and thus application of Euclidean geometry to it on large scales would be inaccurate. Einstein's general theory of relativity makes use of non-Euclidean geometry.

The geometry case brings the artificial nature of mathematics into the focus. In a plain world the Euclidean system would have been correct. In real world it turns out to be invalid in many contexts. Abstracting away from the application, it cannot be said that the traditional system was wrong. It was an artifact, after all. Likewise, non-Euclidean geometry is an alternative artefact. Only with the reference to the application context the truth or falsity can be judged.

To conclude the section, here the story of another exciting mathematical concept will be mentioned briefly. The concept is that of the imaginary number (Nahin, 1998). Whole and fractional numbers, both positive as well as negative have long been used by humankind and they are relatively easy to interpret. Irrational numbers had appeared later, and it they are somewhat more difficult to grasp intuitively. In Renaissance Italy many prominent mathematicians took up the challenge for (and succeeded in) solving general cubic equations. Rafael Bombelli was an Italian mathematician who was working on a type of cubic equations. He noticed, that in the process of solving them there was a need of introducing a square root of negatives, even though the final solution would consist of real numbers. Thus the concept of an imaginary number: the square root of minus one was born. However, what could it mean? How could one make sense out of it? Many have regarded imaginary numbers as fictitious, "not real" in some sense, and useless. In short, this seemed to be simply an invention to which no real-life concept seemed to correspond.

With time, however, these numbers started to be used by some prominent mathematicians, such as Euler and Gauss. Nowadays, their use in science and engineering is so wide-spread, that they have long become a part of the standard mathematical education for scientists and engineers. Application of complex numbers ranges from such practice-oriented areas as electrical engineering to a highly theoretical ones, including quantum physics. The story of imaginary numbers shows clear analogies with inventions. This is the case where adoption of the concept initially regarded as an invention can be seen as an evidence of its truth.

ASTRONOMY: THE BEAUTY

Ancient people tended to ascribe meaning to the inanimate nature in belief that a deity, or some sort of consortium of them would not allow for chaos or randomness in the orchestration of the universe. The domain of celestial objects was, perhaps the most important realm towards which humans directed their attention. Study of the sky had important implications for the agricultural activities. Skies, after all for many cultures were the place where the deities resided. The arrangements and movements of the celestial objects had to be perfect and beautiful. Human beings are inventors and designers due to their very nature. It was very natural for them to start imposing their inventions on the skies. Soon there appeared imaginary beautiful objects made up from the stars: the constellations. The stars are naturally arranged in a random fashion. Yet, humans, denying this randomness created designs. There is absolutely no natural criterion to constellation formation, except for the human sense of beauty. Based on the movements of planets through the Zodiac the astrologers had built completely "artificial" apparatus to predict earthly events. Even in astrology, false as it is, one could recognize elements of beauty—perhaps this is one of the reasons that it still thrives nowadays.

But beauty criterion was also behind the sincere and honest attempts to understand the mechanics of the skies, and the aesthetic feeling, as a criterion had sometimes contributed towards eventual scientific progress in Astronomy. Scientists of the past, lacking powerful instruments (such as telescopes) had to invent and design. And the design is very often driven by beauty. Why would one attempt to design ugly artifacts? And if the deity is the grand and most perfect possible designer, then his design must be beautiful. The task of the astronomer is then to unveil this beauty behind the observations of the skies. We will review some interesting historical ideas in Astronomy, where the aesthetic design aspect is most visible.

For the major part ancient Greek philosophers had espoused the geocentric model of the world, where the known planets, the sun and the moon were viewed as being located on different spheres, rotating around the centrally positioned Earth. Then, the Pythagorean Philolaus had come up with a different view (Huffman, 2008). The earth was perceived as being flat, and Philolaus had invented a fiery central spot, located in space under the Earth. All the celestial objects moved around this spot. Moreover, there was a counter-Earth, which was also rotating around the center, but in such a way that it was at all times located opposite to the earth, on the other side of the fiery spot. This is why it couldn't be observed. One would wonder why this seemingly whimsical invention was made by Philolaus?

According to one popular belief, partly inspired by Aristotle, the invention was prompted by the Pythagorean worship of numbers. In particular, number ten was especially sacred for them as it was the basis for tetractys. The latter was a figure of a triangular shaped formed by the ten points. The first raw contained one point, the second one – two, the third one – three, and the fourth one – four. The celestial objects in the ancient world were thought of containing the five visible planets, the sun, the moon, the earth, and the sky with the fixed stars. The total number of objects would add up to nine—just one short of the perfect ten. Thus, it was believed that Philolaus, in the spirit of Pythagoreans have simply invented the non-observable counter-Earth to complete the picture. If it was true, then this would have been a perfect example of how beauty leads to invention of a model depicting the arrangement of things in the universe.

Nowadays, however many think it is doubtful that the sheer desire to complete the cosmic object count prompted the model. Rather, Philolaus seemed to be baffled by the discrepancy of the geocentric model and the observed motions of the planets. Thus, he had suggested that the central point towards which all things fall is located in a spot distant from the Earth and located underneath its flat surface. But then, he would have reasoned, there must be another body, quite equivalent to the Earth and located on the exactly opposite side of the central fiery spot to balance the weight of the Earth. The Earth and counter-Earth would form a kind of a cosmic dumbbell and would balance each other. To Philoluas' credit the sort of reasoning that he had employed proceeding from the discrepancy in observations with the theory to inventing hypothetical; objects had been found to be a fruitful approach in Astronomy. The planets Neptune and Pluto were also initially "invented" as hypothetical objects based on the study of motions of other planets. In similar fashion, a number of planets have been "discovered" recently in distant star systems.

The "invention-oriented" approaches to discovery had created many curious theoretical models in the past. Losee calls such practices "saving the appearances," and much of what follows in the remainder of this section appears in his book (Losee, 1993). The term "degrees" of freedom is well known in Mechanics and Statistics. In Mechanics it relates to the number of dimensions along which a body can move and the number of axes around which it can rotate. In Statistics, one interpretation related to the number of observations in a given sample that could vary, once some statistic(s) is (are) given. For example, if there are 10 observations in a sample, and the average is known, then only nine of them could vary, and the remaining one would have to have a certain value. In geocentric system the model did not fit well with the observations. In particular, the occasional backwards movements of the planets could not have been accounted for by adopting simple circular orbits. A circle with the center on the Earth would just not have sufficient degrees of freedom to explain the motions. A designer would have to come up with the more elaborate system to build a desired mechanism with the sufficient number of degrees of freedom.

Ptolemy had engineered just such a system. In his model, he envisaged the spherical orbits, along which the major paths of planets lied. However, this circle actually described the movement of a point, which was central to the smaller orbit, along which the planets actually moved. These orbits were called epicycles. By adjusting the speeds of the motions along the two orbits, Ptolemy succeeded in reconciling theory with the observations. It is easy to see the very mechanical nature of the model; in fact analogous mechanisms are known and widely used by mechanical engineers. What is even more interesting, Ptolemy had devised another model, which would produce the same results. In this model a planet moves along a circular orbit with the center being at the point, which moved along another circular orbit around the Earth, but in the opposite direction (Losee, 1993). Thus, the true artefact nature of these theoretical models becomes apparent.

Copernicus had essentially simplified the mechanism of planetary motions by shifting the center from the Earth to the Sun. The new model had provided predictions, in some respects better than that of Ptolemy, without the need for the epicycles. However, this model contradicted the biblical teachings. Osiander, a theologist who wrote the preface to Copernicus' book had noted that it was not necessary to assume that the model corresponded to the reality. It was, simply a useful tool, an artifact, which made calculations easier. In other words, just like the design of a clock does not correspond to the nature of time, the heliocentric model doesn't have to reflect the true nature of things. It is due to this "clarification" that the

Church was quite tolerant of Copernicus' ideas; in great contrast to the way it treated Giordano Bruno, who claimed that the heliocentric model was, indeed the true one.

The attempts to impose mathematical beauty upon the organization of the solar system had led Johannes Kepler to invent a model, which, by its sheer composition is anything shorter from being remarkably elegant. Based on Copernicus' data Kepler had managed to fit the orbits of the planets along the spheres circumscribed around, and inscribed within a set of three-dimensional geometrical objects. This arrangement would fit nicely with the belief that world is designed by a mathematician god. Kepler had associated the following series of solids with the planetary orbits: between Saturn and Jupiter – cube, between Jupiter and Mars – tetrahedron, between Mars and Earth – dodecahedron, between Earth and Venus – icosahedron, between Venus and Mercury – Octahedron. Kepler, in essence, was a puzzle solver with various geometric forms at hand to construct the solar system puzzle.

However, when he obtained more accurate set of data based on Tycho Brahe's observations (who had the most accurate instruments at the time) he found that his model didn't fit. Moreover, even for heliocentric system, the circular orbits of planets did not seem to match the observations. He tried to re-design the system by fitting circular orbits to planetary motions with different hypothesized centers. This still did not work, however. A circle did not have sufficient number of parameters. The required artifact simply could not be produced by means of circular components. Some level of simplicity had to be given up. And as a designer would do, he opted for the solution, which was one step more complex. The ellipse as a form can accommodate a larger variety of observations than a circle. Instead of a single center, it has two focal points, such that the total distance from these points to any point on the ellipse is the same. Kepler had successfully engineered a model in which planets moved along ellipses, in one of the foci of which

the Sun resided. Nowadays, the model is known as Kepler's first law.

To conclude the topic of astronomical inventions, one interesting insight into the apparent order behind planetary orbit locations has to be mentioned. In the Eighteen's century a conjecture known as "Bode's law" has been advanced. It suggested that the distances of planetary orbits from the sun approximately followed a geometrical series of the form 0, 3, 6, 12, 24, ... If one adds a constant 4 to each of the numbers in the series, then the following progression is obtained: 4, 7, 10, 16, 28, ... If one accepts the distance to the Earth as 10 (the third number in the series for the third planet), then a striking similarity between the series and the distances of planets from the sun would become apparent. Compare the relative distances from the sun with the "predicted" values: Mercury: 3.9 vs. 4; Venus: 7.2 vs. 7; Mars: 15.2 vs. 16; Jupiter: 52 vs. 52; Saturn: 95.4 vs. 96. There was a gap in the series, namely for number 28 there was a planet missing. Since this would not fit the series prediction, Bode had speculated that there must be a planet between Jupiter and Mars. Soon, astronomers started discovering small planets at approximately predicted distance. The gap between the orbits of Mars and Jupiter now is referred to as asteroid belt. It was once hypothesized that a planet had existed between in the asteroid belt, which for some reason had been destroyed, and the asteroids are the remnants of it. This hypothetical planet had been called Phaeton.

It is truly remarkable, that a simple invention of the mind in the Platonic spirit could yield predictions with a satisfactory degree of accuracy. The cosmos did seem to be orderly, arranged by a grand mathematician. Sure enough there were sceptics, who considered the law to be whimsical. For a given small set of numbers (distances) it could be possible to find a rough match with mathematical series, but it hardly justifiable. Note, however, that in Popper's terms Bode's law was falsifiable, and thus it constituted a legitimate scientific theory that could be tested. In fact, it had made a prediction of the missing planet that was followed by the discovery of asteroid, and a hypothetical planet conjecture. It had survived the test. Moreover, when later Uranus was discovered its relative distance (191.9) was found to be in agreement with the one predicted by Bode's law (196). The law had survived a test again! But, according to Popper this doesn't mean much, only that a theory hasn't been falsified yet. When Neptune was discovered, its distance turned out to be at 300.7, while the law predicted a value 388. Thus Bode's predictive artifact had crumbled.

PHYSICS: THE CREATIVITY

Physics is concerned with the study of nature of material objects and forces. It has been the favourite model science of many philosophers. In their writings they refer often to the discoveries in physical sciences. The term itself was introduced by Aristotle, who is often regarded as one of the fathers of Physics and wrote a book with the same title. Much of Physics aims at uncovering the hidden structures and mechanisms behind the phenomena of the material world. In doing so it inevitably faces the problem of constructing the models involving the entities, which defy direct observation, e.g. electrons, forces, quarks, etc. In fact, as mentioned earlier, some philosophers of Science claim that theoretical laws in science (implying mostly the physical science) must state relationships between the unobservable (Carnap, 1966).

Since Physics looks to explain the structure and behaviour of observable objects and related phenomena using unobservable, hypothetical entities, it requires a substantial degree of inventiveness and creativity—the qualities frequently associated with design and invention. Thus, physicists create artifacts, which would fit the observable phenomena of the real world. These artifacts are subsequently put to the test through collecting new observations either passively or through active experimentation. System designers could readily see the parallels between system design and development and the subsequent testing (by means of system tests, and alpha and beta tests). The artifacts of physical science, which pass the tests successfully become adopted by the scientists and engineers, because they work. Whether they truly reflect the reality, or are just artificial inventions or computational devices is a matter of debate among the philosophers of science. The artefact nature of physical theories, laws, principles, and models becomes evident when one considers developments at the forefront of progress in physical sciences.

Ever since early Greek philosophy, attempts had been made at explaining the multitude of worldly forms in terms of simpler basic principles. Thales was the first known Western philosopher who tried to reduce the different kind of substances to a single basic substance, from which others derive. He had conjectured that this basic substance was water. More interestingly, his pupil Anaximander had noted that none of the existing elements has properties that would explain properties of other substances. Fire cannot be wet, water cannot be dry, thus none of these could serve as a mother of all substances. Therefore, he suggested the existence of a primordial matter, which gives birth to all other elements (Copleston, 1993). He named this infinite indefinite, not directly observable substance *apeiron*. Thus, Anaximender was the first Western proto-physicist who had stepped into the realm of the unobservable. He had invented the abstract matter, the mother of all the concrete matter.

Plato was another ingenious inventor whose speculations were driven by his belief in the mathematical and aesthetic origins of the world. He had correlated a number of solids with the basic elements often referred to by ancient Greek thinkers (Losee, 1993). Fire is the most sharp and penetrating element, therefore the corresponding solid should be sharp. Fire was thus connected with tetrahedron. Earth is a solid matter, thus it was associated with a cube. Air is hardly felt, and thus it was connected with Octahedron. Water flows freely, as if it is made of tiny round objects; therefore it had been linked with icosahedrons. He had also introduced the fifth element: celestial matter that was correlated with dodecahedron. It is curious to see how Plato's fascination with the perfect mathematical forms had led him to invent the unobservable structures behind all the matter.

The history of the concept of atom provides another example of "designing" the invisible. Leucippus and Democritus were the first Western philosophers to propose an atomist view of the world. While Parmenides held that there could not be motion, since it requires existence of the void, and the latter cannot exist, because it is "nothing," the atomist had contended that there are only atoms and the void. They did not accept teleological view in explanation of physical phenomena, but maintained that all events are due to mechanistic interactions between material objects, the basic components of which are atoms. There are only atoms and the void. How did they come up with the idea that there must be small indestructible and eternal particles, which could not be divided any further? Why one would conjure up that an object cannot be divided further and further on into smaller and smaller pieces indefinitely? Adopting constructiveness stance could provide an explanation (admittedly, a hypothetical one). A designer must always start with some basic components. A hypothetical designer of the world must start with something given, with basic elements, smallest possible pieces. If the matter was divisible infinitely, the designer would have had to start with infinitely small, e.g. nothing. Out of nothing comes nothing. Therefore, there must be some, however small non-divisible pieces of matter to start with. The atomist went on to "invent" different type of atoms, e.g. for the solids, for air, and so on, which could mechanically link with each other, for example, by means of hooks.

The atomic approach to re-engineering the reality is preferable because it suggests discreteness at the base of matter. The imaginary grand designer would have probably opted for discreteness, since, as it shall be seen in the next session, it provides a simple and robust basis for evolving complex organisms. The game of Life has distinct elements, which could be either on or off. Computers are digital devices that do their processing of bytes and bits: the discrete entities. In the past, there were attempts to build analog machines, which would process continuous inputs. However, the discrete approach has proven to be far superior. Computer engineers thus have shifted their efforts in the direction of exploiting the digital paradigm. The grand designer would probably have had chosen the same path. The ideas of the ancient atomists have stayed around for millennia as one possibility out of other views. John Dalton had discovered that substances react in certain proportions. This had immediately led to the support of the discrete view of organization of matter. Atoms, after all, seemed to be real, though it was not until Einstein had interpreted the Brownian motion the atomist view became a commonly accepted knowledge.

Yet, if the matter consists of discrete particles, the question remains of how these would stick together to form different substances. What is the nature of "hooks" of Leucippus and Democritus (if not taken literally)? Early models of electricity had envisioned the presence of electric negative and positive fluids. Then it had been found that electricity comes in discrete units – again the discrete nature of basic elements had appeared to be the "grand designer's" choice. Ernest Rutherford had discovered that atom was not a solid indestructible entity, but had a structure of its own. Thus, a model of the atom with the nucleus at the center surrounded by the orbiting electrons had appeared. This solar system-like arrangement of the atom is commonly taught at schools, though it cannot be taken as the accurate representation of reality according to Quantum Physics. It is an artifact that is easy for everybody to picture.

Again, the question remains unanswered: how to make atoms stick together? Here, the grand designer would have to come up with the rules: the design principles. First, he (or she) would have to decree that electrons could not be located at arbitrary orbits, but there would be fixed definitive orbits which they could occupy. This is very much in the spirit of discreteness and it makes further design much simpler. Second, there would be a limit on how many electrons could occupy a certain orbit. In actuality, the maximum number of electrons is determined by four parameters, which dictate when a given orbit is "full." This design decision goes by the name of Pauli Exclusion Principle. Having it in place means that some orbits will be underpopulated and the elements, which have such orbits, could share electrons. Voila, the hooks are in place!

Quantum Physics has revealed strange behaviour of particles, which is difficult for humans to grasp. Deterministic views of the past looked to invent models using which the state of any mechanical system could be predicted definitively. Laplace had conjectured that given the state of all objects in the world any future state of the universe could, in principle, be predicted. The world was viewed as a well-organized mechanical system. Yet Quantum Physics had discovered randomness to be an integral part of nature. The existence of randomness was doubted by some prominent Physicists, including Einstein. Randomness did not seem to fit well with the picture of a well-designed world. There must be deeper level structures and mechanisms, which Physics is yet to discover, they suggested. Bohm had introduced the idea of implicate order, which implies deeper structure of the reality and the suggests the unity behind the observed phenomena of the quantum realm (Bohm & Peat, 2000). His conception of the implicate order and hidden non-local variables was an invention designed to explain the weird behavior of the quantum world, including the apparent paradoxes, e.g. the famous paradox of Schrödinger's cat.

To conclude the section, the cutting-edge research in Physics that yields the amazing models of subatomic world will be briefly mentioned here. It is interesting to note that modern physics tends to move away from purely mechanistic view to that featuring the elements of information processing. In particular, particles like photons are often described as "messenger" particles, rather than mechanical objects (Greene, 1999). The design of the atomic nuclei includes protons and neutrons, which, in turn are built up from three quarks. What is the nature of the elementary particles? Do they have a definite size, or are they infinitely small? One popular theory models them as vibrating strings (or membranes). The point-like interpretation of particles views them as zero-dimensional objects. The string model suggests that they are one-dimensional objects vibrating in multiple (eleven) dimensions. It is through these vibrations that the known forces are actuated. String theory provides an excellent example of creativity in Science and conveys the artifact nature of scientific models. Strings are invented entities; there is no way to discover them directly. It makes predictions, which are difficult to test in practice. Physicists study the nature by invention and design.

BIOLOGY: THE PURPOSE

Throughout this book examples and metaphors from Biology have been used often. In particular these references mostly came from writings of Richard Dawkins as they contained brilliant insights into the nature of evolution, which he managed to put in a non-technical form easily understandable by the majority of educated people. Biological analogies are well worthwhile of consideration when the subject of discussion is design. The structure and behavior of the living organisms display remarkable imprints of design and purpose. Teleological stance could be well justified in Biology, as opposed to, say, Physics. Certainly, this teleological orientation does not imply the existence of the purpose in a literal sense. Purpose is evoked in an "as-if" fashion. A biologist may ask, for example what kind of features would an organism have, provided the prevalence of certain conditions and the purpose of survival and reproduction?

Descartes believed that animals were machines which did not have souls. In his account they were sort of mechanical automata with a pre-wired circuitry that allowed them to respond in a specific way to the inputs they received. An interesting discussion regarding the closeness of living organisms and humanly designs is presented in (Dawkins, 2006a). Some of the analogies which appear in the above book will be briefly mentioned below. Dawkins starts out by citing Paley's argument from design. He then notes that Paley could not have known to what extent the living creatures display the aspects of good design. The world, in particular the biological domain is much, much better designed than Paley could have imagined.

To make this point Dawkins gives an example of bats. How would they be able to find their way around in complete darkness? In fact, why would they choose to live in darkness? Because this context serves as a niche which living creatures could occupy, since the other lighted contexts have already been populated by many competing forms. Dawkins asks how a human engineer would have solved this problem. The fact that bats navigate by using ultrasonic built-in radars is well-known to many, as well as its similarity to humanly-designed radars. The natural bat radars, though had appeared millions of years before the human re-invention of them. Yet, there are certain intricacies in the design of bat radars.

Bats navigate by producing clicks in ultrasound and then receiving those signals back to allow their brain machinery to re-construct the images of their surroundings. In essence bats "see" the world as series of images, similar to the way movies are made. How frequent should these clicks be? Naturally, the higher the rate of the clicks the more "real-time" the picture would be. It would allow for execution of tasks that require high pre-

cision, e.g. catching an insect. However, higher frequencies are associated with higher levels of energy needed, and that is an economical cost. The solution is to lower the click rate when precision is not required, and increase it automatically when needed, and this is how bat radars work.

Another example engineering problem faced by the bats relates to the necessity of making very loud ultrasonic signals. Since these signals propagate in three dimensions as waves, they quickly lose their energy. When they hit the objects and return, they lose energy again. So, the ear has to be very sensitive. But then a sensitive ear would be deafened by an outgoing initial signal. Dawkins provides an analogy of human radar engineering that came up against a similar problem. This was solved by radar designers through a mechanism, which would turn off temporarily the circuitry for the receiving part while the outgoing signal was being produced. Bats have the same mechanism that shuts their ears while the sound is being sent out.

Thus, the design of different aspects of living creatures is truly remarkable and sophisticated. Yet, there is no need for an intelligent designer to explain it. A perfect intelligent designer could have, hypothetically speaking, produced the designs of incredible sophistication without much waste. Humans, although intelligent, but certainly not perfect can design artifacts while taking many wrong turns in the process. Dennett refers to Hume who had entertained an idea that the designer of the world did not have to be super-intelligent, in fact he or she could possess no intelligence (Dennett, 1995). If one does away with the idea of intelligent design, what kind of process could produce the forms we encounter in this world? In other words, to explain the variety of living forms on Earth one would have to "design" the designer.

Taking it as a problem of process design, let us consider it in the context of representational framework for meta-artifacts. Recall that the framework was adopted from the proposal by Zachman that looked to organize various aspects of software systems, i.e. humanly designed artifacts.

We will just briefly walk through the first three layers of the framework. Analytically speaking the problem is to invent a method, which could, in turn, invent all the variety of living forms on Earth. The method should account for the great variety of creatures, and their exquisite designs that allowed them to occupy all conceivable niches for life. Various organisms are neatly organized along the tree of life, showing the relationships between them. Some of them are closely related, while others appear on distant branches. And, above all the method should involve no intelligent interference.

At a synthetic layer Darwin had managed to invent just such a method. Structurally it had required the presence of a population of creatures with varying features. The variation in the features allowed for some of them to be better fit to their environment than others. Process-wise, the selective pressures favored better-fit individuals to survive in face of competition and environmental hazards. These then would pass their beneficial features on to the descendants. Gradually, then the whole population would move in the direction of better designed organisms than their ancestors. This design method is simple, yet effective. It is also mindless and wasteful, as compared to "intelligent design." But it provides a way of producing designs without having to postulate the pre-existence of a grand deity designer. The method allows for the separation of populations into subgroups, and further into different species. The synthetic layer description focuses on the phenotype, i.e. the features that come into interaction with the environment.

One problem with the method is that it requires a certain kind of mechanism of reproduction. If, let's say two individuals mate to reproduce, then one possibility would be that the offspring would have some sort of the average of the features of parents. In a long term this would bring to the convergence of the population to a state of small variance in terms of features. The lack of diversity

then would be the source of stagnation, as the method requires maintaining the variation in the populations. How could this dilemma be resolved technically? The solution depends on the choice of the way to encode the features. Genes are discrete units and as such are inherited from the parents as units, and not as "averages." In DNA-based life often one of the alternative genes is dominant and it results in contributing towards the feature inherited from one of the parents. Furthermore, mutation, which occurs due to the copying errors of reproductive biochemical machinery (due to such causes as cosmic rays) allow introducing changes ("innovations") in the population. The machinery combats these errors, as many of them are harmful. The rate of mutation as a result is at the levels which balance the exploration of new solutions with the exploitation of the features of known good solutions. Chromosomal crossover is another ingenious trick in the reproductive machinery. During meiosis, the process of division of cells to produce single chromosome cells, the two chromosomes may exchange their parts. So, the resulting cell, which could serve as a basis for new organism, will be a combination of two parental chromosomes. This provides a way of combining elements of the existing solutions to produce a new one.

To conclude the topic, an intriguing passage from Dawkins' book can be cited just to show the degree of similarity between cellular processes and information technology (Dawkins, 2003). "…genetics has become a branch of Information Technology. The genetic code is truly digital, in exactly the same sense as computer codes. This is not some vague analogy, it is the literal truth…a software subroutine (that's exactly what a gene is) can be Copied from one species and Pasted into another species, where it will work exactly as it did in the original species" (pp. 27-28). Software engineers would certainly be able to relate with the above fragment.

REFERENCES

Adami, C. (1998). *Introduction to artificial life*. New York, NY: Springer. doi:10.1007/978-1-4612-1650-6

Adler, I. (1962). *Stories of hoaxes in the name of science*. New York, NY: Collier.

Bohm, D., & Peat, F. D. (2000). *Science, order, and creativity* (2nd ed.). London, UK: Routledge.

Carnap, R. (1966). The nature of theories. In Carnap, R., & Gardner, M. (Eds.), *Philosophical Foundations of Physics: An Introduction to the Philosophy of Science* (pp. 316–332). New York, NY: Basic Books.

Collins, J. (2006). *Perpetual motion: An ancient mystery solved?* Retrieved from http://www.lulu.com.

Copleston, F. (1993). *A history of philosophy: Greece and Rome* (*Vol. 1*). New York: Doubleday.

Davis, P. (1992). *The mind of God: The scientific basis for a rational world*. New York, NY: Simon & Schuster.

Dawkins, R. (2003). Science, genetics and ethics: Memo for Tony Blair. In *A Devil's Chaplain: Reflections on Hope, Lies, Science, and Love* (pp. 27–37). Boston, MA: Houghton Mifflin Co.

Dawkins, R. (2006a). *The blind watchmaker*. London: Penguin.

Dawkins, R. (2006b). *The God delusion*. Boston, MA: Houghton Mifflin Co.

Dembski, W. A. (Ed.). (1998). *Mere creation: Science, faith & intelligent design*. Downers Grove, IL: InterVarsity Press.

Dennett, D. C. (1995). *Darwin's dangerous idea: Evolution and the meanings of life*. New York: Simon & Schuster.

Dudley, U. (1997). *Numerology, or, what Pythagoras wrought*. Washington, DC: Mathematical Association of America.

Gardner, M. (1970). Mathematical games: The fantastic combinations of John Conway's new solitaire game "life". *Scientific American, 223*, 120–123. doi:10.1038/scientificamerican1070-120

Glanville, R. (1999). Researching design and designing research. *Design Issues, 15*(2), 80–91. doi:10.2307/1511844

Greene, B. (1999). *The elegant universe: Superstrings, hidden dimensions, and the quest for the ultimate theory*. New York, NY: Vintage Books.

Huffman, C. (2008). Philolaus. *The Stanford Encyclopedia of Philosophy*. Retrieved from http://plato.stanford.edu/archives/fall2008/entries/philolaus/.

Lightman, A. (2000). *Great ideas in physics*. New York, NY: McGraw-Hill.

Lindstrum, S., Palmgren, E., Segerberg, K., & Stoltenberg-Hansen, V. (Eds.). (2009). *Logicism, intuitionism, and formalism: What has become of them?* (*Vol. 341*). Berlin, Germany: Springer. doi:10.1007/978-1-4020-8926-8

Losee, J. (1993). *A historical introduction to the philosophy of science* (3rd ed.). Oxford, UK: Oxford University Press.

Maor, E. (1987). *To infinity and beyond: A cultural history of the infinite*. Boston, MA: Birkhäuser.

Nahin, P. J. (1998). *An imaginary tale: The story of (the square root of minus one)*. Princeton, NJ: Princeton University Press.

Paley, W. (2006). *Natural theology: Or, evidence of the existence and attributes of the deity, collected from the appearances of nature: Edited with an introduction and notes by Matthew D. Eddy and David Knight*. New York: Oxford University Press.

Penrose, R. (1989). *The emperor's new mind: Concerning computers, minds, and the laws of physics*. New York: Oxford University Press.

Quine, W. V. (1999). On what there is. In Kim, J., & Sosa, E. (Eds.), *Metaphysics: An anthology* (pp. 4–12). Malden, MA: Blackwell Publishers.

Whitehead, A. N., & Russell, B. (1927). *Principia mathematica* (2nd ed.). Cambridge, UK: Cambridge University Press.

Chapter 12
Some Example Meta–Artifacts Inspired by Science and Nature

ABSTRACT

Science reveals the workings of the mechanisms behind the natural phenomena. If one can entertain an idea of nature exhibiting definite features of design, then, perhaps human designers could learn from it some of its structures and methods to solve problems faced by human designers. Imitating the natural may be beneficial to tackle tough problems. The chapter provides few such examples. In the first case, the workings of the nervous system, including the brain as revealed by the science have been forward engineered by researchers in artificial neural networks. In the second case, the most versatile designer, i.e. the evolutionary process, has been employed to design solutions for problems in various areas of human activity. In the third case, the "non-scientific" vagueness inherent in human judgment has been harnessed in a fascinating way to provide useful solutions.

DESIGNING BY IMITATING

Modern design tradition relies heavily on principle of accumulated design. Solutions to a variety of problems invented earlier remain in the common human design repository (e.g. in the form of patents) ready to be re-used for the engineering of new artifacts. This cumulativeness is the major factor contributing towards rapid pace of technological progress and the vast variety of human-made objects. If every new artefact had to be built from scratch, without the accumulated design knowledge, the world of the artificial would have been far, far poorer. The term "re-inventing the wheel" refers to situations where a given solution is invented anew, despite the fact that similar idea had appeared before. To re-invent

DOI: 10.4018/978-1-4666-0131-4.ch012

the wheel means to ignore the principle of accumulated design.

Principles of good design emphasize the processes by which the existing solutions are fit in the context of new designs in an effective and efficient manner. Early software developers had to write volumes of code to produce applications of clumsy monolithic nature. One could only wonder of many times fragments of code performing some common function had to be re-invented again and again. The modularity principle in software engineering had dictated that programs should be broken into modules, i.e. subroutines and functions, which could be re-used in other parts of programs. For most commonly used functions and procedures the libraries had been created, which contained the units of code used commonly by applications.

Object orientation in software engineering had brought about a new level of abstraction: a class. Classes bundled together related properties and behaviour into units, which corresponded to some concepts in a given problem domain. Due to the principles of encapsulation and information hiding object-orientation had promoted relative independence of classes from each other. Object-oriented software is easy to test and maintain as it is well organized in terms of interacting objects. A given class, representing some important business concept, e.g. account, or customer, could now be borrowed and reused in new applications. Class libraries provide a repository for classes which, when re-used make re-invention unnecessary. The advance of components and component-oriented development facilitated easy way for the developers to effortlessly embed existing executable chunks of functionality into their applications. The service orientation allows to obtain a particular functionality within a given system context without having to embed this functionality in the system.

Thus, reuse is a principle of efficient design process. What is interesting, the processes invented by humans in one domain could sometimes be carried over, with appropriate adjustments to the other domain. Some known solutions appear to be transcendental with respect to various areas of human activities. In such cases, it is probably not appropriate to use the term "reuse," but something like borrowing, or imitation.

Consider an example of annealing from metallurgy. Atoms of metals bond together forming microstructures. Initially these microstructures may be far from "perfect" meaning that they cause internal tension in a metal. Such metals may be brittle, which makes them unsuitable in situations where hardness and solidity are required. The trick is to "shake up" the metal so that the atoms would then settle down into more stable formations. This is done by heating the metals, and then cooling down the temperature so that the atoms re-arrange into more stable structure. The process has long been known and used in metallurgy.

In certain types of systems (e.g. decision support systems) optimization feature is often required. When impossible to employ "strong" optimization techniques, such as linear programming, there is a choice of using so-called heuristic algorithms. These produce solutions, which are not necessarily "optimal," but often satisfactory. One simple heuristic optimization method is known as "hillclimbing." It imitates a person trying to climb to the top of a hill, when the top cannot be seen in advance, e.g. due to foggy conditions. The person would take a step in random direction. If the new location is lower than the previous one, the person would return to the previous location. If the new position is higher, then he or she would retain it, and then try a new step. After a number of such steps the person would find out that every random step leads to a lower altitude, which means that he or she had reached the top (or its vicinity).

In optimization problems there is a set of controllable variables and an objective function to optimize. The hillclimbing technique would start out with some random point in the variable space, and calculate the objective function value for that point. Then it would try series of small random changes to the point and check for the improvement in the value of the objective function. If the change has led to an improvement, it is retained; otherwise it is discarded in favour of preserving the status quo. Repeated application of the procedure would end up with the variable values, which translate into a near-optimal solution.

However, there is a catch. If the "terrain" of the surface of the objective function has multiple hills, then it is possible that the process would not lead to the top of the highest hill. That is, the random selection of the initial point would turn out to be on a hill, with the highest top. This drawback of some of the iterative improvement methods is known as "local optima." One way to try to overcome local optima is through imitating the annealing process (Kirkpatrick, Gelatt, & Vecchi, 1983). In "simulated annealing" the process also starts with the random choice of an initial point. Then a step in random direction is taken and the value of the objective function is calculated. Similar to hillclimbing, if the step leads towards improvement, the new point is retained. However, if the step leads to an inferior position, it is not necessarily discarded. The new position is accepted with a certain level of probability. This probability is closely linked to the parameter used by an algorithm, called temperature: the higher the temperature, the higher the probability of accepting "bad" steps. The method initially sets the temperature to a high value. It is then gradually lowered in the process of optimization. Towards the end, as the temperature "cools down," the chances of accepting bad steps become very small, and the process basically becomes similar to that governed by hillclimbing. The method has higher chances of hitting global, rather than local optima.

The previous chapter had entertained an idea of Nature as a designer, and science as a process of reverse engineering. If Nature shows remarkable features of design, then one would wonder if a human designer could borrow some of the "natural" solutions as uncovered by science? There may be processes and structures designed by the nature, which human designers could borrow or "reuse"

in their problem solving. Certainly, adaptations and simplifications would be required to apply the workings of the Nature to the design problems. Yet, at some level of abstraction, these natural vs. human-reinvented processes and structures would become indistinguishable. The purpose of this chapter is to show some examples where the "ideas" of nature have been imitated in the world of artificial to produce useful designs. These "ideas" could be said to be transcendental in respect to the traditional science and humanly design.

MIMICKING THE BRAINS

The questions concerning the nature of the mind, nervous system, and brain in particular had attracted humans since the times of ancient Egypt. Hobbes had thought of human bodies and brains as being mechanical systems. In "Leviathan" he writes: "The cause of Sense, is the External Body, or Object, which presseth the organ proper to each Sense, either immediately, as in the Taste and Touch; or mediately, as in Seeing, Hearing, and Smelling: which pressure, by the meditation of Nerves, and other strings and membranes of the body, continues inwards to the Brain, and Heart…" (Hobbes, 1985, p.85). Thus, to Hobbes all nervous and mental processes were produced by the workings of inner mechanisms. Descartes had also viewed animal behaviour in mechanistic terms, while denying the animals any soul (or consciousness). Much of the human body, according to him, function similarly. However, humans, unlike the animals, do possessed souls. Soul was conjectured to be of a distinct nature than the material body, and had connection with the latter via pineal gland in the human brain. Dennett calls this dualistic matter-soul connection "the Cartesian theatre" (Dennett, 1991).

The late Nineteenth – early Twentieth century findings had revealed that a nervous system, including brain contains special kinds of cells called neurons. A neuron consists of a cell body (soma), which contains a nucleus, an axon, and dendrites (Figure 1). It processes information by accumulating and firing electrical signals. Dendrites are typically numerous, and they are sometimes collectively referred to as a dendrite tree. They serve as the inputs to a neuron, as electrical pulses from other neurons travel through them towards a cell membrane. The charges tend to affect the electrical potential that is built up on the membrane. If the potential exceeds a certain threshold limit, the neuron fires series of pulses through its axon. There is only one axon per neuron and, from signal processing perspective, it acts as an output. Axon connects to the other neurons, typically through their dendrites. By sending an output signal a given neuron, thus affects the state of the other connected neuron.

The connection spot between an axon and a dendrite is called a synapse. The strength of the synaptic connection determines to which extent firing of a signal by a given neuron affects the state of the receiving one. Neurons of the brain are massively connected among each other, leading to highly complex patterns of interactions. There are around 10^{11} neurons in human brains with some $10^{12} - 10^{14}$ connections among them. The strengths of the synaptic connections chang-

es over time, largely affected by the patterns of neuron firings. This lays the basis for important cognitive abilities, such as learning. Many thousands of neurons are lost by the brain on a daily basis. Despite this on-going loss, human beings continue on to function cognitively normally, which attests to the robustness of the brain.

Could human designers imitate the workings of the networks of interconnected neurons to obtain some useful functionality? It would be too ambitious of an attempt to build truly thinking machines, yet perhaps some aspects of pattern recognition and learning could be harnessed. Early attempt to imitate nervous cells was by McCulloch & Pitts (1943). Their neuron included binary inputs, which were summed to be compared with a "threshold" to determine if a neuron produces an output signal. Combination of such neurons could implement any Boolean function. Another example included Rosenblatt's perceptron (Rosenblatt, 1958). The earliest learning rule that explained changing the strengths of inter-neuronal connections was Hebb's rule, which stated that connection between two neurons that fire together frequently tends to grow stronger over time (Hebb, 1949).

Nowadays there is a good variety of different models of artificial neurons. Schematically a gen-

Figure 1. Neuron

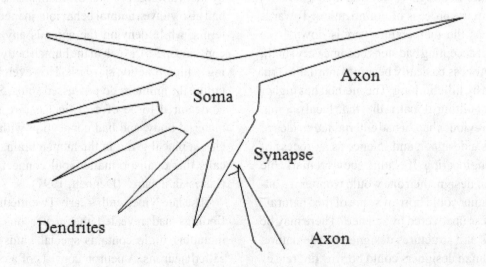

eral model for an artificial neuron is represented in Figure 2. Inputs imitate the dendrites, weights are the analogs of synaptic conductivity, aggregation and transfer functions mimic the process of potential accumulation on a membrane and neuron firing, while the output models the axon. Inputs could be binary or continuous values. The weights are continuous values, either positive or negative. Positive weights tend to increase the potential, while the negative ones decrease it. In natural neural networks, the potential decreasing effect is achieved by inhibitory connections. For example, when somebody is looking at a black rectangle, the sensory neurons perceiving the edges are active, and they tend to inhibit the neighbouring neurons so that the brain is not overloaded with volumes of sensory data. Brain reconstructs the dark area of a rectangle, based on a subset of inputs.

The magnitude of the weights determine how much the arriving signals contribute towards firing or inhibiting of a neuron. The inputs are multiplied by the weights and then aggregated according to some function. The most common aggregation function is summation:

$$S = \sum_{i=1}^{n} w_i x_i$$

Here, w stands for a weight, x is an input and n is the total number of inputs for a neuron. The weighted sum, then is passed through the transfer function. The straightforward analogy with the natural neurons would dictate a threshold-like shape for a transfer function (Figure 3):

$$y = \begin{cases} 1 & if \ S \geq T \\ 0 & otherwise \end{cases},$$

where T is a threshold. In a nutshell, if the weighted sum of all inputs of a neuron exceeds a given threshold value, the neuron fires a signal (i.e. its output is set to 1), otherwise, it remains passive (i.e. the output is 0). Note that while a biological neuron would accept incoming signals continuously, the simulated one receives them at discrete intervals. Mathematically speaking, the threshold function is "inconvenient," in particular for the purpose of training neural networks. The "smoother" versions are much more preferable.

One commonly used transfer function is so called sigmoidal, or S-shaped function (Figure 4):

$$y = \frac{1}{1 + e^{-(S+b)}}$$

Here b is a parameter called bias, which provides an offset for the inflection point of the "smoother" threshold. It can be viewed as an additional default input to a neuron. Unlike threshold function, the value of the sigmoidal function ranges from 0 to 1 (for some other function choices, e.g. hyperbolic tangent it could range from -1 to 1). This implies that a neuron's output would not have to be binary. In cases where bi-

Figure 2. Artificial neuron

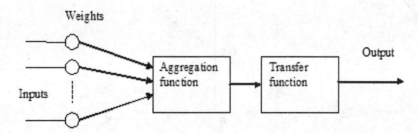

Figure 3. Threshold function

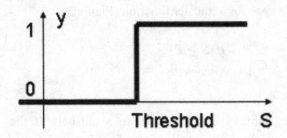

nary output is required, the output could be rounded to 0 or 1.

Simulated neurons are used to build artificial neural networks by linking the outputs of some neurons to the inputs of the others. A variety of such network types could be built, but the most common one organizes neurons by the "layers." In a layered structure a set of neurons is assigned to an input layer, and the other set to the output layer. The input layer neurons act as elementary sensors as they collect signals from outside and simply distribute them to the neurons of the output layer, which perform calculations according to the neural model adopted. Their outputs serve as results of neural network's computation. When there are only input and output layers in a network, it is called a two-layered model (sometimes such networks are called single-layered, as only one layer performs actual computations). Two layered neural networks are limited in their computational capacity. When used for classification purposes

(i.e. the inputs serve as features of an object to be classified, and the outputs are assigned to different classes) their capacity is limited to solving problems, where classes are linearly separable (they could be separated by straight lines). In this respect, A two-layered model can perform something similar to linear discriminant analysis.

Multi-layered networks include additional layers between the input and output neurons. The neurons of each such layer receive input from the neurons of the previous layer, and pass the calculated output signals to the neurons of the next layer. The layers situated between the input and the output one are referred to as "hidden" layers. The term "hidden" implies that these units do not directly interact with the external environment. The more layers a network has, the higher its computational capacity. If signals in a network flow from layer to layer in a forward direction only, such models are called feedforward neural networks. If some of the outputs are allowed to feed back as inputs to the neurons of the same or previous layers, these are called recurrent networks. Figure 5 shows an example of a three-layered feedforward neural network with three inputs, two outputs, and five hidden neurons.

While the number of input and output neurons is defined by the problem context, finding the required number of hidden units requires some expertise and experimentation, although some rules of thumb had been proposed. It had been

Figure 4. Sigmoidal function

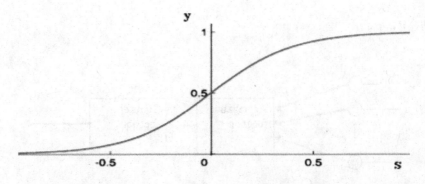

Figure 5. A three-layered feedforward neural network

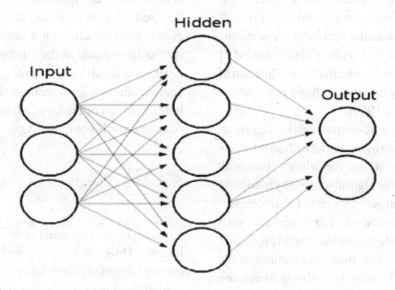

demonstrated that neural networks are universal approximators, i.e. provided a sufficient number of hidden neurons any functional input to output mapping can be approximated to a desired degree (Hornik, Stinchcombe, & White, 1989). The mapping is achieved by finding the appropriate weights of connections (synaptic strengths). This is performed by training a given neural network.

Training involves exposing the neural network to a number of example data (called a training set) and applying training algorithm, which tunes the weights of a network so that the latter captures the important patterns behind the data. Hebb's rule, mentioned earlier leads to a simple training algorithm that changes the weights locally, i.e. based on the activation levels of two neurons. The rule is not effective in many cases, and a variety of algorithms had been devised in the past. Training algorithms could be classified into supervised, unsupervised and reinforcement categories. In supervised training a network is exposed to a set of example input – output pairs and it adjusts the weights to model the required input - output mapping. The network could then be tested on a new, previously "unseen" data set to check the generality of its performance. In unsupervised

training, no output data is provided in the training set. Such a network could perform a type of cluster analysis. In reinforcement training a single "reward/punishment" signal is provided to the algorithm during training. Below we will briefly describe the most common type of supervised training algorithm.

As mentioned earlier, a two-layered neural network can only solve linearly separable classification problems. It fails to solve the problems of the XOR type (i.e. if both binary inputs are 0 or 1, the output should be 0; otherwise it should be 1). It had been known that three-layered networks could solve the problem, but there was no algorithm available to train multi-layered networks. That is, for a two-layer network, provided with sample input, the output could be calculated and compared with the desired one. The discrepancy served as the basis for iteratively adjusting the weights of inputs feeding into the given output neuron. The actual algorithm involved, known as Widrow-Hoff rule would converge to the minimum least square solution. However, in multi-layered networks the problem was that error for the hidden neurons could not be calculated, since there were no explicitly given desired outputs for them.

While hidden neurons enhance the computational capacity of a network, in general it is difficult to say what they actually represent. In port, this deficiency had led to a relative abandonment of research in neural network after the publication of a book by Minsky and Papert, titled *Perceptrons* (Minsky & Papert, 1969).

The advent of error backpropagation algorithm allowed for training of networks with an arbitrary number of hidden layers (Rumelhart, Hinton, & Williams, 1986). The algorithm starts by randomly choosing an initial set of weights for all connections in a neural network. For a given layered feedforward neural network the error of prediction can be calculated as the total of deviations of the network outputs from the desired outputs coming from the training set:

$$E = \sum_c \sum_{i=1}^{n} \left(d_i - o_i \right)^2,$$

where d is the desired output, o is the actual output, c is the number of cases from the training set, and n is the number of output neurons. The weights should be adjusted in a way that decreases the total error. This is achieved by following gradient (steepest) descent path in respect to the error. Thus, the weights of connections leading to the output neurons are attuned in accordance with the formula:

$$w_{ij}(t+1) = w_{ij}(t) - r \frac{\partial E(t)}{\partial w_{ij}(t)}$$

Here, w_{ij} stands for the weight of connection between j^{th} output neuron and i^{th} neuron of the layer adjacent to the output one at a given time t, and r is a parameter called learning rate.. This allows for the adjustment of weights between the output layer and the one feeding into it. However, in a multi-layered network the weights of connections feeding into the hidden layer should also be adjusted. But then what should be the "desired" outputs for these neurons? In error back propagation the error for a given hidden neuron is calculated based on the error of the subsequent layer, weighted by the strengths of outgoing connections of a given neuron. Thus, for a given hidden neuron of the layer adjacent to the output one the error is computed as:

$$e_i = \sum_c \sum_{j=1}^{n} \left(w_{ij} e_j \right),$$

where e_j is the (squared) error for the jth output neuron. Thus, an error for each hidden neuron can be computed. The total error can be used in a similar fashion to attune the weights between any given hidden layer and the previous one. In this truly elegant method, errors are sort of propagated backwards, while the firing of neurons proceeds in a forward direction. The working of the algorithm is shown schematically in Figure 6.

If one could picture an N-dimensional surface, where N refers to the total number of weights in a neural network, then one could imagine that for every point in that space there would be a given magnitude of error. Thus, in a $N+1$ − dimensional space one could picture the error surface. Back propagation starts with a random point in that space and starts descending into a nearest "valley" in the steepest direction. The pace of the descent is set by the learning rate: if set too low, it will take longer to hit the near-bottom; if set too high, the procedure will make the network to jump from one side to the other without settling down (oscillations). The valley may be the local one, i.e. not the deepest one. Neural network, for that matter could set out to explore non-linear patterns that are in fact better modeled by simpler, linear methods. Basic back propagation algorithm described above has been extended and improved significantly to avoid local minima and "overtraining" (modeling complex patterns, when they are not there). Yet, interestingly, one critique of back

Figure 6. Error back propagation

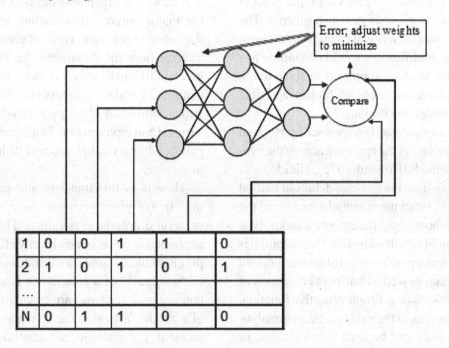

propagation algorithm is often voiced. The error back propagation algorithm *is not biologically plausible*. It is highly doubtful that the natural brain calculates partial derivatives in order to facilitate learning processes. This is an example, where human designers, initially inspired by Nature, eventually went on to deviate from its ways to devise effective avenues to explore its structures. Why would the biological implausibility count against the algorithm?

Business applications of neural networks have been numerous (Smith & Gupta, 2000). Here, we will just consider one example application to stock selection problem. In (Lam, 2004) the authors had sought to combine the elements of fundamental and technical analysis to predict the performance of stocks. Technical and fundamental analyses represent the competing schools of thoughts in financial security analysis. The authors had gathered the data on 364 S&P companies over the period of 1985 to 1995. Examples of their inputs to a neural network include: current assets/current liabilities, net sales/total assets, net income/total assets,

relative strength index, pretax income/net sales, short-term interest rate, and others. The output was used to roughly classify a given company's stock into high, medium, or low return. They had trained the network using historical data, and tested its performance against the market average, and the top third of the best performers on the market. Their findings indicated that the stocks picked by neural network had outperformed the average, but not the "elite" top third of the market.

DESIGNING THE DESIGNER

Human designers use an impressive analytical apparatus in making design decisions. Through billions of years nature has "designed" a huge variety of exquisite life forms well-suited to their respective niches. A hypothetical "intelligent designer" could have used the intelligence to greatly speed up the design process, and would have been much less wasteful than evolution. However, notwithstanding the humongous number of trials and errors, evolution employs a simple process to solve a wide class of design problems. The process is based on survival of the fittest, reproduction, and modification. Could one mimic this tremendously successful process to solve tough problems in various areas of human activity? Could one design the designer?

Genetic Algorithms (GA) devised by Holland represent one successful approach among the evolutionary methods (Holland, 1975). The idea is to abstract away from the intricate details of natural evolution to extract the essential structure of the process and show how different optimization-type problems could be solved by GA. Optimization is a very common type of problem often encountered in engineering, as well as business contexts. For simpler problems (e.g. simple objective function, simple constraints, or their absence) strong analytical approaches could be used, e.g. Calculus, or Operations Research methods. When problems are complex, i.e. not solvable by strong optimization techniques heuristic methods are often the only viable choice. An example is the traveling salesman problem, where a salesman should visit a given number of cities, visiting each one exactly once, while keeping the total distance to a minimum. Heuristic methods allow for finding a near-optimal solution. Hilclimbing and simulated annealing are example heuristic methods.

Similar to the process of natural evolution a distinction between genotype and phenotype is useful in order to understand GA. To remind, genotype refers to the genetic encodings that make up a string of DNA. Phenotype refers to the features of organisms as they come into interaction with the external environment. Phenotype determines the fitness of an organism. A wolf with stronger feet and jaws would be better fit to survive in the wild. These phenotypic features are implicit in the wolf's genetic code. Survival promotes chances of finding mates and producing offspring. In fact, apart from such natural selective pressures, there is also sexual selection, which at times comes at

a cost, as the organisms develop features with the major purpose of attracting individuals of the opposite sex. Both types of pressures in their interrelationship determine the chances of a given individual's survival. Note, that due to the complexity and randomness inherent in reality, a strong individual is not guaranteed a successful survival and reproduction. Due to bad luck it may perish, while a weaker one may be lucky enough to survive.

How does this translate into problem solving? In any given problem, there is a criterion, or several criteria to optimize. These could be expressed in terms of an objective function mapping a candidate solution's features into the degree of "goodness" of a solution. It is also possible, that criterion (criteria) are calculated as outputs of a model, provided the candidate solution as an input. For example, consider how one would use a neural network, similar to the one discussed in the previous section in order to compose an "optimal" portfolio. Suppose a portfolio of ten stocks is being considered. When a given stock is fed into the network, the latter estimates its prospects in terms of the strength of the associated output neuron signal. The problem is to find a set of 10 securities, along with their respective weights in the portfolio, which would maximize the expected return, while limiting the portfolio risk to some acceptable level. GA place very little requirements on the nature of the mapping that measures the "goodness" of solutions. What matters is that there should be a way to calculate criteria values for any given candidate solution.

Based on the objective function (be it explicitly described or inherent in a model implementing the mapping) a "fitness" function is built. All the intricacies of natural and sexual selective pressures are simply "assumed" to be inherent in this function. It accepts a candidate solution as an input and calculates how attractive it is, i.e. what the chances of its "survival" are. The candidate solution is expressed in the representation of a problem context, i.e. it is a phenotype (e.g. a portfolio of selected stocks). Fitness function should have non-negative values and should be of a form that implies maximization. Various sorts of mappings could be chosen to turn the original objective function into the one estimating fitness.

The algorithm works with solution genotypes. Classical GA work with the strings of binary numbers (although GA versions for real-valued strings have also been proposed), which correspond to "chromosomes" containing relevant "genes." The working of GA does not depend on the form of a fitness function; its usage for estimating the fitness of a chromosome is all that is needed by GA. Thus, there is a need for mapping from the binary representation of a given solution to the one that suits the original problem space (i.e. from genotype to phenotype). The choice of this mapping schema often affects the effectiveness and efficiency of the algorithm.

Consider an example of genotype for a portfolio selection problem. It should encode not only the inclusion of a given stock in a portfolio, but also a corresponding relative weight. Suppose we are considering a pool of 100 stocks, of which 10 must be selected. One way to represent candidate solutions would be as follows:

$$\{weight_1, weight_2, weight_3, ..., weight_{100}\}$$

Here, each element of a vector represents a relative weight of a given stock (which are numbered 1 through 100) in a portfolio. A weight of 0 implies that the corresponding stock is left out. All weights add up to unity. Note, that in such representation many randomly generated candidate solutions would not be legitimate, since only 10 stocks can be included. Translating the above string into binary representation would require discretization of the weights. Suppose each weight is discretized to have 128 different levels. This would require 7 bits per weight, for a total of 700 bits. Each set of bits can be regarded

as a gene, and the entire string would correspond to a chromosome:

$$\{gene_1, gene_2, gene_3, ..., gene_{100}\}$$

For example, consider a case of a chromosome that contains the first three genes with some 1s in them, while the rest of the genes are all 0:

$$\{0011010\ 1000000\ 0001111\ 0000000\ ...\ 0000000\}$$

This would translate into:

$$\{26, 64, 15, 0, ..., 0\}$$

Normalizing the string would lead to the following distribution of weights:

$$\{0.25, 0.61, 0.14, 0, ..., 0\}$$

Thus 25% of the portfolio is allocated to stock 1, 61% to stock 2, and 14% to stock 3. Note that this portfolio is indeed "invalid" as it does not have the required number of stocks. As GAs employ randomness in their working, one could expect generation of many such "illegitimate" chromosomes, and much of the search efforts would be in wasteful directions. This is why the choice of the representational schema is so important. An alternative representation would be to have a separate substring indicating an inclusion of a stock in the portfolio (which would require one bit per a stock) in addition to the substring of weights. This way GA could quickly assess the legitimacy of a chromosome and avoid redundant calculations.

Suppose a suitable representation has been chosen and for any chromosome a fitness value can be calculated. One approach to dealing with illegitimate chromosomes is to apply a penalty to a fitness function, which would effectively decrease the fitness value of an inadequate solution. Another way is to try repairing the problematic chromosome. For example, in the above case for an invalid chromosome a random procedure of choosing ten genes to preserve, while setting all the others to zero could be applied, when the number of stocks is too high. Given a binary representation and a way to estimate the fitness, GA can now set to work. Only basic form of GA will be described briefly here. Interested readers could learn more about GA by referring to introductory books (e.g. Michalewicz, 1996).

Darwin had described the evolutionary process starting with the existence of a population of diverse individuals, which actually had become the basis of the criticism of his theory. Notwithstanding the objections regarding where this initial population had come from in the first place, in GA the first step simply generates the initial population of a set size randomly. That is, the algorithm generates N random binary strings. In most cases the size is kept constant throughout the evolution of the strings. This is not biologically plausible, and there are versions in which population size changes in the process (Eiben, Marchiori, & Valkó, 2004). We will assume that the size does not change.

In natural populations some of the individuals will be better fit to survive and reproduce (depending on their phenotypic features) than others. In GA this assessment is performed by calculating a fitness function for each individual. Now the algorithm must decide which individuals (chromosomes) will survive and produce offspring to make up the next generation. Unlike in biological evolution, in simulated one the generations come at discrete times and replace the older ones. In order to do so, often a "roulette wheel" procedure is involved, which sort of mimics the inherent randomness in the organisms' fates. In this procedure the "roulette" is marked by assigning each chromosome a probability of survival according to a formula:

$$p_i = \frac{f_i}{\sum_{i=1}^{N} f_i}$$

Here p_i stands for a probability of survival of the ith chromosome, f_i is its fitness, and N is the population size. Now each chromosome gets, as it were, its own sector on the roulette. The roulette is then spun N times ("life is a game"). This is done by generating a uniformly distributed random number, ranging from 0 to 1 and checking against the markings of the roulette. The lucky chromosome then copies itself into the next generation, i.e. the individual produces an offspring. However, it does not lose its sector on the roulette. Thus, a very lucky chromosome could produce multiple offspring (at the expense of some others). An unlucky chromosome may never win, and thus will produce no offspring at all. As one can easily see, the fitter chromosomes will *tend* to have higher chances of reproduction, but are not *guaranteed* to reproduce.

Why not just keep the better chromosomes and reject the weaker ones deterministically? Why simulate randomness? As shall be seen from further descriptions, due to mutation and crossover processes it is possible that altered and/or recombined weaker chromosomes may lead to promising directions of evolution. In fact, there is a version of algorithm, where a small proportion of strong chromosomes do get their "reservations" in the future generation. This is called the "elitist" approach. An analogy could be drawn with human populations living in relatively harsh conditions, where the rich and noble form such elites and almost assure their survival and reproduction with the offspring often becoming part of the new generation of the elite (unless there is a revolution, of course).

Selection itself does not bring in new variety into the population. In fact, if executed repeatedly, it will diminish the diversity of a population, eventually leading to the convergence. Change is introduced into the algorithm by borrowing from nature. The origins of change are in mutation and crossover. Mutation, in its simplest form flips a bit to its opposite value on a random basis. There may be other variants of mutation if, let's say just flipping a bit would lead to an invalid solution (e.g. changing other related bits maybe required). The probability of a bit being flipped is called mutation rate, and this is one of the key parameters of GA. Therefore, the offspring does not have to be genetically identical to its parent.

Crossover provides another source of producing diversity. By imitating the biologically analogous process taking place during meiosis, it exchanges parts of genetic code between two chromosomes. First, it chooses a set of chromosomes from a population. Then it pairs them up to "mate." It picks up a random position in the chromosome sequence, which serves as a split point. It then exchanges parts of the pair chromosome, producing two offspring. Each of these has a portion of code from one parent, and a portion from another parent. This is a single-point crossover:

the simplest form. Multi-point crossover versions are also used, where several sections of genetic code are interchanged. In terms of solution search in a problem space, crossover provides means of interchanging information between different directions of search. The probability with which a chromosome is picked for crossover is called crossover rate. Figure 7 shows schematically the effects of mutation and crossover.

After the new generation is formed, the selection sets to work again, and the process proceeds in an iterative fashion, until stopping criterion is met. This criterion could be a preset number of iterations, or lack of improvement in fitness over a number of last generations. In basic version of GA the mutation and crossover rates are kept constant throughout the evolution process. However, there are versions, in which they could be adjusted in the process. This is biologically plausible, as mutation rates do seem to evolve in some biological populations (Sniegowski, Gerrish, Johnson, & Shaver, 2000). Why the adjustment of rates in GA would be beneficial. With higher mutation and crossover rates, the algorithm pro-

Figure 7. Mutation and crossover

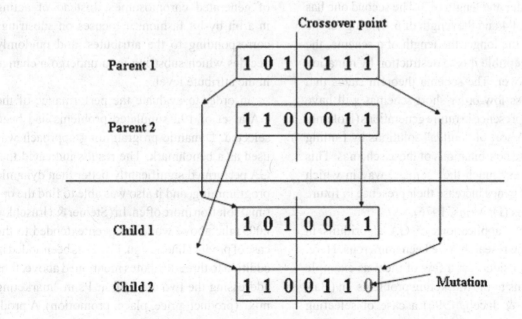

duces many diverse solutions, encompassing large areas of the problem space. This exploration process is helpful in regards with finding promising areas associated with hitting global optima. However, higher rates are not so much helpful in fine-tuning the solutions. Smaller rates lead to fine-tuning of the solutions, but they are susceptible of getting stuck in local optima. This exploration-exploitation dilemma leads to an approach, whereby the rates are set high in the initial stages of evolution, and then gradually reduced to near-zero values (Michalewicz, 1996).

What lies behind the explicit workings of genetic algorithms? Consider the following string: {101*****}. Here, the first three bits have value, while the ones denoted by wildcard characters are allowed to have arbitrary values. This is called a schema and it denotes a subset of all possible chromosomes, where the first three positions are fixed as shown. It is theoretically feasible to estimate the fitness of the schema by comparing the average fitness of the subset covered by it with the entire set of possible chromosomes. Consider another schema: {*1**001*}. The order of a schema is the number of fixed bits in it. The length is the distance between the first and the last fixed bits. Thus, the first example schema has the order and length of 3. The second one has the order of 4 and the length of 6. The higher the order and the longer the length of a schema, the more susceptible it is to destruction by mutation and crossover. The schema theorem states that high-fitness low-order short schemas will have increased presence in future generations (Holland, 1975). GA sort of "builds" solutions by finding appropriate combinations of these schemas. This reminds very much the "selfish" way in which biological genes increase their presence in future generations (Dawkins, 1976).

Business applications of GA algorithms in design-type research have been numerous. Here, we will consider just a few of them as example applications to the Marketing problems. In (Balakrishnan & Jacob, 1996) a case of selecting product design features which would maximize consumers' total utility has been proposed. This is an example case of designing the designer. A product is specified in terms of its key attributes, and a set of discrete values for each attribute. An example of soap with shape, color and scent as the attributes is presented. A chromosome is made up of concatenated binary substrings for each attributes indicating the presence or absence of a specific attribute level. Conjoint analysis was performed to assess the utilities for various combinations of product attribute values. The utilities were used in order to build a fitness function. Elitist approach to selection has been employed, whereby a number of fittest chromosomes would be guaranteed their reproduction into a new generation. Crossover operator, if employed in the basic form could lead to invalid chromosomes. For example, there could be a solution, indicating that the color is both red and green. Therefore, crossover was allowed to split the strings in locations, which precisely separated two neighboring attributes. The crossover rate was set to 0.5, implying that each chromosome in the population had 50/50 chances of being selected for exchanging parts with some other chromosome. Mutation operator has also been adapted to ensure the validity of generated chromosomes. Instead of acting in a bit-by-bit fashion, it focuses on substrings corresponding to the attributes, and randomly decides which substring is to undergo a change in the attribute level.

In order to evaluate the performance of the GA a set of 192 simulated problems had been selected. Dynamic programming approach was used as a benchmark. The results indicated that GA performed significantly better then dynamic programming, and it also was able to find the optimal solution more often. In (Steiner & Hruschka, 2003) the above work has been extended to the case of product line design. Price has been added in addition to three attributes mentioned above, thus addressing the two out of four Ps in "marketing mix" (product, price, place, promotion). A product line included series of products of the same type. Thus, several substrings corresponding to product attribute levels of different products have been concatenated to form a single chromosome. Monte-Carlo simulations have been employed for evaluation of a given candidate product line implicit in a particular chromosome encoding. A comparison with the other heuristic known as "greedy" (which is based on a similar philosophy as hillclimbing) revealed the superiority of GA.

To continue on a topic of Marketing applications, in (Fazlollahi & Vahidov, 2001) the marketing mix problem has been tackled, now covering product, price, and promotion categories (3 out of 4 Ps). The authors have used a business game environment, which simulates a hypothetical business environment, where a number of firms compete for three products (*x*, *y*, and *z*) in an olygopolistic market. Teams of graduate-level business students manage firms aiming at improving profitability and market share. Teams make marketing, production, and financial decisions for each simulated quarter using traditional decision support tools, e.g. simple optimization and Monte-Carlo simulations. Marketing-related decisions include the mix and amounts of goods to produce, pricing, advertising expenses, and production capacity needed. The DSS for marketing decisions incorporates a Monte-Carlo simulation model. The objective of the decision making is to maximize the so-called "marketing value," which is based on the total expected profit, as well as the future value of the inventory. There are constraints related to the total production volume for three products and controlling the probabilities of stocking out for the three products. The problem is thus defined in terms of finding such a combination of decision variables (*Price*, *Advertising*, *Quantity*) for each of the three products, which improves the total value subject to constraints.

Monte-Carlo simulations have been used to deal with the uncertainty regarding competitors' decisions. A decision maker has to use judgment to estimate the uncertain variables, including average industry price, advertising expenses, and R&D expenditures for the current quarter. In Monte-Carlo simulations the values for average industry price, advertising expenses, and R&D expenditures were generated from triangular distributions set by a decision maker. Given trial decisions on three products a number of runs, with different values for uncertain variables is executed using a fairly complex model, which included predictive components. The output of this process was the expected marketing value, which will be used as the basis for the fitness function. Now, instead of a human searching for the best decision by means of "what-if" analysis, the authors let GA evolve promising decisions. In their approach, each chromosome represents a set of nine variables: quantities to produce, prices, and advertising expenses for three hypothetical products. They employed 10 binary digits per each of the continuous variables (resulting in 1024 discrete levels per variable) which resulted in 90-bits long chromosomes. A chromosome was encoded as: $\{P_x, P_y, P_z, A_x, A_y, A_z, Q_{x/y}, Q_{x/z}, Q\}$, where P, A and Q correspond to substrings encoding price, advertising, and quantity for each of the three products. Actually, quantities are represented in ratio form to circumvent the capacity constraint in order to avoid invalid chromosomes.

The authors had compared the performance of GA with the results of "what-if"-based search performed by a set of business student subjects. The algorithm employed elitist strategy as it evolved a population of 50 chromosomes with the mutation and crossover rates set to 0.007 and 0.7 respectively. The algorithm has outperformed human decision makers both after 1000 and, even after 100 generations. An interesting extension of this work has been presented in (Fazlollahi & Vahidov, 2001). Typically, GAs are used to find a single "optimal" solution. However, nature produces a diversity of living form, each sort of "optimized" to occupy its own niche. The authors noted that in decision support context alternative generation is a vital part of decision making. They used the power of GA to produce several alternatives, each one good in its own way in a single run. The alternatives were fitted to different decision contexts, e.g. maximizing profits, or increasing market share. Analysis of results showed that the alternatives generated by GA were truly diverse.

BACK TO THE VAGUE

Human ways of reasoning are susceptible to inconsistencies and vagueness. Aristotle was concerned with the sloppiness of human reasoning. He set out to derive the prescriptive rules to outline the correct ways of thinking. Thus, he could be considered the father of Logic. In his Analytics he spelled out the ways of making correct conclusions from given premises – the so called syllogisms (Aristotle, 1965). One of his famous postulates can be stated as either a statement is true, or it is not. It cannot be true and not true at the same time. Thus, abandoning the natural vagueness of human thought he had introduced a scientific approach to describing "correct" ways of reasoning. Whole of the subsequent Western Logic has developed from the foundations laid by Aristotle.

Reasonable as it may sound, the strict Aristotelian logic leads to non-intuitive results. For example, consider the case of a teenager turning of legal age (suppose the legal age is eighteen). One day before his or her birthday he or she is not considered of legal age. Yet, this is a matter of a single day, and intuitively this does not make sense. If that person tries to enter a bar or a dance club one minute before midnight, then he or she should not be allowed to. A single minute makes a huge difference. In countries with judicial systems based on the civil code, there may be rules that define, say what constitutes major embezzlement. If the embezzler steals one cent less than the set limit, the corresponding punishment could be much lighter. To use another example, how would one define "warm weather"? Take the lower limit of

any such definition and subtract one (or one-tenth, or one-thousands of) degree, and suddenly you are in "not warm" region. Somehow, this defies common sense.

The above examples are curious, yet consistent. But crisp Aristotelian logic leads to paradoxes as well. Consider the well known heap paradox. Say, there is a heap of sand. If you take away one grain, the heap would still be there. Applying this logic iteratively one would eventually end up with no sand at all. But still, by logic this no-sand place would still be considered a heap. Kosko in his book titled "Fuzzy thinking" provides many such examples (Kosko, 1993). If somebody takes a bite from an apple, would it still be categorized as an apple? Take another bite, then another. When does an apple become a non-apple? These examples might seem curious and amusing, but the crispiness of classical sets has important implications for intelligent systems design. Consider the case of expert systems, which utilize their knowledge base containing a set of "if-then" rules. Let's say it is an expert system for approving credit line increase. Suppose it has rules of a kind:

"IF Outstanding_Debt = Medium AND Income = High THEN Credit_Increase = Somewhat_ High."

Now, one has to define all these mediums and highs. One dollar could make a substantial difference. The rules are too rough. One way to deal with this is to introduce finer gradations, i.e. "medium," "slightly higher than medium," "rather high than medium" etc. But this leads to the substantial increase in the number of rules required. If there are five variables to consider with nine possible values for each, then technically speaking the knowledge base should contain 59,049 rules to be defined by experts.

The time to revive the vague, and to harness it! How could the vague be of any use at all? Surprisingly, it could. Vagueness is not only characteristic of human thought. The Nature employs it at its very basic level. It is common to think that quantum processes are intrinsically random. However, as Penrose clarifies, the randomness only appears when the micro- level processes are "brought into" the macro- world (Penrose, 1997). Only by means of observation the randomness comes into the picture. At a micro- level, there is no randomness, but possibilities. A particle that may take one path or the other and interact with other particles, leading to new possibilities kind of maintains the suspended state, until an observable outcome of the process leads a random choice from the possibilities. Physicists can calculate the different possibilities. Nature maintains vagueness until forced by an observer to make its choices. Nature "uses" the vague.

Lotfi Zadeh in his seminal article had introduced the concept of a fuzzy set (Zadeh, 1965). In traditional set theory an element either belongs to a set, or it does not. In fuzzy sets an element may belong to a set *partially*. Thus, it could have partial membership in a given set, as well as in its complement. For example in traditional set-theoretic terms a person would be considered either to be tall, or not tall. He or she cannot be both tall and not tall. In fuzzy sets, though one can. A and not-A is no longer an absurdity. A book could be expensive and not expensive, a temperature could be cold and not cold, a person could be rich and not rich.

In traditional ("crisp") sets an element's degree of "membership" in a given set is either 0 or 1. An element is either a member, or it is not. In fuzzy sets the membership of an element in a given set could range from 0 to 1, inclusively. A given temperature could be in the "warm" category with, say 0.7 degree of membership, and in the "cold" category with 0.4 degree of membership. Note, that this is not the same as probability. The question is not with what probabilities the temperature would fall in one or the other category. The value

for the temperature is known and given. The issue is to what extent this given temperature could be said to be warm or cold.

This means that for every element in a given domain its membership to a fuzzy set needs to be defined. For example, for every value of possible temperatures, there has to be a corresponding value, which expresses its membership to the set of warm temperatures. This is done by means of membership functions. When elements are discrete in their nature, the membership function could be given in a tabular format. When they are continuous, it is convenient to express membership functions formulaically.

Consider an example of a GMAT score. Fuzzy sets "low," "medium" and "high" could be specified by means of membership functions graphically shown in Figure 8. The form of the membership function for the "medium" set is triangular, while for the other two it is trapezoidal. For a triangular function one has to specify three parameters: the value for the peak, where membership is 1 (in cases of so-called "normal" fuzzy sets), and the values for the points on the left and right sides, where it hits 0. For the trapezoidal form, one has to define four parameters correspondingly. A membership of 1 implies that the corresponding point definitely belongs to a set, while that of 0 means that it does not belong to the set. One could set a condition to only consider those elements, whose membership values are higher than some specified level. This is called an alpha cut of a fuzzy set. An alpha cut of 0 is called the support of a fuzzy set. A set of elements, which have the level of 1 ("definitely belong") is called a kernel of a fuzzy set. There could be other types of functions used for describing fuzzy set memberships, e.g. bell-shaped, or S-shaped. They should be chosen so that their values never exceed 1 or drop below 0. Note, that unlike in the case of density of probability distribution functions, the area under the membership functions is not required to equal unity. Mathematically, the triangular membership function could be described as:

$$\mu(x) = \begin{cases} 1 & \text{if } x = b \\ (x-a)/(b-a) & \text{if } a < x < b \\ (c-x)/(c-b) & \text{if } b < x < c \\ 0 & \text{otherwise} \end{cases}$$

Here, a, b, and c correspond to the leftmost, the peak, and the rightmost defining points of a fuzzy set.

This is all interesting, but how would it translate into useful applications? Fuzzy logic allows building applications, where the rules are specified using fuzzy sets. Consider how one would normally adjust the temperature of water in a shower. If the temperature is very hot, then one would turn the knob in the "colder" direction by a good degree. If it is somewhat cold, one would turn it in the "warmer" direction slightly. This is exactly how the rules are specified in fuzzy systems. In fact, fuzzy sets and fuzzy logic have found a good number of applications in the area of automatic control.

Figure 8. Membership functions

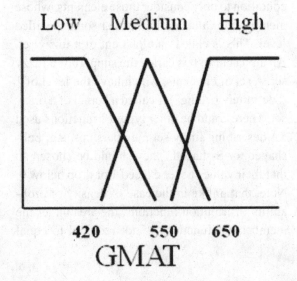

Fuzzy systems contain rules, which describe relationships between the input and output variables. When the (crisp) input values are received, they are first "fuzzified," in other words they are translated into the corresponding membership values of the specified fuzzy sets. Then fuzzy inferencing applies rules to obtain fuzzy value for an output variable. The latter then is "defuzzified" to obtain a crisp value as the output.

An example will make it more clear. Suppose the graduate program office in some hypothetical university considers Grade Point Average (GPA) and GMAT score to decide whether or not to admit an applicant. They want to build a fuzzy logic - based application that generates a suggestion. The GMAT and GPA are considered at the low, medium, and high levels. The system recommendation would be expressed on a scale from 0 to 100. For example, if the output equals 80, then the system supports the applicant's admission to 80%. This could further be used, for example for ranking the applicants.

Figure 9 shows membership functions for the three variables. These variables (GMAT, GPA, and Recommendation) in the context of their fuzzy description are called "linguistic variables," as their values are linguistic terms, which, in turn are defined as fuzzy sets. Assume now that a set of rules has to be defined to specify the relationship between GPA and GMAT on one hand and the corresponding recommendation on the other. Since there are only two input variables with three values per each, there could be a maximum of nine rules. For the simplicity sake, suppose that we only have two rules in the knowledge base (and really simple ones):

If GMAT = High AND GPA = High Then Recommendation = High

If GMAT = Medium AND GPA = Medium Then Recommendation = Medium.

Figure 9. Example fuzzy sets

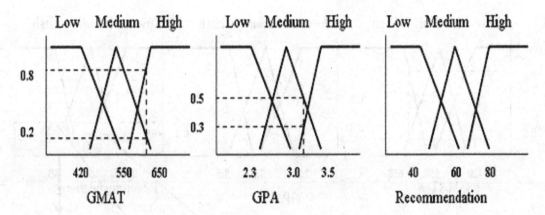

Assume that a particular applicant has a GPA of 3.2 and a GMAT score of 620. These are crisp original values. Fuzzification implies restating these values in fuzzy terms for the corresponding linguistic variables. Assume (according to Figure 9) that GMAT score of 620 could be said to be "high" to the 0.8 degree, medium to 0.2 degree, and low to 0 degree. That is 620 belongs to the set "High" with the membership of 0.8, and to the set "Medium" with the membership of 0.2. For the GPA, applying the same fuzzification procedure, 3.2. would yield membership of 0.5 to the "Medium" set, and that of 0.3 to the "High" set. Now the fuzzification step is complete. Instead of considering initial crisp values, fuzzy inferencing works with their "vague" images.

The fuzzy values are mapped against all of the fuzzy rules in the knowledge base. In our case we only have two. The left ("If") sides of the rules are assessed to assess to what degree the conditions specified are true. The first condition states: "GMAT = High AND GPA = High." Since we already have fuzzified the inputs, this effectively translates into: "0.8 AND 0.3," with the numbers representing the degree of truth of the elements of the condition. Different versions of AND operations have been proposed, with the simple one being minimum of the two operands. Employing this form of "AND" operation we would conclude that the rule is supported to the

0.3 degree. Therefore, the conclusion "Recommendation = High" has a support of 0.3. If there was some other rule that implied a different support for the same output (let's say 0.6) then the results of the two would have to be aggregated by an "OR" operator. The simplest type of "OR" takes the maximum of the two values.

Applying similar reasoning we could find that the second rule gets the support of 0.2 ("0.2 AND 0.5"). This means that the output "Recommendation = Medium" would be supported at 0.2 level. Traditional expert systems may need to employ special conflict resolution techniques if inferencing leads contradictory results. There is no need for such mechanisms in fuzzy systems. The way the resulting output is aggregated is depicted in Figure 10 (again, this is one way of doing so). The shaded area represents the fuzzy recommendation built by combining the outputs of rules 1 and 2. Since the final output should be a crisp number, this fuzzy set needs to be defuzzified in order to obtain a definite numeric value. A popular defuzzification method is known as "center of gravity," whereby the crisp output value is determined according to the formula below:

$$v = \frac{\int_X x \cdot \mu(x)dx}{\int_X \mu(x)dx}$$

Figure 10. Fuzzy inferencing

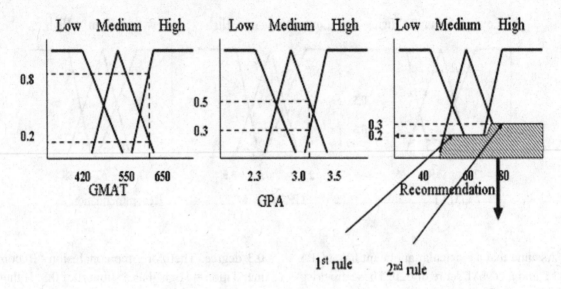

Here *x* stands for some value from the domain of possible values *X*, and *v* is the calculated crisp value for the corresponding fuzzy set. Suppose that the procedure applied to the above scenario yields the value of 77. This represents the final output of the fuzzy system. Note that both input and output values are crisp, and essentially their go through a series of mathematical transformations. Yet, no formulas were explicitly specified to perform the mapping. It was defined by purely verbal means. This is sometimes referred to as "computing by words." Fuzzy approach allows to dramatically decrease the number of rules needed as compared to ordinary expert systems. To learn more about fuzzy approach, the reader is referred to an introductory book on a subject, e.g. (Klir & Yuan, 1995).

Fuzzy sets and fuzzy logic found an impressive number of applications in various contexts, ranging from industrial engineering to consumer electronics. Research into designing fuzzy systems for business applications has also been extensive. Here, we will briefly discuss one such application as an example. In (Pathak, Vidyarthi, & Summers, 2005) the problem of detecting fraud in settled insurance claim is addressed using fuzzy system.

High-value claims are assessed using a number of criteria, including the so-called "ambiguity index," degree of incomplete information, and the level of discretion used in the claim settlement. The possible outputs are "Genuine Settlement" (GS) or "settlement with the Suspect of Fraud" (SF). Each of the input linguistic variables is defined using three fuzzy sets (low, medium, high). This leads to 27 possible rules. An example rule is:

IF Ambiguity index = Medium AND Degree of incomplete information = Medium AND the level of discretion = High, Then Output = SF (suspected fraud).

Provided the data on the claim the system works to produce a crisp output indicating degree to which a given claim is believed to be suspected of fraud.

REFERENCES

Aristotle,. (1965). *Aristotle's prior and posterior analytics: A revised text with introduction and commentary by W. D. Ross*. Oxford: Clarendon Press.

Balakrishnan, P. V., & Jacob, V. S. (1996). Genetic algorithms for product design. *Management Science, 42*(8), 1105–1117. doi:10.1287/mnsc.42.8.1105

Dawkins, R. (1976). *The selfish gene*. New York: Oxford University Press.

Dennett, D. C. (1991). *Consciousness explained*. Boston, MA: Little, Brown and Co.

Eiben, A. E., Marchiori, E., & Valkó, V. A. (2004). Evolutionary algorithms with on-the-fly population size adjustment. In *Parallel Problem Solving from Nature - PPSN VIII* (pp. 41–50). Berlin: Springer. doi:10.1007/978-3-540-30217-9_5

Fazlollahi, B., & Vahidov, R. (2001). Extending the effectiveness of simulation based DSS through genetic algorithms. *Information & Management, 39*(1), 53–65. doi:10.1016/S0378-7206(01)00079-9

Fazlollahi, B., & Vahidov, R. (2001). A method for generation of alternatives by decision support systems. *Journal of Management Information Systems, 18*(2), 229–250.

Hebb, D. O. (1949). *The organization of behavior*. New York: Wiley.

Hobbes, T. (1985). *Leviathan*. London, UK: Penguin Books.

Holland, J. H. (1975). *Adaptation in natural and artificial systems*. Ann Arbor, MI: University of Michigan.

Hornik, K., Stinchcombe, M., & White, H. (1989). Multilayer feedforward networks are universal approximators. *Neural Networks, 2*(5), 359–366. doi:10.1016/0893-6080(89)90020-8

Kirkpatrick, S., Gelatt, C. D., & Vecchi, M. P. (1983). Optimization by simulated annealing. *Science, 220*(4598), 671–680. doi:10.1126/science.220.4598.671

Klir, G. J., & Yuan, B. (1995). *Fuzzy sets and fuzzy logic: Theory and applications*. Upper Saddle River, NJ: Prentice Hall.

Kosko, B. (1993). *Fuzzy thinking: The new science of fuzzy logic*. New York: Hyperion.

Lam, M. (2004). Neural network techniques for financial performance prediction: Integrating fundamental and technical analysis. *Decision Support Systems, 37*, 567–581. doi:10.1016/S0167-9236(03)00088-5

McCulloch, W., & Pitts, W. (1943). A logical calculus of the ideas immanent in nervous activity. *The Bulletin of Mathematical Biophysics, 7*, 115–133. doi:10.1007/BF02478259

Michalewicz, Z. (1996). *Genetic algorithms + data structures = evolution programs*. New York: Springer-Verlag.

Minsky, M. L., & Papert, S. A. (1969). *Perceptrons*. Cambridge, MA: MIT Press.

Pathak, J., Vidyarthi, N., & Summers, S. L. (2005). A fuzzy-based algorithm for auditors to detect elements of fraud in settled insurance claims. *Managerial Auditing Journal, 20*(6), 632–644. doi:10.1108/02686900510606119

Penrose, R. (1997). *The large, the small and the human mind*. New York: Cambridge University Press.

Rosenblatt, F. (1958). The perceptron: A probabilistic model for information storage and organization in the brain. *Psychological Review, 65*(6), 386–408. doi:10.1037/h0042519

Rumelhart, D. E., Hinton, G. E., & Williams, R. J. (1986). Learning internal representations by error propagation. In Rumelhart, D. E., McClelland, J. L., & Group, P. R. (Eds.), *Parallel Distributed Processing: Explorations in the Microstructure of Cognition* (*Vol. 1*, pp. 318–362). Cambridge, MA: MIT Press.

Smith, K. A., & Gupta, J. N. D. (2000). Neural networks in business: Techniques and applications for the operations researcher. *Computers & Operations Research, 27*, 1023–1044. doi:10.1016/S0305-0548(99)00141-0

Sniegowski, P. D., Gerrish, P. J., Johnson, T., & Shaver, A. (2000). The evolution of mutation rates: Separating causes from consequences. *BioEssays, 22*(12), 1057–1066. doi:10.1002/1521-1878(200012)22:12<1057::AID-BIES3>3.0.CO;2-W

Steiner, W., & Hruschka, H. (2003). Genetic algorithms for product design: How well do they really work. *International Journal of Market Research, 45*, 229–240.

Zadeh, L. A. (1965). Fuzzy sets. *Information and Control, 8*(3), 338–353. doi:10.1016/S0019-9958(65)90241-X

Concluding Remarks

The purpose of this book was to show that design-type research (in particular in the Information Systems field) is a legitimate way of conducting a science. The whole argument of the book can be summarized as follows:

Much research in Information Systems in the past had ignored the system artifacts (Chapter 3). Design-type research is steadily gaining popularity in the IS community (Chapter 5). But is design-type research in IS akin to the traditional notion of science (Preface)? Design in general is a problem-solving activity aiming at creation of artifacts (Chapter 1). Science can also be viewed as a kind of problem-solving aiming to create knowledge artifacts; it is akin to reverse engineering (Chapter 2). Although there are differences between design of abstract artifact concepts and the traditional science, these differences are not essential, i.e. they do not distinctly separate the two (Chapter 4). Such traditional scientific concepts as theory, observation and discovery are also applicable to design-type research (Chapter 5). There are ways of representing IS meta-artifacts in light of design theories (Chapters 6, 7). Furthermore, well-known principles of the traditional science, such as Ockham's razor and Popper's falsificationism are applicable to design-type research as well (Chapters 8, 9). Typologies and taxonomies are often used in the traditional science, e.g. in Biology. Although difficult, it is possible to derive a typology of IS artifacts (Chapter 10). Research in different sciences can be viewed as design process (Chapter 11). Moreover, sometimes the workings of nature (e.g. biological evolution) as uncovered by sciences can be (almost) "copied" and "pasted" to build useful artifacts. This is essentially a reverse engineering – forward engineering process (Chapter 12). Therefore, there are no essential differences between design-type research and traditional science. Design-type research is science (Concluding remarks)!

The reader could, if he or she happens to open this concluding section, go through the above claims and read the chapters corresponding to those claims for a more thorough elaboration. The key point here is that design that aims to produce artifact types, or meta-artifacts expressed in form of design theories is at par with the traditional science and deserves as much respect. It is stressed repeatedly in the book that the key output of design-type research is a type of artifact, not the concrete implemented object. At the 5th International Conference on Design Science Research in Information Systems and Technology, the keynote speaker, Dr. Jay F. Nunamaker, had emphasized the importance of delivering the artifact to the respective end user communities. Ideas, however powerful, need to be actually embodied in concrete form to deliver the value ("go the last mile"). He outlined the three phases of artifact development and delivery: proof of concept (it works), proof of value (it is useful), and proof of use (it is used on a sustainable basis).

Surely, the delivery of the artifact as one instance of the corresponding meta-artifact is important. Yet the research output should be knowledge, i.e. the meta-artifact (abstract artifact). Theories are what makes design and science similar (indeed, the same). Throughout the book multiple arguments have been made that design is a kind of science. Some authors had also suggested that science is type of design. It does not matter how one looks at this "dilemma" as long as they are indistinguishable. The position of the book is that design-type research is a proper scientific research. If the reader by this point is confused about what is science vs. what is design, this is the positive result, because this was exactly the purpose of the author.

Compilation of References

Aaboe, A. (1964). *Episodes from the early history of mathematics*. New York: L. W. Singer.

Ackoff, R. L. (1978). *The art of problem solving: Accompanied by Ackoff's fables*. New York: John Wiley and Sons.

Ackoff, R. L., Magidson, J., & Addison, H. J. (2006). *Idealized design: Creating an organization's future*. Upper Saddle River: Wharton School Publishing.

Adami, C. (1998). *Introduction to artificial life*. New York, NY: Springer. doi:10.1007/978-1-4612-1650-6

Adler, I. (1962). *Stories of hoaxes in the name of science*. New York, NY: Collier.

Aggrawal, R., Imielinski, T., & Swami, A. (1993). *Mining association rules between sets of items in large databases*. Paper presented at the ACM SIGMOD Conference on Management of Data (SIGMOD 1993). San-Diego, CA.

Alba, J. W., & Hutchinson, J. W. (1987). Dimensions of consumer expertise. *The Journal of Consumer Research*, *13*(4), 411–454. doi:10.1086/209080

Albrecht, A. J. (1979). *Measuring application development productivity*. Paper presented at the Joint Share, Guide, and IBM Application Development Symposium. Monterey, CA.

Aldag, R. J., & Power, D. J. (1986). An empirical assessment of computer-assisted decision analysis. *Decision Sciences*, *17*(4), 572–588. doi:10.1111/j.1540-5915.1986.tb00243.x

Alexander, C. (1964). *Notes on the synthesis of form*. Cambridge, MA: Harvard University Press.

Alexander, C., Ishikawa, S., & Silverstein, M. (1977). *A pattern language: Towns, buildings, construction*. Oxford: Oxford University Press.

Alter, S. (1977). A taxonomy of decision support systems. *Sloan Management Review*, *19*(1), 39–56.

Alter, S. (2003). 18 reasons why IT-reliant work systems should replace "the IT artifact" as the core subject matter of the IS fiel. *Communications of the Association for Information Systems*, *12*(23), 366–395.

Angehrn, A. A., & Jelassi, M. T. (1994). DSS research and practice in perspective. *Decision Support Systems*, *12*, 267–275. doi:10.1016/0167-9236(94)90045-0

Antonsson, E. K., & Otto, K. N. (1997). Improving engineering design with fuzzy sets. In Dubois, D., Prade, H., & Yager, R. R. (Eds.), *Fuzzy Information Engineering: A Guided Tour of Applications* (pp. 633–654). New York: John Wiley & Sons.

Arciszewski, T., Michalski, R. S., & Wnek, J. (1995). *Constructive induction: The key to design creativity*. Paper presented at the Third International Round-Table Conference on Computational Models of Creative Design. Heron Island, Australia.

Aristotle,. (1965). *Aristotle's prior and posterior analytics: A revised text with introduction and commentary by W. D. Ross*. Oxford: Clarendon Press.

Armour, P. G. (2007). Twenty percent: Planning to fail on software projects. *Communications of the ACM*, *50*(6), 21–23. doi:10.1145/1247001.1247020

Asimow, M. (1962). *Introduction to design*. Englewoods Cliffs, NJ: Prentice-Hall.

Bacon, F. (2000). *The new organon*. Cambridge, UK: Cambridge University Press.

Balabanovic, M., & Shoham, Y. (1997). Fab: Content-based collaborative recommendation. *Communications of the ACM*, *40*(3), 66–72. doi:10.1145/245108.245124

Balakrishnan, P. V., & Jacob, V. S. (1996). Genetic algorithms for product design. *Management Science*, *42*(8), 1105–1117. doi:10.1287/mnsc.42.8.1105

Banker, R. D., & Kauffman, R. J. (2004). The evolution of research on information systems: A fiftieth-year survey of the literature in management science. *Management Science*, *50*(3), 281–298. doi:10.1287/mnsc.1040.0206

Banville, C., & Landry, M. (1989). Can the field of MIS be disciplined. *Communications of the ACM*, *32*(1), 48–60. doi:10.1145/63238.63241

Barki, H., Rivard, S., & Talbot, J. (1988). An information systems keyword classification scheme. *Management Information Systems Quarterly*, *12*(2), 299–322. doi:10.2307/248855

Barki, H., Rivard, S., & Talbot, J. (1993). A keyword classification scheme for IS research literature: An update. *Management Information Systems Quarterly*, *17*(1), 209–226. doi:10.2307/249802

Barr, S. H., & Sharda, R. (1997). Effectiveness of decision support systems: Development or reliance effect? *Decision Support Systems*, *21*, 133–146. doi:10.1016/S0167-9236(97)00021-3

Bartneck, C. (2009). *Using the metaphysics of quality to define design science*. Paper presented at the Fourth International Conference on Design Science Research in Information Systems and Technology. Malvern, PA.

Basadur, M. (1994). Managing the creative process in organizations. In Runco, M. A., & Chand, I. (Eds.), *Problem Finding, Problem Solving, and Creativity* (pp. 237–268). Norwood, NJ: Ablex.

Basalla, G. (1988). *The evolution of technology*. Cambridge, NY: Cambridge University Press.

Baskerville, R. L., & Myers, M. D. (2002). Information systems as a reference discipline. *Management Information Systems Quarterly*, *26*(1), 1–14. doi:10.2307/4132338

Baskerville, R., & Myers, M. D. (2004). Special issue on action research in information systems: Making IS research relevant to practice - Foreword. *Management Information Systems Quarterly*, *28*(3).

Battistini, M. (2007). *Astrology, magic, and alchemy*. Los Angeles, CA: J. Paul Getty Museum.

Baylor, G. W. (2001). What do we really know about Mendeleev's dream of the periodic table? A note on dreams of scientific problem solving. *Dreaming*, *11*(2), 89–92. doi:10.1023/A:1009484504919

Beam, C., & Segev, A. (1996). *Automated negotiation: A survey and the state of art*. Berkeley, CA: Hass School of Business.

Becker, J., Niehaves, B., & Pfeiffer, D. (2008). *Case study perspectives on design science research*. Paper presented at the Third International Conference on Design Science Research in Information Systems and Technology. Atlanta, GA.

Bellifemine, F., Poggi, A., & Rimassa, G. (2001). *JADE: A FIPA2000 compliant agent development environment*. Paper presented at the Fifth International Conference on Autonomous Agents. Montreal, Canada.

Benbasat, I. (2001). Editorial notes. *Information Systems Research*, *12*(2), iii–iv.

Benbasat, I., & Weber, R. (1996). Research commentary: Rethinking "diversity" in information systems research. *Information Systems Research*, *7*(4), 389–399. doi:10.1287/isre.7.4.389

Benbasat, I., & Zmud, R. W. (2003). The identity crisis within the IS discipline: Defining and communicating the discipline's core properties. *Management Information Systems Quarterly*, *27*(2), 183–194.

Berry, P., Peintner, B., Conley, K., Gervasio, M., Uribe, T., & Yorke-Smith, N. (2006). *Deploying a personalized time management agent*. Paper presented at the Fifth International Joint Conference on Autonomous Agents and Multiagent Systems. Hakodate, Japan.

Berry, A. (1961). *A short history of astronomy: From earliest times through the nineteenth century*. New York: Dover Publications.

Bertola, P., & Teixeira, J. C. (2003). Design as a knowledge agent: How design as a knowledge process is embedded into organizations to foster innovation. *Design Studies*, *24*, 181–194. doi:10.1016/S0142-694X(02)00036-4

Bettman, J. R. (1979). *An information processing theory of consumer choice*. Reading, MA: Addison-Wesley.

Billsus, D., & Pazzani, M. J. (1999). *A personal news agent that talks, learns and explains*. Paper presented at the Third International Conference on Autonomous Agents. Seattle, WA.

Bohm, D., & Peat, F. D. (2000). *Science, order, and creativity* (2nd ed.). London, UK: Routledge.

Boose, J. H., & Bradshaw, J. M. (1987). Expertise transfer and complex problems: Using Aquinas as a knowledge-acquisition workbench for knowledge-based systems. *International Journal of Man-Machine Studies*, *26*, 3–28. doi:10.1016/S0020-7373(87)80032-9

Brazier, F. M. T., Van Langen, P. H. G., Ruttkay, Z., & Treur, J. (1994). On formal specification of design tasks. In Gero, J. S., & Sudweeks, F. (Eds.), *Artificial Intelligence in Design* (pp. 535–552). Berlin, Germany: Kluwer Academic Publishers. doi:10.1007/978-94-011-0928-4_31

Briggs, R. O., Vreede, G.-J. D., & Nunamaker, J. F. Jr. (2003). Collaboration engineering with ThinkLets to pursue sustained success with group support systems. *Journal of Management Information Systems*, *19*(4), 31–64.

Brown, J. R. (1993). *The laboratory of the mind: Thought experiments in the natural sciences*. New York: Routledge.

Bruner, J., Goodnow, J. J., & Austin, G. A. (1967). *A study of thinking*. New York: Science Editions.

Buchanan, R. (1995). Rhetoric, humanism, and design. In Buchanan, R., & Margolin, V. (Eds.), *Discovering Design: Explorations in Design Studies* (pp. 23–66). Chicago, IL: The University of Chicago Press.

Bunge, M. (1967). *Scientific research II: The search for truth*. Berlin: Springer Verlag.

Bunge, M. (1984). What is pseudoscience? *The Sceptical Inquirer*, *9*(1), 36–46.

Burstein, F., & Gregor, S. (1999). *The systems development or engineering approach to research in information systems: An action research perspective*. Paper presented at the 10th Australasian Conference on Information Systems. Wellington, New Zealand.

Cambridge. (1997). *The Cambridge illustrated history of astronomy*. Cambridge, NY: Cambridge University Press.

Carbonneau, R. A., Kersten, G. E., & Vahidov, R. (2008). Predicting opponent's moves in electronic negotiations using neural networks. *Expert Systems with Applications*, *34*, 1266–1273. doi:10.1016/j.eswa.2006.12.027

Carlsson, S. (2005). Developing information systems design knowledge: A critical realist perspective. *The Electronic Journal of Business Research Methodology*, *3*(2), 93–102.

Carlsson, S., Henningsson, S., Hrastinski, S., & Keller, C. (2011). Socio-technical IS design science research: Developing design theory for IS integration management. *Information Systems and E-Business Management*, *9*(1), 109–131. doi:10.1007/s10257-010-0140-6

Carnap, R. (1966). The nature of theories. In Carnap, R., & Gardner, M. (Eds.), *Philosophical Foundations of Physics: An Introduction to the Philosophy of Science* (pp. 316–332). New York, NY: Basic Books.

Carr, N. (2003). IT doesn't matter. *Harvard Business Review*, *81*(5), 41.

Carroll, J. M., & Kellogg, W. A. (1989). *Artifact as theory-nexus: Hermeneutics meets theory-based design*. Paper presented at the SIGCHI Conference on Human Factors in Computing Systems: Wings for the Mind. Austin, TX.

Changchien, S. W., Lee, C. F., & Hsu, Y.-J. (2004). On-line personilized sales promotion in electronic commerce. *Expert Systems with Applications*, *27*, 35–52. doi:10.1016/j.eswa.2003.12.017

Chavez, A., & Maes, P. (1996). *Kasbah: An agent marketplace for buying and selling goods*. Paper presented at the First International Conference on the Practical Application of Intelligent Agents and Multi-Agent Technology. London, UK.

Chen, E., Vahidov, R., & Kersten, G. E. (2005). Agent-supported negotiations in the e-marketplace. *International Journal of Electronic Business, 3*(1), 28–49. doi:10.1504/IJEB.2005.006387

Chen, H. (2011). Editorial: Design science, grand challenges, and societal impacts. *ACM Transactions on Management Information Systems, 2*(1), 1–10. doi:10.1145/2037661.2037663

Chernev, A. (2003). When more is less and less is more: The role of ideal point availabilty and assortment in consumer choice. *The Journal of Consumer Research, 30*(2), 170–183. doi:10.1086/376808

Chervany, N. L., Dickson, G. W., & Kozar, K. A. (1971). *An experimental gaming framework for investigating the influence of management information systems on decision effectiveness.* Unpublished manuscript.

Clark, M. (2003). Computer science: A hard-applied discipline? *Teaching in Higher Education, 8*(1), 71–87. doi:10.1080/1356251032000052339

Claver, E., Gonzales, R., & Llopis, J. (2000). An analysis of research in information systems (1981-1997). *Information & Management, 37*, 181–195. doi:10.1016/S0378-7206(99)00043-9

Coehoorn, R. M., & Jennings, N. R. (2004). *Learning on opponent's preferences to make effective multi-issue negotiation trade-offs.* Paper presented at the 6th International Conference on Electronic Commerce. Delft, The Netherlands.

Cole, R., Purao, S., Rossi, M., & Sein, M. (2005). *Being proactive: Where action research meets design research.* Paper presented at the International Conference on Information Systems, ICIS 2005. Las Vegas, NV.

Collins, J. (2006). *Perpetual motion: An ancient mystery solved?* Retrieved from http://www.lulu.com.

Conway, D. G., & Koehler, G. J. (2000). Interface agents: Caveat mercator in electronic commerce. *Decision Support Systems, 27*(4), 355–366. doi:10.1016/S0167-9236(99)00046-9

Cooper, R., & Press, M. (1995). *The design agenda: A guide to successful design management* (Vol. 298). Chichester, NY: Wiley.

Cooper, W. W., & McAlister, L. (1999). Can research be basic and applied? You bet: It better be for B-schools! *Socio-Economic Planning Sciences, 33*, 257–276. doi:10.1016/S0038-0121(99)00017-8

Copleston, F. (1993). *A history of philosophy: Greece and Rome* (Vol. 1). New York: Doubleday.

Coren, S., Ward, L. M., & Enns, J. T. (1999). *Sensation & perception* (6th ed.). Hoboken, NJ: John Wiley & Sons.

Courtney, J. F. (2001). Decision making and knowledge management in inquiring organizations: Toward a new decision-making paradigm for DSS. *Decision Support Systems, 31*, 17–38. doi:10.1016/S0167-9236(00)00117-2

Cross, N. (1984). *Developments in design methodology.* Chichester, UK: Wiley.

Cross, N. (1995). Editorial. *Design Studies, 16*, 2–3. doi:10.1016/0142-694X(95)90004-Y

Cross, N. (2001). Designerly ways of knowing: Design discipline versus design science. *Design Issues, 17*(3), 49–55. doi:10.1162/074793601750357196

Cross, N. (2006). *Designerly ways of knowing.* London: Springer-Verlag.

Cross, N. (2007). Forty years of design research. *Design Studies, 28*, 1–4. doi:10.1016/j.destud.2006.11.004

Culnan, M. J. (1987). Mapping the intellectual structure of MIS, 1980-1985: A co-citation analysis. *Management Information Systems Quarterly, 11*(3), 341–353. doi:10.2307/248680

Culnan, M. J., & Swanson, E. B. (1986). Research in management information systems 1980-1984: Points of work and reference. *Management Information Systems Quarterly, 10*(3), 289–302. doi:10.2307/249263

Davenport, T. H. (1998). Putting the enterprise into the enterprise system. *Harvard Business Review,* (July-August), 121-131.

Davenport, T. H., & Markus, M. L. (1999). Rigor vs. relevance revisited: Response to Benbasat and Zmud. *Management Information Systems Quarterly, 23*(1), 19–23. doi:10.2307/249405

David, J.-M., Krivine, J.-P., & Simmons, R. (1993). *Second generation expert systems*. Secaucus, NJ: Springer-Verlag New York, Inc.doi:10.1007/978-3-642-77927-5

Davis, F. D. (1993). User acceptance of information technology: System characteristics, user perceptions and behavioral impacts. *International Journal of Man-Machine Studies*, *38*(3), 475–487. doi:10.1006/imms.1993.1022

Davis, F. D., Bagozzi, R. P., & Warshaw, P. R. (1989). User acceptance of information technology: A comparison of two theoretical models. *Management Science*, *35*(8), 982–1003. doi:10.1287/mnsc.35.8.982

Davis, F. D., & Venkatesh, V. (2004). Toward preprototype user acceptance testing of new information systems: Implications for software project management. *IEEE Transactions on Engineering Management*, *51*(1), 31–46. doi:10.1109/TEM.2003.822468

Davison, R. M., Martinsons, M. G., & Kock, N. (2004). Principles of canonical action research. *Information Systems Journal*, *14*(1), 65–86. doi:10.1111/j.1365-2575.2004.00162.x

Davis, P. (1992). *The mind of God: The scientific basis for a rational world*. New York, NY: Simon & Schuster.

Davis, P., & Gribbin, J. (2007). *The matter myth: Dramatic discoveries that challenge our understanding of physical reality*. New York, NY: Simon & Schuster.

Dawkins, R. (1976). *The selfish gene*. New York: Oxford University Press.

Dawkins, R. (1982). *The extended phenotype: The gene as the unit of selection*. Oxford: Freeman.

Dawkins, R. (2003). Science, genetics and ethics: Memo for Tony Blair. In *A Devil's Chaplain: Reflections on Hope, Lies, Science, and Love* (pp. 27–37). Boston, MA: Houghton Mifflin Co.

Dawkins, R. (2004). *The ancestor's tale: A pilgrimage to the dawn of evolution*. Boston, MA: Houghton Mifflin.

Dawkins, R. (2006a). *The blind watchmaker*. London: Penguin.

Dawkins, R. (2006b). *The God delusion*. Boston, MA: Houghton Mifflin Co.

Dayal, U., Castellanos, M., Simitsis, A., & Wilkinson, K. (2009). *Data integration flows for business intelligence*. Paper presented at the 12th International Conference on Extending Database Technology: Advances in Database Technology. Saint Petersburg, Russia. DSS-89. (1989, April). Ninth international conference on decision support systems: Call for papers. *OR/MS Today*, 50-51.

De Moor, A., & Weigand, H. (2004). Business negotiation support: Theory and practice. *International Negotiation*, *9*, 31–57. doi:10.1163/1571806041262106

de Vries, M. J. (1996). Technology education: Beyond the "technology is applied science" paradigm. *Journal of Technology Education*, *8*(1), 7–15.

de Vries, M. J. (2008). Gilbert Simondon and the dual nature of technical artifacts. *Techné: Research in Philosophy and Technology*, *12*(1), 23–35.

Dehn, D. M., & Mulken, S. V. (2000). The impact of animated interface agents: A review of empirical research. *International Journal of Human-Computer Studies*, *52*, 1–22. doi:10.1006/ijhc.1999.0325

DeLone, W. H., & McLean, E. R. (1992). Information systems success: The quest for the dependent variable. *Information Systems Research*, *3*(1), 60–95. doi:10.1287/isre.3.1.60

Dembski, W. A. (Ed.). (1998). *Mere creation: Science, faith & intelligent design*. Downers Grove, IL: InterVarsity Press.

Dennett, D. C. (1987). *The intentional stance*. Cambridge, MA: MIT Press.

Dennett, D. C. (1991). *Consciousness explained*. Boston, MA: Little, Brown and Co.

Dennett, D. C. (1995). *Darwin's dangerous idea: Evolution and the meanings of life*. New York: Simon & Schuster.

Descartes, R. (1996). *Discourse on method and meditations on first philosophy*. New Haven, CT: Yale University Press.

Detlor, B., Sproule, S., & Gupta, C. (2003). Pre-purchase online information seeking: Search versus browse. *Journal of Electronic Commerce Research*, *4*(2), 72–84.

Dewey, J. (1910). A short catechism concerning truth. In *The Influence of Darwin on Philosophy and Other Essays* (pp. 154–168). New York, NY: Henry Holt and Company.

Dhar, V., & Stein, R. (1997). *Intelligent decision support methods: The science of knowledge work*. Upper Saddle River, NJ: Prentice-Hall.

DoD. (1994). *Technical architecture framework for information management (TAFIM)*. Reston, VA: DISA Center for Architecture.

Dong, W. M., & Wong, F. S. (1987). Fuzzy weighted averages and implementation of the extension principle. *Fuzzy Sets and Systems, 21*(2), 183–199. doi:10.1016/0165-0114(87)90163-1

Dorst, K. (2001). Creativity in the design process: Co-evolution of problem-solution. *Design Studies, 22*, 425–437. doi:10.1016/S0142-694X(01)00009-6

Dorst, K. (2006). *Understanding design: 175 reflections on being a designer*. Amsterdam, The Netherlands: BIS Publishers.

Dorst, K. (2008). Design research: A revolution-waiting-to-happen. *Design Studies, 29*, 4–11.

Dudley, U. (1997). *Numerology, or, what Pythagoras wrought*. Washington, DC: Mathematical Association of America.

Dufner, D. (2003). The IS core-I. *Economic and systems engineering approaches to IS identity, 12*(31), 527-538.

Dzeng, R.-J., & Lin, Y.-C. (2005). Searching for better negotiation agreement based on genetic algorithm. *Computer-Aided Civil and Infrastructure Engineering, 20*, 280–293. doi:10.1111/j.1467-8667.2005.00393

Eiben, A. E., Marchiori, E., & Valkó, V. A. (2004). Evolutionary algorithms with on-the-fly population size adjustment. In *Parallel Problem Solving from Nature - PPSN VIII* (pp. 41–50). Berlin: Springer. doi:10.1007/978-3-540-30217-9_5

Ein-Dor, P., & Segev, E. (1993). A classification of information systems: Analysis and interpretation. *Information Systems Research, 4*(2), 166–204. doi:10.1287/isre.4.2.166

Einstein, A., & Infeld, L. (1938). *The evolution of physics: The growth of ideas from early concepts to relativity and quanta*. New York, NY: Simon and Schuster.

Eldredge, N., & Gould, S. J. (1972). Punctuated equilibria: An alternative to phyletic gradualism. In Schopf, T. J. M. (Ed.), *Models in Paleobiology* (pp. 82–115). San Francisco, CA: Freeman Cooper.

Estévez, P. A., Held, C. M., & Perez, C. A. (2006). Subscription fraud prevention in telecommunications using fuzzy rules and neural networks. *Expert Systems with Applications, 31*(2), 337–344. doi:10.1016/j.eswa.2005.09.028

Evans, J. R. (1990). *Creative thinking in the decision and management sciences*. New York: South Western Publishing Co.

Faratin, P., Sierra, C., & Jennings, N. R. (2002). Using similarity criteria to make issue trade-offs in automated negotiations. *Artificial Intelligence, 142*(2), 205–237. doi:10.1016/S0004-3702(02)00290-4

Farhoomand, A., & Drury, D. H. (1999). A historiographical examination of information systems. *Communications of the AIS, 1*(19), 1–20.

Fazlollahi, B., Parikh, M. A., & Verma, S. (1997). Adaptive decision support systems. *Decision Support Systems, 20*(4), 297–315. doi:10.1016/S0167-9236(97)00014-6

Fazlollahi, B., & Vahidov, R. (2001). A method for generation of alternatives by decision support systems. *Journal of Management Information Systems, 18*(2), 229–250.

Fazlollahi, B., & Vahidov, R. (2001). Extending the effectiveness of simulation based DSS through genetic algorithms. *Information & Management, 39*(1), 53–65. doi:10.1016/S0378-7206(01)00079-9

Feyerabend, P. K. (1975). *Against method: Outline of an anarchistic theory of knowledge*. London, UK: NLB.

Fisk, D. (1997). An application of social filtering to movie recommendation. In Nwana, H. S., & Azarmi, N. (Eds.), *Software Agents and Soft Computing* (pp. 117–131). Berlin: Springer-Verlag.

Franklin, S., & Graesser, A. (1997). Is it an agent, or just a program? A taxonomy for autonomous agents. In Muller, J. P., Wooldridge, M. J., & Jennings, N. R. (Eds.), *Intelligent Agents III: Agent Theories, Architectures, and Languages* (pp. 21–36). Berlin: Springer Verlag. doi:10.1007/BFb0013570

Gaines, B. R., & Shaw, M. L. G. (1993). Knowledge acquisition tools based on person construct psychology. *The Knowledge Engineering Review, 8*(1), 49–85. doi:10.1017/S0269888900000060

Galle, P. (2002). Philosophy of design: An editorial introduction. *Design Studies, 23,* 211–218. doi:10.1016/S0142-694X(01)00034-5

Galle, P. (2008). Candidate worldviews for design theory. *Design Studies, 29,* 267–303. doi:10.1016/j.destud.2008.02.001

Gardner, M. (1970). Mathematical games: The fantastic combinations of John Conway's new solitaire game "life". *Scientific American, 223,* 120–123. doi:10.1038/scientificamerican1070-120

Gargeya, V. B., & Brady, C. (2005). Success and failure factors of adopting SAP in ERP system implementation. *Business Process Management Journal, 11*(5), 501–516. doi:10.1108/14637150510619858

George, J. F., Valacich, J. S., & Valor, J. (2005). Does information systems still matter? Lessons for a maturing discipline. *Communications of the Association for Information Systems, 16,* 219–232.

Gimpel, H., Jennings, N. R., Kersten, G., Ockenfels, A., & Weinhardt, C. (2007). *Negotiations, auctions and market engineering (Vol. 2).* Berlin, Germany: Springer-Verlag.

Glanville, R. (1999). Researching design and designing research. *Design Issues, 15*(2), 80–91. doi:10.2307/1511844

Glass, R. L., Ramesh, V., & Vessey, I. (2004). An analysis of research in computing disciplines. *Communications of the ACM, 47*(6), 89–94. doi:10.1145/990680.990686

Goldschmidt, G. (1990). *Linkography: Assessing design productivity.* Paper presented at the Tenth European Meeting on Cybernetics and Systems Research. Singapore, Singapore.

Goldschmidt, G. (2004). Design representation: Private process, public image. In Goldschmidt, G., & Porter, W. L. (Eds.), *Design Representation* (pp. 203–217). New York: Springer. doi:10.1007/978-1-85233-863-3_9

Goldschmidt, G., & Tatsa, D. (2005). How good are good ideas? Correlates of design creativity. *Design Studies, 26,* 593–611. doi:10.1016/j.destud.2005.02.004

Goodhue, D. L., & Thompson, R. L. (1995). Task-technology fit and individual performance. *Management Information Systems Quarterly, 19*(2), 213–236. doi:10.2307/249689

Gorla, N., & Paulraj, A. (1999). *On the maturity of the MIS research field.* Paper presented at the Americas Conference on Information Systems. Milwaukee, WI.

Gorry, A., & Scott-Morton, M. (1971). A framework for information systems. *Sloan Management Review, 13,* 56–79.

Gosain, S., Lee, Z., & Im, I. (1997). *Topics of interest in IS: Comparing academic journals with the practitioner press.* Paper presented at the Eighteenth International Conference on Information systems. Atlanta, GA.

Gould, S. J. (1996). *Full house: The spread of excellence from Plato to Darwin.* New York: Harmony Books.

Gower, B. (1997). *Scientific method: An historical and philosophical introduction.* London, UK: Routledge.

Grant, E. (2007). *A history of natural philosophy: From the ancient world to the nineteenth century.* Cambridge, UK: Cambridge University Press.

Gray, P. (2003). Introduction to the debate on the core of the information systems field. *Communications of the Association for Information Systems, 12*(42).

Greene, B. (1999). *The elegant universe: Superstrings, hidden dimensions, and the quest for the ultimate theory.* New York, NY: Vintage Books.

Green, P. E., Krieger, A. M., & Wind, Y. (2001). Thirty years of conjoint analysis: Reflections and prospects. *Interfaces, 31*(3), S56–S73. doi:10.1287/inte.31.3s.56.9676

Gregg, D. G., Kulkarni, U. R., & Vinze´, A. S. (2001). Understanding the philosophical underpinnings of software engineering research in information systems. *Information Systems Frontiers*, *3*(2), 169–183. doi:10.1023/A:1011491322406

Gregor, S., & Benbasat, I. (1999). Explanations from intelligent systems: Theoretical foundations and implications for practice. *Management Information Systems Quarterly*, *23*(4), 497–530. doi:10.2307/249487

Gregor, S., & Hevner, A. (2011). Introduction to the special issue on design science. *Information Systems and E-Business Management*, *9*(1), 1–9. doi:10.1007/s10257-010-0159-8

Gregor, S., & Jones, D. (2007). The anatomy of a design theory. *Journal of the Association for Information Systems*, *8*(5), 312–335.

Gulliver, P. H. (1979). *Disputes and negotiations: A cross-cultural perspective*. Orlando, FL: Academic Press.

Guttman, R., Moukas, A., & Maes, P. (1998). Agent-mediated electronic commerce: A survey. *The Knowledge Engineering Review*, *13*(3).

Hadamard, J. (1954). *An essay on the psychology of invention in the mathematical field*. New York: Dover Publications.

Haubl, G., & Trifts, V. (2000). Consumer decision making in online shopping environments: The effects of interactive decision aids. *Marketing Science*, *19*(1), 4–21. doi:10.1287/mksc.19.1.4.15178

Haverty, M. (2002). Information architecture without internal theory: An inductive design process. *Journal of the American Society for Information Science and Technology*, *53*(10), 839–845. doi:10.1002/asi.10096

Hebb, D. O. (1949). *The organization of behavior*. New York: Wiley.

Heidegger, M. (1971). *Poetry, language, thought*. New York: Harper & Raw.

Heidegger, M. (1977). *The question concerning technology and other essays*. New York: Harper & Raw.

Hevner, A. R., March, S. T., Park, J., & Ram, S. (2004). Design science in information systems research. *Management Information Systems Quarterly*, *28*(1), 75–105.

Hevner, A., & Chatterjee, S. (2010). Design science research in information systems. In *Design Research in Information Systems* (Vol. 22). New York: Springer. doi:10.1007/978-1-4419-5653-8_2

Hevner, A., March, S. T., Park, J., & Ram, S. (2004). Design science in information systems research. *Management Information Systems Quarterly*, *28*(1), 75–105.

Hobbes, T. (1985). *Leviathan*. London, UK: Penguin Books.

Hofstadter, D. R. (1979). *Gödel, Escher, Bach: An eternal golden braid*. New York: Basic Books.

Holland, J. H. (1975). *Adaptation in natural and artificial systems*. Ann Arbor, MI: University of Michigan.

Holmström, J., Ketokivi, M., & Hameri, A.-P. (2009). Bridging practice and theory: A design science approach. *Decision Sciences*, *40*(1), 65–87. doi:10.1111/j.1540-5915.2008.00221.x

Holsapple, C. W., & Sena, M. P. (2005). ERP plans and decision-support benefits. *Decision Support Systems*, *38*(4), 575–590. doi:10.1016/j.dss.2003.07.001

Hornik, K., Stinchcombe, M., & White, H. (1989). Multilayer feedforward networks are universal approximators. *Neural Networks*, *2*(5), 359–366. doi:10.1016/0893-6080(89)90020-8

Hubka, V., & Eder, W. E. (1996). *Design science*. London, UK: Springer-Verlag. doi:10.1007/978-1-4471-3091-8

Hubka, V., & Weber, W. E. (1998). Theoretical approach in design methodology. In Frankenberger, E., Birkhofer, H., & Badke-Schaub, P. (Eds.), *Designers: The Key to Successful Product Development* (pp. 12–28). London, UK: Springer-Verlag.

Huffman, C. (2008). Philolaus. *The Stanford Encyclopedia of Philosophy*. Retrieved from http://plato.stanford.edu/archives/fall2008/entries/philolaus/.

Iivari, J. (2008). *Twelve theses on information systems as a design science*. Paper presented at the Third International Conference on Design Science Research in Information Systems and Technology. Atlanta, GA.

Iivari, J. (2003). The IS core – VII: Towards information systems as a science of meta-artifacts. *Communications of the Association for Information Systems, 12*(37), 568–581.

Iivari, J. (2007). A paradigmatic analysis of information systems as a design science. *Scandinavian Journal of Information Systems, 19*(2), 39–64.

Ingrand, F., Georgeff, M., & Rao, A. (1992). An architecture for real-time reasoning and system control. *IEEE Expert: Intelligent Systems and Their Applications, 7*(6), 34–44.

Ives, B., Hamilton, S., & Davis, G. B. (1980). A framework for research in computer-based management information systems. *Management Science, 26*(9). doi:10.1287/mnsc.26.9.910

Iyengar, S. S., & Lepper, M. R. (2000). When choice is demotivating: Can one desire too much of a good thing? *Journal of Personality and Social Psychology, 79*(6), 995–1006. doi:10.1037/0022-3514.79.6.995

Jani, A. Y. (2001). *IS research relevance: A perspective from the design science and the philosophy of technology*. Paper presented at the Seventh Americas Conference on Information Systems, Boston, MA.

Järvinen, P. (2004). *Supplementing Ron Weber's view on a theory building*. Paper presented at the Information Systems Research in Scandinavia (IRIS 27). Falkenberg, Sweden.

Järvinen, P. (2005). *Action research as an approach in design science*. Retrieved from http://www.cs.uta.fi/reports/dsarja/D-2005-2.pdf.

Johansson, I. (1991). Pluralism and rationality in the social sciences. *Philosophy of the Social Sciences, 21*(4), 427–443. doi:10.1177/004839319102100401

Johnston, R. B., & Milton, S. (2001). *The significance of intentionality for the ontological evaluation of information systems*. Paper presented at the Seventh Americas Conference on Information Systems. Boston, MA.

Kant, I. (1987). *Critique of judgment*. Indianapolis, IN: Hackett.

Kant, I. (1999). *Critique of pure reason*. Cambridge, UK: Cambridge University Press.

Karacapilidis, N., & Moraitis, P. (2001). Building an agent-mediated electronic commerce system with decision analysis features. *Decision Support Systems, 32*(1), 53–69. doi:10.1016/S0167-9236(01)00100-2

Karvonen, K. (2000). *The beauty of simplicity*. Paper presented at the ACM Conference on Universal Usability. Arlington, VA.

Kasanen, E., Lukha, K., & Siitonen, A. (1993). The constructive approach in management accounting research. *Journal of Management Accounting Research, 5*, 243–264.

Kaufmann, A., & Gupta, M. M. (1985). *Introduction to fuzzy arithmetic: Theory and applications*. New York, NY: Van Nostrand Reinhold.

Keen, P. G. W., & Morton, M. S. S. (1978). *DSS: An organizational perspective*. Reading, MA: Addison-Wesley.

Keller, K. L., & Staelin, R. (1987). Effects of quality and quantity of information on decision efectiveness. *The Journal of Consumer Research, 14*(2), 200–213. doi:10.1086/209106

Kelly, G. A. (1955). *The psychology of personal constructs*. New York: Norton.

Kersten, G., Law, K. P., & Strecker, S. (2004). *A software platform for multi-protocol e-negotiations: An InterNeg research report 04/04*. Montreal, Canada: InterNeg Research Center.

Kersten, G., & Noronha, S. J. (1999). WWW-based negotiation support: Design, implementation, and use. *Decision Support Systems, 25*, 135–154. doi:10.1016/S0167-9236(99)00012-3

Khazanchi, D., & Munkvold, B. E. (2000). Is information system a science? An inquiry into the nature of the information systems discipline. *ACM SIGMIS Database*, *31*(3), 24–42. doi:10.1145/381823.381834

Kim, J. B., Strecker, S., Kersten, G. E., & Law, K. P. (2005). *Towards a theory of e-negotiation protocols.* Paper presented at the Group Decision and Negotiation (GDN). Vienna, Austria.

Kim, D., & Benbasat, I. (2003). Trust-related arguments in internet stores: A framework for evaluation. *Journal of Electronic Commerce Research*, *4*(2), 49–64.

Kim, H. S., & Cho, J. H. (2010). Supply chain formation using agent negotiation. *Decision Support Systems*, *49*(1), 77–90. doi:10.1016/j.dss.2010.01.004

Kim, J. B., Kersten, G. E., Strecker, S., & Law, K. P. (2005). *Component-based software protocol approach: InterNeg research papers INR 01/05*. Montreal, Canada: InterNeg Research Center.

Kim, J. K., Cho, Y. H., Kim, W. J., Kim, J. R., & Suh, J. H. (2002). A personalized recommendation procedure for internet shopping support. *Electronic Commerce Research and Applications*, *1*, 301–313. doi:10.1016/S1567-4223(02)00022-4

Kim, J. W., Lee, B. H., Shaw, M. J., Chang, H.-L., & Nelson, M. (2001). Application of decision-tree induction techniques to personalized advertisements on internet storefronts. *International Journal of Electronic Commerce*, *5*(3), 45–62.

Kim, W., Kerschberg, L., & Scime, A. (2002). Learning for automatic personalization in a semantic taxonomy-based meta-search agent. *Electronic Commerce Research and Applications*, *1*(2), 150–173. doi:10.1016/S1567-4223(02)00011-X

Kirkham, R. L. (1992). *Theories of truth: A critical introduction*. Cambridge, MA: MIT Press.

Kirkpatrick, S., Gelatt, C. D., & Vecchi, M. P. (1983). Optimization by simulated annealing. *Science*, *220*(4598), 671–680. doi:10.1126/science.220.4598.671

Klemke, E. D., Hollinger, R., Rudge, D. W., & Kline, A. D. (Eds.). (1998). *Introductory readings in the philosophy of science* (3rd ed.). Amherst, NY: Prometheus Books.

Kline, A. D. (1998). Theory and observation: Introduction. In Klemke, E. D., Hollinger, R., Rudge, D. W., & Kline, A. D. (Eds.), *Introductory Readings in the Philosophy of Science* (3rd ed., pp. 309–315). Amherst, NY: Prometheus Books.

Klir, G. J., & Yuan, B. (1995). *Fuzzy sets and fuzzy logic: Theory and applications*. Upper Saddle River, NJ: Prentice Hall.

Kock, N., Gray, P., Hoving, R., Klein, H., Myers, M., & Rockart, J. (2002). IS research relevance revisited: Subtle accomplishment, unfulfilled promise, or serial hypocrisy? *Communications of the Association for Information Systems*, *8*, 330–346.

Kogan, J. N. (1986). *Information for motivation: A key to executive information systems that translate strategy into results for management.* Paper presented at the Sixtrh International Conference on Decision Support Systems. Washington, DC.

Kohli, R., Devaraj, S., & Mahmood, M. A. (2004). Understanding determinants of online consumer satisfaction: a decision process perspective. *Journal of Management Information Systems*, *21*(1), 115–136.

Kornfeld, W. A., & Hewitt, C. (1981). The scientific community metaphor. *IEEE Transactions on Systems, Man, and Cybernetics*, *11*(1), 24–33. doi:10.1109/TSMC.1981.4308575

Kosko, B. (1993). *Fuzzy thinking: The new science of fuzzy logic*. New York: Hyperion.

Kotler, P., & Rath, G. A. (1984). Design: A powerful but neglected strategic tool. *The Journal of Business Strategy*, *5*(2), 16–21. doi:10.1108/eb039054

Kroes, P. (2002). Design methodology and the nature of technical artefacts. *Design Studies*, *23*, 287–302. doi:10.1016/S0142-694X(01)00039-4

Kroes, P. (2003). Screwdriver philosophy: Searle's analysis of technical functions. *Techné: Research in Philosophy and Technology*, *6*(3), 22–35.

Kuechler, B., & Vaishnavi, V. (2008). *Theory development in design science research: Anatomy of a research project.* Paper presented at the Third International Conference on Design Science Research in Information Systems and Technology. Atlanta, GA.

Kuechler, B., Park, E. H., & Vaishnavi, V. (2009). *Formalizing theory development in IS design science research: Learning from qualitative research.* Paper presented at the AMCIS 2009. New York, NY.

Kuhn, T. S. (1962). *The structure of scientific revolutions.* Chicago, IL: University of Chicago Press.

Kurzweil, R. (1990). *The age of intelligent machines.* Cambridge, MA: MIT Press.

Ladrière, J. (1998). The technical uiniverse in an ontological perspective. *Philosophy and Technology, 4*(1), 66–91.

Lakatos, I. (1980). Falsification and the methodology of scientific research programmes. In Worrall, J., & Currie, G. (Eds.), *The Methodology of Scientific Research Programmes* (Vol. 1, pp. 8–101). Cambridge, UK: Cambridge University Press. doi:10.1007/978-94-010-1863-0_14

Lam, M. (2004). Neural network techniques for financial performance prediction: Integrating fundamental and technical analysis. *Decision Support Systems, 37,* 567–581. doi:10.1016/S0167-9236(03)00088-5

Lawson, C. (2008). An ontology of technology: Artefacts, relations and functions. *Techné: Research in Philosophy and Technology, 12*(1), 48–64.

Le Sage, A.-R. (1972). *The history and adventures of Gil Blas of Santillane.* New York, NY: Garland Pub.

Lea, B.-R., Guptab, M. C., & Yuc, W.-B. (2005). A prototype multi-agent ERP system: An integrated architecture and a conceptual framework. *Technovation, 25*(4), 433–441. doi:10.1016/S0166-4972(03)00153-6

Lee, A. S. (1999). Researching MIS. In Currie, W. L., & Galliers, R. D. (Eds.), *Rethinking Management Information Systems: An Interdisciplinary Perspective* (pp. 7–27). Oxford, UK: Oxford University Press.

Lee, A. S. (2004). Thinking about social theory and philosophy for information systems. In Mingers, J., & Willcocks, L. (Eds.), *Social Theory and Philosophy for Information Systems* (pp. 1–26). Chichester, UK: John Wiley and Sons.

Lee, W., Liu, C., & Lu, C. (2002). Intelligent agent-based systems for personalized recommendations in e-commerce. *Expert Systems with Applications, 22,* 275–284. doi:10.1016/S0957-4174(02)00015-5

Lee, Z., Gosain, S., & Im, I. (1999). Topics of interest in IS: Evolution of themes and differences between research and practice. *Information & Management, 36,* 233–246. doi:10.1016/S0378-7206(99)00022-1

Leff, H. S., & Rex, A. F. (2002). *Maxwell's demon 2: Entropy, classical and quantum information, computing.* New York, NY: CRC Press.

Lemley, B. (2000, February). Do you love this face?. *Discover.*

Lewin, K. (1946). Action research and minority problems. *The Journal of Social Issues, 2,* 34–46. doi:10.1111/j.1540-4560.1946.tb02295.x

Liang, T.-P., & Huang, J.-S. (2000). A framework for applying intelligent agents to support electronic trading. *Decision Support Systems, 28*(4), 305–317. doi:10.1016/S0167-9236(99)00098-6

Lightman, A. (2000). *Great ideas in physics.* New York, NY: McGraw-Hill.

Lindstrum, S., Palmgren, E., Segerberg, K., & Stoltenberg-Hansen, V. (Eds.). (2009). *Logicism, intuitionism, and formalism: What has become of them?* (Vol. 341). Berlin, Germany: Springer. doi:10.1007/978-1-4020-8926-8

Liu, D.-R., & Shih, Y.-Y. (2005). Integrating AHP and data mining for product recommendation based on customer lifetime value. *Information & Management, 42,* 387–400. doi:10.1016/j.im.2004.01.008

Livari, J. (2003). The IS core – VII: Towards information systems as a science of meta-artifacts. *Communications of the Association for Information Systems, 12*(37), 568–581.

Livio, M. (2005). *The equation that couldn't be solved: How mathematical genius discovered the language of symmetry*. New York, NY: Simon & Schuster.

Losee, J. (1993). *A historical introduction to the philosophy of science* (3rd ed.). Oxford, UK: Oxford University Press.

Love, T. (2000). Philosophy of design: A metatheoretical structure for design theory. *Design Studies, 21*, 293–313. doi:10.1016/S0142-694X(99)00012-5

Lucas, H. C. (1999). The state of the information systems field. *Communications of the AIS, 1*, 1–5.

Lurie, N. (2004). Decision-making in information-rich environments: The role of information structure. *The Journal of Consumer Research, 30*(4), 473–486. doi:10.1086/380283

Lyytinen, K. (1999). Empirical research in information systems: On the relevance of practice in thinking of IS research. *Management Information Systems Quarterly, 23*(1), 25–28. doi:10.2307/249406

Lyytinen, K., & Newman, M. (2008). Explaining information systems change: A punctuated socio-technical change model. *European Journal of Information Systems, 17*, 589–613. doi:10.1057/ejis.2008.50

MacCrimmon, K. R., & Taylor, R. N. (1976). Decision making and problem solving. In Dunnette, M. D. (Ed.), *Handbook of Individual and Organizational Psychology* (pp. 1397–1453). Chicago, IL: Rand-McNally.

Mackay, W. E., & Fayard, A.-L. (1997). *HCI, natural science and design: A framework for triangulation across disciplines.* Paper presented at the 2nd conference on Designing Interactive Systems: Processes, Practices, Methods, and Techniques. New York, NY.

Maeda, J. (2006). *The laws of simplicity*. Cambridge, MA: MIT Press.

Maes, P., Guttman, R. H., & Moukas, A. G. (1999). Agents that buy and sell. *Communications of the ACM, 42*(3), 81–87. doi:10.1145/295685.295716

Maher, M. L., Poon, J., & Boulanger, S. (1996). Formalizing design exploration as co-evolution: A combined gene approach. In Gero, J. S., & Sudweeks, F. (Eds.), *Advances in Formal Design Methods for CAD*. London, UK: Chapman and Hall.

Mandviwalla, M., & Gray, P. (1998). Is IS research on GSS relevant? *Information Resources Management Journal, 11*(2), 29–37.

Mankiewicz, R. (2000). *The story of mathematics*. London, UK: Cassel & Co.

Maor, E. (1987). *To infinity and beyond: A cultural history of the infinite*. Boston, MA: Birkhäuser.

March, S. T., & Hevner, A. R. (2005). Integrated decision support systems: A data warehousing perspective. *Decision Support Systems, 43*(3), 1031–1043. doi:10.1016/j.dss.2005.05.029

March, S. T., & Smith, G. F. (1995). Design and natural science research on information technology. *Decision Support Systems, 15*, 251–266. doi:10.1016/0167-9236(94)00041-2

March, S., Hevner, A., & Ram, S. (2000). Research commentary: An agenda for information technology research in heterogeneous and distributed environments. *Information Systems Research, 11*(4), 327–341. doi:10.1287/isre.11.4.327.11873

Markus, M. L., Majchrzak, A., & Gasser, L. (2002). A design theory for systems that support emergent knowledge processes. *Management Information Systems Quarterly, 26*(3), 179–212.

Markus, M. L., & Tanis, C. (2000). The enterprise system experience: From adoption to success. In Zmud, R. W. (Ed.), *Framing the Domains of IT Management: Projecting Future...through the Past* (pp. 173–207). Cincinnati, OH: Pinaflex Educational Reseources.

Mason, R. O., McKenney, J. L., & Copeland, D. G. (1997). An historical method for MIS research: Steps and assumptions. *Management Information Systems Quarterly, 21*(3), 307–320. doi:10.2307/249499

Massetti, B. (1996). An empirical examination of the value of creativity support systems on idea generation. *Management Information Systems Quarterly, 20*(1), 83–97. doi:10.2307/249543

Maxwell, G. (1962). The ontological status of theoretical entities. In Feigl, H., & Maxwell, G. (Eds.), *Minnesota Studies in the Philosophy of Science (Vol. 3*, pp. 3–14). Minneapolis, MN: University of Minnesota Press.

McCabe, T. J. (1976). A complexity measure. *IEEE Transactions on Software Engineering, 2*(4), 308–320. doi:10.1109/TSE.1976.233837

McCulloch, W., & Pitts, W. (1943). A logical calculus of the ideas immanent in nervous activity. *The Bulletin of Mathematical Biophysics, 7*, 115–133. doi:10.1007/BF02478259

McNeil, I. (Ed.). (1990). *An encyclopaedia of the history of technology*. London: Routledge. doi:10.4324/9780203192115

Meijers, A. (2000). The relational ontology of technical artifacts. In Kroes, P., & Meijers, A. (Eds.), *The Empirical Turn in the Philosophy of Technology (Vol. 20*, pp. 81–96). New York: JAI Press.

Michalewicz, Z. (1996). *Genetic algorithms + data structures = evolution programs*. New York: Springer-Verlag.

Miles, G. E., & Howes, A. (2000). A framework for understanding human factors in Web-based electronic commerce. *International Journal of Human-Computer Studies, 52*(1), 131–163. doi:10.1006/ijhc.1999.0324

Miner, J. B. (2006). *Organizational behavior 3: Historical origins, theoretical foundations, and the future*. Armonk, NY: M.E. Sharpe.

Mingers, J. (2001). Combining IS research methods: Towards a pluralist methodology. *Information Systems Research, 12*(3), 240–259. doi:10.1287/isre.12.3.240.9709

Minsky, M., & Papert, S. (1969). *Perceptrons: An introduction to computational geometry*. Cambridge, MA: MIT Press.

Modi, P. J., Veloso, M., Smith, S. F., & Oh, J. (2005). CMRadar: A personal assistant agent for calendar management. In Bresciani, P., Giorgini, P., & Henderson-Sellers, B. (Eds.), *Agent-Oriented Information Systems II* (pp. 169–181). Berlin, Germany: Springer. doi:10.1007/11426714_12

Moody, D. L. (2000). *Building links between IS research and professional practice: Improving the relevance and impact of IS research.* Paper presented at the Twenty First International Conference on Information Systems. Brisbane, Australia.

Mooney, R. J., & Roy, L. (2000). *Content-based book recommending using learning for text catecorization.* Paper presented at the 5th ACM Conference on Digital Libraries. San Antonio, TX.

Morrison, J., & George, J. F. (1995). Exploring the software engineering component in MIS research. *Communications of the ACM, 38*(7), 80–91. doi:10.1145/213859.214802

Mylonopoulos, N. A., & Theoharakis, V. (2001). On site: Global perceptions of IS journals. *Communications of the ACM, 44*(9), 29–33. doi:10.1145/383694.383701

Nagel, E. (1961). *The structure of science: Problems in the logic of scientific explanation*. New York, NY: Harcourt, Brace & World.

Nah, F. F.-H., & Davis, S. (2002). HCI research issues in e-commerce. *Journal of Electronic Commerce Research, 3*(3), 98–113.

Nahin, P. J. (1998). *An imaginary tale: The story of (the square root of minus one)*. Princeton, NJ: Princeton University Press.

Nambisan, S. (2003). Information systems as a reference discipline for new product development. *Management Information Systems Quarterly, 27*(1), 1–18.

Neander, K. (1991a). Function as selected effects: The conceptual analyst's defence. *Philosophy of Science, 58*, 168–184. doi:10.1086/289610

Neander, K. (1991b). The teleological notion of function. *Australasian Journal of Philosophy, 69*, 454–468. doi:10.1080/00048409112344881

Nelson, H. G., & Stolterman, E. (2003). *The design way: Intentional change in an unpredictable world: foundations and fundamentals of design competence.* Englewood Cliffs, NJ: Educational Technology Publications.

Neumann, J. V., & Morgenstern, O. (1953). *Theory of games and economic behavior* (3rd ed.). Princeton, NJ: Princeton University Press.

Nguyen, T. D., & Jennings, N. R. (2004). *Coordinating multiple concurrent negotiations.* Paper presented at the 3rd International Conference on Autonomous Agents and Multi-Agent Systems. New York, NY.

Nissen, H. J., Damerow, P., & Englund, R. (1993). *Archaic bookkeeping: Early writing and techniques of the economic administration in the ancient Near East.* Chicago, IL: University of Chicago Press.

Nissen, M. E. (2001). Agent-based supply chain integration. *Information Technology Management, 2*(3), 289–312. doi:10.1023/A:1011449109160

Nolan, R. L., & Wetherbe, J. C. (1980). Toward a comprehensive framework for MIS research. *Management Information Systems Quarterly, 4*(2), 1–19. doi:10.2307/249333

Nunamaker, J. F. J., Chen, M., & Purdin, T. D. M. (1991). Systems development in information systems research. *Journal of Management Information Systems, 7*(3), 89–106.

Nwana, H. S., Ndumu, D. T., Lee, L. C., & Collis, J. C. (1999). *ZEUS: A toolkit and approach for building distributed multi-agent systems.* Paper presented at the Third Annual Conference on Autonomous Agents. Seattle, WA.

O'Keefe, R. M. (1989). The evaluation of decision-aiding systems: Guidelines and methods. *Information & Management, 17*, 217–226. doi:10.1016/0378-7206(89)90045-1

O'Keefe, R. M., & McEachern, T. (1998). Web-based customer decision support systems. *Communications of the ACM, 41*(3), 71–78. doi:10.1145/272287.272300

Orlikowski, W. J., & Barley, S. R. (2001). Technology and institutions: What can research on information technology and research on organizations learn from each other? *Management Information Systems Quarterly, 25*(2), 145–165. doi:10.2307/3250927

Orlikowski, W. J., & Baroudi, J. J. (1991). Studying information technology in organizations: research approaches and assumptions. *Information Systems Research, 2*(1), 1–28. doi:10.1287/isre.2.1.1

Orlikowski, W., & Iacono, C. (2001). Desperately seeking the "IT" in IT research - A call to theorizing the IT artifact. *Information Systems Research, 12*(2), 121–134. doi:10.1287/isre.12.2.121.9700

Orlikowski, W., & Iacono, C. (2001). Desperately seeking the "IT" in IT research - A call to theorizing the IT artifact. *Information Systems Research, 12*(2), 121–134. doi:10.1287/isre.12.2.121.9700

Österle, H., Becker, J., Frank, U., Hess, T., Karagiannis, D., & Krcmar, H. (2011). Memorandum on design-oriented information systems research. *European Journal of Information Systems, 20*, 7–10. doi:10.1057/ejis.2010.55

Owen, C. (1997). Design research: Building the knowledge base. *Journal of the Japanese Society for the Science of Design, 5*(2), 36–45.

Pahl, G., & Beitz, W. (1984). *Engineering design.* London, UK: Pitman Press.

Paley, W. (2006). *Natural theology: Or, evidence of the existence and attributes of the deity, collected from the appearances of nature: Edited with an introduction and notes by Matthew D. Eddy and David Knight.* New York: Oxford University Press.

Palmer, W. J. (2002). Web site usability, design, and performance metrics. *Information Systems Research, 13*(2), 151–167. doi:10.1287/isre.13.2.151.88

Pathak, J., Vidyarthi, N., & Summers, S. L. (2005). A fuzzy-based algorithm for auditors to detect elements of fraud in settled insurance claims. *Managerial Auditing Journal, 20*(6), 632–644. doi:10.1108/02686900510606119

Pattisson, G. (2000). *The later heidegger.* London, UK: Routledge.

Peffers, K., Tuunanen, T., Rothenberger, M., & Chatterjee, S. (2008). A design science research methodology for information systems research. *Journal of Management Information Systems, 24*(3), 45–77. doi:10.2753/MIS0742-1222240302

Penrose, R. (1989). *The emperor's new mind: Concerning computers, minds, and the laws of physics*. New York: Oxford University Press.

Penrose, R. (1997). *The large, the small and the human mind*. New York: Cambridge University Press.

Perkins, D. N. (1986). *Knowledge as design*. Hillsdale, NJ: Lawrence Erlbaum Associates.

Petric, A., & Jezic, G. (2009). Reputation tracking procurement auctions. In *Computational Collective Intelligence: Semantic Web, Social Networks and Multiagent Systems* (pp. 825–837). Berlin, Germany: Springer. doi:10.1007/978-3-642-04441-0_72

Petroski, H. (1990). *The pencil: A history of design and circumstance*. New York, NY: Alfred A. Knopf.

Piirainen, K., Gonzalez, R., & Kolfschoten, G. (2010). Quo vadis, design science? – A survey of literature. In Winter, R., Zhao, J., & Aier, S. (Eds.), *Global perspectives on design science research* (*Vol. 6105*, pp. 93–108). Berlin: Springer. doi:10.1007/978-3-642-13335-0_7

Pirsig, R. M. (1974). *Zen and the art of motorcycle maintenance: An inquiry into values*. New York, NY: Morrow.

Plato,. (1973). *Theaetetus*. Oxford, UK: Clarendon Press.

Polyzotis, N., Skiadopoulos, S., Vassiliadis, P., Simitsis, A., & Frantzell, N.-E. (2007). *Supporting streaming updates in an active data warehouse*. Paper presented at the 23rd International Conference on Data Engineering. Istanbul, Turkey.

Popper, K. R. (1962). *Conjectures and refutations: The growth of scientific knowledge*. New York, NY: Basic Books.

Popper, K. R. (1968). *The logic of scientific discovery*. London: Hutchinson.

Popper, K. R. (1969). *Conjectures and refutations: The growth of scientific knowledge*. London: Routledge & K. Paul.

Popper, K. R. (1978). Natural selection and the emergence of mind. *Dialectica*, *32*, 339–355. doi:10.1111/j.1746-8361.1978.tb01321.x

Poser, H. (1998). On structural differences between science and engineering. *Philosophy and Technology*, *4*(2), 81–93.

Prasad, B. (2003). Intelligent techniques for e-commerce. *Journal of Electronic Commerce Research*, *4*(2), 65–71.

Preston, B. (1998). Why is a wing like a spoon: A pluralist theory of function. *The Journal of Philosophy*, *95*, 215–254. doi:10.2307/2564689

Pries-Heje, J., & Baskerville, R. (2008). The design theory nexus. *Management Information Systems Quarterly*, *32*(4), 731–735.

Purao, S. (2002). *Design research in the technology of information systems: Truth or dare*. Unpublished Working Paper. Retrieved from http://purao.ist.psu.edu/working-papers/.

Purao, S., Baldwin, C. Y., Hevner, A., Storey, V. C., Pries-Heje, J., Smith, B., et al. (2008). The sciences of design: Observations on an emerging field. *Communications of the AIS, 23*(29).

Quine, W. V. (1999). On what there is. In Kim, J., & Sosa, E. (Eds.), *Metaphysics: An anthology* (pp. 4–12). Malden, MA: Blackwell Publishers.

Raiffa, H. (1982). *The art and science of negotiation*. Cambridge, MA: Belknap Press of Harvard University Press.

Rao, A. R., & Monroe, K. B. (1988). The moderating effect of prior knowledge on cue utilization in product evaluations. *The Journal of Consumer Research*, *15*(2), 253–264. doi:10.1086/209162

Richey, R. C., & Klein, J. D. (2007). *Design and development research*. Mahwah, NJ: Lawrence Erlbaum Associates.

Rittel, H., & Webber, M. (1973). Dilemmas in a general theory of planning. *Policy Sciences*, *4*, 155–169. doi:10.1007/BF01405730

Rizzi, S., Abelló, A., Lechtenbörger, J., & Trujillo, J. (2006). *Research in data warehouse modeling and design: dead or alive?* Paper presented at the 9th ACM International Workshop on Data Warehousing and OLAP. Arlington, VA.

Robey, D. (1996). Research commentary: Diversity in information systems research: Threat, promise, and responsibility. *Information Systems Research*, 7(4), 400–408. doi:10.1287/isre.7.4.400

Robey, D., & Markus, M. L. (1998). Beyond rigor and relevance: Producing consumable research about information systems. *Information Resources Management Journal*, 11(1), 7–15.

Roger, N. S. (2007). The genetic basis of human scientific knowledge. In G. R. Bock & G. Cardew (Eds.), *Ciba Foundation Symposium 208 - Characterizing Human Psychological Adaptations,* (pp. 23-38). Chichester, NY: John Wiley & Sons.

Rohde, M., Stevens, G., Brödner, P., & Wulf, V. (2009). *Towards a paradigmatic shift in IS: designing for social practice.* Paper presented at the 4th International Conference on Design Science Research in Information Systems and Technology. Malvern, PA.

Rojcewicz, R. (2006). *The Gods and technology: A reading of Heidegger.* Albany, NY: State University of New York Press.

Ronan, C. A. (1982). *Science, its history and development among the world's cultures.* New York, NY: Facts on File.

Ropohl, G. (1999). Philosophy of socio-technical systems. *Philosophy & Technology*, 4(3), 59–71.

Rosemann, M., & Vessey, I. (2008). Toward improving the relevance of information systems research to practice: The role of applicability checks. *Management Information Systems Quarterly*, 32(1), 1–22.

Rosenblatt, F. (1958). The perceptron: A probabilistic model for information storage and organization in the brain. *Psychological Review*, 65(6), 386–408. doi:10.1037/h0042519

Rosenburg, N. F. M., & Dorst, K. (1998). Describing design as a reflective practice: Observations on Schön's theory of practice. In Frankenberger, E., Birkhofer, H., & Badke-Schaub, P. (Eds.), *Designers: The Key to Successful Product Development* (pp. 29–41). London, UK: Springer-Verlag.

Rosen, R. (1985). *Anticipatory systems: Philosophical, mathematical and methodological foundations.* Oxford, UK: Pergamon Press.

Rowley, J. (2000). Product search in e-shopping: A review and research propositions. *Journal of Consumer Marketing*, 17(1), 20–35. doi:10.1108/07363760010309528

Rueda, S. V., Garcia, A. J., & Simari, G. R. (2002). Argument-based negotiation among BDI agents. *Journal of Computer Science & Technology*, 2(7), 1–8.

Rumelhart, D. E., Hinton, G. E., & Williams, R. J. (1986). Learning internal representations by error propagation. In Rumelhart, D. E., McClelland, J. L., & Group, P. R. (Eds.), *Parallel Distributed Processing: Explorations in the Microstructure of Cognition* (Vol. 1, pp. 318–362). Cambridge, MA: MIT Press.

Rumelhart, D. E., Hinton, G. E., & Williams, R. J. (1986). Learning representations by back-propagating errors. *Nature*, 323, 533–536. doi:10.1038/323533a0

Russell, S. J., & Norvig, P. (2003). *Artificial intelligence: A modern approach* (2nd ed.). Upper Saddle River, NJ: Prentice Hall.

Saaty, T. L. (1980). *The analytic hierarchy process.* New York, NY: McGraw Hill.

Sagan, C. (1996). *The demon-haunted world: Science as a candle in the dark.* New York: Random House.

Sandholm, T. (2002). Algorithm for optimal winner determination in combinatorial auctions. *Artificial Intelligence*, 135(1-2), 1–54. doi:10.1016/S0004-3702(01)00159-X

Sarwar, B. M., Karypis, G., Konstan, J. A., & Riedl, J. (2000). *Analysis of recommendation algorithms for e-commerce.* Paper presented at the ACM Conference on Electronic Commerce. New York, NY.

Saunders, C. (1998). Editorial preface: The role of business in IT research. *Information Resources Management Journal*, 11(1), 4–8.

Schafer, J. B., Konstan, J. A., & Riedl, J. (2001). E-commerce recommendation applications. *Data Mining and Knowledge Discovery*, 5(1/2), 115–153. doi:10.1023/A:1009804230409

Schmitt, C., Dengler, D., & Bauer, M. (2002). *The MAUT machine: An adaptive recommender system.* Paper presented at the ABIS Workshop 2002: Personalization for the Mobile World. Hannover, Germany.

Schön, D. A. (1983). *The reflective practitioner: How professionals think in action.* New York, NY: Basic Books.

Searle, J. (1980). Minds, brains and programs. *The Behavioral and Brain Sciences*, *3*, 417–457. doi:10.1017/S0140525X00005756

Searle, J. R. (1980). Intrinsic intentionality. *The Behavioral and Brain Sciences*, *3*, 450–456. doi:10.1017/S0140525X00006038

Searle, J. R. (1995). *The construction of social reality.* London: Penguin Books.

Selnes, F., & Troye, S. V. (1989). Buying expertise, information search, and problem solving. *Journal of Economic Psychology*, *10*(3), 411–428. doi:10.1016/0167-4870(89)90032-9

Senn, J. (1998). The challenge of relating IS research to practice. *Information Resources Management Journal*, *11*(1), 23–28.

Seo, Y.-W., & Zhang, B.-T. (2000). *Learning user's preferences by analyzing Web-browsing behaviors.* Paper presented at the Fourth International Conference on Autonomous Agents. Barcelona, Spain.

Shakshuki, E., & Jun, Y. (2004). Multi-agent development toolkits: An evaluation. In Orchard, B., Yang, C., & Moonis, A. (Eds.), *Innovations in Applied Artificial Intelligence* (pp. 209–218). Berlin, Germany: Springer. doi:10.1007/978-3-540-24677-0_23

Sharda, R., Barr, S. H., & McDonnell, J. C. (1988). Decision support system effectiveness: A review and an empirical test. *Management Science*, *34*(2), 139–159. doi:10.1287/mnsc.34.2.139

Sidorova, A., Evangelopoulos, N., & Valacich, J. (2008). Uncovering the intellectual core of the information systems discipline. *Management Information Systems Quarterly*, *32*(3), 467–482.

Sierra, C., Jennings, N., Noriega, P., & Parsons. (1998). A framework for argumentation-based negotiation. In M. P. Singh, A. Rao, & M. J. Wooldridge (Eds.), *Intelligent Agents IV: Agent Theories, Architectures, and Languages: 4th International Workshop,* (pp. 193-208). Berlin: Springer-Verlag.

Silver, M. (1991). *Systems that support decision makers: Description and analysis.* New York: Wiley.

Simondon, G. (1989). *Du mode d'existence des objets techniques* (2nd ed.). Paris: Aubier.

Simon, H. A. (1977). *The new science of management decision.* Englewood Cliffs, NJ: Prentice-Hall.

Simon, H. A. (1996). *The sciences of the artificial* (3rd ed.). Cambridge, MA: MIT Press.

Smith, G. E., & Wortzel, L. L. H. (1997). Prior knowledge and the effect of suggested frames of reference in advertising. *Psychology and Marketing*, *14*(2), 121–143. doi:10.1002/(SICI)1520-6793(199703)14:2<121::AID-MAR2>3.0.CO;2-F

Smith, K. A., & Gupta, J. N. D. (2000). Neural networks in business: Techniques and applications for the operations researcher. *Computers & Operations Research*, *27*, 1023–1044. doi:10.1016/S0305-0548(99)00141-0

Smith, V. (1982). Microeconomic systems as an experimental science. *The American Economic Review*, *72*(5), 923–955.

Sniegowski, P. D., Gerrish, P. J., Johnson, T., & Shaver, A. (2000). The evolution of mutation rates: Separating causes from consequences. *BioEssays*, *22*(12), 1057–1066. doi:10.1002/1521-1878(200012)22:12<1057::AID-BIES3>3.0.CO;2-W

Sowa, J. F., & Zachman, J. A. (1992). Extending and formalizing the framework for information systems architecture. *IBM Systems Journal*, *31*(3), 590–616. doi:10.1147/sj.313.0590

Spewak, S. H. (1992). *Enterprise architecture planning.* New York: John Wiley & Sons.

Srikumar, K., & Bhasker, B. (2004). *Personalized recommendations in e-commerce.* Paper presented at the Management of Electronic Business: 25th McMaster World Congress. Hamilton, Canada.

Stace, W. T. (1967). *Man against darkness, and other essays*. Pittsburgh, PA: University of Pittsburgh Press.

Stahl, B. C. (2008). *Design as reification, commodification and ideology: A critical view of IS design science*. Paper presented at the 16th European Conference on Information Systems in an Innovative Knowledge-Based Society. Galway, Ireland.

Stanford. (2008). *Encyclopedia of philosophy*. Palo Alto, CA: Stanford University Press.

Steiner, W., & Hruschka, H. (2003). Genetic algorithms for product design: How well do they really work. *International Journal of Market Research, 45*, 229–240.

Stohr, E. A., & Viswanathan, S. (1999). Recommendation systems: Decision support for the information economy. In Kendall, K. E. (Ed.), *Emerging Information Technologies* (pp. 21–44). New York: SAGE Publications.

Strahler, A. N. (1992). *Understanding science: An introduction to concepts and issues*. Buffalo, NY: Prometheus Books.

Sultan, F., Urban, G. L., Shankar, V., & Bart, I. Y. (2002). *Determinants and role of trust in e-business: A large scale empirical study*. MIT Sloan School of Management Working Paper 4282-02. Cambridge, MA: MIT Press.

Tedre, M. (2007). Know your discipline: Teaching the philosophy of computer science. *Journal of Information Technology Education, 6*, 105–122.

Tegarden, D. P., Sheetz, S. D., & Monarchi, D. E. (1995). A software complexity model of object-oriented systems. *Decision Support Systems, 13*(3-4), 241–262. doi:10.1016/0167-9236(93)E0045-F

Thalhammer, T., Schrefl, M., & Mohani, M. (2001). Active data warehouses: Complementing OLAP with analysis rules. *Data & Knowledge Engineering, 39*(3), 241–269. doi:10.1016/S0169-023X(01)00042-8

Thiessen, E. M., Loucks, D. P., & Stedinger, J. R. (1998). Computer-assisted negotiations of water resources conflicts. *Group Decision and Negotiation, 7*(2), 109–129. doi:10.1023/A:1008654625690

Todd, P., & Benbasat, I. (1999). Evaluating the impact of DSS, cognitive effort, and incentives on strategy selection. *Information Systems Research, 10*(4), 356–374. doi:10.1287/isre.10.4.356

TOGAF. (2001a). *The open group architectural framework, version 7, December, 2001*. New York: The Open Group.

TOGAF. (2001b). *The open group architectural framework, version 8, December, 2002*. New York: The Open Group.

Toms, E. G. (2000). Understanding and facilitating the browsing of electronic text. *International Journal of Human-Computer Studies, 52*(3), 423–452. doi:10.1006/ijhc.1999.0345

Toulmin, S. (1953). Do submicroscopic entities exist? In *The Philosophy of Science: An Introduction* (pp. 134–139). London, UK: The Hutchinson Publishing Group.

Vahidov, R. (2006). *Design researcher's IS artifact: A representational framework*. Paper presented at the 1st International Conference on Design Science Research in Information Systems and Technology, DESRIST 2006. Claremont, CA.

Vahidov, R., & Neumann, D. (2008). *Situated decision support for service level agreement negotiations*. Paper presented at the 41st Hawaii International Conference on System Sciences (HICSS). Waikoloa, HI.

Vahidov, R., Chen, E., & Feng, Z. (2005). *Experimental evaluation of agent-supported e-negotiations*. Paper presented at the Group Decision and Negotiation 2005. Vienna, Austria.

Vahidov, R. (2007). Situated decision support approach for managing multiple negotiations. In Gimpel, H., Jennings, N. R., Kersten, G., Ockenfels, A., & Weinhardt, C. (Eds.), *Negotiation and Market Engineering* (*Vol. 2*, pp. 179–189). Berlin, Germany: Springer-Verlag. doi:10.1007/978-3-540-77554-6_13

Vahidov, R., & Fazlollahi, B. (2004). Pluralistic multi-agent decision support system: A framework and an empirical test. *Information & Management, 41*(7), 883–398. doi:10.1016/j.im.2003.08.017

Vahidov, R., & He, X. (2010). Situated DSS for personal finance management: Design and evaluation. *Information & Management, 47*(2), 78–86. doi:10.1016/j.im.2009.11.001

Vahidov, R., & Ji, F. (2005). A method for infrequent purchase decision support in e-commerce. *Electronic Commerce Research and Applications, 4*(2), 143–158. doi:10.1016/j.elerap.2004.09.001

Vaishnavi, V. K., & Kuechler, W. Jr. (2008). *Design science research methods: Innovating information and communication technology.* Boca Raton, FL: Auerbach Publications.

Vamvacas, C. J. (2009). Xenophanes of Colophon. In *The Founders of Western Thought – The Presocratics* (pp. 85–99). New York: Springer. doi:10.1007/978-1-4020-9791-1_8

Van Aken, J. E. (2004). Management research based on the paradigm of design sciences: The quest for field-tested and grounded technological rules. *Journal of Management Studies, 41*(2), 219–246. doi:10.1111/j.1467-6486.2004.00430.x

Vanegas, L. V., & Labib, A. W. (2001). Application of new fuzzy-weighted average (NFWA) method to engineering design evaluation. *International Journal of Production Research, 39*(6), 1147–1162. doi:10.1080/00207540010023592

Venable, J. R. (2006). *The role of theory and theorising in design science research.* Paper presented at the First International Conference on Design Science Research in Information Systems and Technology. Claremont, CA.

Vermaas, P. E., & Houkes, W. (2003). Ascribing functions to technical artefacts: A challenge to etiological accounts of functions. *The British Journal for the Philosophy of Science, 54*(2), 261–289. doi:10.1093/bjps/54.2.261

Walls, J. G., Widmeyer, G. R., & El Sawy, O. A. (1992). Building an information system design theory for vigilant EIS. *Information Systems Research, 3*(1), 36–59. doi:10.1287/isre.3.1.36

Wand, Y., & Weber, R. (1988). *An ontological analysis of some fundamental information systems concepts.* Paper presented at the International Conference on Information Systems. Minneapolis, MN.

Wand, Y., & Weber, R. (1990). *Towards a theory of deep structure of information systems.* Paper presented at the International Conference on Information Systems. Copenhagen, Denmark.

Wand, Y., & Weber, R. (1990). An ontological model of an information system. *IEEE Transactions on Software Engineering, 16*(22), 1282–1292. doi:10.1109/32.60316

Wang, Y.-F., Chuang, Y.-L., Hsu, M.-H., & Keh, H.-C. (2004). A personalized recommender system for the cosmetic business. *Expert Systems with Applications, 26*(3), 427–434. doi:10.1016/j.eswa.2003.10.001

Watson, R. T., DeSanctis, G., & Poole, M. S. (1988). Using a GDSS to facilitate group consensus: Some intended and unintended consequences. *Management Information Systems Quarterly, 12*(3), 463–478. doi:10.2307/249214

Weber, S. (2010). *Design science research: Paradigm or approach?* Paper presented at the Americas Conference on Information Systems, AMCIS 2010. New York, NY.

Weber, M., Kersten, G., & Hine, M. (2006). Visualization in e-negotiations: An inspire ENS graph is worth 334 words, on average. *Electronic Markets, 16*(3), 186–200. doi:10.1080/10196780600841571

Weber, R. (2003a). Editor's comments: Still desperately seeking the IT artifact. *Management Information Systems Quarterly, 27*(2), iii–xi.

Weber, R. (2003b). Editor's comments: Theoretically speaking. *Management Information Systems Quarterly, 27*(3), iii–xii.

Wells, D., & Kurien, A. (1996). *Groupware & collaboration support.* Washington, DC: Object Services and Consulting, Inc.

Whewell, W. (1967). *The philosophy of the inductive sciences.* London: Cass.

Whinston, A. B., & Geng, X. (2004). Operationalizing the essential role of the information technology artifact in information systems research: Gray area, pitfalls, and the importance of strategic ambiguity. *Management Information Systems Quarterly, 28*(2), 149–159.

Whitehead, A. N., & Russell, B. (1927). *Principia mathematica* (2nd ed.). Cambridge, UK: Cambridge University Press.

Wieringa, R. (2009). *Design science as nested problem solving.* Paper presented at the 4th International Conference on Design Science Research in Information Systems and Technology. Malvern, PA.

Winter, R. (2008). Design science research in Europe. *European Journal of Information Systems, 17*, 470–475. doi:10.1057/ejis.2008.44

Wooldridge, M., & Jennings, N. (1995). Intelligent agents: Theory and practice. *The Knowledge Engineering Review, 10*(2), 115–152. doi:10.1017/S0269888900008122

Wurman, P. R., Wellman, M. P., & Walsh, W. E. (1998). *The Michigan Internet auction bot: A configurable auction server for human and software agents.* Paper presented at the Second International Conference on Autonomous Agents. Minneapolis, MN.

Zachman, J. A. (1987). A framework for information systems architecture. *IBM Systems Journal, 26*(3), 276–292. doi:10.1147/sj.263.0276

Zadeh, L. A. (1965). Fuzzy sets. *Information and Control, 8*(3), 338–353. doi:10.1016/S0019-9958(65)90241-X

Zamenopoulos, T., & Alexiou, K. (2007). Towards an anticipatory view of design. *Design Studies, 28*, 411–436. doi:10.1016/j.destud.2007.04.001

Zeng, Y., & Cheng, G. D. (1991). On the logic of design. *Design Studies, 12*(3), 137–141. doi:10.1016/0142-694X(91)90022-O

Zopounidis, C., Doumpos, M., & Matsatstinis, N. F. (1997). On the use of knowledge-based decision support systems in financial management: A survey. *Decision Support Systems, 20*, 259–277. doi:10.1016/S0167-9236(97)00002-X

About the Author

Rustam Vahidov is an Associate Professor of Management Information Systems at the Department of Decision Sciences and MIS, John Molson School of Business, Concordia University (Montreal, Quebec, Canada). He received his Ph.D. from Georgia State University in 2000. Dr. Vahidov has published papers in a number of academic journals, including *Journal of MIS*, *Decision Support Systems*, *Information and Management*, *E-Commerce Research and Applications*, *IEEE Transactions on Systems, Man and Cybernetics*, *Fuzzy Sets and Systems*, and several others. His primary research interests include: decision support systems, design science research, software agents, e-commerce systems, distributed artificial intelligence and multi-agent systems, negotiation systems, data mining, fuzzy logic, and genetic algorithms.

Index

U

ultimate concrete 9, 11
Unified Modeling Language (UML) 18

W

wicked problems 13

X

XOR problems 226

Z

Zachman's framework 120-121, 123, 125-126
Z-specifications 17, 89